Youth Justice

This book provides a comprehensive, student-friendly and critical introduction to youth justice in England and Wales, offering a balanced evaluation of its development, rationale, nature and evidence base. It explores the evolution of definitions and explanations of youth offending and examines the responses to it that constitute youth justice.

Bringing together theory, policy and practice, this book provides a balanced exposition of contemporary youth justice debates, including detailed discussions of governmental rationales, policy developments, practical issues and an extensive evaluation of critical academic positions. It includes a range of features designed to engage and inspire students:

- 'Stop and think': Activities challenging students to reflect on important issues.
- 'Conversations': Discussions of key themes and issues from the perspectives and experiences of relevant stakeholders, including policy-makers and activists.
- 'Telling it like it is': Testimonies giving voice to the personalised, subjective and contentious viewpoints of youth justice influencers.
- 'Controversies and debates': Prompts to stimulate students to question and critique established knowledge and understanding by considering alternative angles.
- 'Recurring theme alerts': Boxes that flag recurring themes in the developing construction of youth offending and youth justice.

The new edition has been fully revised and updated and includes discussion of revised National Standards in Youth Justice, the new 'Child First' strategic objective for youth justice, the 'trauma-informed practice' movement, the impact of coronavirus on children in the Youth Justice System and the continued impact of austerity on policy and practice.

This book is essential reading for students taking courses in youth justice, youth offending, youth crime, youth work and social policy.

Stephen Case is Professor of Criminology in the Department of Criminology, Sociology and Social Policy at Loughborough University, UK. He has conducted large-scale funded research projects for the Nuffield Foundation, the Leverhulme Trust, the Youth Justice Board, the National Institute for Social Care and Health Research, the Economic and Social Research Council and the Welsh Government.

Steve Case's *Youth Justice: A Critical Introduction* provides an essential introduction to youth justice in England and Wales, indeed I'd say is *the* essential introductory text, and as such fills a gap last occupied when Donald West first published his seminal *The Young Offender* in 1967. Stimulating, balanced, but with a committed and challenging edge to it, no student, youth justice practitioner or policy maker should allow themselves to be far away from a copy.

John Drew,
Professor at University of Bedfordshire and
former chief executive of the Youth Justice Board for
England and Wales (2009–2013)

Youth Justice

A Critical Introduction

2nd Edition

STEPHEN CASE

Routledge
Taylor & Francis Group

LONDON AND NEW YORK

First published 2022
by Routledge
2 Park Square, Milton Park, Abingdon, Oxon OX14 4RN

and by Routledge
605 Third Avenue, New York, NY 10158

Routledge is an imprint of the Taylor & Francis Group, an informa business
© 2022 Stephen Case

British Library Cataloguing-in-Publication Data
A catalogue record for this book is available from the British Library

Library of Congress Cataloging-in-Publication Data
Names: Case, Stephen, author.
Title: Youth justice : a critical introduction / Stephen Case.
Description: 2nd edition. | Abingdon, Oxon ; New York, NY : Routledge, 2021. |
    Includes bibliographical references and index.
Identifiers: LCCN 2020056948 | ISBN 9780367417789 (hbk) |
    ISBN 9780367417796 (pbk) | ISBN 9780367816209 (ebk)
Subjects: LCSH: Juvenile justice, Administration of—Great Britain. |
    Juvenile justice, Administration of. | Juvenile delinquency—Great Britain.
Classification: LCC HV9145.A5 C3673 2021 | DDC 364.360942—dc23
LC record available at https://lccn.loc.gov/2020056948

ISBN: 978-0-367-41778-9 (hbk)
ISBN: 978-0-367-41779-6 (pbk)
ISBN: 978-0-367-81620-9 (ebk)

Typeset in ITC Stone Serif Std
by Apex CoVantage, LLC

Contents

Figures and tables

FIGURES

TABLES

Acknowledgements

I am extremely indebted to friends and colleagues who took the time to review developing drafts of this book. Their comments were always constructive, insightful and in the spirit of making this text more accessible and engaging for the reader. I would particularly like to thank the excellent reviewers who were officially recruited by Routledge and those unofficially recruited by me (Tim Bateman, Roger Smith and Roger Hopkins-Burke), who were all very generous with their time and feedback. In this vein, I'd also like to offer sincere gratitude to the numerous youth justice experts who kindly participated in the 'Conversations' and 'Telling it like it is' features that animate my arguments and take this so far beyond the traditional textbook, in my humble opinion. Finally, many thanks to my editors, Tom Sutton and Jessica Phillips, for their dedication and support throughout this project, in particular for their ambition to produce an original and innovative textbook for students.

Introduction

Youth justice

Welcome to *Youth Justice*, a critical introduction to the development of youth justice in the industrialised Western world. The intention of this book is to provide the reader with an engaging and accessible overview of why the concepts of 'youth offending' and 'youth justice' should not be understood as taken-for-granted facts or realities, but rather how each is a dynamic, contested and contingent social construction – a constructed reality, if you like. The nature of youth justice is shaped by how a society chooses to define (construct) 'youth offending' at any given point in time, which in turn can influence how youth offending is explained, which then can influence how it is responded to through the philosophies, systems, structures, strategies, processes and practices that constitute youth justice. A classic example of this interrelationship between definitions, explanation and responses is the creation/construction of official crime statistics. Their construction tells us more about the activities of the Youth Justice System and the behaviours and people that the system chooses to construct as 'criminal' than about the 'reality' of youth offending. *Youth Justice* will introduce you to the 'triad of youth justice' (Figure 0.1) – a framework for understanding that sees definitions, explanations and responses as three interrelated and mutually reinforcing elements working together in the social construction of youth justice.

Youth Justice encourages you, the reader, to 'Always Be Critical' (the ABC approach to academic study; Case *et al.* 2017) about everything that you read, hear and do relating to youth justice; critical in the sense of balanced, reasoned, evidenced, analytical and evaluative. The book attempts to offer a critical balance to reconcile what can be a polarised youth justice literature consisting of critical criminologists challenging current manifestations of youth justice and more supportive, less critical academics and policy-makers championing the benefits of contemporary youth justice in practice. This textbook challenges the reader to balance the available evidence/arguments and to formulate their own critical views on how best to understand and respond to youth offending in the modern world. Evaluation of contemporary youth justice (let us define 'contemporary' as from the 1990s onwards – you'll understand why later), will be informed by a thorough thematic analysis of the socio-historical construction of youth justice; one that identifies a series of conceptual **dichotomies** (pairs or divisions of opposites) such as innocent–dangerous child definitions, individual-critical explanations and welfare-justice responses in order to provide a further framework for developing your knowledge and understanding. Critical discussion in this book aims to have more breadth and depth than

FIGURE 0.1 THE 'TRIAD OF YOUTH JUSTICE'

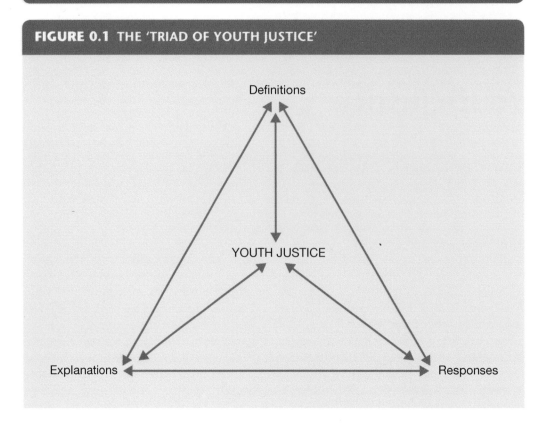

you might find in historical-criminological reviews of youth justice (which tend to focus on pre-twentieth-century developments) or in textbooks from critical youth justice academics that may privilege the Crime and Disorder Act 1998 as the 'year zero' starting point for their critique of contemporary youth justice. That is not to say that you shouldn't engage with these often excellent texts, but rather that you might find it more useful to start here. In this book, you will embark on a structured journey through the socio-historical construction of youth offending and youth justice at each point of the triad – a journey that seeks to incrementally improve your knowledge and understanding of youth justice. We will consider the perspectives of academics, politicians, policy-makers, practitioners, media, children and families and their contributions to the social construction and reconstruction of knowledge and understanding about youth offending and youth justice. I will also offer you my insight as an experienced youth justice academic and researcher as a way of animating the discussions. I'll also help you to demystify the (often unnecessary) complexity of academic debates surrounding youth justice so that you're better able to engage with, challenge and build on existing knowledge. For example, you will be provided with clear explanations of the myriad of technical academic concepts and practice jargon that you'll encounter on your journey to understanding youth justice (see also Goldson 2008). A series of 'key features' will be integrated throughout the chapters to engage you in critical thinking about youth justice and to motivate you to construct knowledge of your own:

KEY FEATURES

1 **Stop and think**: encourages you to reflect and challenge what you think about key youth justice issues and arguments.

2 **Conversations**: stimulates you to listen and engage with key issues and arguments by providing you with the valuable personal experiences and insights of key stakeholders (interviewed specifically for this book) who have contributed to the construction of youth justice.

3 **Telling it like it is**: promotes understanding and analysis by giving access to the personalised, subjective and contentious viewpoints of youth justice influencers.

4 **Controversies and debates**: prompts the reader to question and critique established knowledge and understanding by considering alternative angles and provocative perceptions of controversial issues and debates in youth justice.

5 **Recurring theme alerts (RTAs)**: consolidates and challenges knowledge and understanding by alerting you to recurring themes in the developing construction of youth offending and youth justice, often in the form of conceptual dichotomies.

The key features combined with the 'triad of youth justice' model are provided to make complex and challenging arguments more accessible and digestible. They are supplemented by a third heuristic (practical, learning) method known as '5 easy pieces'. Each chapter and each section within each chapter is broken down into five parts (often chronologically) to set you on a logical journey to understanding the key areas that contribute to the construction of youth justice (see the key features above for your first example). The '5 easy pieces' boxes within each chapter are logical places to start if you want an initial overview or framework for understanding of the chapter. The book itself is divided into three sections that map onto the 'triad of youth justice': defining youth offending (Chapter 1), explaining youth offending (Chapters 2 and 3) and responding to youth offending (Chapters 4–6; see Figure 0.2).

Chapter 1 explores the first point of the 'triad of youth justice': definitions. It introduces you to the importance of operationalising the key behaviour that is being explained and responded to through clear, consistent definitions. The central argument is that youth offending is a social construction, the definitions of which are created and manipulated by key socio-economic, statistical, political, professional and intellectual influences and influencers. The chapter traces the historical development of the concept of 'youth offending' from the pre-Victorian social construction of 'childhood' and the resultant dichotomy of the innocent–dangerous child

FIGURE 0.2 STRUCTURE OF THE BOOK

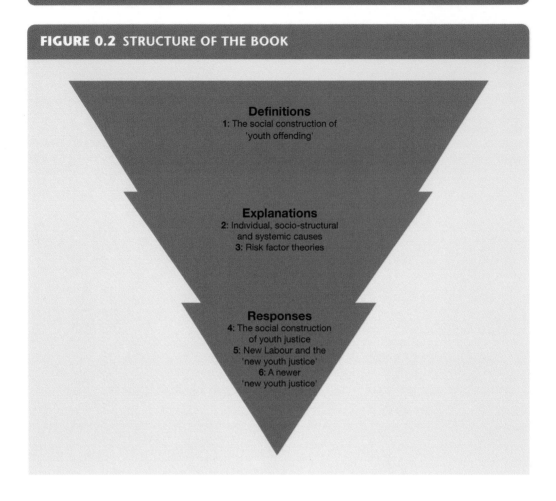

Definitions
1: The social construction of
'youth offending'

Explanations
2: Individual, socio-structural
and systemic causes
3: Risk factor theories

Responses
4: The social construction
of youth justice
5: New Labour and the
'new youth justice'
6: A newer
'new youth justice'

in understandings of children who offended in the second half of the nineteenth century. Discussion moves on to the social construction of 'adolescence' in the early twentieth century and the way the concept was employed to address the innocent–dangerous child issue, leading into associated developments in the second half of the twentieth century regarding how best to understand and respond to non-adults who offended – as children needing welfare services or as youths deserving justice. The chapter concludes with a review of the post-1990s 'punitive turn' in constructions of young people who offend and their reconstruction in England and Wales as irresponsible and immoral 'youth offenders'.

Chapter 2 presents an historical overview of the development of explanatory theories of offending. Discussion begins with explanations focused on the individual, from the eighteenth-century classical theories emphasising the role of free will and rational choice to the positivist theories of the nineteenth and early twentieth centuries that examined the criminogenic (crime-inducing) and predetermined influence of biological factors (e.g. physical characteristics, genetics, brain development) and psychological factors (e.g. personality, learning). We will then explore the socio-structural explanations of sociological positivism that emphasise the role of social disorganisation, strain and membership of subcultures. The penultimate section introduces the critical theories that emerged from the 1950s to explicitly challenge positivist explanations by viewing offending as a social construction resulting from the labelling and criminalisation of behaviours and individuals by powerful groups, notably white, middle-class men. The final set of explanations is the integrated forms of positivist and realist theories developed from the 1970s to provide more comprehensive and valid understandings of (youth) offending by challenging the reductionism (restricted, oversimplified nature) of single-theory positivist explanations and the left idealism (offending as a social construction visited on the powerless, rather than necessarily a real-world, problematic behaviour) of critical theories.

The second explanations chapter (Chapter 3) explores the chronological and simultaneous explanatory evolution of a group of theories that understand youth offending as the result of exposure to 'risk factors', which predicts an increased likelihood of offending in the future. The chapter discusses the quasi-positivist nature of many of these theories, resembling key aspects of positivism (e.g. use of empirical research methods, biopsychosocial foci) but differing slightly in other aspects (e.g. preferring surveys to empirical experiment and observation, identifying predictors rather than causes). We will explore the early biopsychosocial developmental theories (1930s–1970s) that identified biological, psychological and sociological risks (quantified into 'factors') experienced in childhood and early adolescence as predictive of later offending (i.e. developmental theories). This is followed by an investigation of integrated developmental theories (1980s onwards) that considered the role of interactions between biopsychosocial risk factors, socio-structural risk factors, rational choice and context in early life as criminogenic predictors of later offending. The integrated explanations of these theories were extended by interactional developmental theories (1990s onwards), which added in the potential for reciprocal interactions between risk factors and youth offending (e.g. that youth offending could cause or exacerbate risk factors) and the potential for criminogenic interactions between young people and the Youth Justice System. The penultimate section focuses on age-graded life course theories, which trace the predictive influence of interactions between psychosocial risk factors, structural context, informal social control and agency (rational choice) beyond childhood and youth and into adulthood (i.e. life course theories). Finally, there is a detailed discussion of the explanatory outlier, constructivist pathways theories. These explanations consider young people's ability to construct, make meaning of, negotiate and resist their experiences of risks (factors and processes) and the effects of these constructions of young people's pathways into and out of offending.

The first of three youth justice chapters, Chapter 4 explores the historical development of different systems, structures, philosophies, strategies and practices of youth justice internationally. Discussion begins by focusing on early (pre-1850) social constructions of youth justice in an era of custody and control, particularly youth justice structures and mechanisms such as prison statistics and the first youth prison. We move on to the 1850–1900 period of more welfare-based and less punitive custodial youth justice, which legislated for differentiated structures and strategies for responding to children who offended (e.g. custodial reformatories) and children who were neglected and needy (e.g. the industrial school). There follows an examination of youth justice developments in the first half of the twentieth century, including the introduction of new structures (the juvenile court, borstals, professional social work departments for troubled children) that pursued welfare and justice objectives simultaneously. The penultimate section outlines a period of youth justice developments (1950–1990) characterised by conflict and ambivalence in terms of how youth justice legislation, strategies and practices were constructed and implemented, once again characterised by a twin-track (bifurcated) approach that attempted to address the tensions between welfare and justice priorities. Finally, international youth justice is brought up to date through consideration of contemporary strategic models that have extended the welfare-justice debate to include neo-liberalism, minimal intervention and restorative justice, before setting out three identifiable 'movements' in contemporary youth justice: punitive approaches based on control, correction and custody; practical approaches grounded in risk management; and protective approaches linked to a rights-compliant 'child-friendly justice'.

Chapter 5 provides a detailed exploration of the significant youth justice developments in England and Wales under the New Labour Government that seized power in 1997. Discussion coalesces around the 'new youth justice' model that offered a radical reorientation of youth justice responses – a move away from traditional welfare-justice priorities and towards 'new', modernising and neo-liberal/neo-correctionalist strategies of responsibilisation, prevention and risk-focused early intervention (i.e. implementing the risk factor prevention paradigm), net-widening and interventionism. Rest assured that these and other ostensibly complex concepts will be explained in detail as we move forwards. The chapter traces the origins of the 'new youth justice' from the birth of New Labour (1992–1995) and their support for strategies of communitarianism and responsibilisation – support informed by political expedience, research evidence and personal/professional experience. Discussion moves to the *Misspent Youth* and *No More Excuses* reports (1996–1997), which recommended modernising and managerialist strategies for the more effective, efficient and economical delivery of youth justice. We then examine the newly constructed, fully formed 'Youth Justice System' created by the Crime and Disorder Act 1998, which was to be managed (strategically) by a new structure, the Youth Justice Board, and mobilised (in practice) by new, multi-agency Youth Offending Teams. There follows a statistical and thematic evaluation of the central strategies of the 'new youth justice' that emerged from the Crime and Disorder Act 1998 and its associated legislation, concluding with an equivalent evaluation of the final years of New Labour – both of which identify the throughgoing conflict and ambivalence reflected by the strategies and practices of the 'new youth justice', in particular simultaneous use of support and control mechanisms with the same young people.

The final chapter brings youth justice up to date by evaluating contemporary developments in youth justice in England and Wales since the fall of New Labour in 2010. Discussion begins with an examination of youth justice developments under the Coalition Government (2010–2015), a period in which Prime Minister David Cameron introduced the 'Big Society' idea and his Government produced the *Breaking the Cycle* Green Paper (2010); the Legal Aid, Sentencing and Punishment of Offenders Act 2012; and the revised assessment and intervention framework, AssetPlus. Each of these developments contained recommendations to progress youth justice policy and practice (e.g. localising youth justice governance, significantly revising the out-of-court and assessment-intervention systems), yet also consolidated key strategies of the 'new youth justice' (e.g. responsibilisation, prevention through risk-focused early intervention). The second chapter section contains an evaluation of the extent to which Coalition youth justice was 'new' as opposed to simply an updated version of the 'new youth justice' (the underpinning focus of the chapter). There follows a detailed discussion of youth justice developments under the Conservative Government that came to power in 2015 – in particular the commissioning and recommendations of a thorough review of the Youth Justice System (Taylor 2016) and the continued significance of the youth custody debate. The penultimate section explores the special case of youth justice in Wales and evaluates the extent to which a distinct 'dragonised' youth justice (the dragon being the national symbol of Wales) has emerged structurally, strategically and in practice. Finally, there is an examination of new frontiers in youth justice nationally and internationally, paying special attention to conceptual, principled and practical developments in relation to the 'children-first' model of positive youth justice.

The summative conclusion section asks, 'What do we know about youth justice?' We address this challenging question by revisiting and re-evaluating the 'triad of youth justice' and the interrelationships between the definitional, explanatory and responsive dichotomies identified on our journey through the socio-historical construction of youth justice. Our book concludes by re-emphasising the complexity, hybridity and socially constructed nature of 'youth justice' and the knowledge and understandings associated with youth justice.

Defining youth offending

The social construction of 'youth offending'

CHAPTER OUTLINE

Our opening chapter explores the pivotal issue of how youth offending is defined. It is crucial to examine how *definitions* of youth offending have been created (constructed) and revised (reconstructed) over time through the activities of various social, cultural, economic, political, professional, academic and media influences and influencers. These definitions determine how, what and who is measured and studied in our search for better understandings of the extent, nature and causes of youth offending. Definitions help us to identify the key influences on youth offending behaviour in order that it can be explained more accurately. In turn, *explanations* and theories of youth offending inform youth justice *responses*. Accordingly, the definitions, explanations and responses associated with youth offending can be seen as interrelated and mutually reinforcing – as illustrated by the 'triad of youth justice' (see Introduction).

A central argument throughout this book is that how 'youth offending' is defined and measured (i.e. socially constructed) shapes how it is understood, explained and responded to socially, legally, politically, practically, academically and in the media. In this way, 'official data are social products' (Box 1981: 208). Therefore, 'youth justice' is best defined as the label given to the formal, systemic responses to offending behaviour by children and young people. Youth justice consists of the philosophies, systems, structures, policies, strategies, processes and practices associated with youth offending – typically informed by official (police and court) statistical measures of the extent and nature of youth offending, but also by self-report studies of offending and victimisation.

CONTROVERSIES AND DEBATES

Measuring youth offending

Much discussion in academic textbooks and student essays focuses on examining statistical trends and patterns in the extent and nature of officially recorded offending by young people over time. These forms of analyses are very useful, of course, because they establish a baseline for how the measurement of youth offending has evolved over time within and between countries and demographic subgroups in these countries (e.g. relating to age, gender and ethnicity). Equivalent analysis of youth justice statistics is possible, for example, examining the trends and patterns in the extent and nature of sentencing in and diversion from the formal Youth Justice System. These youth offending and youth justice statistics are typically labelled 'official' in that they represent data on offending behaviour and justice responses recorded by agencies within the official, formal Youth Justice System of a given country; for example, the police, courts, youth justice teams, the probation service and the prison service. As you will already know from your broader study of criminology, official crime and justice statistics can be reliable (consistent) indicators of the levels, distributions and trends in offending reported by the public and recorded by criminal justice agencies. By their very nature, these forms of official statistics do not measure the 'dark figure' of unreported and unrecorded crime. This issue does not make official statistics any less reliable or useful, as long as we reflect on the extent to which it can render them incomplete and invalid. However, official statistics *can* be unreliable if the recording practices of official agencies change over time or vary within and between countries – such as the inconsistency in police recording statistics between local force areas in the UK until 2002. In other words, if recording practice is unreliable, the resultant statistical trends and any international comparisons may be unreliable.

When the neglect of the dark figure of crime is considered alongside the potential for unreliable recording practices, official criminal justice statistics offer a limited, incomplete measure of (youth) crime. However, if these limitations are accounted for, official statistics can provide reliable baseline indicators of the extent and nature of officially reported and officially recorded youth offending within and between different countries and demographic groups. Also, the neglect of the dark figure of crime can be compensated for to some extent through self-report offending and victimisation surveys, such as the Crime Survey for England and Wales (CSEW – which until 2009–2010 did not survey young people), the International Crime Victims Survey (Europe) and the National Crime Victimization Survey (US). Indeed, the CSEW victimisation survey is now considered to be the 'official' source of crime statistics in England and Wales. However, even self-report surveys can be unreliable. They may employ different or additional questions over time, which is highly likely where new offences enter a country's law and other 'offences' drop out due to being decriminalised or legalised. These surveys may also lack validity if respondents lie, exaggerate, withhold information, mislead, forget or otherwise misrepresent their experiences (Thornberry and Krohn 2003). Therefore, self-report surveys come with a series of caveats to bear in mind when examining their methods and interpreting their findings. That's not to say that we shouldn't use self-report surveys or other official sources for that matter, but that we should do so with caution and criticality. This is the 'ABC' mindset – Always Be Critical. By 'critical' I mean reflective, analytical and balanced, rather than seeking to undermine everything that you read or hear!

Arguably the most important benefit of official statistics to our understanding youth offending is not what they tell us about the ostensible reality of youth crime and justice, but more what they tell us about the preferred definitions, explanations, responses, activities and political priorities of governments and formal criminal justice agencies in different countries at different points in time. In order to better understand these activities and their consequences (e.g. the production of official statistics), it is crucial to take a step back from the statistics themselves to examine the very concept they purport to measure – youth offending.

So, what exactly do we mean by 'youth offending'? What exactly is this behaviour, this category, this phenomenon that official and self-reported statistics have been created to measure? In order to fully understand the extent, nature and influence of youth justice, it is imperative that we **operationalise** youth offending. By operationalise, I mean to clarify the behaviour it seeks to respond to – how we intend to define, understand and work with our central concept. The preceding 'Controversies and debates' box introduces the idea that official (statistical) measures of crime and justice are social constructs (Stephen Box's 'social products'). But what is the behaviour that these measures purportedly represent, and how is it defined? The category of 'youth offending', like its historical predecessor 'juvenile delinquency', is not an uncontested fact. Youth offending is a **social construction** – the creation of institutions and people in specific societies in specific historical periods through the definitions, labels and measures given to specific behaviours, groups and individuals. What we define and understand as 'youth offending' is *dynamic* – it can vary wildly and rapidly over time and place. The definition of youth offending can also be viewed as *contingent* – dependent on (dynamic) historical, cultural, social, economic and political contexts. Such change and variability results in definitions of youth offending being *contested* – subject to debate and disagreement (i.e. a lack of consensus) across history and between and within countries, organisations, professions and individuals. Consequently, youth offending is best viewed as a 'constructed reality' rather than a fact – a reality that is constructed at a given point in time and then subject to reconstruction in the future. The dynamic, contingent and contested nature of youth offending is the reason why you may often see the phrase presented within inverted commas, as if to imply some degree of ambiguity and variability in its definition. The social construction of youth offending and the youth justice responses to it will be clearly illustrated as we progress using the example of the UK (latterly England and Wales), the political, social, cultural, professional and academic context in which this book was written. However, throughout the book I intend to reflect on international variations and similarities in how youth offending and youth justice have been socially constructed (see, for example, Arnull and Fox 2016) across different legal cultures in the industrialised Western world[1] and to utilise international examples where relevant. As such, it is hoped that the arguments presented will be of interest and utility to students and youth justice stakeholders across the globe.

So, let's consider why it is instructive and appropriate to understand youth offending as a social construction. I would argue that there are at least three benefits to knowledge and understanding in adopting this view, relating to the enhancement of:

1   *Validity*: examining youth offending as a social construction provides the most accurate, comprehensive and realistic understanding of what the phenomenon actually is – the complex product (constructed reality) of a series of dynamic, contingent and contested influences, rather than a universal fact that can be uncritically accepted.
2   *Reliability*: if we are clear about exactly what we are focusing on and how it has been operationalised, then we can be consistent and replicable in how we study (e.g. measure) and explain the concept.
3   *Explanatory utility*: the dynamic, contingent and contested definitions of youth offending give us the intellectual space to explain the behaviour differently in different contexts. This social constructionist perspective also allows us to examine the historical, social, political, media and academic influences (and influencers) that have shaped our definitions, explanation and responses regarding youth offending.

Reflecting on the 'triad of youth justice' from the Introduction: how we define youth offending can and should (at least) shape and (at best) determine how we explain it, which in turn can and should determine how we respond to it – how we construct and deliver youth justice. Therefore, it is essential to be explicit about what we mean by youth offending at any given point in time. As I have indicated, pinning down the definition of youth offending is a highly complex exercise because the concept is a dynamic social construction subject to a variety of different and sometimes competing influences. A similar problem is faced when seeking to understand the generic

category of 'crime' or 'offending'. Defining youth offending becomes further complicated when we consider cultural differences, such as how certain cultures and countries
prefer to use the term 'delinquency' to 'offending' and 'juvenile' to 'youth'. In their
review of 'juvenile' justice systems in the non-Western world, Friday and Ren (2006)
attempt to distinguish between 'delinquency' and 'youth offending'. They assert that
in non-Western juvenile justice systems, for example, delinquency is the label given to
less serious offending behaviour committed by a young person in need of protection,
whereas youth offending is considered more serious and deserving of punishment.
However, the authors caution that 'the fine distinction between youthful offender and
delinquent and between the need for help and the demand for punishment is cultural'
and that 'definitions and interpretations are fluid' (Friday and Ren 2006: 16).

CONTROVERSIES AND DEBATES

Is it 'youth offending' or 'juvenile delinquency'?

I am not convinced that the distinction between 'youth offending' and 'juvenile
delinquency' is necessarily valid, helpful or relevant, especially when examining
the social construction of youth offending and juvenile delinquency in the Western
world. In my experience as a youth justice scholar and researcher, more often than
not, the terms 'youth offending' and 'juvenile delinquency' are used interchangeably by youth justice stakeholders such as academics, politicians and practitioners.
My advice is to view the concepts as largely synonymous unless the source you are
using clearly indicates to you that there are differences in how these terms have been
operationalised. For example, some research studies may employ the term 'delinquency' as a catch-all concept to encompass both offending (i.e. legally prohibited
behaviour) and other 'deviant' or 'antisocial' behaviours that may not by legally
prohibited at a given point in time. Similarly, I seldom perceive much difference
in how the terms 'youth' and 'juvenile' are applied, unless their operationalisation
has been clearly differentiated. The key learning point here is to Always Be Critical
(ABC) – analyse every source that you use, engage with them closely to ensure a
full and accurate understanding of their central concepts, and evaluate whether the
authors have fully and accurately operationalised their concepts and evidenced their
arguments (see also Case *et al.* 2017).

Note for the reader

For clarity and consistency, I will employ the term 'youth offending' as standard
throughout the book, although at times it may be used interchangeably with 'youth
crime' and 'juvenile delinquency' (especially when exploring historical debates where
the latter term was more common). Similarly, I will refer to 'youth justice' rather than
'juvenile justice', unless the latter is more appropriate, for example when it is more
faithful to the original source or historical period (e.g. 'juvenile justice' was preferred
to 'youth justice' for much of the period prior to the Crime and Disorder Act 1998).
I will also try to avoid the term 'young offender' (apologies if I occasionally slip up)
in preference to alternatives such as 'children/young people who have offended', as

I consider the former to be a negative label loaded with stigmatising connotations. Please consider all of my personal preferences for terminology as examples of how professional values and accepted practices can influence the social construction of 'youth offending' and our understandings of it.

So where does this leave us? I've argued that youth offending is a social construction, moreover a 'constructed reality', rather than an unequivocal reality or fact. I'll present the evidence for this assertion as we progress through the chapter. However, there is a bigger immediate issue; one that predates any quest to understand 'youth offending' in socio-historical, political, legal or academic terms. Simply put, in order to understand youth offending we need to understand exactly *who* is committing the behaviour – exactly who or what is a 'youth'?

WHAT PUTS THE 'YOUTH' IN 'YOUTH OFFENDING'?

You may think that pursuit of a comprehensive and accurate understanding of the social and historical (socio-historical) evolution of youth offending would need to start by examining what is meant by 'youth', followed by what is meant by 'offending'. Well, no. The social construction of the category of 'youth' is a relatively modern development, so any exploration of youth offending must go even further back to the socio-historical construction of the category of 'child'.

STOP AND THINK

Socially constructing 'youth offending'

How would you define and measure the following concepts?

- Child
- Juvenile
- Adolescent
- Youth

What criteria did you employ to make your judgements? Are there any differences between your judgements, and if so, why?

Would you say that these categories are facts that we can all agree on, or labels that may differ between people and countries?

Now ask yourself the same questions about how you would define youth offending. What factors influence your view?

At what age do you think someone becomes old enough to be arrested and convicted as a 'youth offender' in the country you live in?

- At what age does this youth offender become an adult offender?
- Has this always been the case?
- At what age do you think someone *should* be classified as a young offender, and why?

The 'Stop and think' activity is intended to get you to employ your ABC mindset about how the categories of child, youth and youth offending are socially constructed and are contingent on historical, social, legal, political and cultural influences (cf. Ariès 1962). From here, this chapter will adopt a chronological approach to exploring and explaining how the definitions of child and youth have evolved through the social construction of distinct developmental periods: childhood and adolescence (also known as 'youth'). As stated, the focus will be the UK in order to illustrate and explore these developments within a consistent, detailed social context.[2] Particular attention will be paid to the socio-historically constructed views of 'childhood' as a developmental period of innocence, dependence, protection and socialisation, compared to the post-industrialisation construction of 'adolescence' (the precursor to 'youth') as a period of disruption and corruption. The social construction of adolescence ultimately led to the identification of juvenile delinquency as a distinct legal and behavioural category requiring special treatment, strategies, processes and explanations (Brown 1998; Hopkins-Burke 2016). Chapter discussions will illustrate how this special category of 'juvenile delinquency', otherwise known as 'youth offending', can only be properly understood within its broader socio-historical context (Hendrick 2015). To understand the origins and development of youth offending, the chapter starts by explaining childhood and youth as specific, socially constructed, age-related categories (similar to youth offending as a specific behavioural category) that have undergone multiple constructions and reconstructions over time in response to the specific socio-economic, cultural and political challenges in particular periods. Adding in developments in academic thought, research and media representations around childhood and youth presents us with a complex set of interrelated and contrasting influences on how 'youth offending' has been constructed and understood.

The study of youth offending and youth justice can be a complex, impenetrable exercise at times, so it is my intention throughout the book to provide clear, accessible and coherent exposition of key issues. With this in mind, the definitions chapter is structured as five stages that follow and build on each other chronologically,[3] with each of these five stages summarised by five key points ('5 easy pieces'). Every other chapter will be structured in an equivalent way. The socio-historical construction of 'youth offending' will be traced from the pre-1850s conception of 'childhood', 'youth' and subsequently 'youth offending' through to the construction of the child as innocent and the youth as dangerous in the second half of the nineteenth century (1850–1900), and from there, to the resolution of this innocent–dangerous dichotomy in the first half of the twentieth century (1900–1950). The remaining two stages trace the emergence of the child welfare–youth justice (welfare versus justice) dichotomy across the later twentieth century (1950–1990) to the radical post-1990 'punitive turn' towards harsher forms of justice (reconstructing the child as 'evil'), which was part challenged and part consolidated by a practical risk management approach to youth justice, with both punitive and practical movements being challenged by a more positive 'child-friendly justice'. The five stages will be reflected in subsequent chapters, including being mapped directly onto the discussions of youth justice responses in Chapter 4. There will be ongoing exploration of how these definitions and social constructions may have informed and shaped explanation of and responses to youth offending historically – thus the throughgoing focus will be on the 'triad of youth justice'. At each stage, a number of key influences on the social construction and explanation of childhood, adolescence/youth and juvenile delinquency/youth offending can be discerned, and these will be explored throughout the chapter. These influences and influencers, largely reciprocal and interconnected, can be variously defined as the following:

Socio-economic: widespread changes due to industrialisation and urbanisation, the emerging influence of middle-class values and behaviours, the creation of juvenile-specific institutions, the economically driven representations of children and young people by the media.

Political: lawmaking, evolving government legislation and policy regarding the behaviours and treatment of children and young people, rhetoric from politicians.

Statistical: the creation of new sources of statistical information to categorise groups and behaviours in order to measure the extent and nature of (youth) crime and justice-based responses to it.

Professional: the investigations, experiences and arguments of key stakeholders who practice in the criminal and youth justice systems (with practice differentiating them from the so-called intellectuals), including lawyers, magistrates, police and social workers.

Intellectual: the changing perceptions of children and young people promoted by key thinkers such as philanthropists, moral entrepreneurs and social reformers, combined with the explanations of behaviour provided by academics through empirical research and critical scholarship.

5 EASY PIECES

Defining youth offending

1   *The early social construction of youth offending (pre-1850)* traces the development of early understandings of youth offending/juvenile delinquency from nascent constructions of childhood in the eighteenth century and post–Industrial Revolution notions of children as threats to mid-nineteenth-century arguments for bespoke responses to children who offend.

2   *Socially constructing the innocent–dangerous child dichotomy (1850–1900)* explores the evolution of the innocent–dangerous dichotomy of innocent, vulnerable children in need of care and protection versus the dangerous, threatening child deserving of reform and control when they offend.

3   *Socially reconstructing the innocent–dangerous child dichotomy: innocent children– dangerous adolescents (1900–1950)* discusses the growing influence of the social construction of a distinct developmental period of 'adolescence' on explanations of and responses to offending by younger people (non-adults) as a vehicle to resolve the innocent–dangerous child dichotomy.

4   *Child welfare versus youth justice (1950–1990)* introduces the welfare versus justice debate through discussion of legislation, labelling/moral panic and conflict and ambivalence regarding the most appropriate ways to respond to non-adults who offend.

5   *Reconstructing the child as a 'youth offender' (1990 onwards)* examines the 1990s 'punitive turn' in understanding of children and young people who offend and the associated Government project to reconstruct children/young people as immoral, irresponsible and evil when they offend.

1 THE EARLY SOCIAL CONSTRUCTION OF YOUTH OFFENDING (PRE-1850)

Childhood has long been the subject of wide-ranging academic interest, not least because of widespread concerns about the problems associated with 'youth' and the sense of threat sometimes associated with the idea of young people being out of control (Case *et al.* 2017). Prior to the seventeenth century in Western Europe, however, the notion of 'childhood' as a distinct developmental stage in a person's life did not exist (cf. Ariès 1962). Consequently, prior to the seventeenth century, there was no such thing as a 'youth' and so there was no such thing as 'youth offending'. There was offending. There was even offending by people of an age that we now label as 'youth'. However, the terms 'youth' and 'juvenile' were not used to refer to specially identified groups within the broader population at that time, so there could be no youth offending or juvenile delinquency. This point may seem a bit like 'If a tree falls in the woods and no one is there to hear it, does it make a sound?' Not so – it illustrates clearly how people and behaviours need to be categorised, labelled and constructed before they can be defined, explained and responded to. Philippe Ariès (a French medievalist and historian of the family, 1914–1984), for instance, believed that childhood was effectively a modern invention, only discovered in the Middle Ages. Recognising that children were virtually absent from artistic works before this time and that there was an absence of any distinctive form of dress, he suggested that this indicated 'a marked indifference . . . to the special characteristics of childhood' (Ariès 1962: 73). Although the arguments of Ariès have been the subject of debate since they were introduced, notably regarding their narrow cultural, **ethnocentric** bias (cf. Pollock 1983), he is widely credited for introducing important considerations of how childhood has been socially constructed and thus divorced from its biological/physiological basis (cf. Shore 2011). Notwithstanding debates around the veracity of Ariès' claims, it is fair to say that up until the mid-1700s in the UK, children were generally treated in the same way as adults, with the same social standing, socio-cultural and legal expectations of them (Case and Smith, in Case *et al.* 2017). This state of affairs may help to account for the apparent liability of children in pre-modern times to the same, often extreme, forms of punishment as their elders. In fact, prior to the Victorian era (1837–1901), distinguishing a period of 'childhood' was arguably irrelevant and unnecessary anyway, as three-quarters of working-class children died before the age of 5! The Victorian era increase in life expectancy, therefore, had an influence upon the social construction of childhood. In the early nineteenth century, therefore, children in society were basically smaller, younger adults in terms of appearance, lifestyle, culture, employment (e.g. children were typically put to work from the age of 5 – obviously if they were still alive at that point) and in the eyes of the legal system. Until well into the nineteenth century, there were no differentiations accorded to age in the method of bringing offenders to trial, or in the form of trial itself, in the punishments that could be imposed or, generally, in the way in which they were enforced (Radzinowicz and Hood 1986). Children were subjected to **adulterisation** – being understood and receiving treatment equivalent to that of adults because they were seen as (little) adults. Then came the historical period of 'modernity'.

From the middle of the eighteenth century, the Industrial Revolution swept across Western Europe, expanding the influence of modernity and significantly impacting upon economic structures, means of production and, most importantly, the role of the child in society. New capitalist market economies built on modernised factory production enhanced by new technologies were accompanied by rapid urban expansion, such as the building of houses in industrial towns and cities in previously rural areas. A by-product of these developments was increasing demand for child labour in the factories and mills, a demand that was easily met by the booming child population. Put simply, children worked cheap and were more expendable than adults. This situation was just as well because they were often forced into more dangerous jobs due to their small size, such as crawling behind and inside machinery to clean and repair it. However, very soon, social reformers such as Mary Carpenter and Matthew Davenport Hill began to campaign against the use of child labour for reasons of philanthropy and protection, often grounded in Christian religious values and the growing social attitude that children were innocent and vulnerable beings. These campaigns were strengthened by a resistance to the exploitation of children as cheap labour (which also undermined the value of adult labour) and the need for more skilled workers and hence more educated children to enter the workplace when they were older – what eminent criminologist-historian Roger Hopkins-Burke calls 'deferring the age of wage' (Hopkins-Burke 2017, personal correspondence). Consequently, with fewer available jobs and no compulsory education provision (until the late 1800s), newly unemployed children were increasingly forced onto the streets during the daytime. While on the streets, children socialised with their peers, formed groups (the precursors to gangs) and behaved like children do – loudly, energetically and childishly. With such a change in social dynamics, children and their behaviours became much more visible than ever before and they were increasingly identified as a different, special and other social group that looked, sounded, thought and behaved differently to adults. One manifestation of this difference was that children[4] were now starved of legitimate employment opportunities and so were increasingly turning towards petty crime and other nuisance behaviours for financial reasons and due to youthful exuberance and boredom (Muncie 2014).

On a global scale, during the seventeenth century, the ways in which the world and human behaviour were examined, understood and responded to changed dramatically. Gone was the dominant culture of religious beliefs and folk traditions in shaping our knowledge bases. In came more secular, scientific and rational ways of understanding the world. Out went feudal economic and legal systems that based society around relationships between landowners and labourers (peasants) in rural contexts. In came industrialised processes (e.g. market economies, waged labour) and urbanised living arrangements in new towns and cities. Therefore, the period known as 'modernity' heralded 'the development of a secular, scientific, rational, increasingly industrialized and urban tradition' (Hopkins-Burke 2016: 24). Concurrent to these cultural and economic changes, a modern conception of 'childhood' was emerging, driven by the growing middle-class population that was becoming discernible from the more traditional working class (peasant) and upper class (landowner). Middle-class influence on the social construction of childhood, youth and youth offending is a recurrent theme across this chapter. The new middle class lived in houses in towns and cities – all of which were relatively new constructions (pardon the pun). They valued formal education (although only for the sons at that time) and viewed the child as essential to the family (Ariès 1962). The importance of understanding, nurturing and socialising the immature, innocent, vulnerable child in their formative years (soon to be labelled 'childhood') became a dominant middle-class attitude and quickly came to represent an 'acceptable' and ultimately enforceable model of parenting (Arthur 2016; Hopkins-Burke 2016).

Children as threats

The newly identified and publicised differences between children and adults inevitably caused anxieties among the general public (of adults), who struggled to understand and explain this emerging social group and their peculiar, chaotic ways. In particular, there was a stark contrast between social attitudes portraying children as innocent and perceptions of the same group as newly visible, threatening and dangerous to the general public. Indeed, this struggle to resolve conflicting views of children based on their behaviour has arguably never ended and constitutes a recurring theme in youth justice – what will be labelled a 'Recurring Theme Alert' (**RTA**) across the book. The acknowledgement of differences in behaviour between children and adults ushered in the modern notion of childhood as a distinct developmental period requiring bespoke explanation and treatment. An equivalent social movement was occurring in the US in the early nineteenth century, as middle-class values and urbanisation/industrialisation encouraged new attitudes about children as innocent/vulnerable/fragile and emphasised society's obligations to them (Soung 2011). Notably, these changing attitudes only related to white children at that time in the US, with post-slavery black children retaining their status as property and labour providers exempt from the innocent child perception and the nurture, protection and political/economic rights afforded to white children (Feld 1999; Soung 2011). The social construction of childhood offered societies a framework for understanding the unknown. Interestingly, these differences were represented as more of a social problem to be addressed than a normal element of growing up. For example, social reformer Lord Ashley scathingly categorised working-class children who offended as a 'fearful multitude of untutored savages'. As children grew more visible due to spending more time on the streets with one another, their behaviours became viewed as ever more different and therefore threatening to adults. These public concerns inevitably evolved into governmental concerns. As a result, behaviours that were once seen as little more than a nuisance were now increasingly criminalised (May 1973). Criminal justice responses began to focus more on types of visible street 'crime' such as drunkenness, gambling, mischief and dangerous play (Muncie 1984). Furthermore, the category of 'status offences' was introduced to tackle criminal behaviours to children and young people, such as truancy and sexual precociousness. These status offences could be seen as an early construction of 'youth offending', as they identified behaviours by children that should be defined, measured, explained and responded to differently to those of adults. Indeed, status offences remain an important element of youth justice systems across a number of Western and Eastern European countries including England and Wales, Scotland, Bulgaria, Estonia and Finland (Dunkel *et al.* 2010). A new category of 'juvenile delinquency' began to emerge, initially covering the offending behaviour of children, with public and governmental discussions focusing on the need to create penal and legal strategies and structures to respond to the ostensibly growing problem of children breaking the law (Shore 1999).

CONTROVERSIES AND DEBATES

The pre-nineteenth-century social construction of juvenile delinquency?

Evidence suggests that the social construction of juvenile delinquency through bespoke language, structures, strategies and processes comfortably predates the common starting point for historical analysis, the beginning of Victorian era (1837–1901). It is possible to trace the use of specialised language to categorise juvenile delinquency back to the sixteenth century. For example, Paul Griffiths has identified evidence of 'places of confinement for the young', specialised forms of policing for disorderly youth and attempts at reformation as far back as the pre-nineteenth century (Griffiths 2002: 25). Furthermore, courts were shaping their judgements in relation to the defendant's age prior to the late eighteenth century (Shore 2011). Raymond Arthur (2016) asserts that concern over the causes of juvenile crime, the issue of criminal responsibility and the remedy for youthful misbehaviour can be traced back to the 1790s and the formation of the earliest voluntary societies aimed at addressing the juvenile delinquency problem. The best example of a voluntary society is the 'Philanthropic Society', which was essentially a 'new youth justice' structure responding to public and political concerns from the 1780s regarding disorderly and idle children and a need to increase the provision of basic educational facilities for the poor (King 2006). The Philanthropic Society signified a new sensibility towards the criminal and delinquent child (Straker and Sons 1988, in Shore 2011) through its focus on 'those who most need instruction [and] have been most neglected; and those who did not find friends in their parents [and] have found none in the Public, but have been abandoned to infamy and ruin' (Philanthropic Society 1792: 6, in Shore 2011). In the 1790s, the Philanthropic Society placed delinquent boys into the 'Reform', where they were provided with a moral and social education. Once 'sufficiently reformed', they were transferred to the 'Manufactory', where they were taught practical skills and undertook employment. Another bespoke institution, the 'Refuge for the Destitute' (founded in London in 1806) exemplified how the Government worked closely with the philanthropic (voluntary) sector, such that by the mid-1830s the Refuge was essentially a (partially) state-funded juvenile reformatory (King 2006; Shore 2011).

These late eighteenth-century linguistic and structural/institutional developments suggest that socio-economic and intellectual influences on the social construction of juvenile delinquency were evident long before the Victorian era and even prior to the nineteenth century.

Notwithstanding evidence of even earlier social constructions of juvenile delinquency, it is clear that from the mid-1700s to the early 1800s, the notion of a child crime 'problem' (remember that we did not have 'youth' at this time) was legitimised by the production of official statistics and research data measuring the extent of crime committed by children and indicating that this behaviour was increasing rapidly (cf. Pearson 1983). Purported increases in child crime amounted to something of a self-fulfilling prophecy, therefore, because the category of child crime had been created, whereas previously it had not existed, so there were no statistics or data relating to it. The consequent emphasis on its investigation and targeting by criminal justice agencies (e.g. the police and courts), Government, academics, public and media exacerbated the extent of the perceived problem. As such, crime by children was becoming 'a vehicle for articulating mounting anxieties about issues, which really have nothing to do with crime at all: social change in the stability of social hierarchy' (Gatrell 1990: 249). Several academic historians have identified the period 1820–1850 as particularly significant in the social construction of juvenile delinquency due to the creation of legislation, statistics, structures and empirical evidence to address offending by children as a distinct phenomenon.

CONTROVERSIES AND DEBATES

Juvenile delinquency as a cause for alarm in 1816

The empirical identification of children (more precisely, working-class children) as a distinct group of offenders arguably predates even the 1820–1850 period that this chapter goes on to discuss. The social construction of juvenile delinquency was influenced by statistics and data from an early research study in 1816, boasting the snappy title *Report of the Committee for Investigating the Causes of the Alarming Increase of Juvenile Delinquency in the Metropolis* (cf. Pinchbeck and Hewitt 1981). (We will call it the Alarming Increase Committee study so that I stay under within the required word count for the book.) The Alarming Increase Committee was initiated and formed by a group of philanthropists and penal reformers responding to political and public concern (which they had helped to construct) in London, UK, that 'juvenile delinquency existed in the Metropolis to a very alarming extent' (Alarming Increase Committee 1816: 5, in Pinchbeck and Hewitt 1981). In reality, the alleged alarming increase that prompted the study was but one small part of a much broader public debate around penal policy and policing practices that had been stimulated by an increase in recorded crime – adult crime (King 2006). Juvenile delinquency represented a brand-new focus for public concerns about the negative outcomes of industrialisation and urbanisation: outcomes such as insubordination, idleness, public disorder and increases in recorded crime. As such, children were held up as 'powerful representatives of the shape of the future . . . dangerous manifestations of these broader social problems' (King 2006: 106). This would not be the last time that children and young people would be scapegoats for adult misbehaviours and adult anxieties regarding the future cohesion of society. The newly created 'problem' of juvenile delinquency prompted the establishment of the Committee with the objective 'to obtain every possible information respecting the nature and causes of the evil in question' (Alarming Increase Committee 1816: 6, in Pinchbeck and Hewitt 1981).

A list of 190 boys held in Newgate Prison was compiled by the Committee, and its members set out to interview each of these boys regarding their delinquent behaviour – although some parents were resistant to allowing their child to be interviewed. Following the interviews, the Committee concluded that there were thousands of boys under the age of 17 in the metropolis daily engaged in crime, thus establishing an early focus on the criminal behaviour of boys (rather than girls) and identifying 17 as an upper age limit for youth offending (where it stays to this day in England and Wales). The causes of juvenile delinquency were poor parenting (e.g. improper conduct, excessive punishment), lack of education (including frequent truancy), lack of employment and delinquent lifestyle (e.g. gambling, drinking alcohol) – all combining to produce an immoral character in the child (cf. Goldson and Jamieson 2002). Subsidiary systemic causes were also identified: lax criminal code (ineffective laws), defective policing and poor prison discipline. The emphasis upon parenting, education, employment, lifestyle and ineffective system responses as the main explanations for juvenile delinquency are key socio-historical themes that persist today, having evolved into the positivist and risk factor theories have subsumed the explanatory project (see Chapters 2 and 3) and that continue to shape youth justice responses (see, for example, Chapters 4–6).

The pre-Victorian social construction of juvenile delinquency: 1820–1850

A particular focus of developing constructions of juvenile delinquency is clearly the 1820–1850 period, which both predates and overlaps the Victorian era beginning in 1837. Similar developments were occurring in the US at that time (Platt 1969). Several notable criminologist-historians, including Heather Shore (2011), Peter King (2006), Paul Griffiths (2002), Susan Magarey (1978), Margaret May (1973) and Ivy Pinchbeck and Margaret Hewitt (1973), have challenged the accepted assertion that the social construction of juvenile delinquency was a development of the Victorian era (cf. Radzinowicz and Hood 1986). Some have focused on the language of the State and emerging political debate about child crime before this era (e.g. Magarey, May), while others have combined socio-cultural analyses of contemporary debates with more empirically led approaches to provide a more meaningful measure of the growth of juvenile delinquency in the nineteenth century (e.g. Shore, King).

In political, *legislative* terms, the Vagrant Act 1824 and the Malicious Trespass Act 1827 were introduced, and as a result, a wider range of typical youthful behaviours began to be criminalised. This criminalisation was consolidated by the Metropolitan Police Act 1829, which empowered police officers to target and arrest:

> all loose, idle and disorderly Persons whom he shall find disturbing the Public Peace, or whom he shall have just Cause to suspect of any evil Designs, and all Persons whom he shall find between Sunset and the Hour of Eight in the Forenoon lying in any Highway, Yard, or other Place, or loitering therein, and not giving a satisfactory Account of themselves.
>
> (in Magarey 1978: 21)

In other words, those people more likely to behave in rowdy ways, cause nuisance and be on the streets after dark were more likely to be targeted and arrested – a practice that disproportionately prioritised the behaviour of children. These new police powers were extended in the follow-up Metropolitan Police Act 1829 (which largely established the modern professional police force) to include 'people found in a thoroughfare or public place flying a kite, playing any game "to the Annoyance of the Inhabitants or Passengers", or making a slide in the ice or snow' – again, targeting behaviours disproportionately likely to be committed by children rather than adults, particularly by the 'street children' of the poor, working classes (Magarey 1978). Consequently, the identification of 'delinquency' as a specific and escalating social problem requiring a distinct response was influenced by legislation, particularly relating to police practice.

An arguably even more important influence on the nineteenth-century (pre-Victorian) social construction of juvenile delinquency was the creation of official crime *statistics* and their delineation by age (May 1973). Following the Gaol Act 1835 (inspired by contemporary developments in the French and Belgian criminal justice systems), the Home Office Criminal Registrar began requiring detailed statistical returns from local prisons, which enabled the collection of localised prison statistics categorised by age. The statistical category of 'juvenile' generally referred to children aged up to 17 years old. In 1838, 9,686 under-17s were committed to prison in England and Wales, rising to 11,720 in 1843. Despite regional inconsistencies in terms of measurement, these new prison statistics indicated that the numbers of under-17s formally registered as 'delinquent' (by spending time in prison) was increasing during the 1840s, and increasing faster than the population in that age group (Magarey 1978). However, these increases and the growing juvenile crime 'problem' that they appeared to implicate did not continue into the 1850s, despite the claims of middle-class reformers. Consequently, historians concluded that the perceptions of the growing problem of juvenile delinquency (largely middle-class perceptions) were paradoxically accurate and inaccurate – they were broadly justified by the statistical evidence throughout the 1830s and 1840s, but they were 'wildly imprecise' in their judgement of the extent and duration of the problem (Magarey 1978).

The creation of official prison statistics for juveniles, running concurrently to new legislation that created more juvenile offenders (reflected in these statistics) by extending police powers, led to the creation of specific *structures* to respond to this 'new' phenomenon of juvenile delinquency (see Chapter 4 for more detailed discussion). Prior to the reformatory and industrial schools of the 1850s (see Section 2 of this chapter), Parkhurst Prison was established in 1838, designed largely with the male juvenile criminal in mind (Pinchbeck and Hewitt 1973). Training was to be a key feature of the new prison, with the objective of producing better and more useful colonial citizens for transportation to Western Australia. However, Parkhurst as a juvenile-specific prison was relatively short-lived and ceased receiving juveniles in 1864, this being recognised by historians as a failed experiment (Shore 2011).

Thus far, we have seen how political/legislative, statistical and structural influences played crucial roles in the social construction of juvenile delinquency in the 1820–1850 period that predated and overlapped with the onset of the Victorian era. A final notable influence during that time was the *intellectual/professional*, which sought to make sense of the growing statistical trends in juvenile delinquency and the associated political and public anxieties that they caused. Public fears precipitated a wave of unofficial intellectual/professional inquiries (studies) in the 1830s and 1840s, which typically confirmed current statistical trends in juvenile delinquency and thus consolidated the perception of juvenile delinquency as a distinct and growing social problem (May 1973). Unofficial (non-governmental) studies during that period (and even earlier) accumulated and analysed detailed information regarding the extent and nature of juvenile delinquency as a behaviour distinct from other social problems such as general crime. Most were empirical studies conducted by professionals who had everyday experience of children who committed crime. These professionals constructed understandings of 'juvenile delinquents' based on their expertise, values and biases – although the extent of this subjectivity was often overlooked by politicians and the public due to their status as 'credible' professionals (May 1973).

According to May (1973), the most authoritative group of social investigators throughout the 1830s and 1840s was drawn from the numerous statistical societies, so merging statistical and professional influences on the social construction of juvenile delinquency. The work of these 'moral statisticians' was highly influential in creating a 'science' of criminology that could focus in detail on the age of the offender – in other words, being able to examine youth offending empirically and through the identification of verifiable facts and patterns of offending. Consequently, moral statisticians were able to identify the first clear concept of 'juvenile delinquency' (May 1973) and by the 1840s, juvenile delinquency was being treated as a separate social problem, distinct from crime. A notable influence on this distinction was the identification of the 'age-crime curve' that demonstrated the correlation between age and the extent and nature of offending. However, the social construction of a distinct juvenile delinquency perpetuated a largely negative view of children who offended as

> a youthful population . . . devoted to crime, trained to it from infancy, adhering to it from education and circumstances . . . differing from the rest of society not only in thoughts, habits and manners but even in appearance.
> (W. A. Miles 1835 – Select Committee of the House of Lords on the Present State of the Several Gaols and Houses of Correction in England and Wales)

Here we have another Recurring Theme Alert (**RTA**) with relation to the socio-historical construction of juvenile delinquency and youth justice – placing the focus and blame for child offending disproportionately upon the working classes, their chaotic, disorganised lifestyles (demonstrated by the behaviour of street children) and (particularly) inadequate parenting (an **RTA** in its own right). Middle-class commentators spoke of 'parents destitute of all sense of parental responsibility', with juvenile delinquency resulting from 'too early and exposure to the hardships and temptations of life [so] children were driven to crime and vagrancy by sheer necessity' (Matthew Davenport Hill, in Muncie *et al.* 2002: 106). In contrast to the prison reformist views of children as experiencing socio-structural deprivation and neglect, moral statisticians and empiricists began to define 'youth offending' in individualised, pathological ways as the results of abnormality, immorality, impulsivity, poverty and living in criminogenic, socially disorganised neighbourhoods. Whichever view was taken, it seemed that inadequate parenting among the working class was ultimately seen as the main culprit (May 1973).

5 EASY PIECES

1 The early social construction of youth offending (pre-1850)

1 *Little adults*: until the eighteenth century, children in society were viewed as 'little adults', equivalent to adults in appearance, leisure pursuits and subject to the same social norms and laws.
2 *The social construction of childhood*: the concept of 'childhood' was socially constructed; created/invented as a distinct developmental stage characterised by dependence, innocence and vulnerability, in order to structure understandings/explanations of the increasingly visible behavioural, psychological and physical differences between children and adults (Ariès 1962).
3 *Industrial Revolution social changes*: the post–Industrial Revolution modernisation and urbanisation of the mid-eighteenth century onwards moved children out of the factories and increasingly onto the streets.
4 *The visible, threatening child*: the increased visibility of working-class street children became a source of public concern and these children started to be viewed as dangerous and threatening, rather than innocent and vulnerable.
5 *Constructing specific responses to juvenile delinquency*: the 1820–1850 period progressed the social construction of 'juvenile delinquency' through the creation of specific institutions, statistics and professional bodies for responding to children who offended – although some commentators have traced these social construction processes even further back.

2 SOCIALLY CONSTRUCTING THE INNOCENT–DANGEROUS CHILD DICHOTOMY (1850–1900)

By 1851, 'juvenile delinquency' was established among the upper and middle classes (Magarey's 'journal reading, servant-employing Britons') as a major social problem in England (Magarey 1978). The perception of a juvenile delinquency 'problem' was vindicated by the creation of official crime and justice statistics and emerging research data, notably during the 1820–1850 period but traceable back to at least 1816. The Government further legislated juvenile delinquency into existence (Muncie 2004) in the 1850s and throughout the rest of the nineteenth century. For the first time, juvenile delinquency was recognised as a distinct social phenomenon and behavioural category, notably through the Juvenile Offenders Act of 1847 and the Youthful Offenders Act of 1854. In between these acts, social reformer Mary Carpenter published *Reformatory Schools for the Perishing and Dangerous Classes and for Juvenile Offenders*, consolidating her arguments in 1853 with *Juvenile Delinquents – Their Condition and Treatment*. The latter publication contended that society had assigned to children who offended 'qualities the very reverse of what we should desire to see in childhood; we have beheld them independent, self-reliant, advanced in the knowledge of evil'. Carpenter believed the very opposite, that children were physically and mentally very different from and less developed than adults, so the negative qualities assigned to them were inappropriate and should not guide society's responses to children who offended.

RTA = ADULTERISATION

Children are assigned adult capabilities when they offend and are subject to criminal justice responses reserved for adults, in contravention of prevailing views of children in society as innocent, immature and incapable.

Demands for remedial state action inevitably followed the discovery/creation of juveniles as social and institutional outcasts. Social reformers such as Mary Carpenter and Matthew Davenport Hill led a prolonged campaign for reform, often dubbed the 'child-saving' movement, which harnessed support from a powerful cross-section of religious, political and professional stakeholders. Central to this reform campaign was to reinvigorate the legal principle of doli incapax, outlined by Blackstone in 1796 – 'the capacity of doing ill, or contracting guilt, is not so much measured by years and days, as by the strength of the delinquent's understanding and judgement'. At that time, children up to the age of 7 were presumed incapable of criminal intent and could not be held personally responsible for violations of the law; children between the ages of 7 and 14 were presumed innocent unless the prosecution proved their ability to 'discern between good and evil' (the presumption of doli incapax); thereafter they were fully responsible. Social reformers reanimated the argument that the child's capacity to understand right and wrong in regard to offending behaviour should take into account their chronological age and associated immaturity and lack of cognitive and emotional development, along with parental neglect. However, there was much ambiguity surrounding the definition (social construction) of the child's (age of) criminal culpability and the State's right to interfere with parents and parenting practice. Even social reformers were uncertain as to the age at which the distinction between (irresponsible) child and (responsible) adult should be made, the degree of guilt exhibited by children and the purpose of punishment itself. The most disputed indicator of criminal responsibility was age (May 1973). For example, the 1852–1853 Select Committee heard conflicting evidence on the delinquent's capacity to distinguish between right and wrong and the age at which this capacity was reached, with opinion ranging from 10 to 16 years old. At the same time, there were increasing middle-class anxieties about working-class children upsetting the social order – anxieties that were to potentially worsen with the imminent abolition of transportation for offenders. The division of opinion regarding children's culpability for their offending and the pressure of growing middle-class anxieties produced a legislative compromise in the animation of Mary Carpenter's proposals for reformatory schools (Youthful Offenders Act 1854) for convicted offenders and industrial schools (Industrial Schools Act 1857) for the potentially criminal and neglected child (with similar measures being passed in both Scotland and Ireland at around the same time).

So, by the mid-nineteenth century, the children of the working classes had become viewed as a serious threat to the social order. Social reformers such as Mary Carpenter spoke of working-class children as the 'dangerous' classes and the 'perishing' classes. Social constructions of working-class children as dangerous threats were counterbalanced by middle-class representations of children as perishing victims of widespread poverty caused by rapid industrialisation and poor parenting. Reflecting contemporary views of children, these more sympathetic perceptions were largely reserved only for children who did not break the law. Accordingly, there was an urgent need to theorise 'childhood' so that social and penal responses could be appropriately targeted. For example, existing penal responses to children who offended emphasised punishment or rehabilitation (responding to children as if they were a threat), which was incongruous with the perception of children as victims of social disadvantage, poverty, inadequate parenting and unmet needs. The major structural development within the Youthful Offenders Act 1854 was the establishment of the reformatory school as a structure/institution to reform and rehabilitate threatening children who were delinquent, notably by inculcating them with the Protestant work ethic that they would need to carry with them into adult employment (Hopkins-Burke 2016). Soon after, the Industrial Schools Act of 1857 introduced the industrial school to treat the neglected and victimised children (aged 7 to 14 years) of the perishing classes and to prepare them for a life of work – a direct alternative to the reformatory school intended for the more threatening, dangerous classes. This development illustrates a dichotomy in how children and their behaviour were viewed, explained and responded to until the late 1800s – as dangerous threats when they offended and as perishing victims when they did not. In short, reformatory schools were to be reserved for convicted offenders (the 'dangerous classes'), while industrial schools took the potential delinquent and neglected child (the 'perishing classes'). It is also possible to discern the beginnings of the welfare-justice debate here, a debate that would be a recurring theme in youth justice responses from that point. Put simply, industrial schools can be seen as a welfare-based response to the perishing classes, while reformatory schools were a justice-based response for the dangerous classes of convicted offenders (see also Chapter 4).

The social construction of young working-class males as distinct, threatening entities was consolidated in the second half of the nineteenth century by changes in their lifestyle related to leisure time. The growing affluence of the working class relative to previous generations coincided with and stimulated the growth of a range of new leisure opportunities such as variety theatres, public houses, gambling dens, travel opportunities (e.g. day excursions) and sporting events such as boxing and football (cf. Hopkins-Burke 2016). However, these new entertainment forms were viewed by the middle classes as cheap, nasty and dangerous pursuits. They were considered to be ungodly and reflective of a moral failure within the working class and, of course, a failure of appropriate parenting. Anxieties were exacerbated because the middle class lacked control over these working-class leisure pursuits, whereas they retained control over other working-class experiences such as education, employment and criminal justice responses. Here we see further evidence of how growing social differences between subgroups of the population can be constructed as indicating a threat to social order and the need for control – enduring themes in the socio-historic construction of juvenile delinquency.

The changing role of children

In the latter part of the 1800s, as the birth rate and family sizes fell in the UK, the middle-class ideal of the child as essential to the family transferred into working-class attitudes. In the same period, the philosopher Rousseau asserted childhood to be a state of innocence and vulnerability, in line with middle-class conceptions of needy children and perishing classes. The dominant social construction of children became one of younger, less mature individuals who needed to be protected by adults from the harm caused to them by other adults. This social attitude of children as innocent, vulnerable and in need began to influence the way that all parents, not just the middle classes, socialised their children (Muller 1973) – an early incarnation of the welfare approach (as opposed to justice- or punishment-based approaches) to working with children who offend (see Chapter 4; see also Haines and Case 2015). With fewer jobs available, a vastly diminished need for child labour and increasing moral resistance to the exploitation of child workers, children became much more dependent on their families – a financial burden rather than a source of income. A significant influence on the changing views of children at this time was legislation that introduced compulsory education for all children aged between 5 and 13 years old (Education Act 1870) and the 1876 Royal Commission on the Factory Act, which advocated compulsory education as a means of abolishing child labour. This legislation took children out of the working world and would further increase the financial burden they imposed upon the families. In turn, families were now more consumers and producers (e.g. of food and other commodities) due to increasing urbanisation and industrialisation, which further increased the financial burden placed upon them by the child. However, the short-term financial burden of the child became a long-term financial benefit, as families began to rely on the child's earning capacity in later life as a means of sustaining and supporting them. Therefore, the role of the child in the family and in society had changed and children were established as a distinct social group, whose behaviour required different explanations and responses (e.g. sentences, interventions, treatments, services). Understandings of the 'child' were being reconstructed by legislation, child savers, philosophers and changing social attitudes towards an emphasis upon children as innocents in need of protection, education and socialisation, as opposed to expendable commodities or dangerous entities in need of control. Accordingly, children's ignorance, weakness and innocence began to be emphasised, and they were viewed now as 'fragile creatures . . . who needed to be both safeguarded and reformed' (Ariès 1962: 133). The implications of this argument are that childhood itself has only come to be seen as a separate life stage in tandem with, and as a result of, wider social changes, such as industrialisation, the specialisation of labour and the associated need for longer periods of education and preparation for work (cf. Case 2017; www.youtube.com/watch?v=QYWPyiZIpV8).

The second half of the nineteenth century (our chronological second stage in this chapter) evidenced an increasing focus on the *reform* of children who offended and a move away from punitive responses to these children (see also Chapter 4 discussion of youth justice responses). The period 1850–1900 was highly significant in the developing social construction of juvenile delinquency through a series of socio-economic, political/legislative, statistical and professional influences and marked increasing blurring of society's explanations of and responses to children who offended (as dangerous threats) and children who were neglected (as vulnerable, innocent and dependent).

5 EASY PIECES

2 Socially reconstructing the innocent–dangerous child dichotomy (1850–1900)

1   *Perishing or dangerous children*: in the early 1850s, the social reformer Mary Carpenter identified children from the 'perishing classes' who were socially disadvantaged and neglected, comparing them with children from the 'dangerous classes' who were more threatening and criminal.
2   *Doli incapax*: at the same time, the legal principle of doli incapax was reemphasised in understandings of and responses to children who offended – the presumption that children aged 7 to 14 were unable to distinguish between right and wrong in relation to their offending behaviour unless this could be proven otherwise.
3   *Legislating youth offending into existence*: the Youthful Offenders Act 1854 was a major legislative influence on the social construction of juvenile delinquency through its introduction of reformatory schools for the reform (not punishment) of convicted offenders (from the 'dangerous classes'). It was followed in 1857 by the Industrial Schools Act and its introduction of industrial schools for the potentially criminal and neglected child (from the 'perishing classes').
4   *Middle-class values*: the social construction of a dichotomy between the dependent, innocent, perishing child and the threatening, chaotic, dangerous child offender was perpetuated by the middle classes as a response to their anxieties regarding working-class lifestyles/leisure pursuits and their perceptions of inadequate parenting and working-class children's misbehaviour as threats to the social order.
5   *Children as innocent*: at the end of the nineteenth century, the prevailing social attitude to children reflected in legislation was that they were typically innocent, vulnerable, dependent and in need of care and protection. However, children who offended were increasingly viewed as dangerous, threatening and in need of reform (although with less of a punitive focus than before).

3   SOCIALLY RECONSTRUCTING THE INNOCENT–DANGEROUS CHILD DICHOTOMY: INNOCENT CHILDREN–DANGEROUS ADOLESCENTS (1900–1950)

It is in the nexus between child welfare, juvenile delinquency and the emergence of the adolescent that much of the work on the twentieth century juvenile justice system has sought to place itself.

(Shore 2011: 122)

The late nineteenth-century reconstruction of the child as innocent and vulnerable presented a serious social problem: how should society understand children who were behaving in troublesome ways and causing concern to the public, while maintaining this new construction of children as innocent and in need? What of the 'dangerous' classes and the notion of children as threats? An answer to this apparently complex dilemma came in the social construction of a new developmental category of 'adolescence', later known as 'youth'. Towards the turn of the twentieth century, social scientists (mainly psychologists) began to explore adolescence as a specific developmental stage experienced by older children around the age of puberty and in their teenage years. According to Muncie (2014), however, it was not until the late nineteenth century, influenced by the advent of compulsory education, that the concept of adolescence began to shape understandings of the children of the working classes. Adolescence was purportedly characterised by series of biological, psychological and sociological (also known as **biopsychosocial**) factors and pathologies that conspired to make adolescents more threatening, disruptive and deviant than younger children (Brown 1998). Indeed, as Chapter 2 will illustrate, the dominant academic explanations of youth offending continue to focus on biopsychosocial influences. G. Stanley Hall (1904) famously described the stage of adolescence as one of 'storm and stress', where adolescents experience predetermined biological and psychological stresses (e.g. hormonal changes, puberty) that render their behaviour chaotic and difficult to manage. The biopsychological determinism employed to explain adolescence was based on a perceived contrast between the collective behaviour of working-class youths and the 'normal adolescent demeanour' of their more conformist middle-class peers, the argument being that the behaviour of the middle classes was desirable for all adolescents. Once again, the working classes were judged and treated based on middle-class standards and values (Griffiths 2002). If they failed to live up to those standards, working-class adolescents were labelled deviant and immoral (see Chapter 2's discussion of labelling theories as an explanation of youth offending), while their parents were blamed for inadequate socialisation. The social construction of adolescence as a distinct developmental and pathological stage (with a particular wave of social construction taking place from 1870 to 1914; see Gillis 1975; Springhall 1986; Hendrick 1990) provided an ideal vehicle with which to explain offending behaviour by older children, while retaining the view of younger children as vulnerable and innocent. Adolescence became the dominant framework for explaining the transition from childhood to adulthood. The discovery of the 'adolescent' as a problematic category of younger person (too old to be a child and too young to be an adult) began to shape public attitudes and Government policy regarding youth offending from the later nineteenth century (Davies 1982), encompassing a range of categories that were developing to describe problematic (older) children and maintaining the juvenile delinquent as the key focus group for reformers.

Government legislation animated the perceived need for distinct responses to the behaviours of this newly constructed group of adolescents, who would later become better known as 'youths' (see Section 4 of this chapter). The Youthful Offenders Act 1901 and the Probation of Offenders Act 1907 both extended the use of alternatives to custody for children, typically adolescents. This legislation was followed by the Children Act 1908, which sought to reconcile welfare and justice imperatives through the introduction of juvenile courts that had simultaneous civil jurisdiction over needy children and criminal jurisdiction over children (typically adolescents) who offended (Hopkins-Burke 2016; see also Chapter 4). The Act also abolished the use of imprisonment for young people below the age of 14 and only permitted imprisonment for 14- to 15-year-olds in exceptional cases (Joyce 2017). These legislative measures essentially established the child as a special category of person requiring special treatment in different domains of their life. The Children Act 1908 reflected the 'conflict and ambivalence' (Gelsthorpe and Morris 1994: 951) with which children were viewed (**RTA = conflict and ambivalence in understandings and treatment of children demonstrating problematic behaviour**), simultaneously deserving of saving (as children) and of punishment (as young people), depending on their behaviour and often small variations in their age. In the same year, borstals (custodial institutions) were established for 16- to 21-year-olds, with the dual purpose of instruction (socialisation) and reformation (treatment), as well as discipline and the repression (control) of crime (Garland 1985). Borstals also taught trades such as carpentry, painting and decorating and farming, along with emphasising physical training such as running, gym work and swimming. These legislative and structural/institutional developments in the first decade of the twentieth century began to address the innocent–dangerous child dichotomy by moving slowly towards a perception of children as (typically) innocent and adolescents as (more likely to be) dangerous, for example, being more likely to offend. Furthermore, the middle-class construction of adolescence was a major step towards enabling politicians, penal reformers, the public and youth workers to construct the behavioural category of 'juvenile delinquency', the precursor to 'youth offending'. This new social construction would allow the othering and marginalisation of the working class, singling them out as a troublesome group warranting surveillance, control and punishment (Garland 1985). However, it should be noted that the category 'working class' in the analyses of most historians and criminologists more specifically refers to working-class 'boys', indicating that the social constructions, explanations and responses to juvenile delinquency were fundamentally gendered in the early twentieth century (**RTA = Androcentrism: male dominance in the construction of social, cultural, political and academic understandings of youth offending**). Indeed, much of the influential academic work focused on this period (e.g. Springhall 1986; Gillis 1975) has privileged the experience of the male 'problem adolescent', with only limited, marginal focus on young female criminality, with the notable exception of the pioneering *Gender, Justice and Welfare Bad Girls in Britain, 1900–1950* by Pamela Cox (2003).

STOP AND THINK

The youth crime 'problem'

The notion of a newly identified problematic group of young people with newly identified problematic behaviours that the public should fear (e.g. indicated by rising crime rates) was arguably as unoriginal in the early twentieth century as it is today. The social construction and reconstruction of juvenile delinquency/youth offending has been historically characterised by recurring perceptions (cf. Pearson 1983):

1 Youth offending is a new phenomenon.
2 Youth offending is increasingly problematic.
3 Youth offending is much worse than it was in the past.

Each of these perceptions has reflected middle-class concerns regarding the behaviours and lifestyles of working-class adolescents (typically boys) and has motivated legislative responses to understanding and dealing with this 'problematic' behaviour and 'problematic' group in a manner distinct from the responses adopted for younger children. Ask yourself:

- To what extent is this distinction helpful in political, practical and academic ways?
- To what extent is this distinction valid in the sense of accurate, truthful and comprehensive, as opposed to the social construction of key stakeholders with subjective agendas?

As we will see in the following chapter, working-class adolescent boys have been the focus of most subsequent academic research and scholarship seeking to explain youth offending, indicating that the typical 'young offender' remains socially constructed as a working-class male teenager, and explanations of offending behaviour have been constructed accordingly.

From innocent child to dangerous adolescent

The discussion thus far has illustrated how modernity, particularly manifested by the Industrial Revolution, the onset of capitalism and the advent of compulsory schooling, led to the social construction of distinct developmental categories of 'childhood' and 'adolescence'. Previously, children had simply been considered to be mini-versions of adults, working, socialising and living with adults (Pollock 1983) without special treatment or distinction on the basis of their relative age and (im)maturity. Once the child's position in the family changed as they moved away from the labour market and spent more time on the streets with their peers, the professional middle classes (e.g. social reformers, child savers, politicians, academic researchers) distinguished children as a group whose behaviour require bespoke definitions, explanations and responses. The dichotomy of children as simultaneously victims (the perishing classes) and threats (the dangerous classes) necessitating both saving and reforming had turned into a paradox that began to be resolved with the social construction of two distinct developmental categories based on age and class:

- *Childhood*: a period of innocence, vulnerability and need, necessitating protection by adults (welfare-based responses).
- *Adolescence*: a period of tumultuous biological and psychological 'storm and stress', deviance, disruption and chaos requiring control and punishment by adults (justice-based responses).

Focusing on the behaviour of visible adolescents as a social 'problem' encouraged targeting by Government legislation, criminal justice agencies, academic researchers and the media, which in turn led to production of official statistics and research data confirming the existence of 'youth crime'. This is not to say that offending behaviour by youths had not occurred before this point, but rather that the category of 'youth crime' (just like the category of 'youth') had been socially constructed – invented through the activities of key stakeholders and allocated a label in order to categorise an existing behaviour. This newly labelled behaviour was subsequently measured, self-fulfilled and arguably exaggerated by the definitions, explanations and responses of key stakeholder groups (influencers on social construction such as politicians, criminal justice professionals, media and academics). From the early twentieth century onwards, periodic anxieties about juvenile/youth crime would be married to the broader narrative of the 'problem adolescent' or 'problem youth' (**RTA**), especially in periods of national vulnerability, whereupon the juvenile delinquent becomes the scapegoat and focal point for governmental fears (Shore 2011). The resultant 'moral panic' around this newly created 'problem' in the early twentieth century precipitated further targeting and criminalisation of working-class adolescent males. This in turn increased their presence in youth crime statistics, supported existing research data and justified further research into this group, thus creating a self-fulfilling prophecy that the phenomenon of 'juvenile delinquency' was new, real and getting worse. Consequently, the social construction of adolescence provided common-sense and scientifically justified explanations for the 'problematic' behaviour of young people. The construction promoted a pathological view of working-class adolescent boys as experiencing a chaotic period of physiological and psychological development, while detracting attention from a serious examination of the impact of material inequality and broader socio-structural influences (see Chapter 2), despite developing understandings that the perishing classes were harmed by poverty. As such, explanations of juvenile delinquency grounded in adolescence, coupled with theories of the negative impact of inadequate parenting, were sustained as the dominant explanation of youth offending into the 1950s (Hopkins-Burke 2016). Significant elements of these theories persist today, most notably the identification of psychosocial influences on youth offending and the **responsibilisation** of parents for adolescent behaviour – the shift of primary responsibility for offending and its prevention away from the State and towards the parent (another **RTA**).

In the first half of the twentieth century, key stakeholders from the political and professional middle classes addressed the innocent–dangerous child dichotomy (which was becoming a paradox) through the social construction of a distinct developmental stage of 'adolescence' – a disrupted, volatile developmental period in later childhood more suited to explaining 'youthful' offending behaviour. Consequently, 'childhood' was consolidated through legislation and academic theory as a stage of innocence and vulnerability requiring protection by adults, while adolescence/youth became constructed as a stage of psychological and physiological disturbance and pathology exacerbated by poor parenting and inadequate socialisation – a stage that rendered youths more prone to offending behaviour.

5 EASY PIECES

3 Socially reconstructing the innocent–dangerous child dichotomy (1900–1950)

1 *The construction of adolescence*: as childhood increasingly became seen as a period of innocence and vulnerability, so the distinct developmental period of adolescence was constructed and employed as a vehicle to help to explain juvenile delinquency.

2 *Legislating youth justice into existence*: Government legislation reflected the need to respond to children and adolescents in a manner different from one another

and distinct from adults when offending behaviour occurred, marking the early social construction of legislative youth justice responses.

3   *The nature of adolescence*: adolescence was conceived as a distinct developmental period when pubescent and teenaged children experienced biological, psychological and social stresses that explained their propensity for troublesome behaviour.

4   *The typical delinquent*: explanations of juvenile delinquency began to focus almost exclusively on the behaviour of adolescent working-class males.

5   *Responsibilising parents*: alongside adolescence, parenting emerged as a key influence of the construction of explanations of youth offending, viewed as a vital factor in encouraging and inhibiting juvenile delinquency.

4   CHILD WELFARE VERSUS YOUTH JUSTICE (1950–1990)

The post–World War Two period from the mid-1900s to 1990 was marked by two clear responses to the (re)construction of youth offending (Hopkins-Burke 2016):

1   A raft of legislation prioritising the welfare of children who offended over the more justice-based, punishment-led approaches reserved for dangerous, threatening youths.

2   Growing perceptions of delinquent (antisocial and misbehaving, although not necessarily offending) working-class youth subcultures as problematic – very much the post-industrialisation street children of the time.

During this period, the distinction between children and adolescents (youth) was the starkest it had ever been. From the late 1940s, youth offending/juvenile delinquency became an increasingly hot topic for political legislation, professional discourse and academic debate. The Children Act 1948 established a series of welfare-based, social work provisions for children, including care services located in new local authority children's departments staffed by the first professional social workers exclusively for children. The Act also introduced remand centres, attendance centres and probation hostels as a means of restricting the use of custody for children who offended. The overriding perception was that imprisoning children was damaging and inappropriate, incongruous with their vulnerability and need for protection and support. Conversely, the requirement persisted for the punishment of adolescents who offended (see also Chapter 4), notably from magistrates, with the introduction of detention centres to provide 'short, unpleasant sentences' for 'young offenders'. Once again, the contrasting views of how to understand and respond to the child and adolescent when they offend are apparent.

The Children Act 1948 foregrounded a period in which the 'cult of youth' rose to prominence in society and increasingly came to represent the 'state of the nation' (Davis 1990). From the Teddy Boys of the 1950s to the Mods and Rockers of the 1960s (cf. Cohen 1973 and his identification of 'moral panics') and the Skinheads and Punks of the 1970s, delinquent working-class youth subcultures took centre stage in political, professional, public and academic discourses (see Cohen 2011). The behaviours of these youth subcultures were typically explained as the negative outcomes of class conflicts, post-war structural and economic changes (e.g. the diminishing influence of the UK internationally), the growing influence of American culture, scientific and technological advances and modern trends in family and sexual life (Hopkins-Burke 2016). The key point here is that 'youth' (a label that was beginning to take over from 'adolescent') became *the* focal social group whose behaviour required explanation and response because they caused anxieties and represented social problems, all the while consolidating views of children as (comparably) innocent, non-threatening and in need. The frequent result of these anxieties was the creation of a moral panic, which occurs when a 'condition, episode, person or group of persons emerges to become defined as a threat to societal values and interests' (Cohen 1973: 9).

RTA = MORAL PANICS ABOUT 'PROBLEM YOUTH' POPULATIONS

Groups (subcultures) of children and young people are identified by politicians, the media, academics and the public as a threat to social order and values, and then depicted as a threat, typically by the media. The group's portrayal as a threat increases public concern regarding their behaviour, motivates political responses in the form of legislation, new institutional structures and so on, and can also lead to legal and social changes (e.g. lowering the age of criminal responsibility).

The distinction between innocent child and dangerous adolescent/youth was formalised further by the Ingleby Report in 1960. The report highlighted the confusion in the youth court system between having regard to children's welfare when they offended and promoting a just deserts, justice-led response to this behaviour (**RTA = welfare versus justice as the main driver of youth justice responses**). This confusion indicated a contradiction within the criminal justice system (particularly among police and courts) in how to explain and respond to juvenile delinquency, explained as a welfare/needs issue when committed by children but explained in biopsychological, pathological terms when committed by adolescents (Bottoms 2002). Such contradiction and ambivalence regarding how to understand and respond to children's offending behaviour at different developmental stages of their life (e.g. childhood versus adolescence/youth) have been recurring themes in the history of youth justice. Subsequent legislation in the mid-1900s refocused on a crucial determinant on how juvenile delinquency is socially constructed – the age of criminal responsibility.

CONTROVERSIES AND DEBATES

Socially (re)constructing the age of criminal responsibility

The Children and Young Persons Act 1963 raised the age of criminal responsibility in the UK from 8 to 10 years old. The Act also gave local authorities new powers to conduct preventative social work focused on family relationships, thus enabling a dual response to the child both as threat and victim, incorporating an emphasis on effective parenting. Accordingly, preventative and therapeutic work became the domain of a wider range of professionals – social workers, teachers, psychologists, doctors and probation officers. The subsequent Children and Young Persons Act 1969 from the Labour Government intended to raise the age of criminal responsibility still further, to 14 years old. This increase was to be accompanied by non-criminal proceedings in place of criminal procedures for 10- to 14-year-olds and more liberal use of care proceedings for 14- to 17-year-olds. The authority and discretion for responding to young people who offended was to be given to local authorities and the Department of Health and Social Security, rather than being the primary domain of criminal justice agencies. It appeared that 'the hour of the "child-savers" had finally arrived' (Thorpe *et al.* 1980: 6).

But . . . the proposed increase in the age of criminal responsibility never occurred due to a change in Government and an accompanying radical shift in youth justice agenda. The incumbent 1970 Conservative Government was much more sympathetic to criminal justice agencies such as the police and courts, and the proposals of the Children and Young Persons Act 1969 were never fully implemented. The minimum age of criminal responsibility remained 10 years old in the UK, where it stays to this day in the modern Youth Justice System (YJS) for England and Wales (see also Chapter 5 discussion of the abolition of doli incapax). Residential community homes with education and Intermediate Treatment programmes were introduced following the Act (see Chapter 4) alongside a new range of welfare-based sentences (e.g. care and supervision orders), which were available for both youth offenders and children in need. However, detention centres and borstals were never abolished. Consequently, Government legislation that had been intended to promote child welfare, in part by raising the age of criminal responsibility, retained considerable powers to punish young people as offenders. The tension and ambivalence with which children and young people who offended were understood and responded to was reflected in the tensions between the juvenile court (with his range of punitive sentences) and the newly created social services departments (with their host of welfare interventions). Once again, welfare and justice priorities were at odds and could not be reconciled within a single piece of legislation.

Constant changes to the age of criminal responsibility in the UK (just as in other countries) have served to reconstruct our understandings of what constitutes a 'youth offender'. Historically, these age-based constructions can be somewhat at odds with what society constructs as a 'child' and an 'adolescent'. The outcome has been paradoxical on at least three fronts:

1 A child can be considered a youth if they break the law in their pre-teenage, pre-adolescent years (i.e. 10–12 years old).
2 A child who offends will have their behaviour explained using biopsychosocial theories of adolescence.
3 A child is considered innocent, immature and irresponsible until they offend, at which point they are considered to be dangerous, mature and responsible for their actions.

However, the legal safety net of doli incapax remained in place during the post-war period – the presumption that a child aged between 10 and 14 years old was not necessarily able to distinguish between right and wrong and so should not be convicted unless this presumption can be refuted in court. Notwithstanding this presumption, the age of criminal responsibility introduces further conflict and ambivalence into explanations and responses to the behaviour of children and adolescents by blurring the innocent child–dangerous youth distinction when a non-adult offends.

The 1970s and 1980s proved to be a decade of further confusion and ambivalence over how to define, understand and respond to children and young people who offended (see Chapter 4). The 1970s, for example, was dominated by a twin track (bifurcated) approach to meeting the welfare needs of young people who offended by using Intermediate Treatment programmes (children as vulnerable) alongside the use of juvenile courts and punitive sentences for more serious young offenders (youths as dangerous). In the 1980s, youth justice responses ranged from punitive political rhetoric to more liberal diversionary and systems management practice to more mechanised, tightly managed approaches (see Chapter 4). Consequently, the 1970s and 1980s were less about the (re)construction of youth offending (definitions) and more about (re)constructions of youth justice (responses). Margaret Thatcher's Conservative Government in the UK talked tough about crime throughout the 1980s and continued to fuel the fires of a youth crime 'problem', thus constructing young offenders publicly as the same dangerous threats of old. However, beneath this strong political rhetoric, the practice reality was one of extensive use of diversion from the formal Youth Justice System (through cautioning) and increasing use of community alternatives to custody. These progressive movements towards the more child-friendly treatment of children who offended were grounded in ethical, political and academic arguments that youth offending had become an exaggerated phenomenon in extent and nature (cf. Rutherford 2002) and that formal intervention was harmful (cf. Becker 1963; Cohen 1985; Barry and McNeill 2009). The reality of responding to young people (adolescents) who offended as potentially vulnerable children whose offending behaviour had been overstated or over-constructed in extent and severity clashed with the get-tough, dangerous offender rhetoric given to the public. However, this practice reality resulted in dramatic decreases in the numbers of young people receiving custodial and court sentences during what became known as the 'decade of diversion' and the 'successful revolution' in youth justice (Jones 1984; Allen 1991). The successful revolution in official responses to youth offending introduced a hitherto unseen paradox in the social construction of youth offenders – rhetorical, public, political constructions of youth offenders as threats and contrasting private practice constructions of youth offenders as vulnerable and damaged by formal youth justice interventions. This contrast between (political) rhetoric and (practice) reality is a persistent theme within the youth justice literature, as we will explore across the book (RTA = **political rhetoric versus practice reality**).

The post-war period until 1990 consolidated much of the trajectory of the first half of the century – employing legislation, academic knowledge and media representations to construct youth offending as the domain of adolescent working-class males and male subcultures (thus introducing more sociological foci into dominant biopsychological academic explanations) and continuing to blame inadequate parenting for youth offending and youth justice responses. Alongside these sustaining influences on the social construction of youth offending, there emerged a new legislative focus on the age of criminal responsibility, a dynamic entity that introduced further conflict and ambivalence into perceptions of children and youth in society. Underpinning this conflict were growing debates as to whether welfare or justice approaches should take precedence in responses to children and young people who offended.

5 EASY PIECES

4 Child welfare versus youth justice (1950–1990)

1 *Welfare-based legislation for children*: legislation prioritising the welfare of children who offended gained increasing prominence in the post-war period.
2 *Justice-based legislation for adolescents*: contrasting legislation focused on more justice-based responses to adolescents who offended, slowly reintroducing a punitive element into youth justice.
3 *The typical youth offender*: the juvenile delinquent/young offender was represented as typically an adolescent working-class male, often a member of a delinquent subculture.
4 *Conflict and ambivalence*: juvenile delinquency legislation introduced conflict, ambivalence and confusion within and between agencies working with children and young people, particularly focused on the welfare versus justice debate.
5 *Diversion from labelling and harm*: the 'successful revolution' of the 1980s introduced further conflict between rhetorical, political constructions of young people who offended as social threats compared to the reality of practice constructions of these young people as vulnerable and potentially harmed by formal youth justice intervention, which they should be diverted away from.

5 RECONSTRUCTING THE CHILD AS A 'YOUTH OFFENDER' (1990 ONWARDS)

Our chronological journey to this point has demonstrated that 'childhood' and what it means to be a 'child' are dynamic social constructions, frequently reconstructed over time and place in response to socio-economic and political demands, class positions, culture, public opinion, and professional and academic discourses. In particular, there has been conflict and ambivalence around whether to define children and explain and respond to their behaviour as though they were victims or threats when they offend. These age- and class-related social constructions and ambiguities have been reflected in the treatment of children, especially those labelled 'juvenile delinquents' (more recently 'young offenders') across the Western world in the past 200 years (Goldson 2014).

The 1990s introduced a get-tough governmental attitude to youth offending and a 'punitive turn' (Muncie 2008) towards more punishment-based justice responses across Western Europe, with an equivalent punitive turn occurring concurrently in the US (Feld and Bishop 2011). Gone was the tolerance and diversionary optimism of the 1980s, dismissed as too liberal and soft on crime by the new Conservative Government. Children who offended were reconstructed as 'youth offenders' who were irresponsible, immoral and dangerous, with an accompanying belief that children and young people were 'in some way turning feral' (Jeffs and Smith 1996: 1). This radical reconstruction of children who offended was in part based on the desire of the new Government to stamp its authority on lawmaking and distinguish itself as different from its predecessor – yet another recurrent theme across youth justice and one repeated by the next Government in 1998 (see also Chapter 5). However, the necessity and urgency for a new approach to youth justice policy and practice, animated by reconstructing youth offenders, was largely precipitated by a single horrific event in England – the murder of Jamie Bulger.

Reconstructing the child offender as evil: the Bulger murder

On 12 February 1993, 2-year-old Jamie Bulger was abducted, tortured and murdered by two 10-year-old boys in Bootle, England. The brutality of the offence was dubbed 'an act of unparalleled evil and barbarity' by the presiding judge (Pilkington 1993). The moral panic that ensued in the news media motivated a significant reconstruction of the category of children who offend as representing 'evil' (Davis and Bourhill 1997), where previously 10-year-olds were considered more akin to innocent children requiring welfare and protection. With one horrific act, the perception of children who offended was reconstructed in the minds of politicians, the media, the public and some academics to indicate wicked, immoral and rational individuals who should be assigned full responsibility for their actions (responsibilisation) and as such should be treated as if they were adults (adulterisation). In some ways, the responsibilisation and adulterisation agendas pursued by politicians and the media harkened back to pre–Industrial Revolution times when children were considered to be little adults, although this 1990s reconstruction seemed only to apply to children who offended. The social consensus was that children were too immature to be (legally) responsible in many key areas of their life, such as being allowed to leave school, to vote, to drive, to drink alcohol or to have sex; however, they were assigned full responsibility for their actions when they offended. Here we have the paradox of the irresponsible–responsible child, unable to make significant life decisions until the age of 16 or above but held fully responsible for offending behaviour from the age of 10, an age at which they could not be categorised as a 'youth' in developmental terms (Case 2006, 2007). This irresponsible–responsible child (offender) paradox had first entered the political spotlight due to legislative changes in the 1960s concerning the age of criminal responsibility. The Bulger murder further motivated 'the politicization of juvenile crime' and significantly influenced the way in which child 'offenders' were socially constructed from that point (Goldson 2013). A climate of 'institutionalized intolerance' emerged (Muncie 2004) and any debate regarding raising the age of criminal responsibility above 10 years old was quashed, as if young offenders had been 'removed from the category of "child" altogether' (Jenks 1996: 128). The socio-political response to the murder of Jamie Bulger in 1993 is a cogent example of the growing influence of the mass media on shaping social constructions of youth offending and youth offenders. It is to this increasingly powerful influence that we now turn our attention.

CONTROVERSIES AND DEBATES

Media social constructions of youth offending

It has been made clear in this chapter that definitions of youth offending over history have been socially constructed through the explanations offered by powerful 'primary definers', such as the politicians who make laws and influence government legislation (Hall *et al.* 1975) and the criminal justice agencies who enforce laws and legislation. You may want to add academics to this powerful group if you're feeling optimistic, but whatever you decide, the majority of these influencers fit neatly into the category of white, middle-class males (**RTAs = androcentrism, ethnocentrism and class-centrism** – the dominance of male, white westernised and middle-class individuals and cultures in the social construction of youth justice). According to Ericson (1991: 223), a 'deviance-defining elite' has been able to set its own moral and legal agendas regarding (youth) crime. Another key influencer, the mass media, has a history of seeking out and promoting authority views from these primary definers (Schlesinger and Tumber 1994). Therefore, it can be argued that the mass media, politicians and criminal justice (law enforcement) agencies (less so academics, especially critical criminologists) are inextricably related when socially constructing the 'realities' of crime and justice (Muncie 2009). Critical academic commentators contend that media contributions to the social construction and (mis)representation of youth offending have employed a series of mechanisms that bias and diminish the validity of the definitions, explanations and responses they inform, including:

Distorting reality: the media does not reflect the reality of crime. Instead, they define it in particular ways; acting as a prism that sidesteps reality and distorts the extent and nature of offending by young people (Jewkes 2004).

Privileging newsworthiness: crime news is a commodity with a market value that overrides the necessity for accuracy or relevance (McQuail 1993). Public images of youth offending are typically provided by criminal justice agencies that have a vested interest in crime control and by media sources with a vested interest in newsworthiness – thus questioning the validity of the information each provides.

Stereotyping: the media presents stereotypical images of 'young offenders' and youth offending behaviour in order to perpetuate dichotomies of good (adult, victim) and evil (young offender), driven by pejorative labels (see labelling theories) of young people as 'folk devils' and the 'criminal other' (Cohen 1973; Hall *et al.* 1975).

Presenting the atypical as stereotypical: the media presents atypical crime events (e.g. crimes of extreme violence by children) as stereotypical, symptomatic of the moral decline of children/young people and more newsworthy than normal, law-abiding childhood behaviour (Young 1974).

Creating crime waves: public fears are fuelled by the media's extrapolation of single, isolated incidents into socially constructed 'crime waves' and problems (Cohen 1973), such as the 'youth crime problem'. Consequent public reaction is based more on the fear of social transformation than any shifts in the actual behaviour of young people (Taylor 1981).

Creating moral panics and amplifying deviance: the stoking of public fears around perceived crime problems is a process known as **moral panic** (Cohen 1973). Its
extension into the social construction of crime waves and excessive public fears
is known as **deviancy amplification** (Wilkins 1964), whereby the extent and
nature of an undesirable behaviour (either in reality or perception) is exacerbated
by the increasing frequency and severity with which it is reported.

Creating moral crises: since the late twentieth century, media (mis)representations
have evolved isolated moral panics into perpetual moral crises, where the fact
and fiction of (youth) crime has been blurred and crime as news has blended
into crime as entertainment through reality TV, crime reconstructions, live news
broadcasts and closed-circuit television (Muncie 2014);

Fuelling misconceptions: critics assert that the media wilfully distorts the extent and
nature of youth offending, perpetuating misrepresentations that youth crime is
always increasing, that most youth crime is violent and that the courts are too
lenient in their sentencing of young people – misrepresentations that are consolidated by a steady repetitive stream of atypical and unrepresentative stories
(Hough and Roberts 1998).

STOP AND THINK

Media and public opinion

A common insinuation in academic literature and student essays (in my experience) is
that media misrepresentations of youth offending can exert a linear, deterministic and
negative influence on public opinion of young people and youth offending. However,
the reality is more nuanced than this, and there is not a necessarily simple deterministic relationship between media reporting and the formation and expression of public
opinion (Muncie 2014). Of course, youth offending is a politically sensitised topic and
media coverage contributes to public opinion, as does government rhetoric (often
presented in the media). Indeed, the media and politicians regularly claim that they
are simply responding to the popular punitive public view of youth offending (known
as **populist punitiveness**) in their representations and responses, understanding this
public opinion as homogenous and simplistic. However, public attitudes to youth
offending and youth justice are more divergent and complex than the media and government would have us believe. In fact, as I know from my own research, public opinion is often more tolerant than generalised statements about causes and sentencing
preferences suggest. Indeed, when presented with concrete and detailed descriptions
of actual cases and individual contexts, public attitudes to youth offending and youth
justice can be less punitive and more tolerant and constructive (Case *et al.* 2011).

Notwithstanding the more nuanced relationship between media and public
opinion, it is valid to suggest that the mass media can distort and misrepresent
the extent and nature of youth offending, thus making a significant contribution
(arguably unwelcome) to the social construction of youth offending in terms of its
definitions, explanations and responses.

The Crime and Disorder Act 1998 dramatically reorientated and reconfigured the YJS of England and Wales[5] and perceptions of children who offend by introducing a 'new youth justice' that was less concerned with welfare and justice approaches and more focused on tightly managed, risk-based prevention and early intervention activity (see Chapter 5 for more detailed discussion). A highly significant development within this legislation was to abolish doli incapax – the legal presumption that children aged from 10 to 14 years old were not necessarily capable of discerning between right and wrong and so could only be convicted of an offence if this presumption was refuted in court. In a sense, doli incapax represented the presumption of innocence in childhood and provided for children up to the age of 14 to be kept out of the formal YJS. However, the abolition of doli incapax represented 'an effective lowering of the age' of criminal responsibility (Bateman 2012: 5) and led to the 'statutory construction of the 10-year-old child "offender" as a fully responsibilised and adulterised agent [which] confirms England's and Wales' status is the jurisdiction of the lower stage of [unmitigated] criminal responsibility in Europe' (Crofts 2009: 268).

The abolition of doli incapax and the institutionalised responsibilisation and adulterisation of children who offend in the UK, it has been argued, contradicts a wide range of scientific evidence regarding children's cognitive maturity and moral reasoning capabilities (cf. Goldson 2013) and promotes the 'judicial internalisation of the discourse of moral panic' (Douglas 1998: 266). Many critical academics and children's rights advocates have castigated this development as a gross oversimplification of children's cognitive, moral and social maturity between the ages of 10 and 14 (Crofts 2009), not to mention being founded on uncritical over-generalisations that all children mature at the same rate. This oversimplified reconstruction of the child offender as responsible (although too irresponsible to be assigned power over any other significant areas of their life) appeared to be based in large part on a knee-jerk (over-)reaction to the Jamie Bulger murder and the simplistic assumption that children develop more quickly in modern society thanks to advances such as compulsory education and technological developments (Crofts 2009). The issue of the age of criminal responsibility, in particular the relatively low age in England and Wales compared with westernised countries, is discussed in more detail in Chapter 5.

The abolition of doli incapax under the Crime and Disorder Act 1998 exacerbated the contradictory understanding and treatment of children and young people in England and Wales, depending on their behaviours and the problems they experienced. In particular, the Act contrasted with the more welfare-based Children Act 1989, which assigned the status of 'child' to individuals below 18 years of age. Both of these parliamentary acts accorded with Article 1 of the United Nations Convention on the Rights of the Child (UNICEF 1989) by distinguishing a child as 'every human being below the age of 18 years'. However, there were stark differences between the acts in how the 'child' should be understood and treated if they demonstrated problematic behaviour, by acknowledging their vulnerability, need and right to protection when they were non-offenders (under the Children Act 1989 that shaped the social care system) compared to punishment, control and the prevention of risk (under the Crime and Disorder Act 1998 that shaped the YJS). In this way, the same child could be subject to drastically different and competing sets of responses depending on the form of behaviour (or label given to their behaviour) that manifested from their exposure to a range of personal and social problems.

The growing reconstruction of children and young people as immoral, irresponsible and feckless when they offended was supported (cynics may say 'self-fulfilled') by a review of the YJS of England and Wales on the eve of the 1997 General Election. The 1996 review was conducted by the Audit Commission, an independent public body responsible for ensuring that Government money is spent wisely. The Audit Commission concluded that the YJS was operating inefficiently, ineffectively and uneconomically and that it was comprised of agencies that worked very poorly together; the commission strongly recommended that a reconfigured, joined-up system should prioritise the prevention of youth offending through a focus on risk and early intervention (Audit Commission 1996; see also Case and Haines 2009). Perhaps the most notable element of the review, however, was its title. The *Misspent Youth* report confirmed the political reconstruction of children (aged 10 and above) and young people (up to the age of 17) who offended as out of control, feckless and irresponsible, wasting their teenage years and in urgent need of control and correction by adults (see Chapter 5).

Critics have described the *Misspent Youth* review as a largely subjective, politically motivated exercise (cf. Pitts 2003), a conspiratorial partnership between the Audit Commission and the soon-to-be Labour Government seeking a new approach to understanding youth crime and delivering youth justice. Although the review authors, Judy Renshaw and Mark Perfect (later appointed chief executive of the Youth Justice Board for England and Wales by Home Secretary Jack Straw), consulted fairly widely with academics and other stakeholders, their work clearly benefited from a strong political steer (including from the Labour Party preparing for government), and it drew heavily on 'psychologically oriented criminologists' and a pathological explanation of youth offending as the result of deficits, weaknesses and flaws in the individual (see Case and Haines 2009). The incoming Labour Government wanted to break from the justice-based policies of the 1980s and 1990s and assert the need for a new approach to youth justice. In practice, *Misspent Youth* provided this break – it rather overlooked the achievements and successes of the youth justice of the 1980s and 1990s (on which, see Haines and Drakeford 1998) and recast the era as one of doing nothing about youth crime. *Misspent Youth* articulated a move away from traditional welfare- and justice-based models of youth justice towards more technical, 'system-first' and individualised 'offender-first' conceptions of how to understand and respond to offending behaviour by children (Haines and Case 2015) as the product of individual deficit (exposure to risk factors that predict and lead to offending; see Chapter 3) that demands adult-led management through intervention informed by risk assessment. There was a consequent culture shift towards a technical, administrative form of youth justice focused on risk-based reduction (as prevention) that individualised the causes of offending and thus individualised responsibility for this behaviour (i.e. blamed children for not resisting the influence of risk factors). Representations of 'youth offenders' and how to respond to them exemplified several newly introduced political strategies (discussed in more detail in Chapter 5), including:

- *Neo-correctionalism*: prioritising the correction of deficits and flaws in the individual.
- *Individualisation*: blaming young people for the personal, psychological and immediate social (familial, educational, peer group, lifestyle) deficits and flaws that allegedly lead to offending.

- *Neo-liberal responsibilisation*: maintaining that children and young people possess sufficient agency to choose to offend and to wilfully contravene their obligations to wider society (neo-liberal); therefore, they should be held primarily responsible for committing and correcting their offending behaviour (responsibilisation).

The negative tone of *Misspent Youth* was consolidated in the 1997 White Paper, *No More Excuses: A New Approach to Tackling Youth Crime*, from the incoming Labour Government (Home Office 1997). As its name suggests, the *No More Excuses* White Paper established the Labour Government's responsibilising approach to preventing and responding to offending by children (see also Bessant *et al.* 2003) by representing offending behaviour as the product of irresponsibility and individual deficit (exposure to and failure to resist risk factors), rather than by addressing the needs of children or the criminogenic (likely to cause crime) influence of socio-structural circumstances. The underpinning risk focus of *No More Excuses* was employed to justify recommendations for responsibilising young people (and their families) for their offending behaviour and implementing pre-emptive early intervention to prevent 'at-risk' children from becoming offenders (disregarding the attendant potential of this approach to label, stigmatise and criminalise – see Hine 2006; McAra and McVie 2005).

The recommendations of *Misspent Youth* and *No More Excuses* underpinned the central piece of legislation during the Labour Government's tenure (1997–2010), the Crime and Disorder Act 1998 (see Chapter 5 for a full discussion). It is at this point that we end our historical journey through the changing definitions of 'youth offending' and how these have been contingent upon dynamic reconstructions of the 'child', 'youth' and 'youth offender'. This apparently premature ending is because the Crime and Disorder Act 1998 provided such a sweeping, radical reorientation of the principles and processes of the YJS of England and Wales, accompanied by a significant reconstruction of the 'youth offender', that critical discussion merits its own chapter (see Chapter 5). These discussions follow logically from the 1990s reconstructions of the child offender as evil, immoral, rational and responsible threats to society in urgent need of control and punishment.

5 EASY PIECES

5 Reconstructing the child as a 'youth offender' (1990 onwards)

1 *Get-tough policies*: the 1990s UK Government rejected the successful revolution of the 1980s in favour of espousing a rhetorical get-tough punitive approach to children who offended.
2 *Irresponsible and immoral 'youth offenders'*: children who offended were reconstructed as irresponsible (yet responsible), immoral and rational individuals.
3 *The evil youth offender*: the perception of child offenders as evil was largely the product of the horrific murder of Jamie Bulger by two 10-year-old boys.
4 Misspent Youth *and* No More Excuses: legislation reconstructed children and young people who offended as irresponsible yet rational individuals who required control and punishment – perceptions reflected in the political rhetoric of *Misspent Youth* and *No More Excuses* for children who broke the law.

5   *Crime and Disorder Act 1998 and doli incapax*: the Crime and Disorder Act 1998 radically reorientated the YJS of England and Wales, notably abolishing the doli incapax presumption of innocence and effectively reducing the age of criminal responsibility to 10 years old, in stark contrast to welfare and rights-based legislation that viewed the child as aged up to 18 (Children Act 1989) and 25 (United Nations Convention on the Rights of the Child 1989).

DEFINING YOUTH OFFENDING: SO, WHAT DO WE KNOW?

In this, our first chapter, we have explored the socially constructed nature of 'youth offending' (also known as 'juvenile delinquency') and its associated concepts of 'childhood' and 'adolescence' or 'youth'. Throughout, discussion has focused on how youth offending and youth justice responses to it have been dynamic, contested and contingent, subject to perpetual socio-historical reconstruction due to a series of socio-economic, political, statistical, professional and media influences. The implication here is that neither youth offending nor youth justice should be viewed uncritically as unequivocal facts, but rather as constructed realities. We have seen how prior to the mid-eighteenth century, the role and status of children in society was ambiguous – they were essentially little adults in the world of work, home and leisure. Once modernity had introduced a more secular, scientific and rational society characterised by rapid industrialisation and urbanisation, constructions of children developed equally rapidly. The Industrial Revolution drove children out of the workplace and onto the streets, prompting conceptions of these children as a distinct social group and conceptions of childhood as a distinct developmental stage – both in urgent need of specialised explanations and appropriate responses that were differentiated for those given to adults. Perceptions of children and their behaviours as problematic became difficult to reconcile with welfare-led views of the child as innocent and victimised by poverty – producing conflict and ambivalence in constructions of the child as victim and threat, as deprived and depraved, and in need of care and control. The newly constructed category of 'adolescence' as a developmental period of biological and psychological 'storm and stress', rebelliousness and erratic behaviour, provided youth justice stakeholders (e.g. politicians, professionals and academics) with a convenient vehicle for reconciling this ambivalence. Utilising the social construction of adolescence, stakeholders could begin to explain and respond to the equally new construction of 'juvenile delinquency', now known as 'youth offending'. The new concepts of 'adolescence' and 'juvenile delinquency' were social constructions of the professional middle classes in response to the behaviour of working-class youths, typically boys.

Social constructions of adolescence/youth and juvenile delinquency/youth offending and their associated explanations (see Chapters 2 and 3) have been employed historically to justify the social control, surveillance, punishment and treatment/reform of your offenders by organisations in the YJS and beyond – organisations controlled by the same middle classes largely responsible for constructing the definitions and explanations of youth offending. This situation has changed little in the past 200 years. The social construction of 'adolescence' (latterly 'youth') has been a vehicle for explaining juvenile delinquency/youth offending based on individualised, biopsychosocial causes. Parenting has also become a go-to explanation for youth offending, enabling the responsibilisation of the family for offending behaviour by their children and thus drawing explanatory attention away from external influences such as poverty and material inequalities (see Chapter 2). What is particularly interesting here is how (re)constructions of youth offending appear to have been bookended by constructions of the child as little adults – be they the factory workers predating the concept of childhood or the responsibilised and adulterised child offenders of the 1990s and beyond.

STOP AND THINK

Acknowledging the limiting isms

This chapter has intended to demonstrate that the socio-historical construction of childhood, adolescence and ultimately juvenile delinquency/youth offending has been a product of class and age relations interacting with a complex mix of historical, social, political, economic, cultural and academic influences, at least in the industrialised Western world. However, social constructions at all points of the 'triad of youth justice' (definitions, explanations, responses) have been simultaneously influenced and limited by a group of isms that must be accounted for when evaluating and applying the arguments made and knowledge acquired across this book. For example:

- *Ethnocentrism* to some degree characterises understandings of youth offending and youth justice responses to it (e.g. philosophies, structures, strategies, policies, practices). Most socio-historical constructions of youth offending (along with understandings of childhood and youth) have been developed in the white Western world by white Western politicians, academics and media (typically middle-class men), largely due to the more developed and formalised political, civil service, economic and academic structures in these countries (cf. Friday and Ren 2006). It is when these constructions, explanations and responses are applied uncritically to non-white and/or non-Western populations and systems (legal, criminal justice) that ethnocentrism can occur (cf. Pollock's [1983] criticism of Ariès), so it is crucial to acknowledge and challenge the Western-centric nature of the discussions throughout this book.

- *Androcentrism* emerges as a key issue in the social construction of youth offending (also childhood and youth) – the dominance of male perspectives on our understandings of offending behaviour. The vast majority of research and political attention on youth offending has focused on middle-class men explaining the behaviours of adolescent boys. While boys may be responsible for the majority of youth offending over history, this behaviour is not the exclusive domain of boys, so constructions developed solely with these boys (not to mention their associated explanations and responses) may lack validity and relevance when uncritically applied to girls. This can lead to an explanatory shortfall in terms of offending by young females, with similar explanatory shortfalls related to youth offending by non-white and/or non-Western world populations (ethnocentrism) and for youth offending by the middle classes (i.e. class-centrism).

These various isms remind us to ABC (Always Be Critical), that who, what and how we choose to construct and define as 'youth offending' and 'youth offenders' can influence the validity and utility of the explanations we produce and the responses we recommend. Furthermore, who has had the power to do the constructing (typically white, westernised, middle-class men) can have a huge impact on the who, what and how of youth offending and youth offenders. It is valid to conclude that the concept of 'youth offending' should be understood as a free-floating, dynamic, ambiguous and subjective construction, therefore, rather than a socio-historical 'fact'. Accordingly, explanations of and responses to youth offending may indicate less about the behaviours that youth offending encompasses and far more about social, cultural and political perceptions of children and young people in specific societies at specific times (Case and Haines 2010).

Throughout this chapter, we have traced the varied and often recurring influences on the socio-historical construction of definitions and perceptions of children, youth/young people and juvenile delinquency/youth offending. These influences have been identified as socio-economic, political/legislative, statistical and intellectual/professional (including academics and media). At different points in our history, different understandings of children, youth and youth offending have become established as the norm – the 'constructed reality' of (middle-class) stakeholder groups. As we will come to see in future chapters, the socially (re)constructed definitions of 'youth offending' have influenced and been influenced by similar dynamic and (re)constructed explanations and responses to youth offending, exemplifying the 'overlapping practices, strategies and ideologies that have shaped juvenile justice over the two centuries in which the modern system evolved' (Shore 2011: 131). Indeed, at the outset of the book, the 'triad of youth justice' represented the idea that how youth offending is defined can (or should) influence how it is explained, which should then influence how it is responded to through youth justice. All of this brings us logically to the next point on the triad – explanations of youth offending.

5 EASY PIECES

Recommended further reading

For students interested in exploring the arguments in this chapter in more detail, an ideal starting point is *Young People, Crime and Justice* by Roger Hopkins-Burke (2016). The opening section (six chapters) of this accessible and insightful text focuses on the historical development of social constructions of youth offending and youth justice. As such, it is highly recommended.

Another relevant and dynamic exploration of social constructions of youth offending and youth justice is provided in *Histories of Youth Crime and Youth Justice* by Harry Hendrick (2015), a chapter available in the also excellent edited text *Youth Crime and Justice* by Barry Goldson and John Muncie (2015).

More in-depth, historically specific discussions are provided in three further recommended texts: the book *Children in English Society: From the Eighteenth Century
to the Children Act 1948* by Ivy Pinchbeck and Margaret Hewitt (1973), and two key
journal articles that inform this chapter: 'The Invention of Juvenile Delinquency in
Early Nineteenth-Century England' by Susan Magarey (*Labour History*, 1978) and
'Innocence and Experience: The Evolution of the Concept of Juvenile Delinquency
in the Mid-nineteenth Century' by Margaret May (*Victorian Studies*, 1973). Each of
these texts adopts a more historical than criminological style, but each is a valuable addition to broaden understandings of the key issues addressed in our opening
chapter.

NOTES

1   Although a dynamic, contested and contingent term, 'industrialised Western world' is
    employed in this book to refer to countries in the Western world (e.g. Western Europe, North
    America, Australasia) with highly developed technological infrastructures and service-sector
    economies that have surpassed previous industrial, manufacturing economies. Conversely,
    'non-westernised countries' or 'developing nations' (typically in Asia, Africa and Latin Amer-
    ica) retain industrial or even pre-industrial economies.
2   Many of the arguments have resonance with other international jurisdictions, and com-
    parisons will be made where possible. However, for the purposes of coherence and depth,
    the UK context will take priority. Detailed expositions of the social construction of child-
    hood, adolescence/youth and youth offending in other national contexts are available, and
    I would strongly recommend engaging with these in conjunction with this chapter for a glo-
    balised perspective on the issues discussed. For the US, see Burfeind and Bartusch (2016); for
    Canada, Ksenych (2011); for Australia, Cuneen *et al.* (2015); and for non-Western juvenile
    justice systems, see Friday and Ren (2006).
3   The chronological periods have been drawn in a generalised, approximated way to provide
    you with a framework for understanding and to render their information more coherent,
    accessible and digestible. Consequently, they are subjective 'constructions', not universally
    agreed historical 'facts', and there is a necessary degree of overlap between them.
4   By 'children', what is really meant here is boys. Once girls were taken out of the factories,
    they were subject to other forms of social control (e.g. kept at home for domestic labour pur-
    poses), supported by middle-class notions of their passivity and the need to control female
    sexuality and child-bearing potential (Heidensohn 2000).
5   By the late 1990s, responsibility for youth justice policy-making had been devolved to the
    newly independent governments in Scotland and Northern Ireland, so the YJS encompassed
    England and Wales only, not the whole of the UK.

Explaining youth offending

Individual, socio-structural and systemic causes

The opening chapter explored the socio-historical construction of 'youth offending' and its predecessor, 'juvenile delinquency'. You were presented with a chronology tracing the social construction of 'childhood', which precipitated the need to socially construct 'adolescence' as a way of explaining the new phenomenon of 'juvenile delinquency', which ultimately became known as 'youth offending'. The chapter noted how, since the Industrial Revolution of the mid-1700s, the notion of childhood was distinguished as a separate life stage, with its own very specific characteristics (Hendrick 2015). Before that time, children were thought of as essentially little adults, working and socialising with older adults. The distinction between children and adults, closely followed by the further distinction of adolescents as a category of older children (young people), was based on identified differences in relation to biological, psychological and social development and behaviour. These differences motivated the social construction of new, specialised legislation, provisions and institutional arrangements reserved for children and young people in the criminal justice context. Consequently, a clear understanding emerged over time that children were not to be subjected to the same expectations and treatment as adults (Case *et al*. 2017). This understanding involved a series of dynamic, contingent and contested assumptions (constructions) about what it means to be a child, what should be expected in terms of children's development, and at the same time, how children should be expected to come to terms with increasing levels of responsibility and social obligation. This, in turn, clearly flowed through into a set of dynamic, contingent and contested assumptions about children's behaviour and how this was to be explained and managed (Case *et al*. 2017). The contentious issues surrounding how to construct and understand 'children', 'adolescents/youths' and 'youth offending' precipitated arguments about the degree to which children should be held responsible for their actions (e.g. through establishing an appropriate age of criminal responsibility) and introduced debates about how youth offending should be responded to through official 'youth justice' measures.

We now move to the second point of the 'triad of youth justice': explanations. It is informative to explore how youth offending (however defined or constructed) can be explained and understood, in order to evaluate the influence of these explanations on subsequent definitions of 'youth offending' and 'youth offenders' and their influence on youth justice responses to youth offending (the third point of the triad). The historical development of explanatory theories of youth offending will be (in broad terms) mapped onto the five chronological periods outlined in Chapter 1. As will become evident, this is not an exact science and there is a degree of overlap between the evolution of definitions and explanations, as there are with the responses explored in the second half of the book.

EXPLAINING YOUTH OFFENDING

In Chapter 1, it was argued that 'youth offending' is a subjective, dynamic, contingent and contested socio-historical construction subject to a series of socio-economic, political, statistical, professional and intellectual influences. However, the constructed nature of youth offending should not prevent it from being viewed as a *real* social problem with tangible effects on individuals and societies. Youth offending is, after all, a 'constructed reality'. Socio-historical constructions of youth offending in the Western world have shaped how the phenomenon has been defined and measured.

The perennial (re)construction of youth offending as a social 'problem', the public and political anxieties/uncertainties that have resulted and the economic, social and personal costs of youth offending in the real world have demanded the construction of appropriate explanations of this 'problem'. Over the past 200 years, a series of explanatory theories have been advocated, typically by professionals and intellectuals (predominantly academic social scientists) that claim to identify the causes, influences, predictors and correlates associated with offending, whether offending is defined and measured as an objective fact or as a dynamic social construction. A significant number of these explanatory theories have privileged the study of young, working-class, white males as the archetypal 'offender' – a focus of clear relevance to our ongoing study of youth offending. At the same time, in the spirit of ABC (Always Be Critical), we should also recognise the explanatory limitations of these theories due to their inherent androcentric, ethnocentric and class-centric biases (see Chapter 1, 'Stop and think: Acknowledging the limiting isms').

A central tenet of this book is that definitions of youth offending can influence how it is explained, and the explanatory theories produced can have a reciprocal influence on how youth offending is defined going forwards. In broad terms, definitions help us to understand 'crime'; explanations help us to understand 'criminal' behaviour. But why bother to explain offending behaviour by young people at all? Well, if we can explain youth offending, then we are able to define it with more accuracy and completeness (validity). Explanations also enable us to respond to youth offending more effectively, for example, by identifying appropriate objectives and suitable targets for sentences and interventions or justifications for minimal intervention and diversion (see Chapters 4 and 5). Explanations have been sought to aid understandings of the 'problem' of youth offending, thus reducing public and political anxieties/uncertainties and informing suitable (youth justice) legislation and political, structural, philosophical, strategic and practical responses to youth offending. In this way, it is clear how the definitions and explanations of youth offending can be related to responses.

Theoretical explanations of youth offending have been generated by academics, intellectuals, politicians and the media ever since juvenile delinquency was first marked out as a distinct category of behaviour. The dominant explanations have been utilised to inform and shape youth justice responses to any behaviour defined as juvenile delinquency/youth offending at a given point in time. Equivalent to the definitions of youth offending that they seek to explain, explanations are also social constructions – the products/creations of the institutions and individuals within them in particular societies at particular times. Explanations of youth offending have been as dynamic, contingent and contested as the social constructed definitions of youth offending – evolving over time and place through debate, evidence generation, research, challenge, refinement and reconstruction. Some of the **theories** (frameworks for understanding) have been generated through applied research and the production of evidence and data; others through scholarship, **polemic** (controversial argument or attack) and direct challenge to existing theories. Some theories have emerged from research with children and young people (typically the working class), while others have resulted from the study of adult offenders (typically the working class) and have had their findings and conclusions applied to children and young people as a way of explaining youth offending. It is important to understand the origins and bases of theoretical explanations of offending and to explore their **validity** (comprehensiveness, accuracy, honesty, appropriateness) when explaining *youth* offending and for informing responses to it.

STOP AND THINK

What do you need to know about explaining youth offending?

What exactly do you need to know about how criminology has explained 'offending' since its socio-historical construction? For our purposes, there are five main points to consider when evaluating a theory of offending:

1 How does a theory explain offending?
2 Is the theory relevant and applicable to *youth* offending?
3 What is the relationship between the theoretical explanation and definitions of youth offending?
4 How good is the explanatory theory? To what extent is it valid, reliable, evidence based, universal, practical?
5 What are the implications of the explanation for responding to youth offending?

What do you think?

For the purposes of this chapter, you will be introduced to the most influential explanatory theories of (youth) offending produced in criminology, several of which have been heavily influenced by criminology's big brothers in the social sciences, psychology and sociology, with additional contributions from biology, geography, ecology, politics and other subject areas (see also Case *et al.* 2017). Following the '5 easy pieces' format adopted throughout the book, the chapter and its individual sections will be summarised into five broad explanatory schools of thought[1] and mapped onto the broadly equivalent five-stage chronological structure of Chapter 1 where possible. This approach has been employed to minimise unnecessary complexity and to help you to develop digestible knowledge and understanding to feed into your studies, your research, your scholarship, your practice and your policy-making. The central arguments, methodologies and evidence base of each theory will be outlined, and the theory's relevance and validity for explaining the offending behaviour of young people will be evaluated. Starting and ending each section with a review of its '5 easy pieces' is intended as an effective way of providing a framework for understanding that section's structure and central knowledge base – its arguments, theories, conclusions and practical recommendations. There is neither the space nor the necessity in this book to provide you with great detail on hundreds of specific theories and their associated evidence bases and research studies. In any case, other sources provide a depth and breadth of theoretical coverage with far more eloquence than I ever could, so you are urged to engage with these works. The excellent *Youth and Crime* by John Muncie (2014) and *An Introduction to Criminological Theory* by Roger Hopkins-Burke (2013) are particularly recommended. This chapter will provide you with the need-to-know essentials for understanding the key explanations of offending and their relevance to youth offending, contextualised within our book's working model of interacting definitions, explanations and responses (i.e. the 'triad of youth justice').

The first section of this chapter introduces 'individual' explanations of youth offending, starting with a discussion of the earliest explanatory theories in criminology, which emerged from **classicism** – a school of criminological thought asserting that individuals offend due to their rational choice, free will and desire to maximise the benefits/rewards of crime and to minimise the costs (e.g. punishment). What follows is a detailed examination of the explanatory theories from **positivism** – an approach to studying the social world and identifying the causes of human behaviour using the methods of the natural sciences. Positivists claim to be able to identify the causes of offending and as such produce what are known as **aetiological** theories – explanations that identify the causes of abnormal behaviours and disorders. We start by exploring the theories of **individual positivism** that dominated criminological understandings of (youth) offending over the first half of the twentieth century – theories that explain (construct) the causes of youth offending as internal forces located within the individual young person. The initial focus will be on the theories of **biological positivism** that developed in the latter part of the nineteenth and early twentieth centuries, which focused on the **criminogenic** (crime-causing) nature of physical characteristics, genetic inheritance and latterly neuroscience (brain development). This discussion is followed by an examination of the key theories of **psychological positivism**, which have focused on psychological criminogenic influences, notably learning and personality, from the early twentieth century onwards. Next comes discussion of the socio-structural theories of offending produced by **sociological positivism**, which challenges individual positivism by explaining the causes of offending as rooted in socio-structural problems external to the individual, seeking out explanations of crime patterns rather than individual motivations. Exploration of sociological positivism will pay particular attention to concentric zone, anomie/strain and subcultural theories (largely developed from the 1930s onwards).

In Section 4, we move on from the positivist search for causes into an evaluation of the critical (of positivism) explanatory theories of **critical criminology**. Critical theories have gained popularity in criminology since the 1950s as a means of explaining how behaviours and individuals such as young people become labelled and criminalised – or (re)constructed as criminal – by powerful others (e.g. adults, politicians, criminal justice professionals). This **systemic** focus (on criminal justice systems and processes) offers a direct challenge to the conclusions of classicism and positivism, which can be seen as **reductionist** (oversimplifying) and **deterministic** (viewing certain factors as inevitably and irresistibly causal). In particular, we will consider the central arguments of labelling theory, Marxist/conflict theories, the new criminology and gendered perspectives of feminism and masculinities.

In the final part of the chapter, we examine the integrated forms of positivist theory that came to prominence in the 1970s to challenge the reductionism and determinism of traditional positivism. This is followed by an exploration and the integrated realist theories that emerged in the 1980s to challenge the idealism of critical theories by treating crime as a real (non-constructed) phenomenon typically committed by the working class. We will examine how right and left realist perspectives differ starkly from one another, with right realism promoting a **neo-classical** (new, updated, revised), rational choice understanding of youth offending that is disinterested in the search for causes, compared to left realism's emphasis on relative deprivation and criminogenic interactions between the individual, the public, the state (e.g. police, law) and the victim.

5 EASY PIECES

Explaining youth offending: individual, socio-structural and systemic causes

1 *Individual explanations of offending: classicism (pre-1850)* explores the earliest explanatory theories that focused on the role of free will and rational choice in the aetiology of offending.

2 *Individual explanations of offending: biological positivism (1850–1900)* examines the first (individual) positivist theories that offered 'scientific' explanations of offending by identifying the causal influence of biological/physiological factors such as physical characteristics, genetics and (more recently) neuroscientific theories of brain development.

3 *Individual to socio-structural explanations of offending: psychological and sociological positivism (1900s onwards)* introduces theories of (individual) psychological positivism that highlight the criminogenic nature of personality and learning, leading into discussion of (socio-structural) theories of sociological positivism based on the criminogenic influence of social disorganisation, strain and membership of subcultures.

4 *Critical explanations of offending: labelling and critical theories (1950s onwards)* investigates the role of power (mediated by gender, class and ethnicity) in the social construction of (youth) offending through criminalisation processes such as labelling and control of lawmaking and law enforcement.

5 *Integrated explanations: integrated positivist and realist theories (1970s onwards)* outlines more recent developments in explanatory theories by focusing on integrated (biopsychosocial) positivist theories and integrated (right and left) realist theories; explanations that have evolved to challenge the perceived reductionism of positivism and the idealism of critical theories.

1 INDIVIDUAL EXPLANATIONS OF OFFENDING: CLASSICISM (PRE-1850)

The first academic explanations of offending in the social sciences came from the classical school, or 'classicism', in the eighteenth century, mainly from the work of two criminologist-philosophers: Cesare Beccaria (1738–1794) in Italy and Jeremy Bentham (1748–1832) in England. This historical period can be mapped broadly onto the pre-1850 era, the first chronological stage of our journey into the social construction of youth offending (see Chapter 1). During this period, the concepts of 'youth offending' and 'youth justice' had yet to be recognised and made official through social construction mechanisms, so early criminological theories focused on explaining and responding to the generic category of 'offending' (remember that the category of 'youth' had yet to be constructed). Both Beccaria and Bentham asserted that all individuals (including children and young people) are rational actors (Hopkins-Burke 2013) possessing free will and the capability of making rational choices whether to offend or be law-abiding, based on balancing the benefits of committing crime against the costs of being caught and punished. Bentham believed that offending contravened the principle of **utilitarianism** – that an action (e.g. punishment) should deliver the greatest good to the greatest number of people. The early classical explanations agreed on free will/rational choice as the cause of offending and looked no further for more complex explanations, neither were they concerned with conducting research to provide evidence to support their theories. The main objective of classical explanations of offending was to inform appropriate criminal justice responses, which led to recommendations for proportionate, certain and speedy punishment (Beccaria 1767/1963) that outweighed the benefits of crime (Bentham 1811/1970). Classicists argued that certain individuals will inevitably offend if given the chance and if the benefits of offending are considered sufficient to take the risk, so they advocated a **deterrence** approach to criminal justice – the need to increase the perceived risk of offenders being caught and punished in order to deter (dissuade) them from offending. Classical school recommendations, such as deterrent punishment,[2] supported a **crime control** response to offending, understanding the behaviour as inevitable and thus needing to be controlled, rather than identifying and treating its supposed causes (beyond personal choice).

Classical theorists argued that children and young people have the same capacity for free will, rational thought and considered decision-making as do adults. This assumption has been the subject of much criticism in the light of subsequent theoretical developments that offered a better understanding of children's cognitive development (Piaget 1932) and moral development (Kohlberg 1958) as slower to mature than that of adults, which raises serious questions over whether children and young people should be held fully responsible for their offending behaviour, and if so, at what age (i.e. the age of criminal responsibility).

Subsequent explanatory theories (explored later in this chapter) have questioned the degree to which offending, and youth offending specifically, are influenced by rational choice compared to being influenced by internal biological and psychological factors (individual positivism, right realism), socio-structural factors (sociological positivism) and systemic factors (critical theories, left realism). These critiques, combined with the natural tendency of academic theories to evolve through test and challenge, ultimately led classicists to re-evaluate their overly simplistic view of offending. Neo-classical theorists have reconstructed the role of free will/rational choice as only one (albeit significant) element of more holistic, multifactor, integrated explanations (see later in this chapter). Indeed, the explanatory popularity of rational choice has made a serious comeback in criminology since the 1980s (see, for example, rational choice theory [Clarke 1987] and routine activities theory [Cohen *et al.* 1981]), particularly as a means of informing the **situational crime prevention** methods (reducing the physical opportunities for crime and increasing the effort and risks associated with it) supported by Western governments who have lost faith in the ability of other (mainly positivist) explanations and responses to tackle crime. The neo-classical compromise position advocated from the 1980s onwards (although earlier versions can be traced back to the nineteenth century) views free will and rational choice as **mitigated** (alleviated, made less influential) by other factors in the lives of 'vulnerable' groups such as children and those with mental illness or learning disabilities (e.g. Akers 1991; Wilson and Herrnstein 1985); as such, this is a compromise position between classical and individual positivist theories. The most influential neo-classical theory, right realism, is discussed in the final (integrated theories) section of this chapter, while an integrated version of this theory (right realist biopsychosocial theory) is explored in the same section.

5 EASY PIECES

1 Individual explanations of offending: classicism (pre-1850)

1   *Classical explanations*: the classical school of criminology grew from the work of Beccaria and Bentham in the eighteenth century.

2   *Free will and rational choice*: traditional classicism views offenders as rational actors possessing free will and the capacity for rational choice when making decisions to offend.

3   *Cost-benefit analysis*: individuals who offend make a rational decision that the benefits of crime will outweigh the costs of being caught and punished.

4   *Deterrence and situational crime prevention*: crime can be deterred by the threat of punishment (deterrence theory) and prevented by reducing the physical opportunities for and risks of offending (situational crime prevention), which can lead to the costs of offending (e.g. the physical effort) outweighing the perceived benefits.

5   *Neo-classical compromise*: the neo-classical compromise sees free will and rational choice as mitigated by the biological, psychological, sociological and situational factors present in the lives of vulnerable groups such as children and young people.

2 INDIVIDUAL EXPLANATIONS OF OFFENDING: BIOLOGICAL POSITIVISM (1850–1900)

In the second half of the nineteenth century, a theoretical challenge to classicism came from positivist criminology. Positivists utilised research methods taken from the natural sciences (chemistry, biology, physics) to obtain **quantitative** (numerical, statistical) data regarding the causes of behaviour such as offending. This data/ evidence was considered to be **empirical** – obtained via study and direct experience using experiment and observation.[3] Positivists focused on studying and explaining offending behaviour, whereas classicists were more interested in examining the creation and operation of laws and criminal justice systems (Muncie 2009). They produced causal, aetiological explanations of crime, which were then employed to inform responses that targeted these causes through treatment, rehabilitation and preventative intervention. In direct contrast to classical explanations based on free will and rational choice, positivist theories viewed offending as determined by biological and psychological factors that were internal to the individual, along with sociological factors external to the individual – all of which were largely irresistible by the individual. As such, positivism offered deterministic explanations of offending and perceived the offender as a predetermined actor (someone whose actions are predestined following exposure to certain influences), rather than a rational actor who chooses to offend (Hopkins-Burke 2013). Positivist theories soon became **hegemonic** (dominant) within criminology, offering more complex and evidence-based explanations than classicism, which was largely based on scholarship and polemic. Furthermore, positivists recommended responses that held the promise of changing the individual in the long term, rather than simply deterring them from offending in the short term. According to Burfeind and Bartusch (2006), the social construction of juvenile delinquency has been underpinned by three key influences: the social construction of childhood and adolescence (see Chapter 1), the central arguments of positivism (discussed in this chapter) and the welfare principle of parens patriae (see Chapter 4). Somewhat ironically and uncritically, however, traditional positivist explanations took the definition of crime for granted as an agreed 'fact', yet these theories originated in an historical period wherein the social construction of (definitions of) 'youth' and 'youth offending' was a key socio-political, cultural and academic issue – indicating a degree of disconnect between the points on the 'triad of youth justice'.

The initial positivist theories of offending were individual in nature, concentrating on the internal biological and psychological (also known as biopsychological) influences on an individual's offending behaviour. The earliest theories of individual positivism were biological and developed from the mid- to late nineteenth century onwards. Biological positivist theories focused mainly on the criminogenic potential of physical characteristics and genetic inheritance, moving towards latterly neuroscientific considerations of the role of brain development. From the early twentieth century onwards, theories of psychological positivism also began to gain popularity in criminology. Later, we will examine the key psychological theories of crime, which explore the role of learning and personality in offending behaviour. But let us start where positivist criminology started – with biological explanations.

Biological positivism: physical characteristics

The seminal positivist theory of crime was biological and came from the father of criminological positivism, Cesare Lombroso (1836–1909). It is likely that you're already familiar with Lombroso's biological theory of crime, which he outlined in his book *L'Uomo Delinquente* (On criminal man; Lombroso 1875). Basically, Lombroso compared the physical characteristics of a group of imprisoned offenders with those of a group of non-offenders (at least, men who had not been formally identified or convicted as offenders). He observed that the imprisoned offenders were more likely to have larger ears, sloping foreheads, crooked noses and long arms than their non-offender comparison group. These **atavistic** (less evolved, primitive, throwback) characteristics were correlated (statistically) with established definitions/measures of 'offending' (with no consideration that the category may be socially constructed) and viewed as criminogenic.

Towards the middle of the twentieth century, other criminologists began to consider the potential influence of physique on criminal behaviour. Notably, William Sheldon (1949) utilised **somatotyping** (the categorisation of the human physique) to conclude that physique is correlated with individual temperament and mental well-being, all of which could influence criminality. Sheldon studied 200 boys who had been housed in a reformatory school in Boston, US, and found that boys with the more muscular and athletic mesomorph physique were most likely to have an aggressive and violent personality correlated with offending. In contrast, boys with small, weak, fragile **ectomorph** physiques were more likely to be intellectual and introverted, while the heavier, softer **endomorphs** were more likely to be friendly and sociable in personality. Sheldon's conclusion, therefore, was that delinquents were more likely to have the mesomorphic physique, linked to aggression and violence.

Evaluation: physical characteristics

Although Lombroso's 'scientific' methodology seems rather crude by today's standards, at the time it was a truly groundbreaking and innovative means of criminological investigation – a world away from the armchair theorising of classical criminologists. Lombroso's biological positivism was the first criminological theory to utilise controlled comparisons in order to identify the differences between 'offenders' and 'non-offenders', differences that were then explained as potential causes of offending. Sheldon's somatotyping did likewise, categorising individuals by physique (observing physical differences between these groups), then correlating these differences with offending behaviour. As such, both studies employed a quasi-experimental method – almost an experiment, but without direct manipulation of the variables under examination (physical characteristics) to generate an evidence-based theory. Their method can be criticised as inherently biased, however, because the so-called experimental group had already formed itself and been officially constructed – offenders had already been identified, convicted and placed in a prison or reformatory for reasons unconnected to their physical characteristics. Consequently, neither Lombroso nor Sheldon was able to conclusively determine whether physical characteristics exerted any causal influence on offending behaviour. Findings were simply correlated with offending behaviour; identified as present at the same time as offending behaviour in the lives of offenders. But correlations are not causes (see Case *et al.* 2017). Indeed, certain physical characteristics may even have been symptoms that are caused by offending or imprisonment (e.g. obtaining a broken nose in a prison fight, developing a muscular physique while in custody doing manual work); they may have been the products of other influences (e.g. biological, psychological, sociological); or they may have had no relationship with offending behaviour at all. Consequently, it could be argued that Lombroso's and Sheldon's conclusions were largely based on supposition rather than conclusive proof of any (causal) relationship with offending.

It should be noted that neither theory of biological positivism had anything to say about offending behaviour by young people specifically, even though the concept of juvenile delinquency was gaining momentum as a social construction at the time of the research. As such, the early biological positivist theories that focused on physical characteristics lack a degree of relevance as contemporary explanations of youth offending. It could be argued that their **ecological validity** (ability to accurately represent real-world behaviour) is significantly diminished because children and young people are yet to fully develop into adults physically, so they may lack the (full) physical characteristics that Lombroso and Sheldon identified as criminogenic. Therefore, the **explanatory utility** (usefulness, scope) of the theory is restricted to explaining offending by white, westernised males and, as such, can be accused of **androcentrism** (privileging male viewpoints and experiences in the development of knowledge and understanding) and **ethnocentrism** (privileging westernised perspectives in knowledge development). The subsequent uncritical and negative application of Lombroso's findings and conclusions to black males and to females also merits accusations of racism and sexism (for more discussion of these issues, see Hopkins-Burke 2013).

In conclusion, Lombroso and Sheldon employed progressive (at that time) methodologies to identify the physical differences between offenders and non-offenders, and then offered common-sense, quasi-scientific suppositions as to the link between these characteristics and offending behaviour. Their conjectures were extrapolated into an assumption (not an explanation) that physical characteristics somehow predetermine offending – a form of **biological determinism.** There was no consideration at the time of the possible influences of other factors, be they biological, psychological, sociological (socio-structural) or systemic, so the explanations are somewhat simplistic and reductionist. Nor was there any acknowledgment of the socially constructed nature of definitions of (youth) offending. However, Lombroso's later work did acknowledge the limitations of this single-minded, reductionist focus on a specific group of biological, physical factors, and he extended his theory to incorporate a dominant role for environmental factors such as climate, poverty and urbanisation – thus representing an early form of integrated positivist theory (see Section 5 of this chapter).

Biological positivism: genetic inheritance

Towards the end of the nineteenth century, Lombroso's groundbreaking biological explanation of offending was falling out of favour within criminology, although many criminologists remained committed to exploring the criminogenic role of biological factors. The focus of biological positivism turned to genetic inheritance and the possibilities that, pathological genes (causing disease, illness or behavioural disorder) could be passed down through families. In 1877, Richard Dugdale published his study of the Jukes family from New York, who were infamous for their criminality. Having traced over 1,000 family members, Dugdale concluded that over a quarter of family members were criminals, implicating some influence for genetic inheritance. These early suggestions that genetic inheritance could be criminogenic were consolidated by Henry Goddard's (1914) study of the family of Martin Kallikak, who had an illegitimate son by a woman of 'low birth'. Goddard found that the relations of Martin's illegitimate son were more likely to be criminal than those of his 'legitimate' family. The common conclusion from these formative biological studies of genetic inheritance was that it was possible to inherit undesirable genetic characteristics that predisposed the individual to crime (Hopkins-Burke 2013). However, like Lombroso and Sheldon before them, these individual positivist studies employed a quasi-scientific method (with preformed groups/families) and identified biological correlates with offending, not direct causes, despite the manner in which the researchers might have presented their findings. Furthermore, genetic inheritance studies to that point could neither rule out nor account for the influence of socio-environmental/sociological factors (nurture), as criminogenic either in their own right or in addition to the role of biological factors (nature).

Twin and adoption studies gained popularity from the 1970s onwards as a method of addressing the perceived limitations of family studies in pinpointing a causal influence for genetics. Initially, twin studies were advocated as more effective than family studies in isolating the genetic factors associated with crime, as they were able to explore differences in criminality between **monozygotic (MZ) twins** (identical twins developing from a single egg and possessing a near identical biological make-up) and **dizygotic (DZ) twins** (fraternal twins developing from two separate eggs). Two twin studies provided particularly strong evidence that genetic inheritance could play a role in offending behaviour. The first of these by Christiansen (1974) found a 52 per cent correlation in criminality between MZ twins (i.e. in 52 per cent of the cases where one twin had offended, so had the other twin), compared to a 22 per cent correlation between DZ twins. The second study, a review of twin research conducted from 1929 to 1961, identified a 60 per cent correlation between MZ twins in terms of criminality, compared to a 30 per cent correlation between DZ twins (Mednick and Volavka 1980). The conclusion was that MZ twins are more prone to commit crime than DZ twins due to them sharing a greater proportion of genetic make-up. Therefore, twin studies were better able to control for and examine genetic differences than family studies and could be more confident in concluding a genetic influence on offending. Exactly what was inherited and how this influenced offending remained unclear. Rutter and Giller (1983) surmised that what is inherited is an element of personality predisposition (see later discussion of criminogenic personality). However, the evidence base remains inconclusive as to the extent and nature of genetic influence on crime.

The perceived methodological limitations of twin studies led criminologists, most notably Sarnoff Mednick, to advocate for the prioritisation of adoption studies as a more effective test of genetic inheritance of criminal predisposition. Support for the adoption study method was based on the notion that twins often share the same environment, which could in itself contribute to their criminality (i.e. nurture) instead of, or in addition to, the contribution of their biology (i.e. nature). Therefore, studying the criminal outcomes of adopted children with a biological parent who had offended enabled the influence of shared environment to be eliminated. Following a study of 14,000 adoption cases in Denmark, Mednick and his colleagues (Mednick *et al.* 1987) identified that adopted children with a biological parent who had offended were more likely to have offended themselves compared to children with biological parents who had not offended. The logical conclusion was that there must be a degree of genetic inheritance (i.e. a 'criminal gene') passed on biologically between parent and child, as the role of shared environment could be excluded in adoption studies – although environmental influences more generally could not.

Evaluation: genetic inheritance

Although the precise extent and nature of genetic influence on offending is unknown, arguments for potential genetic causes of offending have gained credence from successive biological studies of families. As they have progressed, genetic studies have attempted to rule out or override **socio-environmental** influences (relating to the physical and social settings in which people live) on offending through the use of twin and adoption studies. However, socio-environmental influences can never be entirely ruled out for a number of reasons. For example, twins are highly likely to share the same environment, while the adopted children of criminal parents will still be exposed to environmental factors that could increase their likelihood to commit crime, whether operating as stand-alone influences or interacting with biological propensity. Genetic inheritance studies, by their very nature (no pun intended), have seldom considered, measured or analysed environmental influences. The same could be said of their neglect of psychological factors. Furthermore, these studies have seldom considered the impact of the (processes of) social construction of offending on the validity of their explanations. For example, it is possible that individuals from 'non-offending' comparison groups (e.g. law-abiding twins, non-offending biological parents of adopted children) have actually offended, but that this behaviour has not been identified, reported, recorded or convicted, the so-called 'dark figure' of crime, so they have not been constructed/labelled as 'offenders'. This possibility introduces a validity issue into the quasi-experimental comparisons used in genetic inheritance studies. However, notwithstanding the potential limitations in methodology and explanatory utility, the clear indication from the biological positivist studies discussed is that genetic inheritance has at least some degree of influence on offending behaviour.

Biological positivism: neuroscience

Biological positivist theories of (youth) offending have waned in popularity over the course of the twentieth century, losing explanatory dominance in criminology to psychological positivist theories (see next section). However, the late twentieth and early twenty-first centuries witnessed a return to the spotlight for biological explanations, largely due to the growing significance of neuroscience as a means of physically differentiating the brains of youths (adolescents) from adults in order to explain their (offending) behaviour. New imaging technologies have emerged that are able to map the development of the human brain from childhood to adulthood (Bishop and Farber 2007). These new technologies include computerised tomography (CT) scanning to identify abnormalities in the body, positron emission technology (PET) scanning to capture radioactive tracers moving through the bloodstream to understand brain functions, electroencephalogram (EEG) recordings of electromagnetic fluctuations in various parts of the brain, and functional magnetic resonance imaging (fMRI) to detect changes in brain function when performing specific mental tasks. These technological advances in brain imaging have precipitated major discoveries about the process of adolescent brain development relative to adult brains (Beckman 2004). The first major neuroscientific discovery has been that the adolescent brain massively overproduces grey matter – the brain material responsible for thought – and needs to prune it back. The brain follows this pruning with a myelination process that produces white matter to insulate it and make it work more efficiently (Giedd *et al.* 1999). Secondly, neuroscientists have discovered that the brain's frontal lobe (associated with cognitive reasoning) changes most dramatically during adolescence and is the last region of the brain to fully develop (Sowell *et al.* 1999). These discoveries have indicated that adolescents/youths are not fully developed cognitively, psychologically or socially (Soung 2011). Other neuroscientific studies have demonstrated that stress, trauma and threatening treatment by adults can produce neurochemical changes in adolescents that can affect their attention, impulse control, ability to form healthy relationships and capacity for remorse and empathy (Perry 2001), all of which can be viewed as criminogenic and linked to offending behaviour. These findings support the 'use it or lose it' principle of neuroscience, which argues that adolescent brains become hardwired during a certain time period, and in the absence of key experiences and stimulants, their neurological pathways may be lost and their capabilities compromised, which could also have an influence on offending behaviour (Greenough *et al.* 1987). The RTA of conflict and ambivalence re-emerges here (see Chapter 1). On the one hand, some neuroscientists view adolescents as developing individuals in need of care and protection, but others view adolescents as hardwired during their formative years and so requiring control and punishment. The implication of this conclusion is that social care and treatment interventions would be wasted on adolescents and so should be reserved for younger children (Soung 2011).

Evaluation: neuroscience

Neuroscientific research in the late twentieth and early twenty-first centuries has identified that cognitive and reasoning processes develop more slowly in adolescence than previously thought. Clearly, such conclusions (if accepted) could have significant implications for how we choose to respond to youth offending, in particular, where we set the appropriate age of criminal responsibility and the degree to which youth justice responses should hold young people responsible for that behaviour. Unlike the biological positivists before them (except for Lombroso in his later amended theory), neuroscientists do not claim that biological factors are exclusive explanations for offending behaviour (cf. Jones *et al.* 2009); instead asserting that biology (especially genetics) and environment both play a significant role in shaping the minds, brain development and behaviours of adolescents (cf. Beckman 2004). Therefore, although neuroscience does not constitute an integrated positivist theory due to its predominant focus on biological brain development, it does attempt to contextualise the influence of biology/brain development and identify it as a significant (but not exclusive) influence on offending behaviour.

5 EASY PIECES

2 Individual explanations of offending: biological positivism (1850–1900)

1 *Biological positivism*: the individualised biological/physiological differences between offenders and non-offenders can be identified and correlated with offending (defined in a non-constructed, uncritical way), thus producing explanatory theories.
2 *Physical characteristics*: physical characteristics such as atavistic features (Lombroso) and mesomorphic physiques (Sheldon) have been found to occur more often in offenders than non-offenders and have been assumed to be criminogenic.
3 *Genetic inheritance*: the potential for genetic inheritance of criminal predisposition has been examined through family, twin and adoption studies, all of which have identified higher correlations in criminality between close biological family members.
4 *Neuroscience*: modern explanations from neuroscience have cited research using brain imaging to conclude that the adolescent brain develops more slowly than the adult brain and that the brain's cognitive and reasoning processes are not fully formed during adolescence. This relative underdevelopment can lead to offending behaviour.
5 *The limitations of biological positivism*: studies have identified biological correlates with offending rather than the causes of offending, but they have been unable to pinpoint the exact nature of biological influences on crime and have neglected to fully consider the role of environmental factors (nurture) alongside the role of biological factors (nature).

3 INDIVIDUAL TO SOCIO-STRUCTURAL EXPLANATIONS OF OFFENDING: PSYCHOLOGICAL AND SOCIOLOGICAL POSITIVISM (1900 ONWARDS)

The emergence of psychology as the dominant social science in the first half of the twentieth century increased the popularity of the positivist method in criminology, and with that came a new focus on identifying the psychological influences on crime (see Case *et al.* 2017). A form of individual positivism known as **psychological positivism** emphasised how the dynamic cognitive (mental, psychological, thought) processes and characteristics that constitute individual learning and personality could be criminogenic – arguably more so than biological influences. This section will examine two main categories of psychological positivism related to explaining offending: learning theories and personality theories. Both sets of theories developed across (and slightly beyond) the 1900–1950 period of social construction explored in Chapter 1.

Psychological positivism: personality theories

Personality theories of psychological positivism explain youth offending as result of a criminal predisposition and/or criminogenic personality traits that encourage offending, rather than the learning of criminal behaviour per se. Perhaps the earliest (bio) psychological explanation for youth offending came from the 'storm and stress' theory of adolescence by G. Stanley Hall in 1904 (see also Chapter 1), in which he likened the developmental period of adolescence to a storm of biological and psychological stressors (e.g. puberty, hormonal and biochemical changes) that affect the adolescent personality and its components such as cognition, emotion and behaviour. Hall's theory of adolescence viewed this developmental stage as criminogenic on the basis of the young person's inability to cope with the significant stressors that they experienced. The idea that adolescence was somehow criminogenic was supported by Anna Freud (Sigmund Freud's daughter), who claimed that:

> adolescence is by its nature an interruption of peaceful growth, and . . . resembles in appearance a variety of other emotional upsets and structural upheavals.
> (Freud 1952: 255–278)

These theoretical understandings of adolescence linked **biopsychological** (biological and psychological) changes to adolescent personality traits that were seen to motivate criminal behaviour. Exactly how personality traits led to offending appeared less important to psychological positivists than uncritically asserting that they did, as if this conclusion were common sense (which it may well be) and so didn't need to be evidenced (which it probably should be). A by-product of relying on assertion over evidenced argument, however, is that it can promote an explanatory reductionism and invalidity – blinding the researcher to other potential influences on offending behaviour such as biology, psychological learning, socio-structural factors and systemic issues.

In the second half of the twentieth century, Hans Eysenck produced a multifactor, psychologically driven explanation of offending that he applied to youth offending.

Eysenck (1970) famously identified three dimensions of personality: **extroversion** (lacking inhibition, impulsive, risk-taking), **neuroticism** (anxious, nervous, moody) and **introversion** (passive, reserved). He proposed that individuals are born with a particular structure to their brain's cortex, which affects their ability to learn from and adapt to environmental stimuli. Consequently, extroverts are more prone to criminal behaviour because their cortex is under-aroused and so they require more stimulation, which is obtained through the impulsive behaviour associated with offending. Children with an extrovert personality are more difficult to condition (learn/teach through the modification of behaviour) and have difficulty learning from their environment – deficits which can encourage criminality. Therefore, Eysenck's personality theory combines notions of **biological determinism** (individual behaviour being determined by exposure to biological influences) with conditioning through exposure to socio-environmental factors (Muncie 2009). However, he never convincingly identified a direct correlation between extroversion and criminality, let alone a causal link – a common limitation of the conclusions from positivist theories.

Evaluation: personality theories

Personality theories offer a set of deterministic explanations of abnormal behaviour that have subsequently been applied to explaining offending behaviour. In this case, it is the undesirable criminogenic traits within an individual's personality (sometimes transient traits, such as in adolescence) that encourage youth offending, rather than learned behaviour. As with the trajectory of learning theories, the earliest personality theories were exclusively psychological, whereas later versions attempted to integrate biological determinism with sociological influences such as social learning.

Psychological positivism: learning theories

Psychological learning theories, as the label suggests, explain offending as a learned behaviour. The earliest theories focused on the conditioning (learning, teaching) of behaviour in animals through stimulus–response (classical conditioning; Pavlov 1927/1960) and learning through positive and negative reinforcement (operant conditioning; Skinner 1938). However, these theories offered little to explain human behaviour and less still to explain crime. As interesting as they are, we will not explore them in great detail here (but see Hopkins-Burke 2016).

The influence of learning on (youth) offending was initially hypothesised by the psychodynamic school of psychology. Largely associated with the works of Sigmund Freud and Carl Jung, psychodynamic theories have argued that all behaviour is the result of tensions between the individual's unconscious drives (id) and their conscious understandings of self (ego), morality and social order (superego). Therefore, offending is an outward expression of a psychic conflict when the individual does not learn sufficient measures of self-control to enable them to channel their unconscious drives into socially acceptable acts (cf. Muncie 2009). Indeed, August Aichhorn (1925) asserted that delinquent children have an underdeveloped ego and superego, which means that they cannot control the 'pleasure principle' that is driven by the id and encourages offending behaviour.

The learning-based 'differential association theory' (Sutherland 1947; Sutherland and Cressey 1960) is perhaps of most relevance because it linked learning directly to the explanation of youth offending. Edwin Sutherland's explanatory theory of youth offending emphasised the role of psychological, cognitive learning within a social context. Sutherland (1947) argued that criminal behaviour is learned in interaction with other people in intimate social groups – not necessarily people who commit crime, but certainly those who do not consistently support the law. In this way, individuals learn (from their social group) attitudes, definitions of law, motivations and rationalisations favourable to crime. However, differential association theory has not been able to explain why certain young people choose to (or choose not to) associate with others who approve of crime, nor has it evidenced the precise nature of the associations that can lead to different types of crime. In response to criticisms that his explanation was reductionist and deterministic, Sutherland (with Cressey 1960) revised his theory to argue that offending can occur when young people's associations with group attitudes favourable to crime are early, frequent and intense. There has been much subsequent support for the role of differential association in the learning of crime (cf. Rutter and Giller 1983), most notably for its broader explanatory model that links psychological learning with socio-structural (subcultural) elements to produce a more integrated theory of offending.

The potential role of psychological learning in offending behaviour was consolidated by Albert Bandura's (1973) social learning theory. Bandura offered a mix of explanations based on conditioning and subcultural theories (see later in this chapter) by arguing that aggressive behaviour can be learned by children in social situations through imitating the behaviour of adult role models. Bandura's famous 'Bobo Doll' experiment placed children in a room with a large inflatable doll. An adult entered the room, verbally and physically attacked the doll and was then confronted by the experimenter, who either chastised them or positively reinforced (praised, rewarded) their behaviour. If the child witnessed the adult being positively reinforced, then they were more likely to imitate the aggressive behaviour later in the experiment (due to identifying positively with that adult), suggesting that violent behaviour/offending can be learned in childhood through imitation of and identification with adults.

Evaluation: psychological learning theories

The idea that criminal predisposition can be learned and taught (as opposed to developed from predisposed personality traits) has been advocated by psychological positivists, who cite the influence of subconscious learning (psychodynamic theories) and learning through imitation (social learning theory). Neither theory explicitly examined *offending* behaviour, but the principles of both theories have been applied (logically and neatly) to explaining offending and are particularly relevant to the explanation of youth offending due to their basis in explaining children's behaviour. While these learning theories have offered exclusively psychological explanations, differential association theory broadened out psychological theorising by integrating explanations to understand how psychological processes could be criminogenic in social contexts.

5 EASY PIECES

3a Individual to socio-structural explanations of offending: psychological positivism (1900 onwards)

1 *Psychological positivism*: psychological variants of positivist theory have emphasised the criminogenic influence of individual, psychological factors on offending, most notably the role of personality and learning.
2 *Psychological positivist methodology*: psychological positivists have typically identified the individualised psychological differences between offenders and non-offenders, correlated these differences with offending and then concluded that they exert a causal, deterministic influence on offending.
3 *Personality*: personality theorists argue that criminogenic personality traits such as adolescent 'storm and stress' or extroversion can predispose individuals to offend.
4 *Learning*: learning theorists argue that criminal predisposition and offending behaviour can be learned and conditioned in social situations and within social groups.
5 *Integrated explanations*: later forms of psychological theories (e.g. Eysenck's personality theory, Sutherland's differential association theory) have integrated sociological considerations to broaden their explanatory utility.

STOP AND THINK

Individual explanations of offending and five not-so-easy questions

1 *Rational choice*: does a child or young person have the capacity to make fully informed choices and decisions about their behaviour, including their offending behaviour?
2 *Determinism*: do you agree with the central claim of individual positivism that (youth) offending is predetermined by biological and psychological factors operating in isolation or in combination?
3 *Explanatory utility*: does the single-factor/explanation approach of certain individual theories (particularly the earlier classical and positivist theories) limit their explanatory utility (e.g. due to reductionism), or do these theories provide valid explanations for specific episodes of offending?
4 *Nature or nurture*: to what extent is youth offending the product of biology (nature), psychology (nature or nurture) and sociology/environment (nurture)?
5 *Causes and correlates*: do you agree with the argument that individual positivist theories have only been able to identify correlates with youth offending, rather than causes, and that this limits their explanatory utility?

Now that we have explored the original biological and psychological theories of individual positivism, what about theories of youth offending that do *not* focus entirely on the individual as the central unit of explanation? According to Jeffery (1977: 161):

> We do not inherit behaviour any more than we inherited height or intelligence. We do inherit the capacity for interaction with the environment.

A branch of criminological theory was developed from sociology in the early twentieth century to challenge the biological and psychological basis of individual positivism while retaining a positivist commitment to identifying the deterministic causes of crime. Sociological positivism emphasised the deterministic influence of social factors (e.g. community, peer group) and structural factors (e.g. environment, poverty), external to the individual as opposed to the internal factors privileged by individual positivism. Early sociological positivists explained the distribution of crime within specific areas and populations, as opposed to the biological and psychological focus on explaining individual motivations to offend. In the 1830s and 1840s, French statistician Guerry and Belgian mathematician Quételet analysed official statistics relating to suicide, education and most notably crime within specific geographic areas (1842). Both academics identified statistical differences in crime levels in relation to gender, occupation, religion and age, along with broader **socio-structural** (social and structural) differences in relation to the social, political and economic structures in particular societies. These differences indicated that offending may not be simply the product of individual motivations, but instead may be an interaction between influences at a variety of levels, internal and external to the individual. In the early twentieth century, sociologist Emile Durkheim (1895/1964) began to focus specifically on explaining offending as a normal phenomenon that had a number of important social functions in terms of maintaining social organisation and solidarity, establishing moral boundaries and strengthening shared beliefs and values in society. Such theorising of offending as an everyday behaviour within certain local areas prompted a new academic emphasis on exploring sociological factors as criminogenic. This new focus was further promoted by Italian criminologist Enrico Ferri (1895), who argued that offending was most appropriately explained and responded to by targeting a range of factors: individual (e.g. age, gender, psychological variables); physical/environmental (e.g. race, geography, temperature); and social (e.g. population, religion, culture). The emphasis on sociological foci as potential explanations for offending behaviour was elaborated by two main strands of sociological positivist theory, which will now be explored: concentric zone theory and strain/subcultural theories.

Sociological positivism: concentric zone theory

The concentric zone theory understands cities as organisms that live, grow and evolve as close to the behaviour of the individuals within them. Sociological positivists have noted that urban areas have much higher rates of recorded crime than rural areas, leading them to conclude that there is something criminogenic about certain places and spaces (e.g. local areas, neighbourhoods, communities). The innovators of applying this thesis to criminology were a group of sociologists working at the University of Chicago in the 1920s and 1930s, in particular Robert Park, Ernest Burgess and Clifford Shaw.

These sociologists have become known as the Chicago School. Their sociological positivist theory of crime was formulated by analysing the characteristics, social

FIGURE 2.1 THE CONCENTRIC ZONE MODEL OF PARK AND BURGESS (1925)

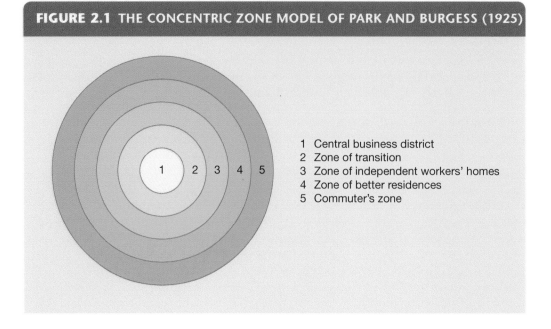

1 Central business district
2 Zone of transition
3 Zone of independent workers' homes
4 Zone of better residences
5 Commuter's zone

changes and distribution of people across Chicago, US. Park and Burgess (1925) were able to divide the city into five concentric 'zones', or areas of increasing size, with a common centre: (1) central business district; (2) transition from business to residences, or the zone of transition; (3) zone of independent workers' homes (working-class homes); (4) zone of better residences (middle-class homes); and (5) commuter's zone (suburbs; see Figure 2.1).

The zone of transition was identified as having the highest rates of adult and youth crime by far. The apparently criminal nature of this area was explained by identifying several criminogenic social characteristics that differentiated it from other areas in the city, notably social disorganisation animated by the regular displacement of residents, undesirable living facilities and deteriorating and transient neighbourhoods – thus lacking social control of its residents. In other words, sociological positivists were identifying the differences between high- and low-offending neighbourhoods and understanding them as explanations for crime, as opposed to the individual positivist method of identifying differences between individuals. A Chicago School colleague, Clifford Shaw, observed that

> in this state of social disorganization, community resistance is low. Delinquency and criminal patterns arise and are transmitted socially just as any other cultural and social pattern is transmitted.
>
> (Shaw 1930: 205)

Evaluation: concentric zone theory

The Chicago School researchers explained crime as the product of neighbourhood factors rather than criminogenic individuals and the product of environmental and cultural determinism rather than biological and psychological determinism

(Case *et al.* 2017). By suggesting that it was the nature of neighbourhoods rather than the nature of individuals that was criminogenic, the concentric zone theory downplayed the influence of broader structural factors (e.g. poverty, overcrowding) and foregrounded the role of space and place (Hopkins-Burke 2013). Like their biological and psychological counterparts, the sociological positivists of the Chicago School were not clear as to exactly how their central concept (space and place) caused crime. In explanatory terms, concentric zone theory has been criticised for advocating contradictory notions of crime causation. On the one hand, the theory explains individual behaviour as predetermined by social disorganisation (the predetermined actor; Hopkins-Burke 2013), but it also assigns an element of free will (the rational actor; Hopkins-Burke 2013) to the learning of patterns of criminal behaviour – explanations that are (arguably) theoretically incompatible (Taylor *et al.* 1973). Accordingly, later studies from the Chicago School employed research methods that were more 'appreciative' of the lives, circumstances and perspectives of individuals in different communities (e.g. ethnographies, life histories). As a consequence, concentric zone theory moved away from strict positivist, deterministic (quantitative) explanations and towards multifactor explanations of offending in criminal neighbourhoods as resulting from individual motivations, social interactions and **psychosocial** (psychological and social) processes of learning and differential association (see previous section).

Sociological positivism: strain and subcultural theories

Durkheim's functionalist perspective that the social construction of offending is a necessary tool for establishing moral, social and legal norms and boundaries also viewed offending as a consequence of society's focus on competitive individualism and a highly structured division of labour (Durkheim 1893/1933). Durkheim argued that unless society regulates and restricts individual aspirations, a state of anomie (normlessness) will occur, leading to social disorganisation (cf. concentric zone theory), from which crime and disorder can result (Durkheim 1895/1964). The concepts of anomie and competitive individualism spawned Robert Merton's 'strain theory' (Merton 1938), which explained offending as a response to the socio-structural strains and pressures (e.g. to succeed, to gain wealth, to achieve recognised status) faced by individuals. Therefore, 'strain' results when there is a disparity between socio-cultural *goals* (defining success and status) and the institutionalised *means* available to the individual to achieve those goals. This strain is criminogenic. Strain theory provides a highly Americanised explanation of crime, focusing on the American dream of boundless opportunity for all, a dream that encourages individual aspirations (goals) that are often blocked by socio-structural restrictions and limited means, especially for young people. Put simply, society encourages individuals to develop unrealistic, unachievable aspirations and expectations, which leads to strain, which then can lead to crime in order to alleviate the strain. According to Merton (1938), when an individual's goals cannot be realised because they are infeasible based on that individual's capabilities and means, then any one of five adaptations occurs:

- *Conformity*: the acceptance of goals and means (the most common adaptation).
- *Innovation*: the value of attaining goals is accepted and acted out irrespective of the impropriety, immorality or illegality of the means used to pursue them.

- *Ritualism*: individual goals are abandoned in favour of adherence to institutionalised means.
- *Retreatism*: the individual rejects cultural goals and institutionalised means.
- *Rebellion*: the individual rejects cultural goals and institutionalised means, with the intention of altering the social structure.

As such, strain theory explains offending as the result of individual adaptations to the strain caused by a mismatch between their goals and means. Adaptations of a criminal nature typically take the form of innovation, but can also be demonstrated through rebellion, implying that the nature of American society is inherently criminogenic.

The principles of strain theory were built upon in the 1950s and 1960s by two particular forms of 'subcultural theory'. The seminal subcultural theory by Albert Cohen (1955) emerged from his research into delinquent working-class boys and gang culture in Chicago. Cohen identified a series of working-class adaptations (cf. strain theory) that these groups of boys would make to adhere to dominant middle-class social norms and values. However, while its predecessor and influencer (strain theory) did not explicitly explore the forms of adaptation that led to irrational (criminal) behaviours that were not a means to an end (e.g. minor theft, petty vandalism), Cohen's subcultural theory did so through its concepts of **status frustration and reaction formation**. Status frustration is the label that Cohen gave to the phenomenon he had observed whereby the subcultural group (gang) operated collectively by using specialised vocabulary, developing internal beliefs (e.g. norms) of their own and promoting unique ways of dressing and behaving (e.g. committing crime) – all of which demonstrated their frustration at their own inability to attain conventional goals. Status frustration was seen as a reaction formation whereby the group inverted dominant middle-class values in order to offer them a collective solution to that restricted opportunities. Cohen (1955: 28) observed that

> the delinquent conduct is right by the standards of his subculture precisely because it is wrong by the norms of the larger culture.

A subsequent subcultural theory was offered by Cloward and Ohlin (1960) to explain how working-class delinquents in subcultural groups pursue high-status goals through aspiring to meet their own working-class criteria and values, rather than seeking to attain middle-class values (which Cohen had argued). Cloward and Ohlin's (1960) version of subcultural theory combined anomie/strain with differential association theory (Sutherland 1947; see earlier) to explain why working-class individuals preferred certain adaptations to others, in particular due to the differential availability of legitimate/illegitimate means to gain material and social status. Their conclusion was that a criminal subculture develops in working-class neighbourhoods where successful criminals become visible to young people and associate with them, providing a criminal success model of status and achievement based on working-class criteria.

Evaluation: strain and subcultural theories

The sociological positivist theories of strain and subculture explained higher rates of delinquency within the working classes in different neighbourhoods by arguing that young working-class males in these areas were more likely to experience strain and then either to offend or to join a subculture, which may encourage them to offend.

Youth offending was viewed as structurally and culturally determined, elaborating the space and place thesis of the Chicago School, which held that geographical areas can be criminogenic. One limitation of these theories, however, is their bias. Like much positivism, the theories of sociological positivism can be androcentric and class centric, privileging the study of offending by working-class males (typically adolescents) and thus restricting their explanatory utility to this specific group, with limited consideration of offending by the middle classes, females or even adults (less problematic for our explanatory purposes). There is also a cogent argument to be made that young people may drift in and out of crime (see Matza's [1964] 'delinquency and drift' thesis), so they may only have a partial commitment to allegedly deterministic subcultural norms and values at any given point in their lives. This suggests that there is no value consensus in society, but instead a **plurality** (multitude, mixture) of values. Consequently, conventional and delinquent norms may overlap and interrelate, and the key influences on (the social construction of) young people's behaviour may be pluralism rather than consensus and interaction rather than determinism (Matza 1964).

5 EASY PIECES

3b Individual to socio-structural explanations of offending: sociological positivism (1900 onwards)

1 *High crime rates*: early sociological positivist theories set out to explain the causes of higher crime rates in specific areas and populations, not the motivations for crime by individuals.
2 *External influences*: sociological positivism (like individual positivism) identifies deterministic influences on crime but is more interested in general patterns of criminality based on social, geographical and economic circumstances external to the individual.
3 *Social disorganisation*: concentric zone theory identifies social disorganisation and lack of social control as the key influence on crime in particular neighbourhoods.
4 *Strain*: strain and subcultural theories argue that working-class males experience strains based on their inability and/or unwillingness to attain accepted social goals by conventional means and to adhere to conventional (middle-class) norms and values. Consequently, individuals may offend or join subcultures and then offend as a means of reconciling or adapting to these strains.
5 *Integration*: sociological positivism has integrated notions of individual learning into its theories of structural determinism, which are viewed by advocates as enhancing its explanatory utility yet viewed by critics as theoretically incompatible.

Now that we have explored the main theoretical groupings within the school of positivism, it is a useful exercise to step back and critically reflect on what we now know and understand about these positivist explanations. Table 2.1 offers five controversial debates relating to the original forms of positivist theory that have been

TABLE 2.1 POSITIVISM AND FIVE NOT-SO-EASY CONTROVERSIES

Benefits	Criticisms
1 Defining crime	
Consensus: traditionally, positivists take the definition and measurement of crime (e.g. through official statistics) for granted, assuming a consensus in society as to how (youth) offending should be defined and understood.[1] This consensus has been intended to promote valid and reliable theoretical explanations of offending that all relate to standardised definitions of 'crime' and 'offending'.	Social construction: critics have argued that 'crime' is a creation of institutions and individuals in different societies – a social construction. Crime is a dynamic, contested and contingent concept. Therefore, we should not assume consensus in its definition and we should explore the criminogenic properties associated with its construction, such as systemic influences and individual subjective experiences.
2 Defining crime: scientific method	
Objectivity: positivists employ an (allegedly) scientific, neutral, value-free, objective methodology to identify biological, psychological and sociological differences between offenders and non-offenders. These differences have been extrapolated (extended/expanded based on assumption and prediction) into the identification of cause and effect relationships that explain offending.	Subjectivity: critics contend that positivism exaggerates the differences and ignores the similarities between offenders and non-offenders. They also argue that criminological study can never be truly objective or value-free; there will always be a degree of subjectivity influencing the decisions made at every stage of the research and scholarship process. Therefore, researchers should critically reflect on their decisions and subjectivity and consider how these may affect the validity and reliability of their findings and conclusions.
3 Explaining crime: reductionism	
Simplicity: positivist methodology offers a largely quantitative, straightforward, common-sense approach producing findings that can be fed easily into statistical analyses to produce simplified and practical explanations of offending to target with appropriate responses.	Oversimplicity: critics suggest that converting the influences on offending to a quantitative number/statistic significantly reduces the complexity and the qualitative value (meanings, interpretations) that individuals attach to them, so much so their explanatory utility and ecological validity may be compromised.
4 Explaining crime: determinism	
Causes: traditionally, positivists have claimed the ability to identify the *causes* of crime – the biological, psychological and sociological factors that predetermine an individual to offend and that therefore should be targeted by criminal justice sentences and interventions. That said, most contemporary positivists are mindful of data limitations, sampling problems and restricted generalisability, with most responsible researchers reflecting on these pitfalls.	Correlates: critics argue that the causes identified by positivists are more akin to *correlates* with offending and that positivist explanatory theories have been unable to conclude exactly how (or even if) different factors influence offending. Therefore, positivist theory can be over-deterministic and its explanatory utility and validity can be limited.

TABLE 2.1 continued	
Benefits	Criticisms
5 Responding to crime: treatment	
Practicality: positivist explanations have identified the biopsychosocial causes of offending and suggest these can be ameliorated (treated, improved) through treatment and rehabilitation, thus recommending a practical, effective, evidence-based optimistic and arguably humane set of responses to (youth) offending.	Complexity: critics argue that positivist treatments are often reductionist, focused on quantified versions of only one element of biopsychosocial influence (n.b. integrated theories have begun to address this) and are sometimes unethical (cf. biological treatments). Also, positivist responses to youth offending assume that the original theory is a relevant and valid explanation of *youth* offending and that biopsychosocial factors are the only/main influences requiring amelioration, a claim contested by critical criminological arguments regarding systemic influences on the social construction of offending.

Note: [1] This generalisation does not necessarily apply to all contemporary positivists, some of whom do not assume a consensus when defining offending. For example, modern positivist methodologies such as self-report surveys containing open-ended questions have been employed to explore individual differences in personalised understandings and construction of 'offending'.

discussed. These debates have been deliberately dichotomised and polarised (split into extreme, generalised versions of competing positions) for the purposes of clear comparison and to encourage you to employ your ABC mindset when evaluating the arguments that you read. In a sense, these polarised positions represent subjective claims made on the basis of the arguments presented thus far – claims that illustrate the constructed, dynamic, contingent and contested nature of explanations of (youth) offending. The main purpose of the table, therefore, is to stimulate you to engage with and evaluate the polarised claims made and to consider your own perspective on positivism as the dominant explanatory framework in criminology.

4 CRITICAL EXPLANATIONS OF OFFENDING: LABELLING AND CRITICAL THEORIES (1950 ONWARDS)

Positivist theories have attained explanatory dominance in criminology. Indeed, positivist explanations of youth offending remain hegemonic to this day, including quasi-positivist explanations focused on the predictive validity of psychosocial 'risk factors' (see Chapter 3). Positivist notions of consensus continue to shape definitions of offending, while positivist notions of objectivity, quantification, determination and biopsychosocial causality continue to shape explanations and responses to offending, particularly youth offending. Despite a degree of critical reflection on their own explanations by positivists and some internal critique of positivist theory by other positivist theories, there has been a general consensus around positivism's central explanatory ideas. The privileging of positivism reflects the contemporary dominance of psychology across the social sciences in the twentieth century and into the twenty-first century. However, since the 1950s, a school of criminological thought has developed that is more sociological in nature, mounting a strong challenge to positivist theories based on the explanations of 'critical criminology'. Critical theories invert the central historical tenets of positivism: that the definition of crime is agreed upon in society (consensus), that the scientific method is neutral value-free (objectivity), that the causes of crime are predetermined (determinism) and that the key causal explanations for crime are individual and social (biopsychosocial causality). The post-1950 evolution of critical theories maps broadly onto our fourth chronological stage from Chapter 1 (1950–1990). This era produced theoretical explanations that were attendant to the social construction of youth offending and the conflict and ambivalence surrounding how to understand and respond to it.

According to critical criminologists, the 'hubris' of positivism (Goldson and Hughes 2010) and its reductionist measurement and oversimplified conclusions has effectively closed down the criminological imagination (Young 2011; see also Case and Haines 2014). Critical criminologists have argued that 'crime' is not an objective fact but is a social construction (see Chapter 1): the dynamic, contingent and contested product of social processes and interactions between institutions and key stakeholders in particular societies. There is a stark contrast between the social constructionist basis of critical theoretical explanations and the other explanatory theories of youth offending discussed in our explanations chapters (except for constructivist risk factor theory; see Chapter 3). This contrast highlights a striking disconnect within the 'triad of youth justice' concerning explanations of youth offending. Although explanatory theories are all essentially social constructs by academic professionals and other intellectuals, they typically have sought to explain youth offending as an objective, value-free, uncontested fact rather than as a dynamic, contingent and contested social construction. Social constructionist arguments, however, assert that youth offending should be defined, *explained* and responded to as the subjective creation of organisations and individuals interacting together in society. The second key focus of critical criminology is that of power. Critical theorists assert that certain groups in society have much more power to decide how 'offending' and 'offenders' are defined (constructed and reconstructed), explained and responded to through youth justice. For example, whites, the middle class, males and adults (so, white middle-class men) have tended to dominate the key stakeholder groups (e.g. academics, politicians, policy-makers, practitioners, media) that produce knowledge and make and enforce social norms and laws – processes that typically benefit them (e.g. in terms of avoiding prosecution) and help or hinder less powerful groups (e.g. children and young people). In other words, the power to criminalise/decriminalise behaviours and to shape the definitions of, explanations of and responses to (youth) offending sits with a select few. Through their focus on social construction and power as influences on the criminalisation of behaviours, individuals and groups, critical criminologists have offered an alternative to the hegemony of positivist theories but have yet to displace them in academic or political terms. For our purposes, critical criminology is especially relevant because a significant and vociferous body of critical *youth* criminologists have emerged (largely in the UK, Australasia and Canada) to challenge the androcentric, ethnocentric, class-centric and adult-centric status quo in youth justice. This cadre of critics includes academics such as Barry Goldson, John Muncie, Roger Smith, John Pitts, Tim Bateman, Jo Phoenix, Gilly Sharp, Kevin Haines and others. I count myself among this group, but nevertheless I will attempt to provide you with as balanced an argument as possible throughout the book, because criticisms can themselves be criticised, and ultimately you need to decide for yourself about how you take these issues forward into your studies, research and future practice.

STOP AND THINK

Is androcentrism justified when explaining (youth) offending?

It is clear that the **socio-historical** construction (social construction across history) of explanations of offending has more often than not been the product of men (usually white, middle-class men) studying the behaviour of boys/men (usually working-class boys/men). Consequently, explanations of (youth) offending have been androcentric and 'malestream' – placing the male perspective at the centre of our understandings. But is this androcentrism indicative of theoretical and methodological bias, is it reflective of the reality of who offends, or is it a mixture of both? Consider this:

- Do we prioritise explanations of crime that apply to males because they do actually commit the majority of crimes? This would be a realist view (see Section 5 of this chapter).
- Is the androcentric focus of criminology the product of an uncritical assumption that males commit the most crime, which leads to the targeting of empirical research, academic explanations and criminal justice practices (e.g. police activities) on this group to the exclusion of other populations? This would be a **self-fulfilling prophecy** – a belief/prediction that causes itself to come true as a direct result of the new behaviour it creates.
- Is it possible that the androcentric nature of biosocial explanations of crime is (in part) a product of academic theorising by an exclusive group of predominantly white, middle-class, male researchers?
- To what extent have we socially constructed the extent and nature of (the reality of) crime committed by males and the need to respond to this crime?

The following section will explore two main groups of critical criminological theories of (youth) offending, starting with 'labelling theories', which essentially bridge the gap between socio-structural positivist explanations (see Section 3 of this chapter) and the critical movement. This discussion is followed by examination of the most prominent theories identified under the banner of 'critical criminology': Marxist criminology, the 'new criminology' and gendered perspectives (feminist and masculinity theories).

Labelling theories

In the 1950s and 1960s in the US, a set of criminological perspectives began to gain momentum as a challenge to the 'prevailing positivist orthodoxy' (Case *et al.* 2017) and its psychological, deterministic and reductionist basis. A small group of critical sociologists began to explore the potential role of power in shaping definitions of offending, with a particular focus on who had the power to criminalise individuals and behaviours – to decide who and what is considered 'criminal' and how society should respond to it. This led to arguments that those in power undertake processes of **criminalisation** – assigning labels to people and behaviours (e.g. through creating laws) and acting on these labels (e.g. by targeting certain groups) in order to make them 'criminal' – another self-fulfilling prophecy. This theory led critical sociologists to explore how individuals in society may react to being labelled. Therefore, the dual focus of labelling theories was process and reaction. In this way, labelling explanations moved away from (biopsychosocial) positivist understandings and towards a greater appreciation of the systemic influence of the structures, processes and agents of criminalisation.

Labelling theories can be traced historically to the late 1930s and Frank Tannenbaum's (1938) 'dramatization of evil' hypothesis. Tannenbaum believed that only a small proportion of the young males who offend (note the exclusive focus on young males as the archetypal 'offender') are actually identified and caught (i.e. working-class males in working-class neighbourhoods), and that once they are caught, they may be labelled as 'evil' by their community/society. This label can prompt the individual to define themselves as evil, marginalising them from their usual social groups and encouraging specialised treatment and punishment as criminal/youth justice responses. The individual's redefinition of their own identity in line with their label encourages them to offend further, thus dramatising (exaggerating, deepening) that 'evil' behaviour. As such, the criminal label becomes a self-fulfilling prophecy. The dramatization of evil hypothesis was built upon and popularised by Edwin Lemert in his 1951 book *Social Pathology*. Lemert distinguished between two forms of deviance:

- *Primary deviance*: temporary, inadvertent and often hidden behaviour causing no long-term damage to the offender because it does not create a social reaction, or if it does, one that is not particularly strong or stigmatising. Consequently, primary deviance does not lead to an individual becoming labelled or viewing themselves as an offender if they are labelled.
- *Secondary deviance*: a criminalising process caused by the individual to see themselves as an 'offender' due to the social reaction to the original offending. This social reaction is sufficiently strong to create a label that has a negative psychological impact on the individual's self-identity. The individual then internalises the label and subsequently acts in a more deviant way (i.e. a self-fulfilling prophecy) because they now see themselves as a deviant/offender or as part of a group that is viewed as deviant/offending. Therefore, that criminal label has a transformative effect on self-perception and identity (cf. Tannenbaum 1938).

Labelling theories of crime are most closely associated with the work of Howard Becker in the 1960s. Becker (1963) focused on the criminalisation processes conducted by the individuals who construct and enforce criminal labels and categories, rather than the reactions of recipients to these labels (unlike Tannenbaum and Lemert). According to Becker, no behaviour is inherently criminal and a behaviour only becomes criminal when a label is conferred upon it:

> Social groups create deviance by making the rules whose infraction constitutes deviance, and by applying those rules to particular people and labelling them as outsiders. From this point of view . . . the deviant is one to whom the label has been successfully applied; deviant behaviour is behaviour that people so label.
>
> (Becker 1963: 4)

In line with much critical criminology explanation that was to follow it, Becker's central theory was that criminal laws and social rules were made (constructed) by people in power (e.g. adults) and enforced upon those without power (e.g. children and young people). He contended that some laws/rules may be cynically designed to keep the less powerful in their place, while others may be genuinely intended to benefit the powerless (e.g. those produced by the 'social reformers' of Chapter 1). However, such laws/rules may have inadvertent or unforeseen negative consequences, such as the creation (through labelling) of new groups of 'outsiders' (e.g. the wave of youth subcultures that emerged across the 1950s–1990s; see Chapter 1). These newly created groups infringe the new laws/rules and create their own replacements, which prompts the creation of new social control agencies to enforce these new laws/rules (e.g. criminal justice organisations). Becker's thesis concludes that ultimately the new laws/rules, the new social control agencies and the 'deviant' social role start to permeate the collective consciousness and become taken for granted by society, thus creating new stereotypes and labels such as 'youth offender' and 'juvenile delinquent' (see also Case *et al.* 2017).

Evaluation: labelling theories

Labelling theories provided a much-needed challenge and counter-view to mainstream positivist explanations of offending, which arguably lacked a degree of validity due to their neglect of both the systemic influences on the creation of offending and the subjective influences that can influence an individual's reaction to their treatment by society. As such, labelling theories provided a highly innovative and arguably valid set of perspectives on youth offending when they were introduced into criminology. However, critics have accused labelling theories of paying insufficient attention to explaining why specific behaviours are labelled and stigmatised while others are not, and why certain individuals are criminalised and not others – beyond generalised notions of power differences. Arguably, labelling theories have been too focused on small-scale interactions (e.g. between two people) rather than broader interactions between (individuals within) larger social groups and institutions. There is also a lack of specific explanation around why and how individuals internalise labels and become (secondary) deviants. Labelling explanations are also somewhat idealistic, arguing that youth offending is largely created and exaggerated through the application of labels rather than existing as a real phenomenon or problem. Such idealism deprives the explanations of a degree of ecological validity and practical utility for informing youth justice responses in the real world, beyond support for 'minimum necessary intervention' (Lemert 1972; McAra and McVie 2015) approaches that would avoid stigmatising interventions and marking out offending individuals for special treatment.

Critical criminology

As the 1960s progressed, a distinct perspective of 'critical criminology', also known as 'radical criminology', developed to elaborate on the central tenets of labelling theories and to more fully explore the role of power in the criminalisation of individuals and behaviours. The development of the critical theories of critical criminology in the UK can be traced back to the National Deviancy Conference of 1968 held at the University of York. The conference was founded by the forefather of critical criminology, Jock Young, along with other noted critical criminologists such as Stan Cohen, Mary McIntosh, Ian Taylor, Paul Walton, Paul Rock, David Downes and Laurie Taylor. The group were described as 'naughty schoolboys' by the venerable positivist Sir Leon Radzinowicz, the implication being that they were somehow causing trouble within criminology. In a sense, they were. Young, Cohen, McIntosh and their colleagues wanted to shake up criminological explanation by considering why society perceived some acts to be deviant and why it reacted to deviance in the way that it did, in addition to exploring the subjective experiences and opinions of the powerless 'deviant'. All of those issues had been touched upon but somewhat glossed over by labelling theories up to that point. The National Deviancy Conference set out to develop a 'fully social theory of deviance' that integrated elements of labelling with Marxist theories of crime. We already know what labelling theories have argued, so what is Marxist theory and how does it relate to crime?

The philosopher, sociologist and economist Karl Marx created his famous theory to explain behaviour in modern capitalist societies. Marx argued that the capitalist economic system creates a distinct mode of production of goods and services that is controlled by the ruling class (the bourgeoisie) because they own the means of production, while the majority of the wealth-creating work is done by the working class (the proletariat), who own little. Essentially, the ruling class controls the production of the goods and services that society consumes and receives profit for doing so. They employ the working class, who sell their labour for a wage and are exploited because they need money to buy the goods that they themselves have made (see also Chapter 1 discussion of the Industrial Revolution). This unequal power relationship creates conflict between the classes that may need to be resolved through the rule of law. However, the powerful ruling class control the processes of lawmaking and law enforcement, so any laws are likely to reflect their own economic interests and not those of the working class. The Marxist criminologist Willem Bonger (1876–1940) applied Karl Marx's general theory to the explanation of offending. Bonger's Marxist criminology believed that the social, political and economic structures of capitalist society can actually create crime and the social reactions to it, so capitalism is criminogenic. He outlined six propositions that encapsulated his Marxist theory of crime:

1   Immorality and criminality are socio-historically constructed variables.
2   The criminal law exists to protect the interests of the powerful.
3   Capitalism is driven by coercion and exploitation, not cooperation and consensus.
4   Capitalism encourages greed and the pursuit of pleasure, which makes both classes more prone to crime and weakens their sense of responsibility towards one another.

5   Poverty can prompt crime by creating a desperate need for food and other necessities.
6   Crime can occur when there is a perceived opportunity to gain an advantage through legal means or opportunities for pleasure are restricted by a biased legal system.

(Bonger 1916, in Muncie 2014: 128)

Bonger argued that both powerful and powerless groups commit crime through greed and opportunity. He noted, however, that explanatory theories had ignored middle-class offending and any committed study of the 'crimes of the powerful', which can actually cause greater harm than everyday crimes (see also Sutherland 1940) but which may often not even be classed as crime. Therefore, Marxist criminology offers an economic explanation of crime by examining differential power relations between the ruling class and the working class in capitalist societies, centred on control of the means of production of goods and services (see also Quinney 1974; Chambliss 1975).

In 1973, three of the criminologists at the heart of the National Deviancy Conference (Ian Taylor, Paul Walton and Jock Young) published 'a manifesto for critical criminology that has influenced and inspired generations of critical criminologists' (Case *et al.* 2017). The 'new criminology' (Taylor *et al.* 1973) integrated elements of labelling and Marxism with interactionism to create what was claimed as a fully social theory of deviance. The new criminology put forward seven incremental elements required to fully explain offending:

1   *The wider origins of this deviant act* – placing offending in its wider socio-structural context (e.g. neighbourhood socio-economic characteristics, unemployment and poverty levels).
2   *The immediate origins of the deviant act* – explaining the different 'events, experiences and structural developments that precipitate the deviant act' in the wider socio-structural context.
3   *The deviant act* – explaining the relationship between the behaviour and its causes (e.g. status frustration).
4   *The immediate origins of social reaction* – how significant others such as family, peers and police respond to the deviance.
5   *The wider origins of deviant reaction* – the reaction in terms of who holds the power and sets the rules.
6   *The outcome of the social reaction on the deviant's further action* – the labelling process.
7   *The nature of the deviant process as a whole* – the relationship between elements 1–6 in forming a 'fully social theory of deviance'.

(Taylor *et al.* 1973)

In 1998, Walton and Young published an edited text called *The New Criminology Revisited*, which updated and largely reaffirmed their original theory while adding in more detailed consideration of feminist arguments and re-evaluating their position (25 years on) in the contemporary context of criminological theories. The new criminology remains committed to the anti-positivist belief that individuals who commit crime do not need to be corrected (through treatment or punishment). The implication for appropriate criminal/youth justice responses appears to be the need for broader socio-structural changes to address crime, such as the redistribution of wealth and power in society. Such responses should target the power differentials that encourage labelling and social reactions to crime that are disproportionately visited upon powerless, socio-disadvantaged groups, such as the working-class boys who have become the focus of socially constructed definitions and explanations of youth offending over the past 200 years.

Gendered explanations

The New Criminology Revisited reflected how the scope of critical criminological theories had expanded since the 1970s to encompass a more detailed examination of gendered issues, particularly through feminist theories. Feminist criminologists such as Carol Smart and Pat Carlen have attacked the androcentric nature of (critical) criminology and its historic focus on the behaviours and activities of males as offenders, victims, criminal justice professional, academics, politicians and so forth. Studies involving females have tended to view them as weak or corrupt creatures unable to control their actions and female criminality has been largely viewed in terms of biology and sexuality (cf. Lombroso's work). A number of different feminist perspectives have emerged (e.g. liberal, radical, black, lesbian) to explore and explain the lives of women in society, and as such, feminism can be seen as a divided movement which some groups of women (e.g. the socially excluded, black, poorly educated) feel does not speak for them or promote their interests (see Smart 1977; see also Case *et al.* 2017). Indeed, some feminist theorists even reject the term 'feminist criminology', viewing it as reductionist and androcentric in its apparent need to comply with simplistic, 'malestream' (mainstream, androcentric) perspectives on crime. Others assert that a feminist criminology,[4] with its attendant qualitative, appreciative research methods, is much needed in order to reflect and explore the neglected lives of females (including female offenders) and the exploitation of male power to criminalise.

Despite being a somewhat fractured set of theories, the different forms of feminist (criminological) theory cohere around a focus on disparities in power and unequal relations in society. Consequently, they critique the **patriarchal** (controlled by men), androcentric nature of orthodox criminology, viewing it as 'malestream' and gender blind, neglecting and downgrading the behaviours, experiences and needs of women and girls (see Smart 1990). In her book *Women, Crime and Criminology*, Carol Smart (1977) criticised not only orthodox positivist criminology but also interactionist and radical theories (e.g. labelling theories, the new criminology) for not fully considering female criminality or victimisation. Smart's work has prompted a new wave of studies by feminist academics (for a review, see Ugwudike 2015). More recently, feminist criminology has turned its attention towards youth justice issues by exploring the extent and nature of the differential treatment of girls who offend, in particular, whether it occurs, what it looks like and if it is appropriate. I discussed these developments with Dr Gilly Sharp, who has researched and published extensively on youth offending and youth justice issues as they relate to girls (cf. Sharpe 2015, 2011; Sharpe and Gelsthorpe 2015).

CONVERSATIONS

Explaining youth offending by girls

Steve: In your view, to what extent has an understanding of girls who offend been a meaningful component of our explanations of youth crime over time?

Gilly Sharp: Historically, there has been an emphasis on female offending as biological, as well as a preoccupation with its assumed sexual and/or psychological causes. Psychological theories have frequently situated the origins of girls' offending within deficient families. For example, William Isaac Thomas was one of the first writers to focus on the relationship between female crime and sexuality. In his early work, Thomas (1907) described women/girls as 'anabolic' (passive), compared with men/boys who are 'katabolic' (active), thus assuming essential physiological sex differences. He further argued that females have more varieties of love in their nervous systems then males and are thus naturally led into sexual 'offences' such as prostitution. In his later work, Thomas (1923) defined girls according to their domestic and sexual roles – dominated by biological imperatives and emotional and irrational impulses. He viewed offending primarily as a social pathology rather than a biological abnormality, and believed that wayward girls could be 'saved' through early intervention in the form of individual treatment, which would help delinquent, 'undersocialised' girls to readjust.

Several later studies of girls in British institutions in the 1960s and 1970s continued to address an assumed relationship between psychology and delinquency, pointing – with a common lack of critical reflection on the effects of institutionalisation – to high levels of emotional instability, poor self-image and psychological disturbance in incarcerated girls. Others attributed girls' delinquency to a form of psychological 'acting out' due to family dysfunction, sexual dysfunction (ironically, being either under-sexualised or over-sexualised) or loneliness. It is highly likely that the foregrounding of girls' sexuality as both cause and expression of their offending in much theorising historically has both reinforced, and been reinforced by, legal definitions in which girls' delinquent behaviour was understood as sexual, such as the category of 'moral danger' (Sharpe 2011).

The relevance of peers to girls' offending was sidelined or ignored even when sociological theories focusing on gangs and peer associations dominated explanations of crime. While group solidarity, excitement and status-seeking were believed to be the principal causes of boys' offending, delinquent girls continued to be portrayed as loners and misfits. Since the late 1970s, however, these assumptions have been challenged by studies demonstrating the importance of peers in girls' offending. Moffitt and colleagues have gone so far as to suggest that, due to the relative absence of biological factors predisposing girls to offending, 'the bulk of antisocial behaviour, *especially by females*, is best understood as a social phenomenon originating in the context of social relationships' (2001: xvi, emphasis added).

A major advance made by feminist criminologists since the 1980s has been to focus attention on the connections, or 'blurred boundaries', between young women's offending and their victimisation experiences. Although the causal mechanisms between victimisation and offending are not well understood, unresolved traumatic events may result in alcohol and drug (ab)use and behavioural problems, including lawbreaking.

There is substantial evidence that young people of both sexes caught up in the YJS have been victims of crime and harm inflicted at the hands of (usually male) adults (see Smith and Thornberry 1995). Studies of criminalised young women have consistently revealed remarkably high rates of childhood victimisation: one North American review reported rates of sexual abuse among justice system–involved girls of between 40 and 73 per cent (Chesney-Lind and Shelden 2004). Such 'feminist pathways' research underpins the development of 'gender-responsive programming' within the YJS.

Steve: Should we consider having gender-neutral theories of youth offending?

Gilly: There is considerable disagreement among theorists today regarding the extent to which gender-neutral theories of crime, derived as they generally are from studies of (only) boys and men, are able to explain offending by girls and women. Added to this is the near invisibility – in UK-based research, at least – of Black and Minority Ethnic (BAME) young women, whose needs and experiences are implicitly subsumed within those of either their white female, or their BAME male, counterparts. An important criticism is that *both* traditional theories *and* feminist theories are overly deterministic about girls' offending and ignore the historical, social, geographical, patriarchal and racialised contexts in which they live and act. Karen Heimer and Stacey de Coster (1999), examining girls' violent offending in the US, have called for a contextualised explanatory approach, which analyses the interaction of structural and cultural factors that may either inhibit or promote crime and violence among girls and boys. They conclude that, although poverty and economic marginalisation increase the likelihood of violent behaviour for both sexes, patriarchal structures and cultural norms sanctioning female violence serve to limit working-class girls' use of violence, resulting in them committing fewer violent crimes. Simultaneously, Heimer and de Coster's finding that girls' emotional bonds to their families inhibit female violence may go some way to explain why some girls *do* become violent if bonds to their families have been damaged – for example as a result of abuse, conflict or neglect.

Note: This 'Conversation' continues in Chapter 6 with a discussion of whether youth justice *responses* should be differentiated by gender. I conducted a related 'Conversation' titled 'Explaining offending by Black and Ethnic Minority children' with Professor Colin Webster, a scholar and researcher who has studied the area in great detail. The results of this fascinating conversation are detailed in Appendix 1 at the end of this chapter.

Developments in feminist explanations of youth offending and how youth justice is applied to girls reflect broader developments in gender studies – the study of gender as it relates to women, men and sexuality. The popularity, quality and necessity of feminist theories of offending has encouraged critical criminology to expand its explanatory focus to incorporate gendered issues more broadly. This development has contributed to the emergence of 'masculinities' as a key issue for explaining offending by men and boys. The culturally informed scholarship of academics such as James Messerschmidt (1993, 2017) and Raewyn Connell (1995, 2005) has further informed criminological thinking in this area by identifying an hegemonic form of masculinity in the identities of Western males, especially those who offend, which is characterised by personality and behavioural traits including competitiveness, toughness, aggression, power and competence. I had a conversation about the issue of masculinities and youth offending with Dr Eric Baumgartner, author of *And Then There Were the Men – Masculinity and the Youth Justice System in England and Wales* (Baumgartner 2012).

CONVERSATIONS

Masculinity and youth justice

Steve: Why do we need a focus on masculinities when studying youth justice?

Eric Baumgartner: Much of the recent media focus on youth justice has uncovered the lack of concentration on young people's welfare needs and the 'needless criminalisation' of an 'already marginalized, literally disenfranchised and often disproportionately victimized community' (Phoenix 2016: 137) of young people. A recent review of the Youth Justice System (YJS) found that it is only recently beginning to address some of the issues raised by scholars in relation to young people's vulnerability and potential mental health needs, and concludes that the number of people both in custody and entering the YJS has decreased (Taylor 2016). The intersection of youth offending, mental health and issues around vulnerability highlights some of the issues regarding masculinity and youth justice. Although the perceived increase in girls' offending behaviour has received attention in recent years (YJB 2009b), with a focus on mental health and young girls' needs, the dominant group of young people in contact with the YJS is young men and boys (Baumgartner 2014). Coote (1993) argues that crime is a male occupation, and Benstead (1994) elaborates that the source of crime committed by men is to be found in the way masculinity has been defined socially. Gelsthorpe and Sharpe (2006) demonstrate how a key feature of the YJS is to regulate acceptable gender-role behaviour. Ashford *et al.* (1997) elaborate that youth justice responses to girls include the sanctioning of perceived violations of normative gender role expectations. While issues in relation to girls' offending behaviour and their perceived vulnerability has enjoyed increasing attention over recent years, the 'current construction of juvenile crime [continues] to neglect issues of masculinity' (Dominelli 2002: 156) and the vulnerability of young men and boys in the YJS in England and Wales (Baumgartner 2014).

Steve: What is the theoretical basis of the masculinities perspective?

Eric: The basis is social constructionism (Burr 2003), focusing on distinctions between sex and gender. This approach argues that gender is not innate but a social construct. Masculinity is 'performed' as a result of both culturally and socially conditioned 'male socialization' and normative gender roles perceived as gender-appropriate in specific socio-economic contexts (Baumgartner 2014). Indeed, Winlow (2002: 41) demonstrates that 'delinquent lower-class male activities . . . are not entirely divorced from wider male culture'. Collier (1998) argues that dominant debates on masculinity and offending revolve around young men's masculinity and their perceived dangerousness, whereby the bodies of young men are criminalised through signifiers (constructions) of a particular kind of masculinity: white and working-class masculinity. Hatty (2000) explains that aggression and violence come to be socially conditioned ideas whereby males hold an entitlement to aggression, with a clear idea of legitimate forms of aggressive behaviour. The conclusion is that violence and aggression shape a particular form of male identity and masculinity, which in turn is deeply embedded in many forms of violence (Hatty 2000). This link between masculinity and crime has been established by a number of authors (Messerschmidt 2012; Mullins 2006) who all argue that 'doing crime' is 'doing masculinity'. These authors make a clear connection between the ways in which young men define themselves as men and the reasons for their offending behaviour.

Steve: What are the implications of these explanations for youth justice practice with boys and young men?

Eric: Taking into account that the dominant group of young people in contact with youth justice services are male and that scholars have made clear connections between constructions of masculinity and male offending behaviour, the logical consequence would be to address or at least problematise issues around masculinity in the prevention, intervention, assessment and sanction of young men who have been identified as having committed crime (Baumgartner 2014). Indeed, the call for male-focused practice in the wider provision of social and welfare services, has been long-standing (Taylor 2003), but these examples of the importance of male-focused service provision (Cowburn 2010) have not been translated into the context of youth justice practice (Baumgartner 2014).

My recent research into masculinity and youth justice has demonstrated that workers in youth offending teams (YOTs) drew close connections between the masculinity of young men and their offending behaviour. Those working with young men in YOTs in England and Wales construct young men along the lines of 'hegemonic localized masculinity' (Baumgartner 2014). In other words, the ways in which those YOT workers understand masculinity is surprisingly homogenous:

1   The display of a clear form of aggression, low impulse control, and the avoidance of any display of weakness.
2   They link this behaviour to some of the main reasons with which they explain young men's offending – the ways in which the young men perform masculinity is through drinking and fighting, the inability to respond to conflict situations other than through drinking and violent behaviour, and the young men's effort to prove their masculinity through showing bravado and an attempt to gain kudos, respect and a reputation as 'hard' (Baumgartner 2014).

Less attention here is paid to the young men's vulnerability and how some of the issues around their offending behaviour can be addressed by problematising the young men's masculinity in prevention, assessment, and intervention by adapting male-friendly approaches. Paradoxically though, the YOT workers in Baumgartner's study do not think that 'masculinity' is something they are to problematise with the young men with whom they work. Some reasons for this are that (1) the practice guidance set out by the Youth Justice Board (see Chapter 5) does not consider gender as a relevant category in assessment and practice, and (2) they do not feel sufficiently equipped through training to address issues around masculinity. While some gender practices reinforcing negative types of masculinity are clearly present (Baumgartner 2014), the opportunity is being missed to address some of the young men's offending behaviour through addressing issues around masculinity (Baumgartner 2014).

It is important to understand that the findings of my research reflect the ways in which practitioners construct the masculinity of the young men with whom they work. While it is plausible that those are, at least in part, influenced by the bodily practices of those young men themselves, more research with young men is needed to fully establish the role masculinity may play in both offending behaviour and youth justice practice. If indeed young men's offending behaviour is linked to the ways in which they construct their own masculinity, then issues around gender in assessment and intervention in youth justice practice need to be addressed. Therefore, to 'ensure that when young people do offend, the manner and degree of intervention are appropriate to their welfare needs and/or their risk of re-offending or causing harm' (Goldson 2008: 383), gendered issues need to be considered in youth justice practice. Such an approach may not only assist in addressing offending behaviour itself, but also help to uncover some of the vulnerabilities and mental health issues that young people in contact with the YJS face. In a system that is highly gendered (Dominelli 2002), and in which the performance of gender in specific criminal and youth justice spaces has been identified as being central (Reich 2010), the problematisation of masculinity in youth justice work with young men is vital to address both their offending behaviour and some of the wider issues around vulnerability, mental health and their often-complex needs (Haines and Case 2015).

Evaluation: critical criminology

In the second half of the twentieth century, critical criminology emerged as a challenge to the positivist orthodoxy in criminology by attempting to offer a fully social theory of deviance that conceptualised offending as a social construct by examining who has the power to criminalise behaviours and individuals (the 'victimised actor'; Hopkins-Burke 2013) and examining the processes by which this criminalisation occurs. Initially, Marxist criminology argued that capitalism is criminogenic, with the powerful ruling class controlling the means of production in society and the powerless working class selling their labour and consuming what is produced. This disparity, it was argued, resulted in socio-economic power differentials that precipitated crime through greed, strain and poverty (cf. strain theory). Subsequently, the new criminology integrated labelling theories, Marxist criminology and interactionism into a 'fully social theory of deviance', which focused on the wider and immediate origins of the offence, the social reaction to it and the outcomes of this (criminogenic) social reaction. Neither Marxist criminology nor the new criminology specifically examined youth offending. However, both theories constituted an important step towards a more detailed and valid explanation of youth offending, because young people are disproportionately likely to be victims of the criminogenic socio-economic power differentials of Marxist criminology and the stigmatising social reactions of the new criminology. As critical criminology developed, critical gendered perspectives of crime were initiated by feminist theorists, who addressed the neglect of females and girls in explanations and responses to crime. Gendered theories of masculinities have focused on the influence of hegemonic masculine identity on explaining crime and the differential responses to offending committed by men and boys.

Critical criminology subverts the need for responses to offending to correct causal 'deficits' in an individual, instead prioritising broader socio-structural and economic changes such as the redistribution of wealth and power and changing the processes by which marginalised, powerless groups such as working-class boys are criminalised. Clearly, critical theories have offered a necessary alternative explanatory perspective to counter the hegemony of positivism (most notably individual positivism), which (traditionally) has taken the definition of 'crime' for granted and focused on individual deficit as its central explanatory mechanism. However, as we will see in the following section, critical criminology is not without its own critics, who portray its explanations as idealistic and unrealistic – as failing to engage with the 'real' extent, nature and causes of crime as committed and experienced by powerless groups.

5 EASY PIECES

4 Critical explanations of offending: labelling and critical theories (1950 onwards)

1 *Labelling theories*: offending is the product of a 'criminal' label being placed on individuals and behaviours by powerful social groups. By approaching offending as a 'social construction', labelling theories offered the first 'critical' theoretical explanations of offending by young people as an often labelled and stigmatised social group.

2 *Labelling as a reaction and a process*: the early labelling theories of Tannenbaum (dramatization of evil) and Lemert (primary and secondary deviance) focused on the recipient's reaction to being labelled criminal, which can lead to them committing further crime. Becker's labelling theory focused on the processes by which powerful individuals/organisations create criminal labels that then create outsiders in society and the need for social control agencies, which ultimately creates more crime (a self-fulfilling prophecy).

3 *Critical theories and power*: critical criminology emerged as a direct challenge to the positivist hegemony. It focused on the socially constructed nature of offending, socio-structural inequalities and processes of criminalisation by powerful social groups, rather than assuming 'offending' to be a social fact resulting from individual deficits.

4 *Marxist criminology and the new criminology*: the Marxist form of critical theory argued that unequal socio-economic power relations caused by capitalism are criminogenic; the new criminology expanded this thesis by integrating labelling and interactionism into a 'fully social theory of deviance'.

5 *Gendered explanations and responses*: contemporary critical gendered explanations of youth offending have taken the form of adapted feminist theories in order to explore differential explanations of and responses to offending by girls and adapted theories of masculinity to examine offending behaviour by boys.

5 INTEGRATED EXPLANATIONS OF OFFENDING: INTEGRATED POSITIVIST AND REALIST THEORIES (1970s ONWARDS)

The foundation for theoretical development in criminology has been the single factor theory that explains offending as the result of a specific influence, often replacing a previous theory that has either been rejected or has fallen out of favour. For example, as has been discussed, biological positivism replaced the classical theories that it had originally challenged as the hegemonic explanatory theory in criminology, then fell out of favour itself and was replaced by psychological and later sociological forms of positivism (see also Case *et al.* 2017). As also noted, however, several explanatory theories have developed with a degree of acknowledgement and even integration of concepts and arguments from other theories (cf. Agnew 2005). The theories explored thus far in this chapter have offered explanations that have privileged rational choice or a particular form of positivism and typically added other elements to this overarching explanation. A more recent development within criminological explanation has been that of **integrated theories** – hybrid, multifactor explanations of (youth) offending that integrate ideas from different theories, as opposed to single-factor explanations (see Case *et al.* 2017). At least three categories of integrated theory can be discerned from the available literature: integrated positivist theories, integrated realist theories and integrated risk factor theories.[5]

Integrated positivist theories

Criminologists have attempted to address the explanatory limitations of single-factor theories by integrating ideas from multiple positivist explanations – combining their relative strengths and compensating for their individual weaknesses to offer more holistic, universal, generalisable and valid explanations of offending (see Case *et al.* 2017). It is possible to distinguish two categories of integrated positivist theory:

- *Biopsychosocial theories*: an integration of biological, psychological and sociological/environmental influences.
- *Social control theories*: an integration of psychological and socio-structural factors (a largely psychosocial approach).

Integrated positivist theories: biopsychosocial theories

As you have read, the early biological theories of crime employed a positivist methodology that was highly innovative at the time and that had produced a series of groundbreaking findings in explanatory terms. The explanatory utility of biological positivist theories in isolation, however, has been characterised as narrow and reductionist, reducing the causes and explanations of offending to that most oversimplified and basic forms at the expense of a broader focus (Miller 2009). The arguments of biological positivism began to appear reductionist and overly deterministic, and even potentially racist, sexist and classist in their implications regarding the criminogenic nature of physical characteristics and genetic inheritance. In particular, some of the recommended responses to offending promoted by biological positivism, such as chemical castration, electroconvulsive therapy and genetic engineering, came to be considered excessive and unethical in academic and medical circles (Vold *et al.*

1998). That being said, as noted in the neuroscience section, biological positivism has experienced a renaissance in the late twentieth and early twenty-first centuries – a resurgence driven by both neuroscience and new biopsychosocial theories combining different strands of positivism within multifactor integrated explanations (see Vold *et al.* 1998; Bernard *et al.* 2015; see also Case *et al.* 2017).

It was Sarnoff Mednick who popularised the notion of integrating positivist explanations of crime through his 'biosocial theory' of criminogenic interactions between biological and socio-environmental factors (Mednick 1977; Mednick *et al.* 1987). Mednick and his colleagues assisted that 'the value of biological factors is more limited in predicting antisocial behaviour in individuals who have experienced criminogenic social conditions in their rearing' (Mednick *et al.* 1987: 68). Mednick's central proposition was that everybody possesses natural, biological instincts and urges to commit crime, but that the inability to control these urges was more prevalent in individuals who had experienced socio-environmental problems such as inadequate socialisation in the family and social interactions with criminal and antisocial peer groups. His theory was that individuals are born with biological predispositions (nature) towards offending that could be triggered by socio-environmental stressors (nurture). C. Ray Jeffery (1977) added psychological influences into Mednick's theory to produce an integrated biopsychosocial theory of crime. According to Jeffrey, biological and psychological factors (e.g. biochemical imbalances affecting cognition) can cause offending behaviour in their own right (nature) or they can interact with social-environmental processes such as socialisation and poverty in order to cause offending behaviour (an integration of nature and nurture).

Integrated biopsychosocial theories were built upon in explanatory terms in the mid-1980s by the forefather of right realism (see later in this chapter), James Q. Wilson, and his colleague Richard Herrnstein. Wilson and Herrnstein (1985) produced their 'right realist biopsychosocial theory', which argued that most crime is committed by young men and is the product of interactions between biological and sociological factors, asserting that

> it is likely that the effect of maleness and youthfulness on the tendency to commit crime has both constitutional and social origins: that is, it has something to do with the biological status of being a young male and with how the young man has been treated by family, friends and society.
>
> (Wilson and Herrnstein 1985: 69)

To right realists, being male in terms of biological sex meant that young men possess certain constitutional/biological characteristics (e.g. gender, age, intelligence, personality) that positively/negatively affect their ability to learn/internalise social norms and to learn from reinforcement or punishment of behaviour (cf. psychological learning theories). Being male can result in experiencing differential treatment and social interactions compared to those experienced by females. For example, boys may be less likely to receive reinforcement for positive behaviour but may be more likely to be rewarded for negative behaviour, so they are more likely to choose to become criminal (in a given situation) and to persist with criminal behaviours (cf. differential association and subcultural theories). As such, right realist biosocial theory is an integration of rational choice and biopsychosocial positivist explanations. Right realists recommend responses around the prevention, treatment and punishment of crime that focus on influencing young males' rational choices to commit crime and to comply with social norms (i.e. their self-control).

Contemporary biopsychosocial theories have identified and targeted biopsychosocial (risk) factors in early life (pre-birth, childhood, adolescence, young adulthood) that increase the risk of later offending and antisocial behaviour (see next chapter for more detailed discussion). For example, biopsychosocial theorists have explained crime as the result of complications during pregnancy creating problems with central nervous system functioning and subsequent well-being (Moffitt 1993), which then interact with maternal rejection and cause violent behaviour (Raine *et al.* 1997) and mix with poverty to predict physical aggression (Arseneault *et al.* 2002). Biopsychosocial theories have also identified poor parenting as criminogenic, with poor parenting defined variously as unresponsiveness and rejection (e.g. Shaw *et al.* 2003) or harsh, controlling behaviour and lack of acceptance of the child (e.g. Younge *et al.* 1996).

Evaluation: biopsychosocial theories

The integration of biological, psychological and sociological explanations has arguably benefited criminological theory by providing broader and more versatile explanations of offending (e.g. Vold *et al.* 1998). Integrating different positivist explanations has mediated the reductionism and determinism of biological theories and provided more holistic, comprehensive explanations of (youth) offending that can fit more crimes at more times for more people (Akers and Sellers 2013). However, androcentric, ethnocentric and class-centric biases remain due to the prevailing focus on explaining the offending of white, working-class, westernised males – biases compounded by the fact though these explanations have been produced predominantly by white, middle-class, westernised males.

Integrated positivist theories: social control theories

In contrast to biopsychosocial theories (indeed most explanatory theories of offending), social control theories have focused on explaining why people *do not* commit crime. Social control theories integrate elements of neo-classical rational choice with explanations from psychological and sociological positivism to produce a set of theories based on arguably the largest body of empirical evidence in criminology[6] (Hopkins-Burke 2013). Building on the mid-twentieth-century psychological control theories concerned with the psychological influences (e.g. personality) controlling people's behaviour and stopping them from offending (e.g. Reiss 1951; Nye 1958), social control theories have examined the *social* factors that bond people to the norms of a given society (e.g. socialisation in the family, school and peer group).

The forefather of social control theories is Travis Hirschi (1969), who produced the original 'social control theory' to explain why some people obey the law and why others don't. Hirschi (1969: 16) explained that 'delinquent acts result when an individual's bond to society is weaker or broken', so being law-abiding results from a strong social bond to the rules and norms. Social control theory divides this social bond into four elements (see Case *et al.* 2017):

- *Attachment* to significant and important people, organisations and institutions (e.g. relationships).
- *Commitment* to conventional, traditional, normal behaviours and actions (e.g. a rational choice to conform).

- *Involvement* in conventional behaviours and activities (i.e. being too busy to commit crime).
- *Beliefs* in the importance of normal behaviour and in each of the other elements of the social bond.

The emphasis on social bonds produced a hybrid, holistic explanation of offending that fuses rational choice theory with elements of psychosocial positivism (e.g. strain theory). As with other explanatory theories, critics have tended to focus on what the theory cannot explain, such as the extent and nature of offending behaviour that may result from weak social bonds (cf. Agnew 2005), the nature of influence that delinquent friends may have and the influence of historical and structural contexts on social bonds and offending behaviour (Case *et al.* 2017).

Hirschi's original social control theory was built upon by Elliott *et al.* (1979), who argued that offending is the product of the weak social bonds resulting from inadequate socialisation in a child's early life. Therefore, strong social bonds and non-offending are the result of effective socialisation. According to Elliott *et al.* (1979), social bonds are further weakened/strengthened by later socialisation experiences in the home, school and community and especially exposure to delinquent peer groups. Elliott *et al.* (1979) added a structural element to social control theory by suggesting that blocked opportunities, social disorganisation, unemployment and economic recession can further weaken social bonds and function as criminogenic, thus integrating arguments from strain and social learning theories.

Twenty-one years on from his original theory, Travis Hirschi collaborated with Michael Gottfredson to produce the 'general theory of crime' (Gottfredson and Hirschi 1990), also known as 'self-control theory' – an attempt to offer a universal explanation of 'all crimes, at all times' (Gottfredson and Hirschi 1990: 117). The central explanatory mechanism was low self-control – individuals with low self-control were seen as more likely to make rational choices to offend, especially when they also experienced ineffective parenting during childhood. This single-factor cause, low self-control, provided a universal explanation for all types of crime, something that social control theory could not offer. However, the general theory of crime is not strictly a social form of control theory because it largely ignores sociological influences in favour of the psychological motivations and immediate rational choices producing low self-control and leading to crime. Due to this very specific explanation, the theory has much more difficulty explaining white collar and corporate crimes, which are typically the product of long-term, detailed, patient and considered planning, characteristics that seem incompatible with the immediate rational choices implied by the low-self-control hypothesis.

A group of modified social control theories have been developed since the turn of the twentieth century, including:

- *Power control theory*: integrates considerations of gender within social control theory to argue that patriarchal attitudes in the home can explain gender differences in offending (Bates *et al.* 2003). Bates *et al.* propose that girls are controlled socially far more than boys in the family setting (usually by mothers who were themselves controlled as girls) and so are less likely to take risks and commit crime. Offending by girls occurs if the balance of power in controlling the child is shared more equally between parents, and girls are not subjected to excessive control (Bates *et al.* 2003; see also Hagan 1989).

- *Control balance theory*: offending results from imbalances in the amount of control an individual has over their own behaviour and the behaviour of others (Tittle 2000). If a person is subjected to excessive amounts of control (i.e. they experience a 'control deficit'), then this can lead to resentment, anger, weak social bonds and ultimately to offending. An excess of control over others and over their environment produces a 'control surplus' that can lead to greed, corruption and an obsession with dominance, all of which can lead to offending. Control balance theory introduces a need versus greed dichotomy – the need to alleviate a control deficit versus the greed to extend a control surplus.
- *Differential coercion theory*: offending is the product of exposure to coercion, the pressure to behave in a certain way (Colvin 2000). High levels of consistent coercion (actual or threatened) in the family (e.g. removal of social support), school (e.g. physical force) and neighbourhood (e.g. gang violence, poverty, unemployment) can produce psychosocial deficits that encourage criminal behaviour. Such deficits include weak social bonds (see also Hirschi 1969), low self-control (see also Gottfredson and Hirschi 1990) and an increased commitment to using coercion to achieve personal goals, a process known as 'coercive ideation'.

Evaluation: social control theories

As arguably 'the most tested theory of crime causation' (Hopkins-Burke 2013: 218), social control theory (and its spin-off theories) has an impressive amount of empirical/evidential support – indicative of a reliable/replicable set of explanations that are appropriate, relevant and valid to a range of populations (see Case *et al.* 2017). These strengths may be attributable (at least in part) to the wide range of criminogenic influences identified, which include socio-structural factors that have been traditionally overlooked and downplayed by positivist explanatory theories. However, critics assert that social control theories offer an oversimplified and reductionist explanation of crime (cf. Downes and Rock 1998), one that reduces offending to the gratification of basic appetites – acquisitive (to obtain goals, property), aggressive or sexual (see Hopkins-Burke 2013).

5 EASY PIECES

5a Integrated explanations of offending: integrated positivist theories (1970s onwards)

1 *Integrated explanations*: integrated explanatory theories of offending have gained popularity since the 1970s as a way of consolidating the benefits of specific individual and socio-structural theories while compensating for their particular limitations (e.g. reductionism, exclusive focus). However, integrated theories retain elements of androcentrism, ethnocentrism and class-centrism.
2 *Integrated positivist theories*: an approach to integrating elements of different positivist theories to form more holistic explanations of (youth) offending has

gained popularity since the latter part of the twentieth century, most notably through biopsychosocial theories and social control theories.

3 *Biopsychosocial theories*: several positivist theories have combined the influence of biological, psychological and sociological factors into a broader explanation of (youth) offending. Mednick and Jeffrey (biosocial theory) viewed offending as the product of biopsychological urges and characteristics interacting with criminogenic social-environmental conditions, while the right realist biopsychosocial theory of Wilson and Herrnstein added an element of rational choice, arguing that biopsychosocial factors influence an individual's decision-making to commit crime or to adhere to social norms.

4 *Social control theories*: integrating elements of rational choice with psychological and sociological positivism, social control theories argue that the strength of an individual's social bonds to their family, school and neighbourhood determines their likelihood to offend or be law-abiding. More contemporary theories have considered the criminogenic role of power, control over self/others and coercion, along with their influence upon social bonds.

5 *Self-control*: both biopsychosocial theories and social control theories focus on the individual's capacity for self-control of their biological and psychological instincts and drives to commit crime in specific social contexts.

Integrated realist theories

As noted in Section 4, critical criminology has been subject to criticism regarding its explanatory bases and the consequent limitations that this places on recommendations for realistic, pragmatic policies and practices to address crime. In particular, the view that individuals who offend are somehow victims of labelling and criminalisation by powerful groups (the 'victimised actor' model; Hopkins-Burke 2013) has been criticised as overly romantic and as unrealistic 'left idealism' by a new wave of 'integrated realist theories'. Realists do not view offending as a social construction that results from criminalisation processes led by the powerful, nor necessarily as the political expression of class conflict and status of frustration on the part of the powerless (e.g. young working-class males). Realists view offending as a real phenomenon that takes place in the real world and is committed and experienced by (young) people who are members of so-called powerless social groups such as the working class, females, ethnic minorities and notably, young people.

You have already been introduced to 'right realism' in its biopsychosocial positivist form as a neo-classical explanatory theory of crime. This politically right-wing branch of realist theory has reimagined classical theory in the late twentieth century, re-emphasising the criminogenic role of rational choice and the necessity for crime control policies based on situational crime prevention, deterrence and increased **punitiveness** – emphasis on punishment. Right realism has also favoured biological positivist explanations of offending as having a genetic basis (e.g. lower intelligence; Herrnstein and Murray 1994), which has encouraged the perception that there is a feral, feckless and moral 'underclass' among the working class who are disproportionately responsible for crime (Murray 1990). Platt and Takagi (1977) identified three common themes that unite and cohere right realist theory:

1 *Focus on street crime*: focusing on legal definitions (not social constructions) of 'crime', mainly street crime. According to James Q. Wilson (1975), the most serious crime is 'predatory crime for gain, the most common forms of which are robbery, burglary, larceny, and auto theft'. These forms of street crime are almost exclusively located within working-class groups and as a result, the corporate and state crimes of powerful groups are ignored.

2 *Anti-intellectualism*: dismissing the need to identify the causes of crime as 'misplaced'. The rationale for this rejection is the increase in post-war crime despite economic increases in the distribution of wealth, which allegedly contradicts critical theory notions of economically motivated crime.

3 *Focus on punishment*: maintaining that the appropriate response to the problem of predatory street crime is tough, punitive responses and crime control policies based on soft deterrence (e.g. situational crime prevention, changes in police activity) and harder deterrence (e.g. longer court sentences, indeterminate prison sentences). Social order and crime control are prioritised over broader issues of social justice and individual welfare.

The two most influential right realist criminologists have been James Q. Wilson and Charles Murray. In *Thinking about Crime*, Wilson (1975) asserted that the individual is the source of crime and that social causes are of no significance. Wilson alleged that previous criminological theorising had been dominated by ideology and conjecture as opposed to empirical evidence, and so the 'facts' of crime were being ignored. Crime was seen as a moral issue, with a view that appropriate levels of blame and responsibility should be assigned to individuals when responding to crime. The central thesis, therefore, was that some individuals are criminal by nature and have an innate disposition to offend. In short, 'Wicked people exist. Nothing avails except to set them apart from innocent people' (Wilson 1975: 235).

In *The Emerging British Underclass*, Charles Murray (1990) identified a criminal subculture from within the working class that he dubbed the 'underclass'. According to Murray, the underclass suffers from a 'moral poverty' that compounds their economic poverty. The group is characterised by violent, feckless males (often young adults) and similarly immoral and feckless females, who may be less violent but are prone to teenage pregnancy and substance use. This widespread immorality and irresponsibility perpetuates high illegitimacy rates and low levels of participation in the workforce, along with high levels of offending. In Murray's view, the underclass has to be given the tools to help itself (e.g. social and financial incentives) to take individual responsibility for its plight and to engender a collective moral and social responsibility among the group. As you can imagine, underclass theory has become highly controversial. Perhaps the biggest criticism is that the theory is both reductionist and inflammatory – it pathologises (represents as flawed, ill) the very individuals who suffer most from the deeply entrenched socio-economic disadvantage that can limit their life choices, thus further stigmatising, disadvantaging and criminalising these individuals. For our explanatory purposes, it is instructive to note (again) that young people in general and the young offenders specifically are disproportionately likely to be members of socially disadvantaged, deprived groups (Gray 2005; Barry 2006). In other words, the underclass theory encourages the (re)construction of young people as 'offenders'.

A body of 'left realism' has been developed to challenge the left idealism of critical criminology (blaming the powerful) and the pathologising notions of rational choice and moral poverty promoted by right realism (blaming the powerless). Left realists are sceptical of critical criminology's idealistic view of offending as the political expression of victimised actors and of the consequent unrealistic, impractical recommendations for youth justice responses based on limited intervention at the individual level. Left realists believe that it is equally mistaken to neglect the harmful behaviour of the powerless because the public's greatest fears of crime focus on street crime (perpetuated by powerless groups), so this issue must be addressed in explanatory and response (policy) terms. Consequently, left realism explicitly challenged right realist perspectives on criminal justice and crime control. Left realism was developed by a group of criminologists from Middlesex University, Jock Young, John Lea and Roger Matthews. Locke outlined the central principle of the theory as

> to reflect the reality of crime, that is in its origins, its nature and its impact. This involves a rejection of tendencies to romanticise crime or to pathologise it, to analyse solely from the point of view of the administration of crime or the criminal actor, to underestimate crime or exaggerate it . . . most importantly it is realism which informs our notion of practice; in answering what can be done about the problems of crime and social control.
>
> (Young 1986: 21)

Left realism has been more inclined towards sociological positivist explanations than its neo-classical right realist counterpart, in particular, the socio-structural elements of strain and subcultural theories. The central explanatory mechanism for left realism has been **relative deprivation** – the individual's perception and experience of being deprived of what they feel entitled to when compared themselves to other individuals in the modern, competitive society (Lea and Young 1984). In this way, relative deprivation is a subjective perception, whereas **absolute deprivation** is a measurable fact based on statistical ratings of levels of poverty, income, unemployment and so forth. According to Young (2007: 488), in certain conditions, relative deprivation is

> a major cause of crime. That is, when people experience levels of unfairness in their allocation of resources and utilise individualistic means to attempt to right this condition. It is a reaction to the experience of injustice.

Left realists have illustrated their theoretical explanation through the 'Square of Crime', which depicts the (potentially criminogenic) interactions between the 'offender', the State (e.g. the criminal justice system, local crime prevention partnerships), the public and the victim (see Figure 2.2).

Left realism has been subject to a series of criticisms and has provided appropriately 'realistic' responses to each of these. For example:

- *Defining crime*: criticisms of left realism's uncritical reliance on State definitions of what constitutes 'crime' and 'offending' have been countered by arguing that the priority was to challenge right realism and to offer practical policies for responding to youth offending in the real world. Therefore, left realists argue that they needed to work to the same definitions of offending as right realism.
- *Explanatory utility*: criticisms that left realism abandons the explanatory gains of critical criminology by neglecting the crimes of the powerful are refuted in similar

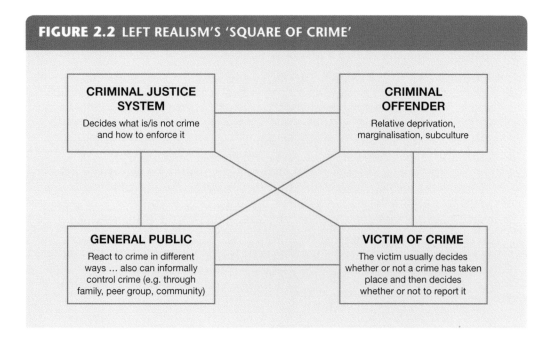

FIGURE 2.2 LEFT REALISM'S 'SQUARE OF CRIME'

CRIMINAL JUSTICE SYSTEM
Decides what is/is not crime and how to enforce it

CRIMINAL OFFENDER
Relative deprivation, marginalisation, subculture

GENERAL PUBLIC
React to crime in different ways … also can informally control crime (e.g. through family, peer group, community)

VICTIM OF CRIME
The victim usually decides whether or not a crime has taken place and then decides whether or not to report it

fashion, arguing that the primary focus has been on the lived realities of excluded, powerless groups in order to challenge right-wing recommendations for the deterrence and punishment of these groups.

- *Explanatory confusion*: left realism has been accused of offering a theoretically contradictory integration of labelling, strain, control and critical theories of crime. The response has been that left realism seeks to develop understandings of crime, the processes of criminalisation and techniques of crime control in rapidly changing times. This urgent, practical, and realistic set of objectives should not be encumbered by unnecessary concerns about resolving appropriate theoretical contradictions and should always be seen as a work in progress.
- *Evidence base*: the weak empirical evidence base of left realism (especially when compared to positivism) and the over-reliance upon local victim surveys has also been criticised. Left realists accept this limitation but argue that local victim surveys address the dark figure of crime and so target the real, hidden crime problems in communities which require realistic solutions (see Case *et al.* 2017).

5 EASY PIECES

5b Integrated explanations of offending: integrated realist theories (1970s onwards)

1   *The reality of offending*: integrated realist theories examine offending as a real phenomenon with real effects on victims (including working-class victims) and communities, effects that must be addressed through realistic and practical policies.

2   *Challenging left idealism*: realist theories explicitly challenge the 'left idealism' of critical criminology, specifically the claims that crime and offending are social constructions produced by the criminalisation of the (victimised) powerless by the powerful and/or a political expression of discontent by the powerless.

3   *Right realism*: right realists offer a neo-classical explanation of crime (notably street crime) as a predominantly working-class behaviour caused by rational choice and moral poverty, which are mediated by low intelligence, irresponsibility and immorality. Recommended responses focus on crime control through situational crime prevention, deterrence and increased punishment.

4   *Left realism*: left realists integrate labelling, strain, control and critical theories to explain crime as the product of relative deprivation and interactions between offender, state, public and victim in a 'Square of Crime'. Recommended responses focus on community and social crime prevention approaches, such as local multiagency partnerships.

5   *Realist explanations*: both right and left realism privilege state definitions of crime rather than crime as a social construction, both prioritise integrated explanations of offending by the working class and both argue for policy responses that are relevant to the real-world experiences of offenders and victims.

EXPLAINING YOUTH OFFENDING: SO, WHAT DO WE KNOW?

When asked in 2015 how they see the study of crime evolving over the next ten years, the cultural criminologists Jeff Ferrell and Keith Hayward responded:

> We suspect that criminology will continue to bifurcate. On the one hand the logic of positivism and positivist methodologies operates as an intellectual self-fulfilling prophecy, creating methodological residues that masquerade as objective research findings. . . . On the other hand, and largely in opposition, alternative criminological paradigms continue to percolate and build momentum.
>
> (Ferrell and Hayward 2015 – Promotional quote for SAGE
> 'Voyages of Critical Discovery' retrospective)

The discussion across this chapter has illustrated the **bifurcation** of criminological theory (journey/spilt along two separate pathways or branches) outlined in the quote, reflecting the social-historical conflict and ambivalence surrounding how offending by children and young people should be understood. The individual and socio-structural deterministic theories of positivism, along with integrated positivist explanations (including right realism) have promoted a view of children and young people who offend as hopeless, helpless and damaged individuals struggling to resist the criminogenic effects of exposure to predetermined causes of offending without adult intervention and treatment (an issue explored further in Chapter 5). In contrast, critical and (left) realist theories have offered a more systemic focus on the socio-structural and economic contexts and interactions that can encourage offending among (working-class) young people. They have also focused on the socially constructed nature of youth offending, notably the role of power in the processes by which individuals/behaviours are criminalised.

The relationship between explanations of youth offending and the socio-historical definitions of youth offending is not always clear or logical. Indeed, this relationship may often be non-existent in the real world that exists beyond theory. Many explanatory theories have taken the definition of (youth) 'offending' for granted as an uncontested and agreed 'fact', rather than as a dynamic and contingent social construction. Consequently, there has been an insensitivity to the socio-structural and political contexts within which young people live and interact. The academic search for an all-encompassing, universal (or at least dominant) explanation of youth offending has encouraged over-generalisation of conclusions and a lack of criticality regarding the socially constructed nature of youth offending and how definitions may differ over time and place, along with a lack of attention to the different (non-academic) influences upon our understandings of youth offending (see Chapter 1). The explanations explored in this chapter have highlighted a degree of disconnect within the 'triad of youth justice'. Explanations of youth offending, especially those with an empirical basis, have been predominantly the domain of academic professionals/intellectuals. In contrast, the (socially constructed) definitions of youth offending (see Chapter 1) and the (youth justice) responses to it (see Chapters 4 and 5) have been influenced far more by politicians and other professionals (e.g. social reformers, policy-makers, practitioners, media). Often, these influences have been a response to anxieties/uncertainties resulting from changing social and economic circumstances (see Chapters 4–6). That is not to say, however, that academics have exhibited no influence upon definitions and responses, but rather that their influence has been (arguably) most significant with regards to constructing theoretical and empirical explanations of youth offending.

As will be made clear in Chapter 4, the relationship between explanations of youth offending and the responses of youth justice systems to youth offending in different places at different times has been many and varied. Linking these youth justice responses to 'evidence-based' explanations has become a political priority internationally, a priority exemplified in the contemporary Youth Justice System of England and Wales (see Chapter 5). The political necessity to inform youth justice responses with evidence drawn from the research underpinning explanatory theories (supplemented by 'evidence' from other sources such as academic polemic, official statistics, and media representations) has created an explanatory **zeitgeist** (defining spirit/mood of the time) within youth justice for evidence-based policy and practice. This zeitgeist has been animated by the rapid rise to dominance of the group of explanatory theories that integrate elements of neo-classicism and integrated positivist theories (occasionally, some elements of critical and realist theories) in order to identify the risk factors that predict youth offending, rather than to identify its causes. This hegemonic explanatory movement has been defined as 'risk factor theories' of youth offending (Case and Smith, in Case *et al*. 2017; Case and Haines 2009) and will be explored in detail in the following chapter.

5 EASY PIECES

Recommended further reading

For students keen to explore the arguments from this chapter in more detail, an ideal starting point (once again) is *Young People, Crime and Justice* by Roger Hopkins-Burke (2016). The book's second section, 'Explaining Offending Behaviour by Children and Young People', covers the main classical and positivist theories in Roger's usual accessible and engaging style. For an even broader theoretical discussion that encompasses these theories, but also critical and realist theories, Roger's very popular *An Introduction to Criminological Theory* (2013) is perhaps the most thorough and wide-ranging text available and is highly recommended.

An outstanding breadth and depth of theoretical coverage is provided in the 'Explaining Crime' section of *Criminology* by Case *et al.* (2017), which also includes a co-authored chapter by Professors Stephen Case and Roger Smith titled 'Explaining Youth Crime and Youth Justice'. *Criminology* is arguably the most accessible, engaging and student-friendly general textbook on the market, even though I may be somewhat biased here!

The final two recommendations are for texts that move beyond positivism to examine critical and realist explanations with clarity, dynamism and exceptional insight. *The New Criminology Revisited* by Paul Walton and Jock Young (1998) offers a vibrant, engaging and challenging critical discussion of the major explanatory developments since *The New Criminology* was published (Taylor *et al.* 1973), exploring feminism, critical criminology and realism alongside commentaries from the original authors. As a complement to this text and to the current chapter, you could do no better than reading *The Criminological Imagination* by Jock Young (2011), a provocative and entertaining critique of positivism combined with a passionate argument for a more critical and broad-minded criminology. A truly thought-provoking book.

NOTES

1   As with the five chronological stages in Chapter 1, the five theoretical categories have been drawn in deliberately broad terms for the purposes of simplicity, coherence and accessibility. Therefore, the categorical distinctions are themselves (my) subjective social constructions, which others may contest. For example, in his 1993 text *Inventing Criminology*, Piers Beirne challenges the distinction between classicism and individual positivism. Others have challenged the validity of sociological positivism as a theoretical category in its own right and as distinct from symbolic interactionism and pragmatist sociology (see Znaniecki and Thomas 1918).

2   A famous example of this approach is Bentham's total surveillance 'panopticon' prison, a multilayered, circular structure with a central inspection house from which all prisoners could be observed at all times (Bentham 1798/1970).

3   Subsequently expanded to incorporate surveys and other research methods (see Case *et al.* 2017).

4   I do not discuss broader versions of 'feminist criminology' in great detail for reasons of coherence in this chapter, but feel free to explore the debate yourself elsewhere in other expert texts (cf. Smart 1977; Ugwudike 2015).

5   This latter category of explanation has become so large and dominant that it requires a much fuller discussion than is possible here, so the entire next chapter is dedicated to an exposition of integrated risk factor theories.

6   At least until the advent of the risk factor theories discussed in the next chapter.

APPENDIX 1

CONVERSATIONS

Explaining youth offending by Black and Minority Ethnic children

Steve: Is it important and informative to adopt a critical perspective when explaining offending by children from ethnic minority groups?

Colin Webster: A clear conceptual and theoretical basis is required for specifying the processes and mechanisms through which institutional and individual decisions and actions operate to disadvantage certain groups over others. So, to explain offending by and youth justice responses to Black and Minority Ethnic (BAME) children, we must find ways of explaining the interplay of societal structures, individual and institutional actions, and the influences of economic conditions and ideas on this interplay. When BAME children meet the police, enter youth justice or appear in the courts, their experience may be of being 'racialised' or 'criminalised', processes that can operate together. 'Criminalising' processes emphasise those aspects of *certain* groups' behaviour which can be defined or labelled as criminal, hence reinforcing the likelihood of members of such groups encountering the police and youth justice. 'Racialisation' means the ways in which race is constructed and made meaningful in the context of unequal power relations, which can result in 'race' becoming a salient factor in the way social resources are allocated, that is, racialised. 'Race' is made to work by becoming a salient element of social relationships, frequently as a normal part of the actions of the State and its agencies with social actors. Racialisation draws attention to the process of making 'race' relevant to a situation or context, and thus requires an examination of the precise circumstances in which this occurs: who the 'agents' are; who the actors are. In other words, who does what and how? An example of racialisation can be found in Katie Hunter's work (in Webster 2018) whereby at the arrest stage, black children are overrepresented in arrest for robbery, weapons possessions and drug offences – those offences for which police officer's discretion and proactivity is key to securing arrests – suggesting police targeting.

Steve: How does the 'racialisation' of BAME children operate?

Colin: Phillips' (2011) model argues that processes and mechanisms that may result in institutional racialisation and ethnic inequalities, operate at three levels – the micro, meso and macro – producing ethnically disparate welfare outcomes as well as ethnic inequalities in education (attainment) and policing (stop-and-search practices). Micro-level racialisation is framed by the influence of familial socialisation and shared cultural values among individuals positioned within various ethnic, classed and gendered groups, and influenced significantly by neighbourhood environmental conditions. Meso-level racialisation involves individual decision-making in institutions like schooling, youth justice, care and welfare. These institutional decisions are in turn influenced by socio-economic disadvantage; neighbourhood composition and effects; political, media and popular discourses; political incorporation and power; and institutional processes and practices. Finally, institutional racialisation recognises cumulative disadvantage experienced across interrelated welfare experiences (housing, education, employment and so on), produced through institutions' routine operations, regardless of the intentionality of individual actors. Macro-level racialisation considers structural forces beyond individual decision-making and institutional practices and processes. Here, structural determinants of material conditions provide the frame through which institutional processes and practices at the meso level are enacted. Globalising forces change the economy, social relations and structure, transnational politics and crucially, the unequal distribution of resources, in Britain as elsewhere.

Steve: How does a focus on racialisation and criminalisation processes help us to better explain offending by BAME children?

Colin: Retrospectively applying these sorts of theoretical and conceptual analysis to explaining ethnicity, youth justice and offending (see Webster 2018), we might point to a number of dimensions including change and continuity in the experiences of successive generations of BAME children. For example, there is little disagreement that child poverty has very significantly increased over the last decade, perhaps particularly among children from black and minority backgrounds, and yet the adverse influence of concentrated, long-term poverty on children's behaviour is well known. For example, the chances of being a persistent young offender increases by 45 per cent for those experiencing poverty at age 9 years and by 80 per cent for those experiencing enduring poverty throughout the first decade of life (Hay and Forrest 2009). At a micro level, familial socialisation under conditions of persistent or recurrent poverty induces extreme stress among children and parents. At a macro level, often marginalised and disadvantaged, black and Asian young people have faced a series of cumulative crises and disruptions in their transitions to adulthood as they adopted new identities and adapted to economic and social change (see Webster 2018). Thus, the recent history of youth transitions to adulthood in Britain is marked by increased precariousness and vulnerability visited on marginalised young people by social and economic crisis.

A legacy of racialisation and criminalisation of BAME children at the micro and meso (institutional) levels described above is easily evidenced, as Feilzer and Hood's (2004) groundbreaking study of minority ethnic young people in the youth justice system shows. They found that at different stages of youth justice decision-making processes, different outcomes were consistent with discriminatory treatment of Asian and black males, and especially mixed-parentage males and females, in respect of prosecution, remand, conviction, the use of more restrictive community penalties and longer sentences of penal custody. A key finding was that large differences or discriminatory treatment of BAME children were found between YOT areas which were tantamount to youth justice by race and geography. An important question is whether it is different treatment by the police that leads to young people entering the youth justice system in the first place. A study by May (2010) presented evidence to help explain how children are brought into the YJS and what happens to them as they pass through it. They found that police-initiated arrests account for a significant number of all arrests, leaving ample room for different treatment on grounds of class and ethnicity (particularly about drug and road traffic offences). Furthermore, having entered the youth justice system May (2010) found that the way young people pass through it involved discrimination against ethnic minorities, given that the different outcomes between ethnic groups could not be accounted for by any specific features of the offences or criminal histories of the suspects or defendants. More recently, Uhrig (2016) revealed a persistent pattern of disproportionate BAME contact with the YJS and that there appeared to be different and discriminatory treatment of BAME children in respect of arrest, prosecution, magistrates' proceedings and committal for trial. Most troubling, BAME children are being unduly processed into the lower courts and unnecessarily elevated to the higher courts, despite these children being no more likely to commit crime than their white counterparts (Sharp and Budd 2003).

Drawing conclusions from Phillips' (2011) multilevel framework of analysis, none of each of these levels of analysis – micro, meso and macro – should take primacy explaining ethnicity, youth offending and justice because racialisation and ethnic inequalities are produced and reproduced at each of these levels in interaction. If institutional racialisation can be placed at the meso level, and micro-level racialisation is found in individual decisions and interactions, then macro-level racialisation considers structural forces beyond individual decision-making and institutional practices and processes, albeit that institutional processes are developed, formulated and implemented by individuals constrained or enabled by structural factors.

Explaining youth offending

Risk factor theories

CHAPTER OUTLINE

The previous chapter explored classical, positivist, critical and integrated (positivist and realist) theories and how these have been applied and developed to explain youth offending. It is clear that there has been an explanatory evolution in criminology, from the earliest individual explanations of classicism that were based on free will and rational choice, to their subsequent challenge by the individual and socio-structural deterministic (causal) explanations of positivism (see Case *et al.* 2017). Deterministic positivist theories were then challenged by critical theories that focused on the criminogenic role of power in constructing offending by criminalising individuals and behaviours. These critical explanations were themselves criticised by (integrated) realist theories that understood offending as a real-world behaviour (not a social construction) necessitating real-world, practical responses. We are left with a variety of theories offering a variety of explanations of, and responses to, youth offending. Notwithstanding the theoretical diversity and lack of consensus surrounding explanations of offending, one definitive conclusion is possible – positivism sustains as the dominant method of explaining youth offending and informing and shaping (youth justice) responses to it. However, the nature of the positivist theory that dominates explanations of youth offending has changed (beyond contemporary integrated versions of positivism), as has the nature of the theories that seek to critique, challenge and involve it. Enter **risk factor theories**.

This chapter will examine the rise to prominence of risk factor explanations of youth offending – the rapidly expanding body of evidence-based, practical theories that have come to dominate how youth offending is constructed, understood and responded to in the contemporary Western world (see also Appendix 2). Discussion is divided into five branches of risk factor theory, which have emerged since this form of explanation came to prominence in criminology.

5 EASY PIECES

Explaining youth offending: risk factor theories

1 *Biopsychosocial developmental risk factor theories* identifies biological, psychological and immediate social factors in early life (e.g. childhood, early adolescence) as predictive of offending in later life (e.g. late adolescence, adulthood).

2 *Integrated developmental risk factor theories* explores interactions between biological, psychological and immediate social factors, socio-structural factors, rational choice and context in early life as predictive of later offending.

3 *Interactional developmental risk factor theories* extends integrated theories by considering the influence of reciprocal interactions between risk factors and offending (e.g. that each may cause the other) and criminogenic interactions between the young person and the Youth Justice System.

4 *Age-graded life course risk factor theories* traces the criminogenic and predictive influence of interactions between psychosocial risk factors, structural context, informal social controls and agency over the life course.

5 *Constructivist pathways risk factor theories* examines young people's ability to construct, negotiate and resist risk factors/processes and the influence of their constructions on pathways into and out of offending.

It is perhaps not valid to claim that risk factor theories per se have attained explan-atory and practical dominance, but rather that a particular form of risk factor theory has come to the fore (see Case *et al.* 2017). These theories explain youth offending as the result of exposure to adverse, damaging influences and experiences in early life (e.g. childhood, early adolescence) situated in biological, psychological, sociological and (less so) structural domains, which can be identified as predictive of offending behaviour in later life (e.g. later adolescence, adulthood). These potentially complex influences and experiences are quantified and converted into numerical, statistical 'factors' or 'artefacts' – hence the theories have been described as **artefactual** (cf. Kem-shall 2008). The biopsychosocial influences are converted into **risk factors** – under-stood as increasing the risk/likelihood/probability of future offending, which renders them 'risk factors'. The explanations offered by artefactual risk factor theories differ from traditional positivist explanations and can be described as quasi-positivist for at least three reasons:

1   They emerged from research that employed *surveys* as the preferred research method, rather than the empirical experiments and observations favoured by tra-ditional positivism.
2   They identify risk factors as *predictors* of offending, rather than causes of offending.
3   They elaborate the traditional biopsychosocial focus of positivism by considering a *broader range of influences*, including socio-structural factors, mediated rational choice and situational elements, thus integrating positivism and neo-classicism/ right realism.

However, quasi-positivist, artefactual risk factor theories retain the positivist desire to employ 'scientific', objective and value-free research methods to identify the universal influences that can explain youth offending, even if these explanations are based on identifying 'predictor and effect' relationships rather than cause and effect relationships. Like positivist theories, the dominant quasi-positivist, artefactual risk factor theories focus their explanations on the individual, rather than looking further afield for critical and systemic explanations.

The origins of the risk factor theories explosion: the 'risk society'

In the 1990s, a global *risk* perspective began to shape political and academic under-standings (constructions) of crime in the industrialised Western world, based on two key claims:

1   *Globalisation and uncertainty*: modern society has been described as a 'risk society' (Beck 1992), characterised by rapid social and economic changes driven by **glo-balisation** – increasing interconnections across the world as a result of expansions and advancements in trade, cultural exchange, international travel, media/social media and other technology. This can lead to populations feeling unsafe, uncer-tain and urgently needing to control their environments.
2   *Increasing youth offending*: crime is rapidly increasing in the risk society, especially youth offending committed by young males. This suggests that the responses of official criminal/youth justice systems (e.g. deterrence, incapacitation, treatment, prevention) are not working and need to be improved to tackle the risk of crime.

The claim that youth offending was increasing strongly implied that the theoretical explanations provided by criminological theories to that point (largely constructed by academics) were no longer fit for purpose and neither were the youth justice responses they informed. Sceptics argued that criminological theories were not identifying the most appropriate causes of youth crime to inform effective criminal/youth justice interventions, and so a new perspective was needed. Western governments throughout the 1990s (perhaps most notably the UK Government under Tony Blair; see Chapter 5) challenged key stakeholders to provide an explanatory theory of youth offending that was valid (appropriate, relevant, accurate), straightforward and practical – with the tacit implication that it should be politically acceptable (e.g. not necessarily highlighting government influences on the social construction of offending as a 'problem'). Governments wanted a political explanation of offending that focused predominantly on individual-level dynamic factors amenable to change (Andrews and Bonta 2010), while the role of broader structural and systemic factors such as unemployment, poverty, social disorganisation and economic recession (far less amenable to change, particularly in the short term) were neglected. Enter **artefactual risk factor theories**.

At the time of the political search for a new hegemonic explanation of youth offending to guide youth justice responses, a significant movement of artefactual risk factor theory was developing in the industrialised Western world, especially in Western Europe, North America and Australasia. Much of the underpinning research was quasi-positivist and empirically led – depicting risks as quantifiable, objective, value free and scientific 'facts', 'factors' or 'artefacts'. The artefactual risk factor theories of the 1990s onwards were not new constructions – they had emerged from a long-term project of longitudinal research dating back to the 1930s – research that largely employed quantitative methodologies such as structured observation, standardised surveys, psychometric testing, secondary data analysis, random/representative sampling and the statistical control and analysis of quantified variables to reach definitive conclusions (cf. Case and Haines 2009). This research and the theories it generated was explicitly **developmental** – explaining youth offending as the product of exposure to risk factors in early life that develop into and determine offending behaviour in later life.

This chapter will explore and evaluate the development of risk factor theories, paying most attention to their dominant artefactual forms, mapping their trajectory towards becoming the hegemonic modern-day explanations of youth offending and the most significant influences on westernised youth justice responses. As with previous chapters, discussion will be divided into five stages ('5 easy pieces') across the chapter and will be summarised in this way within each section. However, at this point we depart from the chronological stages of other chapters, primarily because risk factor theories have evolved chronologically, conceptually and empirically over a much shorter period of time.

1 BIOPSYCHOSOCIAL DEVELOPMENTAL RISK FACTOR THEORIES

The original risk factor theories in criminology were developmental and deterministic in explanation and biopsychosocial in focus, measuring biological, psychological and **immediate social** (family, educational, neighbourhood, lifestyle) factors in early life (childhood, early adolescence) and suggesting that these predicted later offending.

A highly influential body of developmental risk factor theories emerged from studies that utilised longitudinal designs and multiple (positivist) methods to identify these predictive relationships between biopsychosocial risk factors and youth offending.

Biopsychosocial developmental theories: multifactor developmental theory

The seminal risk factor theory in criminology, the forefather of biopsychosocial developmental theories, was the 'multifactor developmental theory' of Sheldon and Eleanor Glueck (1930, 1950). The Gluecks were interested in improving the effectiveness of criminal justice responses to young offenders who entered custody. In *500 Criminal Careers*, Glueck and Glueck (1930) investigated 510 young male adults imprisoned in Massachusetts Reformatory (US) from 1911 to 1922. They conducted observations and interviews with the young men and their families, tracing their life histories before sentence, during their imprisonment, while on parole and for the five years post-completion of their sentence. The 80 per cent reoffending rates during the post-parole period suggested that the reformatory was failing in its reform objectives. The Gluecks began to question whether there were factors present in the young men's life histories (e.g. personal characteristics developed prior to incarceration) that predisposed them to offending/reoffending and that could be more effectively addressed by reformatory and post-parole programmes. From their interviews, the Gluecks identified a series of shared psychological and social (psychosocial) characteristics, circumstances and experiences in the lives of the young man prior to their incarceration. Following quantification of these characteristics/circumstances/experiences into factors using ratings and categorisation tables, they concluded that exposure to certain factors in early childhood and adolescence was related to later (recorded) offending – the earliest incarnation of the 'risk factor' for offending. The most influential factors were located in the psychosocial domains of family (e.g. parental criminality), school (e.g. educational underachievement), lifestyle (e.g. keeping bad company) and individual/personality (e.g. low intelligence).

RTA = PERSISTENT REPLICATION OF PSYCHOSOCIAL RISK FACTORS

The main risk factors identified by the Gluecks reflected those identified by the Alarming Increase Committee in England over a hundred years prior, in 1816 (see Chapter 1), so they did not actually introduce an original understanding of youth offending. Developmental, artefactual risk factor explanations ever since have departed little from the persistent replication and validation of this narrow, restricted body of psychosocial risk factors (see Case and Haines 2009).

The developmental influences on offending identified by the Gluecks constituted the earliest form of criminological 'risk factor', or as they chose to define it, 'the early genesis of antisocial careers' (Glueck and Glueck 1930: 142–143). The implication was that these risk factors should be targeted by reformatory and post-parole responses/interventions in order to prevent and reduce youth offending – an early example of the explanations–responses relationship from our 'triad of youth justice'. However, the Gluecks' main conclusion was that 'the reform of criminals . . . is now bought about largely by the natural process of maturation' (Glueck and Glueck 1937: 206). This conclusion implies that the role of early, intensive and formal intervention may have been overstated, especially if most children are likely to grow out of offending naturally. Such a conclusion could be seen as incongruous when you reflect that artefactual risk factor explanations of youth offending have significantly influenced youth justice responses, especially those underpinned by methods that are **interventionist** – based on an increasing breadth and depth of intervention in young people's lives (see also Chapter 5).

In 1950, the Gluecks moved their developmental agenda forward by incorporating a focus on identifying (risk) factors that were predictive of first-time, official offending (rather than reoffending) in order to inform preventative interventions, on the grounds that targeting interventions on identified offenders was 'to close the barn door after the horse has been stolen' (Glueck and Glueck 1950: 257). In *Unraveling Juvenile Delinquency*, the Gluecks researched 500 officially delinquent and 500 officially non-delinquent white males aged 10–17 years old from lower-class neighbourhoods in Boston, US, studying their lives **prospectively** (from the present into the future) over a 14-year period (1949–1963). The groups were matched on key demographic and psychosocial characteristics: age, race/ethnicity, measured intelligence and residence in underprivileged neighbourhoods. The Gluecks collected a wide range of biopsychosocial data through official records and interviews with the boys and their significant others (e.g. parents, teachers, neighbours, criminal justice staff). Once the data had been quantified or **factorised** (converted to a factor), it was cross-tabulated with officially recorded offending to identify a series of risk factors that were biological (e.g. physique), psychological (e.g. personality, attitudes, thinking) and immediate social (e.g. parental) – reflecting their previous findings and implying that their methods and findings were both valid and **reliable** (consistent, repeatable).

Biopsychosocial developmental theories: developmental crime prevention theory

With their seminal risk factor studies, the Gluecks introduced an innovative new strand of (quasi-)positivist theory that explained youth offending in developmental and deterministic terms as a consequence of exposure to biopsychosocial risk factors in early life. Crucially, their developmental theory was more concerned with *predicting* future offending than identifying the *causes* of prior or current offending. The groundbreaking conclusions of the Gluecks were built upon by a subsequent study that focused its attention on the potential for targeting biopsychosocial risk factors through intervention. The 'developmental crime prevention' theory that resulted continues to influence youth justice responses in the Western world in its modern incarnation as the 'risk factor prevention paradigm' (see Chapters 4 and 5). The 30-year longitudinal Cambridge-Somerville Youth Study began in 1939 under the supervision of Richard Clarke Cabot, a contemporary and neighbour of the Gluecks in Massachusetts, US (Cabot 1940). Cabot studied 650 boys aged between 7 and 12 whose behaviour and personality had been rated as either 'average' or 'difficult' by a committee of judges. Following an examination of data from home visitor interviews with the boys and their mothers/chief carers, the judges quantified and rated psychosocial (predictive) influences on the boys' 'developmental history' relating to their habits, recreation, personality, family and home conditions and neighbourhood (Powers *et al.* 1951). Following this predictive ratings exercise, half of the boys were randomly allocated (by coin toss) to a control group. The other half were randomly allocated to a treatment group and given interventions to reduce and prevent the perceived predetermined impact of these predictive childhood risk factors – interventions such as counselling, academic assistance, family guidance and extracurricular leisure opportunities.

The Cambridge-Somerville Youth Study was the earliest example of a developmental approach to crime *prevention*, an approach that shapes and guides 'evidence-based' youth justice responses internationally in the present day (see, for example, discussion of the 'new youth justice' in Chapter 5). Incredibly, despite the subsequent pervasiveness of risk-focused development prevention across youth justice responses, the evidence of its effectiveness from this seminal study is at best counter-intuitive and at worst non-existent. Follow-ups of the sample identified no significant effect for the risk-based in intervention and in some case, even **iatrogenic** (harmful, negative) effects such as reoffending, due to labelling and criminalisation through contact with the formal youth justice system (McCord 1978). These are counter-intuitive conclusions from what has been heralded as the best designed longitudinal-experimental study of delinquency prevention in the twentieth century (cf. Tremblay, Vitaro, Nagin, Pagani and Seguin, in Thornberry and Krohn 2003).

Biopsychosocial developmental theories: criminal careers model

The most significant and influential risk factor study of all time began in the UK in 1961 and produced the 'criminal careers model' explanation of youth offending. The Cambridge Study in Delinquent Development (better known as the Cambridge Study) aimed 'to investigate the development of juvenile delinquency in a normal population of boys. . . (and why) certain groups, identifiable at an early age, are peculiarly vulnerable' (West and Farrington 1973: xiii). The Cambridge Study was inspired by Unraveling Juvenile Delinquency and the Cambridge-Somerville Youth Study. According to the Cambridge Study founder, Donald West, both of these previous studies had 'pointed to the strong and continuing influence of early upbringing and family circumstances in determining who became delinquent' (West 1982: 3). The Cambridge Study aimed to enhance the explanatory utility of these existing biopsychosocial developmental theories in two key methodological ways (see West and Farrington 1973, 1977):

1   By focusing on *ordinary children*, not experimental comparisons between identified offenders and a non-offending control group.
2   By employing a *prospective longitudinal design* to identify risk factors prior to offending behaviour and tracing their development into the future, not using retrospective bias to identify influential factors in the past lives of identified offenders.

The Cambridge Study was led by Donald West, working with his research partner and future successor David Farrington. West and Farrington identified 411 working-class males born in South London in 1953–1954 and tracked the group prospectively from the age of 8. They employed a multi-method approach of regular interviews with sample members and their peers, psychological testing and secondary data analysis of official records in order to measure the impact of life events and risk factors for youth offending. The Cambridge Study researchers identified risk factors in childhood (between the ages of 8 and 10) in the psychosocial domains of family, school, neighbourhood, peer and individual (West and Farrington 1977) associated with offending across the life course, thus extending the developmental focus of risk factor influence beyond adolescence and into adulthood. The Cambridge Study has also linked these risk factors to the **criminal career** – the trajectory (course, pathway) of offending over the life course that is made up of different aspects including onset, duration, frequency, continuity, escalation, specialisation and desistance. Therefore, the criminal careers model suggests that certain individuals have lifelong offending trajectories, the extent and nature of which are influenced by exposure to biopsychosocial risk factors (see Farrington 2007). The strongest predictors (identified at 8–10 years old) of official and self-reported offending (measured at 14–15 years old) were poor parenting, family criminality, family poverty, academic underachievement, hyperactivity/ impulsivity/attention deficit disorder and antisocial behaviour (West 1982). At a later stage in this study, the researchers began to investigate the role of **protective factors** – factors that insulate the young person against future offending and against the harmful impact of exposure to risk factors (West 1982). Thus, protective factors were seen as the polar opposites (dichotomies) of risk factors.

The Cambridge Study has been described in glowing terms as 'a point of reference for discussion of juvenile delinquency and criminal behaviour for many years to come' (Radzinowicz, in West and Farrington 1973: v) and as 'among the most complete studies of the relationship between risk and offending' (Armstrong 2004: 105). Indeed, it is indisputable that the Cambridge Study has been hugely influential in explanatory and response/policy terms (cf. Case and Haines 2009). The Cambridge Study established and popularised biopsychosocial developmental risk factor theories and has become the touchstone for youth justice prevention policy and practice with young people in the UK, especially since the 1990s (see Chapters 4 and 5). It is now the longest running criminological (risk factor) study and is currently tracing the influence of early risk factors on the adult lives of the children of the original sample. As such, the underpinning criminal careers model has evolved from a developmental theory into a 'life course' theory that explores the influence of risk factors across the lifespan, not just from childhood into early adulthood.

Evaluation: biopsychosocial developmental risk factor theories

Collectively, the Gluecks, Cabot and West, and Farrington introduced an innovative, quasi-positivist approach to explaining youth offending as the inevitable, predetermined outcome of exposure to biopsychosocial risk factors in early life – a concept known as **developmental determinism**. Each developmental theory built on its predecessor, with the Gluecks' revolutionary predictive, multifactor developmental approach being elaborated by Cabot to incorporate risk-focused responses to identified risk factors (developmental crime prevention). Both theories were then elaborated in methodological and explanatory terms by the Cambridge Study's prospective design, non-experimental sample and criminal careers model explanation that was sensitive to specific aspects of offending across the entire life course. While retaining the deterministic, quantified and scientific emphasis of traditional positivism, biopsychosocial developmental risk factor theories offered more integrated, comprehensive explanations of youth offending when compared to (non-integrated, standalone) biological, psychological or sociological positivist theories and a more explicit practical focus on identifying appropriate targets for responses and interventions to reduce and prevent future offending.

There are, however, several issues with biopsychosocial developmental theories in methodological and explanatory terms. Firstly, the nature of the predominantly white, male, working-class samples in each study demonstrates an androcentrism, ethnocentrism and class-centrism that limits their explanatory utility and the validity of any conclusions and recommended interventions, especially where these have been applied/generalised to non-white, female and middle-class populations. Secondly, the quantification of 'risk' across biopsychosocial theories could be seen as an act of reductionism that (over)simplifies complex experiences by converting them into generalised, crude numerical measures that may not adequately represent the (qualitative) realities and meanings that young people attach to their experiences of risk (cf. France and Homel 2007). Thirdly, the biopsychosocial focus of these developmental theories could be viewed as further reductionist, **psychosocial bias** – privileging psychosocial influences on offending over other potential explanations such as socio-structural factors (e.g. poverty, unemployment; see Webster *et al.* 2004), criminogenic interactions with youth justice agencies (McAra and McVie 2007) and young people's personalised constructions of their risk experiences (see Section 5 of this chapter).

5 EASY PIECES

1 Biopsychosocial developmental risk factor theories

1 *Developmental determinism*: experiences in early life (childhood, early adolescence) in the biopsychosocial domains can be quantified (factorised) and identified as statistically predictive of offending in later life (late adolescence, adulthood). Therefore, these 'risk factors' are both developmental and deterministic.

2 *Multifactor developmental theories*: the Gluecks' multifactor developmental theory employed a longitudinal design to identify biopsychosocial risk factors in childhood that predicted officially recorded offending in adolescence by an incarcerated sample. It was concluded that these risk factors should be the target of intervention during and post-release from custody.

3 *Developmental crime prevention*: the developmental crime prevention theory of Richard Cabot extended the Gluecks' theory by targeting risk factors for officially recorded offending for prevention purposes, but ultimately concluded that such risk-focused responses were ineffective and even harmful.

4 *Criminal careers model*: the explanatory model produced from the Cambridge Study used a prospective longitudinal design to identify psychosocial risk factors in childhood that influenced different aspects of official and self-reported offending (e.g. onset, escalation, desistance) over the life course, along with protective factors that insulated the individual against offending.

5 *Evaluating biopsychosocial developmental theories*: biopsychosocial developmental risk factor theories offer more integrated and practical explanations of youth offending than stand-alone positivist theories, but they can be criticised for their androcentrism, ethnocentrism, class-centrism, reductionism and psychosocial bias.

2 INTEGRATED DEVELOPMENTAL RISK FACTOR THEORIES

Biopsychosocial developmental theories are essentially 'integrated' quasi-positivist theories, certainly more integrated in nature than standalone positivist theories. However, developmental risk factor theories have sought to evolve their explanatory utility since the 1980s by integrating neo-classical, socio-structural and contextual influences into their explanations to supplement the focus on biopsychosocial risk factors. Three theories have progressed developmental risk factor explanations in a more integrated direction: the 'social development model' (Hawkins and Weis 1985), 'ecological theory' (Wikstrom and Loeber 2000) and 'rational-contextual theories' (Farrington 2007; Wikstrom 2008).

Integrated developmental theories: social development model

The 'social development model' produced by David Hawkins, Richard Catalano and Joseph Weis at Washington University (US) provided a multifactor explanation of how risk factors operate to influence antisocial behaviour and youth offending. Hawkins and Weis (1985) reviewed a group of prevention programmes and conducted secondary analysis on data provided by the National Center for the Assessment of Delinquent Behavior and its Prevention. They identified multiple 'correlates and causes' (i.e. risk factors) of antisocial behaviour/youth offending within the standard psychosocial (not including biological) risk factor domains of family, school, peer and community. Hawkins and Weis (1985) integrated social control theory (Hirschi 1969) and social learning theory (Akers 1985) to argue that correlates and causes differed in importance at different developmental stages in a young person's life. For example, the key units of socialisation (family and school) were identified as potential causes of both antisocial behaviour/youth offending and prosocial behaviour/conformity (cf. social control theory), implying that these correlates functioned as both risk and protective factors. Furthermore, reinforcement was the *process* by which antisocial/offending behaviour was learned or extinguished (cf. social learning theory), adding elements of dynamism, change and flexibility to previous deterministic explanations of the static influence of *risk factors*. The social development model hypothesised that interactions between four mutually reinforcing, interdependent (risk) factors influenced antisocial and offending behaviour:

1　Perceived opportunities for involvement and interaction with significant others in conventional activities.
2　Degree of involvement and interaction.
3　*Skills* of the young person to participate in these involvements and interactions.
4　*Perceived reinforcements for behaviour* that determine whether association with family, school or peers produces a strong bond.

(Hawkins and Weis 1985)

In 1996, Catalano and Hawkins extended their social development model explanation by adapting ideas from differential association theory (Sutherland and Cressey 1960) to enable the identification of distinct *causal pathways* for antisocial behaviour/offending that were related to association with delinquent peers. The revised social development model also included three new sets of variables to expand its explanatory breadth: biological, demographic and exogenous (external):

1   *Constitutional and physiological traits* (*biological*): cognitive ability (reading, verbal), difficult temperament, aggression, depression, hyperactivity, attention-deficit (factors that influence skills); low arousal of the nervous system (which influences the ability to perceive reinforcement).

2   *Socio-structural status* (*demographic*): age, gender, race, socio-economic status – factors viewed as affecting available opportunities for involvement and interaction with significant others in conventional activities.

3   *External constraints* (*exogenous*): social reactions to behaviour (see also Chapter 2 – labelling theories) that can be formal (police and other official sanction) or informal (ridicule, ostracism, disapproval); the clarity of rules, laws and expectations for behaviour; the monitoring of behaviour (which affects the degree of perceived reinforcement for involvement in behaviour).

(see Catalano *et al.* 2005, in Farrington 2005)

Exogenous variables allegedly increased the likelihood (risk) of antisocial and offending behaviour, but could be 'mediated by other social development model constructs' (Catalano and Hawkins 1996: 160) at different developmental stages (e.g. during primary, elementary, middle and high school), thus identifying the potential for developmental interactions between risk factors, protective factors and offending outcomes (see Section 3 of this chapter). The social development model is perhaps most notable for evolving developmental risk factor theories towards integrated explanations of youth offending based on more developmentally sensitive, process-focused and holistic understandings of the interactions between biopsychosocial risk factors, socio-structural risk factors and external/contextual influences.

Integrated developmental theories: ecological theory

The integrated developmental 'ecological theory' was formulated in the late 1990s by Per-Olof Wikstrom and Rolf Loeber. The theory was constructed to address what the authors considered to be the relative neglect of neighbourhood/community and socio-structural factors within risk factor explanations, both in terms of their stand-alone criminogenic effects and their potential influence on psychosocial risk factors (cf. Wikstrom and Loeber 2000; see also Wikstrom and Loeber 1998). The ecological approach asserted that previous risk factor studies of 'person-context interaction' had focused on the limited interaction between community context and isolated individual and family characteristics, which did not allow comprehensive explanations of youth offending. Wikstrom and Loeber (2000) resolved to explore the interactions between risk factors in the individual and the community on a much broader level to enable more complex understanding of risk factor influence than previous developmental models had allowed, in particular:

•   Interactions between *individual/psychosocial* risk factors, community risk factors and structural risk factors;

•   Interactions between *developmental* risk factors in childhood (individual social situation, individual disposition, community structural characteristics) and risk factors in *current life* (e.g. immediate social context, changes in community structural characteristics).

(Wikstrom and Loeber 2000, in Case and Haines 2009)

The researchers outlined four influential domains of risk that they felt had been much neglected and that could contribute to a more holistic explanation of youth offending:

- *Community structural characteristics* – poverty, high residential mobility, population heterogeneity, family disruption.
- *Immediate social context* – aspects of the environment that affect individual decisions to offend, such as temptations (e.g. attractive commodities), provocations (e.g. insults and threats), risk of punishment (formal and informal sanction).
- *Individual social situation* – family, school, peers.
- *Individual disposition* – impulsivity, guilt.

(Wikstrom and Loeber 2000: 1114)

To illustrate the ecological explanation, analysis of the Pittsburgh Youth Study data (see Causes and Correlates studies discussion in Section 3) concluded that neighbourhood/community risk factors exerted very little independent effect on offending and that most of their influence was mediated by individual risk factors. Further research has concluded that neighbourhood risk factors only exert an indirect effect on offending through their influence on other risk factors such as family functioning (Sampson and Laub 1993, 2005). Indeed, Wikstrom has subsequently extrapolated his ecological explanations into a broader model known as 'situational action theory' (Wikstrom 2008; see next section on rational-contextual theories).

Ecological theory plugged a noticeable gap in previous developmental risk factor theories by examining the influence of interactions between individual and contextual risk factors, including an innovative focus on the influence of risk factors on present-day experiences and behaviours. The theory also introduced a tentative consideration of the role of mediated agency (young people's ability to choose/decide to offend, as constrained by individual and neighbourhood factors). However, ecological theory arguably remains more theoretical than empirical at the time of writing, providing only limited and inconclusive evidence to date.

Integrated developmental theories: rational-contextual theories

Moving further into the twenty-first century, two integrated developmental theories have emerged as extensions of existing risk factor theories, each integrating deeper consideration of interactions between psychosocial risk factors and rational choice in different situational contexts. These contemporary 'rational-contextual theories' have been developed by two of the foremost developmental, artefactual risk factor theorists, David Farrington (criminal careers model) and Per-Olof Wikstrom (ecological theory).

Farrington's 'integrated cognitive antisocial potential' (ICAP) theory introduced a focus on the interaction between *criminal potential* (a long-standing concern of developmental criminology) and the *commission* of offenses (a much-neglected topic within developmental criminology). The ICAP theory (Farrington 2005) synthesised/

integrated elements of several other theories, including strain, social control, social learning, labelling and rational choice theories, to assert that a young person's 'anti-social potential' is determined by the nature and extent of the risk factors that they are exposed to in their everyday lives. This antisocial potential is then **actualised** (made real, brought to life) by cognitive processes (thinking, decision-making) that are influenced by situational contexts (e.g. opportunities to offend, availability of victims), leading to a rational choice favouring the commission of an offence. The ICAP theory makes a distinction between two forms of antisocial potential: long term and short term. **Long-term antisocial potential** is latent until it is actualised by risk factors such as impulsiveness, strain, criminogenic socialisation processes and negative life events, such as losing a job or a relationship. This long-term antisocial potential is further energised/activated by the desire for material possessions, status-seeking and the pursuit of excitement (e.g. sexual satisfaction). Conversely, positive attachments, prosocial socialisation and positive life events (e.g. marriage, obtaining a good job) are protective factors against the actualisation of long-term antisocial behaviour. **Short-term antisocial potential** is shaped by exposure to sociological and socio-structural risk factors (e.g. academic failure, unemployment, low income), which are energised/ activated into offending behaviour by exposure to individual risk factors (e.g. bore-dom, anger, drunkenness, peer pressure) combined with situational/contextual risk factors such as suitable opportunities to offend and available victims. The ICAP theory contends that long-term antisocial potential can be activated in later life by the choices that young people make, whereas short-term antisocial behaviour is more explicable as the result of interactions between active risk factors, agency, cognition and situational factors (Farrington 2005). Youth offending and antisocial behaviour, therefore, are the products of rational choices made during interactions between individual characteristics (e.g. short- and long-term antisocial potential) and environmental influences (situational and contextual factors). Consequently, the ICAP theory has elaborated previous developmental risk factor explanations by offering a new focus on young people's current lives and by extending deterministic explanations through considerations of agency and situational-contextual elements as triggers for youth offending. However, it is unclear as to what empirical evidence (if any) underpins the conclusions of this theory. Some critics suggested that it offers little more than a hypothetical, reductionist and negative explanation of youth offending as being the product of interactions between the 'flawed' young person and a similarly dysfunctional community (cf. Case and Haines 2009; O'Mahony 2009).

The integrated 'situational action theory' (SAT) of Per-Olof Wikstrom (see the previous subsection on ecological theory) and his colleague David Butterworth was produced to address the problem of determining causality within risk factor theories. The researchers adopted an explanatory approach focused on identifying the *causal mechanisms* linking risk factors with offending in different social situations (Wikstrom, in King and Wincup 2008; see also Farrington 2005). Unlike the ICAP, the SAT was empirically grounded, drawing its evidence from the cross-sectional Peterborough Youth Study of nearly 2,000 schoolchildren aged 14–15, a study designed explicitly to expand on the ecological theory's individual-contextual understanding of risk factor influence by

> studying the relationships between family social position (parents occupational social class, family structure and family ethnicity), the adolescents' social situation

(family and social bonds), their individual dispositions (morality and inability to exercise self-control) and lifestyles (as implicated by their peers' delinquency, their own activities and alcohol and drug use) and how these factors relate to their involvement in crime as offenders.

(Wikstrom and Butterworth 2006: 6)

Analyses of self-reported offending and interview data highlighted a group of 'explanatory factors' located within young people's routines, lifestyles, dispositions (morality, self-control) and the social situations to which they were exposed. For example, young people who had limited involvement with their family or school, but who spent time with delinquent peers in high-crime environments, were being exposed to an increased situational risk of offending. As such, traditional psychosocial risk factors were viewed as only indirect causes of crime (the causes of the causes, if you like); they influenced the individual and environmental factors that themselves influenced young people's capability to perceive alternative courses of action ('action alternatives') in different situations and to take decisions to commit crime. According to Wikstrom and Butterworth (2006: 241):

Adolescent offending is best interpreted as the consequence of perception of action alternatives and processes of choice made against the background of the interplay between the youths' individual characteristics and their behavioural contexts.

The SAT explains youth offending as the result of an intersection (interaction) between the *individual* (their current characteristics and experiences) and the *setting* (the people, objects, events and locations to which the young person is exposed and reacts). These interactions are influenced and activated by situational mechanisms, all of which influence and determine the young person's *perception of alternative actions* (alternatives to crime) and their *process of choice* (whether or not to commit crime). Therefore, a young person's perception of alternative actions and process of choice are affected by the situational settings (contexts) in which they find themselves. According to Wikstrom and Butterworth (2006), these settings consist of two influential elements: *temptations* (perceived opportunities to satisfy their desires unlawfully) and *provocations* (perceived attacks on the person, property or self-respect that precipitate a criminal response), while process of choice is influenced by individual elements such as self-control and morality.

Its creators argue that the SAT provides a dynamic 'theory of action' that is animated by 'explanatory' risk factors for youth offending, but that also integrates considerations of rational choice (e.g. morality, self-control) and situational context in order to move beyond traditional psychosocial deterministic explanations. The researchers are aware of the limitations of their cross-sectional design for the purposes of identifying causality, yet Wikstrom has argued that such designs are able to address the issues of **temporal precedence** that underpin causal conclusions (i.e. whether exposure to risk factors or the offending behaviour occurred first in the young person's life) if they employ sensitive measures of 'time of exposure' to risk factors relative to the onset of offending behaviour. To purportedly achieve this level of sensitivity, Wikstrom gathered additional data from his follow-up Peterborough Adolescent Development Study (PADS), an interview-based study with a sample of 707 young people aged 12 years old in March 2003 (Wikstrom and Butterworth 2006). As with the Peterborough Youth Study and the ICAP theory before it, PADS has thus far made available only limited evidence of its methodology or analysis, which raises the possibility that the researchers involved have to some extent lost faith or interest in their largely hypothetical integrated developmental theories. Either that, or possibly they may be so confident in their conclusions and claims that the necessity for a detailed evidence base and critical reflection is considered unnecessary. Perhaps appropriately for this developmental theory of action, time will tell as to whether new evidence and detailed reflection is forthcoming; we await developments!

5 EASY PIECES

2 Integrated developmental risk factor theories

1 *Integrated individual, socio-structural and contextual influences*: extended the arguments of their biopsychosocial counterparts by considering the criminogenic effects of interactions between biopsychosocial factors, rational choice, socio-structural factors and contextual influences.
2 *Social development model*: hypothesised that perceived opportunities for (and degree of involvement/interaction with significant others in conventional activities, possessing the skills to participate and perceived reinforcement for behaviour all interact to influence antisocial and offending behaviour.
3 *Revised social development model*: added consideration of biographical, demographic and exogenous variables: constitutional and physiological traits, socio-structural status and external constraints.
4 *Ecological theory*: elaborated developmental risk factor theories by examining interactions between psychosocial risk factors, ecological risk factors (e.g. community and structural risk factors) and immediate context (e.g. temptations and provocations).
5 *Rational-contextual theories*: progressed the degree of integration evident within integrated developmental theories to that point and added a current life focus to developmental explanations by considering the influence of rational choice, mediated by criminal potential and individual disposition, in different (immediate) situational contexts.

3 INTERACTIONAL DEVELOPMENTAL RISK FACTOR THEORIES

Two integrated, 'interactional, developmental risk factor theories' have emerged from large-scale longitudinal research studies in the US and Scotland. These studies have developed the existing body of integrated, developmental risk factor explanations of youth offending through an innovative focus on *interactions* of different kinds: reciprocal interactions between risk factors and offending in mutually reinforcing relationships (the Causes and Correlates studies [US]) and criminogenic interactions between young people and the youth justice agencies that they come into contact with (the Edinburgh Study [Scotland]).

Interactional developmental theories: Causes and Correlates studies

In 1986, the Office of Juvenile Justice and Delinquency Prevention in the US began the Causes and Correlates studies, with the central aim 'to improve the understanding of serious delinquency, violence, and drug use by examining how youth develop within the context of family, school, peers, and community' (Browning *et al.* 1999: 1). The Causes and Correlates project was an integration of three prospective longitudinal studies: the Rochester Youth Development Study (Thornberry 1994), the Denver Youth Survey (Huizinga and Espiritu 1999) and the Pittsburgh Youth Study (Loeber and Hay 1997), each of which is detailed further in the excellent book *Taking Stock of Delinquency* (Thornberry and Krohn 2003) and summarised in the almost as excellent *Understanding Youth Offending: Risk Factor Research, Policy and Practice* (Case and Haines 2009).

As the name suggests, the Causes and Correlates studies were designed to investigate the causes and correlates related to delinquent behaviour (youth offending). The programme has since expanded to investigate additional issues such as the antecedents (precursors, causes) of prosocial behaviour and developmental trajectories and transitions in adulthood (see Thornberry and Krohn 2003). The compatibility of design across the projects, employing prospective longitudinal, shared self-reported offending inventory and interviews exploring similar groups of risk factors, was a deliberate attempt to identify universal, generalisable risk factors across the studies. To avoid weighing down discussion with unnecessary descriptive detail here, Table 3.1 summarises the main features of the individual Causes and Correlates studies in relation to their underpinning theory, methods, findings and conclusions.

Table 3.1 illustrates the similarities between the separate Causes and Correlates studies in terms of their samples (i.e. preadolescent and adolescent males) and their chosen methods (i.e. interviews). There are clear overlaps in study findings related to the most influential risk factor domains of family, school, neighbourhood, peers and individual. There are further overlaps in terms of the common risk factors identified within each domain, including poor parenting and lack of parental supervision (family), low academic achievement (school), socio-structural neighbourhood disadvantage (neighbourhood), delinquent peers (peers) and low self-esteem and criminogenic attitudes (individual).

The Causes and Correlates studies evolved the explanatory utility of developmental risk factor explanations to that point by (purportedly) identifying universal, causal risk factors and pathways shared by young people while also considering the potential interactional relationship between these risk factors and offending – the possibility that risk factors might influence one another within and between different risk domains. The authors have laid claim to 'the largest and most comprehensive investigation of the causes and correlates of delinquency ever undertaken' (Thornberry *et al.* 2004: 1). Their examination of the temporal precedence of risk factors has (allegedly) enabled the Causes and Correlates studies to address Farrington's concerns that there has been an absence (in risk factor theories) of understanding of the 'processes or developmental pathways that intervene between risks factors and outcomes' (Farrington 2000: 7). However, in reality, the largely quantitative study methods have not broken free from the static risk factor – offending relationships identified by traditional developmental, artefactual risk factor theories. Most notably, the notion of explanatory and causal risk factors appears to be an invalid extrapolation from the restricted methods and analyses employed (see Case and Haines 2009).

TABLE 3.1 THE CAUSES AND CORRELATES STUDIES

Study	Theory	Method	Findings (Causes and Correlates)	Conclusions
Rochester Youth Development Study	Interactional theory – risk factors and offending have a relationship of reciprocal causal influence (they can cause one another) at different developmental stages. This relationship is mediated by structural disadvantage and weak social controls (cf. Catalano and Hawkins 1996; Hirschi 1969), such as low attachment and commitment to the family and school. Social network theory – young people can become 'enmeshed' in criminal agent networks (e.g. delinquent peer groups) that can be multiple, overlapping, dense and stable (Krohn 1986).	Interviews with 1,000 boys and girls aged 13–14 and their parents/carers.	Family – low parent–child attachment and lack of parental involvement, economic hardship, single-parent family. School – lack of commitment, low academic achievement. Neighbourhood – socio-structural disadvantage, economic hardship, lack of social support. Peers – gang membership, delinquency. Individual – criminogenic attitudes.	A 'wide range of environmental, social, and psychological forces' influence offending (Thornberry and Krohn 2003: 18). Due to increased sensitivity to temporal precedence in the methodology, the study was able to support its underpinning theory by identifying 'bidirectional causal influences and developmental changes in causal effects' (Thornberry and Krohn 2003: 18).
Denver Youth Survey	Integrated developmental – an integration of strain, social control and social learning theories (Elliott *et al.* 1985).	Annual interviews with 1,527 boys and girls aged 7, 9, 11, 13 and 15 when the study began and re-interviews with the 7- and 9-year-olds when they were 22 years old.	Family – family criminality, changing family structure, lack of parental monitoring (risk factors); high levels of parental monitoring, consistent rules and discipline (protective factors). School – low academic achievement (risk factor); academic achievement and graduation (protective factors).	The most important predictors of offending at all developmental stages were association with delinquent peers and psychological problems in adolescents. There is 'typological diversity . . . in etiological or explanatory variables' and multiple 'etiological pathways' to delinquency (Huizinga *et al.* 2003: 75).

TABLE 3.1 (CONTINUED)

Study	Theory	Method	Findings (Causes and Correlates)	Conclusions
			Neighbourhood – social disorganisation (e.g. poverty, lack of mobility, ethnic diversity) and single-parent families (risk factors); socio-structural disadvantage (an indirect influence on family-based risk factors), neighbourhood social control/bonding (protective factors). Individual – psychological problems such as low self-esteem and criminogenic attitudes (risk factors); high self-esteem and self-efficacy (protective factors).	
Pittsburgh Youth Study	Integrated developmental – expanding on ecological theory (Wikstrom and Loeber 2000; Sampson and Laub 1997) and seeking to address the 'adevelopmental' nature of many theories of youth offending (citing the social development model and criminal careers model as exceptions).	Interviews with a random sample of 1,517 'preadolescent' boys aged 5–6, 8–9 or 11–12 when the study began, along with parent interviews. Annual interviews with the youngest and oldest samples at a later stage.	Family – low socio-economic status, broken home, maternal stress, substance use problems and poor parental supervision (the strongest family predictor/risk factor). School – low academic achievement (risk factor); high academic achievement (protective factor). Neighbourhood – socio-structural disadvantage as an indirect influence on family-based risk factors (see also Denver Youth Study). Individual – impulsivity, depression, low self-esteem.	'Offending by most juveniles results from forces within the individual and forces in the individual's social environment (parents, siblings, and peers) in different social contexts (family home, school, neighbourhood)' (Loeber et al. 2003: 129).

Interactional developmental theories: Edinburgh Study of Youth Transitions and Crime

In 1998, the prospective longitudinal Edinburgh Study of Youth Transitions and Crime (better known as the Edinburgh Study) began in the School of Law at Edinburgh University under the direction of David J. Smith, assisted by Lesley McAra and Susan McVie. By integrating knowledge and perspectives drawn from across developmental risk factor theories (e.g. social development model, ecological theory, life course models; see Section 4), the Edinburgh Study sought to better 'understand the causes of youth crime and how offending emerges in the process of development from childhood to adulthood' (Smith and McAra 2004: 14). The original foci for the study were:

1   To explore transitions and personal transformations during adolescence and adulthood, rather than early childhood influences;
2   To identify any gender differences in transitions and transformations;
3   To explain the mechanisms leading to serious, long-term, and frequent offending;
4   To assess the influence of contact with the official systems on subsequent criminal careers;
5   To understand how young people negotiated their pathways into and out of offending (cf. the pathways approach) through a focus on interactions between psychosocial risk factors and social structural neighbourhood factors (cf. ecological theory).

(Smith and McVie 2003: 169–170)

Methodologically, the Edinburgh Study team collected official statistics (e.g. Youth Justice System data, neighbourhood information) on 4,317 young people aged between 11-1/2 and 12-1/2 years who entered Edinburgh secondary schools in autumn 1998. In addition, the team conducted surveys (questionnaires and interviews) with young people, parents and teachers, investigating the psychosocial (largely risk-focused) influences on the young people's lives. The key findings of the Edinburgh Study reflected those of the Causes and Correlates studies and of other developmental risk factor explanations before them. The most influential risk factors for offending were located within the psychosocial risk domains of:

- *Family*: poor parental supervision, dysfunctional family, parent–child conflict. The team concluded that 'parenting had a genuine causal influence of the later behaviour of teenagers' (Smith and McAra 2004: 3).
- *School*: poor relationships with teachers, lack of attachment and commitment to school, misbehaviour in school. This led the researchers to assert that 'there is a role for schools in preventing the development of delinquent behavior' (Smith 2006: 4).
- *Neighbourhood*: socio-structural deprivation (e.g. high unemployment, dense local authority housing, dissatisfaction). Neighbourhood disorganisation was more influential than measures of individual deprivation (e.g. separation from parents, family unemployment) in terms of predicting later offending (Smith 2006).
- *Peer group and lifestyle*: gang membership, contact with the police and local criminal justice agencies (Smith 2006; McAra and McVie 2007).
- *Individual*: impulsivity (Smith 2006).

However, the study moved beyond ecological considerations of **neighbour-hood collective efficacy** – the ability of the neighbourhood and its residents to collectively control the behaviour of individuals/groups within it (Sampson *et al.* 1997) and beyond considerations of community functioning and neighbourhood socio-economic status (Wikstrom and Loeber 1998) to explore broader and much-neglected socio-structural factors (e.g. gender, family structure, social deprivation). Possibly the most important finding from the Edinburgh Study in terms of evolving risk factor explanations was highlighting the criminogenic and criminalising role of contact with the Youth Justice System (YJS). The research team concluded that 'repeated and more intensive forms of contact with agencies of youth justice may be damaging to young people in the long-term' (McAra and McVie 2007: 333), largely due to the resultant labelling, which creates the criminalising master status of 'offender'. The 'damage' here is through the exacerbation of criminogenic socio-structural factors that are already outside of the young person's control (e.g. family structure, social deprivation, gender) and through the processes of targeting of intervention on the family and education, rather than on the individual and the offence (McAra and McVie 2007).

In summary, the comprehensive, innovative design and foci of the Edinburgh Study, reflected in the multi-method design, the breadth of the (largely risk-focused) influences measured and the complexity of the statistical analyses conducted have moved risk factor explanations significantly further forward. The Edinburgh Study examined much-neglected socio-structural influences and identified the criminogenic potential of system contact, a notion largely overlooked in risk factor theories yet championed by supporters of diversionary youth justice approaches (see Chapter 4). However, the overriding study focus remained on psychosocial risk factors and the quantification and simplification of the complexity of young people's experiences, leaving the study open to the traditional risk factor criticisms of reductionism and developmental determinism, despite the advanced nature of its design and innovative conclusions.

5 EASY PIECES

3 Interactional developmental risk factor theories

1   *Interactive risk factors*: interactional developmental risk factor theories have extended integrated theories by examining interactive, mutually reinforcing relationships between risk factors and offending, including the potential for offending to predate and influence risk factors.
2   *Criminogenic interactions with the YJS*: interactional developmental risk factor theories (e.g. the Edinburgh Study) have also identified the criminogenic effects of young people's interactions with the YJS.
3   *Psychosocial causes and correlates*: each of the Causes and Correlates studies identified family, school, neighbourhood and individual risk factors as predictive influences on offending by preadolescent and adolescent boys.

4 *Gendered, socio-structural and systemic correlates*: the Edinburgh Study identified similar criminogenic influences on later offending by preadolescent/adolescent boys (11- to 13-year-olds), but extended these findings to incorporate girls, socio-structural considerations and the potentially criminogenic influence of system contact on criminal careers.

5 *Interactional processes*: both interactional theories discussed have examined the multiple developmental processes and pathways into and out of offending that are shaped by interactions between psychosocial and socio-structural/ecological risk factors, individual young people and youth justice agencies.

4 AGE-GRADED LIFE COURSE RISK FACTOR THEORIES

In their groundbreaking text *Crime in the Making: Pathways and Turning Points Through Life*, Robert Sampson and John Laub (1993) formulated a risk-focused explanation of youth offending that traced individual development from childhood to adolescence and into adulthood – a life course theory. Sampson and Laub's theory was not based on original empirical research but on secondary data analysis of the Gluecks' original *Unraveling Juvenile Delinquency* (1950) data, which they had stumbled upon in the basement of Harvard University Law School in 1985. They set about restoring, rebuilding, validating, computerising and reanalysing this extensive dataset. The challenge they set for themselves was to extend the Gluecks' developmental/childhood focus into adulthood and to explore the possibility that in addition to the stability of behaviour over time (as argued by developmental theories), there could be *change* in offending behaviour over the life course.

Age-graded life course theories: age-graded theory of informal social control

Following a comprehensive reanalysis of the Gluecks' data, Sampson and Laub produced their 'age-graded theory of informal social control' (Sampson and Laub 1993), a three-part, risk-focused explanation of the development of youth offending (operationalised as 'antisocial behaviour') in adolescence and into adulthood. The theory posited three main (interacting) explanations for continuity and change in youth offending over the life course:

- *Structural context* (e.g. social class, ethnicity, gender, poverty, broken home, household overcrowding, parental employment), mediated by informal family and school *social controls*, explains delinquency in childhood and adolescence.
- There is strong *continuity* in antisocial behaviour from childhood to adulthood in a variety of life domains.
- *Informal social bonds* to family and employment in adulthood explain *changes* in criminality over the lifespan despite early childhood propensities.

(Sampson and Laub 1993: 7; emphasis added)

The theory illustrated in Figure 3.1 suggests that a young person's behaviour (antisocial or prosocial) elicits a range of formal and informal responses (e.g.

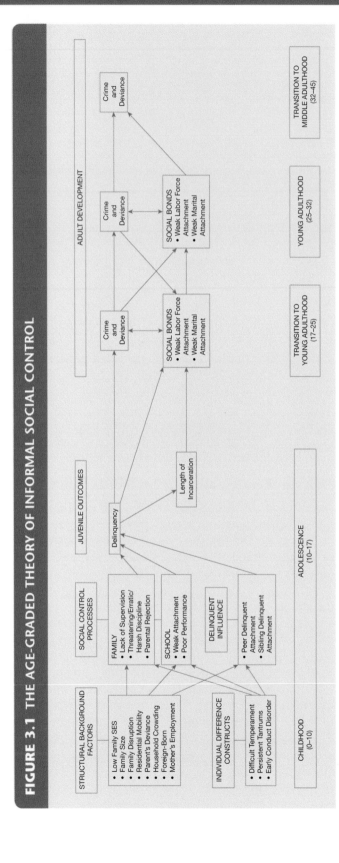

FIGURE 3.1 THE AGE-GRADED THEORY OF INFORMAL SOCIAL CONTROL

punishment from the YJS, parental discipline, approval/disapproval of peers), which interact with existing psychosocial risk factors to shape future behaviour. For example, official punishment could diminish a young person's educational opportunities by incarcerating them or removing them from school, but equally the young person could be encouraged along a prosocial pathway if the punishment makes previously neglected education compulsory. Sampson and Laub viewed the interaction between formal/informal responses and risk factors as providing the context to shape individual decisions regarding behaviour, rather than as deterministic causes of behaviour. They argued that the offending **trajectory** (course, route, pathway) over the life course could change in times of **transition** – significant periods in an individual's life (e.g. moving or leaving school, gaining or losing employment, getting married or separated) or through exposure to critical life events. These changes in trajectory were labelled **turning points**.

Sampson and Laub's age-graded theory of informal social control evolved risk factor explanations beyond narrow, artefactual, developmental understandings of the deterministic impact of childhood experiences on later behaviour and towards **constructivist** (socially constructed) explanations that consider the individual's ability to actively influence and change their *pathways* into and out of crime (see Section 5 of this chapter) over the life course – albeit an ability shaped and constrained by existing risk factors and societal responses to previous behaviour.

Revised age-graded theory of informal social control

Ten years after *Crime in the Making*, Sampson and Laub revisited and extended their age-graded theory of informal social control in *Shared Beginnings, Divergent Lives: Delinquent Boys to Age 70* (Laub and Sampson 2003). They had contacted 52 men from the original *Unraveling Juvenile Delinquency* sample (Glueck and Glueck 1950) and conducted detailed life history interviews with them as they approached 70 years of age, supplemented by analyses of the official criminal histories and death records of all 500 men who formed part of the original (delinquent) sample. The 'revised age-graded theory of informal social control' (Laub and Sampson 2003) integrated an original qualitative, narrative life history approach to build on the Gluecks' original dataset and to expand risk factor theory explanations by obtaining richer, more comprehensive data than the previous quantitative study methods had allowed. This greater breadth and depth of data facilitated explanations across the life course regarding why some of the men persisted with offending and others desisted from offending.

The revised theory focused on four main self-reported transitions in the lives of the delinquent sample that functioned as turning points promoting **desistance** (ending, ceasing) from offending in adulthood: marriage, joining the military, attending reform school and moving to a more prosperous neighbourhood. Interview data suggested that interactions with these age-graded social institutions (e.g. reform school, military, marriage) led to transitions that provided the men with an opportunity to change the direction of their lives; to receive supervision, monitoring and social support; to bring change and structure to their routine activities; and to transform their identity (Laub and Sampson 2003). Consequently, desistance from an offending career was dependent on two central concepts linked to stability and change in offending trajectories (Sampson and Laub 2004: 19):

- 'Knifing off' from one's immediate environment (change).
- Obtaining 'structured role stability' across life domains such as marriage, work and community (stability).

Sampson and Laub concluded that their original theory (Sampson and Laub 1993) had neglected the *progression* (pathways) of change in behaviour over the life course, particularly in relation to desistance from offending. Through collecting new biographical narratives, they were able to develop an integrated, revised age-graded life course theory of offending and desistance that accounted for the influence of risk factors in childhood, adolescence and adulthood, along with the roles of agency and (situated) choice, situational factors, routine activities, culture and historical context. The new focus on the 'inner logic of lives' (Sampson and Laub 2005: 8) and 'transformative action' (Sampson and Laub 2004: 19) introduced a social constructionist element to risk factor explanations more broadly. The revised theory was able to consider how individuals can make meaning of and negotiate (e.g. decide how to respond to) their experiences of risk factors and their pathways into and out of offending (Sampson and Laub 2005), rather than being passive victims of the developmental, deterministic and damaging influence of these risk factors. By 'reconsidering the risk-factor paradigm' (Laub and Sampson 2003: 289) in this way, the researchers produced a richer, more holistic understanding of persistence in offending (stability) and desistance from offending (change) – an understanding that contextualised the role of risk factors as important (but not exclusive) influences on offending across the life course. Taken together, the age-graded life course theories of Sampson and Laub enabled a more detailed consideration of the potential for *stability* and *change* across the life course as the result of complex interactions between risk factors, structural context, social controls and the individual's constructions of these interactions.

5 EASY PIECES

4 Age-graded life course risk factor theories

1   *Reanalysing the Gluecks*: the original age-graded life course theory was formulated by Robert Sampson and John Laub, based on their reanalysis of the Gluecks' original Unraveling Juvenile Delinquency dataset.
2   *A three-way interaction*: the tripartite (three-part) age-graded theory of informal social control (Sampson and Laub 1993) explains youth offending in adolescence and adulthood as the product of interactions between psychosocial risk factors, structural context, formal social controls (e.g. official punishment), informal social controls (e.g. disapproval from parents and peers) and critical life events.

3   *Stability and change across the life course*: interactions at different life stages are seen to shape continuity/stability and change in offending trajectories/pathways, which could lead to transitions and turning points into and out of crime.

4   *Knifing off and structured role stability*: in the revised version of their theory, Laub and Sampson (2003) added narrative life histories to enable closer examination of the progression of change over the life course; arguing that 'knifing off' from a criminogenic environment (change) and obtaining 'structured role stability' from marriage, work or moving neighbourhoods influenced desistance from offending (change).

5   *Integrating the role of constructions*: age-graded life course theories allow a richer, more complex understanding of stability and change in youth offending trajectories as resulting from the individual's constructions of their interactions with risk factors, structural contexts and social controls.

5 CONSTRUCTIVIST PATHWAYS RISK FACTOR THEORIES

A social constructivist (constructionist) pathways strand of risk factor theory has emerged to challenge dominant quantitative/artefactual, developmental understandings of risk. 'Constructivist pathways risk factor theories' (Kemshall 2003) consider young people's ability to construct (e.g. create, make meaning of, negotiate, resist) their experiences of risk and the influence of these constructions on their pathways into and out of offending. Constructivist theories have moved risk factor explanations beyond their fixation with quasi-positivist quantitative methods and the factorisation of risk. They have utilised qualitative methodologies (e.g. life history narratives) to better understand the construction of risk by young people in their everyday lives (cf. France and Homel 2006). Professor Colin Webster has discerned a 'qualitative consensus' across risk factor theories in the UK that has pitted itself directly against deterministic approaches and has emphasised alternative explanations based on the (personal) choice, contingency and context. Constructivist pathways risk factor theories have challenged the alleged causal influence of risk factors on offending (cf. Macdonald 2007) and the deterministic, artefactual conclusion that young people exposed to risk factors can behave in a 'mechanistic and dehumanized fashion abstracted from day-to-day lives and contexts' (Lawy 2002: 408). This criticism attacks the negative, reductionist view of young people perpetuated by artefactual theories. Young people have been constructed as passive recipients (not active constructors) of exposure to risk factors and the harm that this causes – helpless, hopeless and hurtling inevitably towards offending outcomes unless adults intervene – very much the 'crash-test dummies' of Case and Haines' (2009) detailed critique of risk factor research (see Figure 3.2).

Therefore, constructivist pathways risk factor theories provide a less simplistic/reductionist and more interpretive, appreciative and ethnographic (study of people in their own environment) explanation of youth offending that sees risk as experienced, constructed and negotiated in specific social contexts during interactions with significant others and the environment. Three escalating levels of risk construction have been identified across constructivist risk factor theories (Kemshall *et al.* 2006,

Understanding Youth Offending

Risk factor research, policy and practice

Stephen Case and Kevin Haines

in France and Homel 2007), which offer differing views of the relationship between agency and structure (i.e. choice and socio-structural factors) and its influence upon youth offending:

Weak constructivism – agency and the immediate situational context are central. Youth offending results from the interaction between propensity to respond to situational temptations [see also the SAT in Section 4 of this chapter] and the social mechanisms influencing a young person's routines and decision-making processes. This weak form of constructivism prioritises agency and the individual over the social.

Moderate constructivism – pathways into and out of offending are negotiated processes dependent on continuing interactions between agency (individual choice and decision-making) and structure (e.g. power relations and cultural processes within a society). This interaction can determine the contexts and opportunity routes within which decisions whether to offend are made.

Strong constructivism – the role of social structure and cultural understandings of risk are pivotal, rather than the individual's risk decisions. Strong constructivism challenges the processes of *individualisation* and *responsibilisation* surrounding risk [see also Chapter 5], whereby social risks (e.g. unemployment) are transformed into individual faults/deficits (e.g. lack of skill or effort) for which the young person is assigned primary responsibility. Conversely, strong constructivism views risk as an historical, social and political product/construct external to the young person.

(Kemshall *et al.* 2006: 356–357; see also Lupton 1999)

Constructivist pathways risk factor theories have focused on young people's ability to construct and negotiate their own developmental pathways and transitions into and out of crime (Hine 2005; see also Laub and Sampson 2003). There is a particular focus on how young people's experiences and abilities to negotiate risk factors along these pathways can be mediated by different elements of socio-structural context, such as neighbourhood socio-economic status, poverty, unemployment, localised cultural influences and political influence (see France and Homel 2007). In other words, constructivist pathways risk factor theories offer

a life-course perspective that explores the intra-individual and inter-individual aspects of 'experience' as critical to understanding the pathways into and out of crime.

(France and Homel 2007: 4)

The constructivist pathways approach and its understanding of risk as a dynamic process, subject to change and (re)construction by young people, has been animated by two sets of studies in the UK: *Pathways Into and Out of Crime* and the Teesside Studies.

Constructivist pathways theories: *Pathways Into and Out of Crime*

The *Pathways Into and Out of Crime* project was a partnership of longitudinal surveys spanning six UK universities (Sheffield and De Montfort, Nottingham, Newcastle,

Essex and Glasgow Caledonian) sponsored by the Economic and Social Research Council. The partnership studies focused on the potential for young people to (re) construct their pathways into and out of crime (hence the title) and how social processes and demographic characteristics can mediate the constructions and experiences of risk factors in their current lives (Hine 2005). The projects prioritised qualitative methodologies (although certain projects retained quantitative elements) and specifically engaged with so-called hard-to-reach (i.e. often neglected by researchers) and minority groups of young people (substance users, excluded from school, behaviour problems, offenders, those with parents in prison, Black and Minority Ethnic [BAME] groups) in order to:

- Expand understanding and knowledge of the relationship between risk factors and children and young people's pathways into and out of crime;
- Gain a fuller understanding of how children and young people who are identified as being 'at risk' of being future offenders negotiate their pathways into and out of crime;
- Understand the social processes of protection, resilience and resistance that mediate between risk factors and pathways into and out of crime.

(Hine 2006)

The five partnership projects were:

- *Risk and resilience in children who are offending, excluded from school or have behaviour problems*
  Employed interviews with young people and professionals to examine the 'factors that enhance or reduce risk', critical turning points and pathways into and out of crime for first-time offenders working with Youth Offending Teams (see Chapter 5), young people permanently excluded from school and young people with statements of special educational needs (Hine *et al.* 2007).
- *Risk, protection and resilience in urban Black and Asian culture*
  Utilised video stimuli created by young people and focus group discussion with researchers to examine young people's experiences, constructions and negotiations of risk in their area and 'the combination of risk and protective factors which can lead to resilience or susceptibility' in Black and Asian young people (see Haw, in France and Homel 2007).
- *Risk, protection and resilience in the family life of children and young people with a parent in prison*
  Explored the factors, experiences and processes related to risk, protection and resilience for children with a parent in prison, using questionnaires, pre- and post-release interviews with imprisoned parents and interviews with children and young people (Walker and McCarthy, in Preston 2005).
- *Young people, social capital and the negotiation of risk*
  Studied the influence of social and material resources (social capital) on perceptions, experiences and negotiation of risk, decision-making (risk choices) and risk-taking behaviour by young people from secondary schools, Youth Offending Teams and community groups (see Boeck *et al.* 2006). The study employed survey questionnaires, interviews and focus groups with young people.

- *Risk, protection and substance misuse among young offenders*
  Investigated the relationship between substance use and offending, using structured questionnaires, with a particular focus on the 'relationships between substance misuse, offending and personal and social risk factors' (Hammersley *et al.* 2003).

Taken together, the *Pathways Into and Out of Crime* studies emphasised the ways in which individuals negotiate their environments and thus explored the 'chaotic, complex, relative, contextual' relationships between risk factors and offending across diverse cultures, social contexts and political settings (see Ungar 2004). The studies emphasised (but deliberately avoided quantifying) both individual agency (choice) and the structural limitations placed on individual agency (the 'mediated choice' of ecological theory). The main conclusions from the *Pathways* projects were:

- *Context* can be important in determining whether a factor is associated with risk or protection, while circumstances assumed to signify risk (e.g. school exclusion) may actually be protective;
- Young people's *responses* to risk exposure can depend on community context, peer group, family context (e.g. relationships with family) and their relationship with professionals;
- *Resilience* to risk factors and negative influences can be promoted by family and peers;
- *Risk stagnation* can occur when young people are unable or unwilling to remove themselves from their current situation due to feeling hopeless and fatalistic.

  (Hine 2005, 2006; emphasis added)

The constructivist pathways approach acknowledged that young people's lives can be chaotic, unpredictable, diverse and highly individualised, so they are not reducible to neat, predictable factors and deterministic explanations with limited ecological validity. Constructivist explanations from the *Pathways* projects have addressed these complexities and how they impact upon young people's lives, notably young people previously neglected from traditional research samples.

Constructivist pathways theories: the Teesside Studies

Around the same time as the *Pathways* partnership studies were taking place, a group of three interrelated studies were being conducted by researchers at Teesside University under the supervision of Robert Macdonald. The Teesside Studies adopted a constructivist perspective to understand how young people experience risk in different socio-structural contexts and how their resultant perceptions and decisions affect their transitions into adulthood (cf. Case and Haines 2009). The first published study was *Snakes and Ladders: Young People, Transitions and Social Exclusion* (Johnston *et al.* 2000), in which 98 young people aged 15–25 years old from the same neighbourhood, social class and ethnic background were interviewed about their experiences of transitions into adulthood. In the follow-up study, *Disconnected Youth? Growing Up in Britain's Poorest Neighbourhoods* (Macdonald and Marsh 2005), 88 young people aged 15–25 years old living in socially disadvantaged neighbourhoods were interviewed in order to examine how ideas of social exclusion (developed from the first study)

connected to their 'lived realities', with a particular focus on evaluating the explanatory applicability of underclass theory (see discussion of right realism in Chapter 2).
The Teesside Studies concluded with *Poor Transitions: Social Exclusion and Young Adults*
(Webster *et al.* 2004; published prior to *Disconnected Youth* but commencing after it),
which investigated where youth transitions had led members of the original two samples once they had reached adulthood. This final study had the most explicit focus
on examining the influence of risk on offending pathways, so let's explore it further.

The *Poor Transitions* research team reinterviewed 34 members (16 males, 18
females) of the original *Snakes and Ladders* and *Disconnected Youth* samples, then aged
between 23 and 29 years old. The researchers employed retrospective biographical
(life history) interviews supplemented by a reanalysis of the biographical interviews
from the two previous Teesside Studies in order to 'sketch out the *nature* and *shape*
of criminal careers' (Macdonald, in France and Homel 2007: 115). The *Poor Transitions* team identified rough approximations of the influence of risk factors on offending (Webster *et al.* 2006: 9), rather than definitive, deterministic conclusions. These
rough, approximated risk factors were:

- *Family*: living in a single-parent family; domestic violence; having a parent in
  prison; acrimonious parental divorce; living in care.
- *Education*: early and frequent truancy; having no educational qualifications.
- *Lifestyle*: living a troubled, traumatic life.
- *Socio-structural*: socio-economic deprivation.

Poor Transitions criticised traditional artefactual risk factor theories for individualising risk and preferring to 'ignore the role of neighbourhood influence and context in the
emergence of risk factors' (Webster *et al.* 2006: 12). Moving beyond the approximated
(largely psychosocial) risk factors they had identified, the researchers emphasised the
role of **social capital** in the construction and experience of risk – the degree of personal
commitments to the social networks in which the young people lived and operated. In
particular, young people who offended seemed to have been constrained by the limits
of their *bonding* social capital, which restricted their socio-economic opportunities due
to limiting the scope of their social networks to only connect to families and friends.

The *Poor Transitions* team found that the life history biographies of young people
had been clearly influenced by living in a region that had been socially disadvantaged
(cf. socio-structural deprivation, a common risk factor in the Causes and Correlates
studies) by recent sharp increases in poverty and multiple deprivation, combined
with rapid deindustrialisation and economic restructuring (Webster *et al.* 2006).
These socio-economic and socio-structural upheavals were significantly detrimental
to young people due to lowering wages, reducing benefit entitlements and producing a rapid decline in opportunities for employment and training. According to the
authors, such a myriad of structural risk could not have been predicted by artefactual
approaches that inherently neglect the influence of historical, socio-economic and
geographical contexts. The contextualised conclusions of the Teesside Studies were
extended by examining the role of **unpredictable critical moments** (unpredictable
versions of Sampson and Laub's life events) in young people's lives (e.g. experiencing
rape, suffering a road accident), which purportedly increased or decreased the likelihood (risk) of future offending by increasing their vulnerability or resistance to future
risk factors and life stressors.

Professor Rob Macdonald has outlined what he sees as the key conclusions from the Teesside Studies he directed. Although Rob is a friend and respected colleague (like Colin Webster), I can assure you that he wasn't encouraged to present these conclusions in five easy pieces, even though he has! The five main conclusions were:

1   There is a need to *avoid deterministic, reductionist and positivist assumptions* of 'a tight, causal fit between particular risk indicators and later, or concurrent, behaviour'. Instead, the relationships between risk and offending should be understood as 'associations'.
2   It is *infeasible to predict* with confidence which specific young people will offend in the future. Despite the *Disconnected Youth* study confirming the link between having experienced risk factors and being a frequent offender, it also showed that young people experiencing high risk do not necessarily offend.
3   There are inherent *difficulties in establishing which risk factors are most significant* for different young people at different points in their life and in different contexts.
4   Large-scale quantitative studies are less able than qualitative risk factor research studies 'to get close up to actors' *subjective, complicated accounts and life stories*.
5   Risk factor research has over-emphasised individual-level risk and relatively *neglected the influence of historical and spatial contexts* (e.g. deindustrialisation, poverty, the influx of cheap drugs).

(Macdonald, in France and Homel 2007: 118–120; emphasis added)

In order to gain an invaluable insight into the groundbreaking Teesside Studies, I spoke to Rob Macdonald's long-time research partner, Professor Colin Webster, about his research experiences and what he feels that they have contributed to our understandings and explanations of youth offending.

CONVERSATIONS

The Teesside Studies

Steve: What can you tell me about the research?

Colin Webster: The Teesside Studies comprised a series of interrelated projects carried out in Middlesbrough, UK. We interviewed the same people over a fairly long period of time and asked them about their lives, following what happened to them over this time and adding some new older people towards the end of this period. The studies offered an unusually long-term, in-depth view of poor transitions among those stuck in an economically marginalised place. The people we periodically spoke to were aged 15–25 at the start of the studies. By the end, most were in their thirties, some in their forties. Those at the beginning of the project in 1998 were born on the cusp, or in the depth, of the rapid disappearance of well-paid work in the area they lived, while the older group could still remember the better times that had preceded the decline of local industry. By the end of the fieldwork, we had built a compelling picture of young and young adult people often in extreme poverty, getting by through intermittent, insecure work, welfare and in a significant number of cases, through criminal activity.

Steve: What motivated the studies?

Colin: Arriving in Teesside to take up a university post in 1995, I had the good luck to meet new colleagues who were similarly curious about what had happened in one of the most and earliest deindustrialised places in the country. What had it been like to grow up in a place where parents had been occupied in relatively well-paid, skilled jobs, creating prosperity and full employment for most, to then experience economic collapse and the disappearance of opportunity in such a short time? We, too, couldn't help noticing the poverty and dereliction around us in a place that history had forgotten and lives had been apparently thwarted.

One of the main spurs to embark on a study to inquire what had happened among people who had lived and experiencing these changes was a visit by a famous American political scientist, Charles Murray. Murray blamed the people of Middlesbrough for their own worklessness, saying they mustn't want to work, preferring instead to languish on welfare benefits. He accused them of belonging to an amoral 'underclass', possessing values separate from, and in opposition to, those of hardworking, respectable society (see Chapter 2). We were not even sure Murray had visited the area, and he certainly hadn't spoken to anyone on the housing estates he referred to. We decided then to do just that – to speak to people living in Middlesbrough, which was one of the poorest areas in Britain.

The series of studies were funded by the Joseph Rowntree Foundation (a poverty charity) and the Economic and Social Research Council. The questions that drove the initial project, and those that emerged from the subsequent series of studies, hinged around whether choosing to work lifts people out of poverty – as was, and continues to be, claimed by politicians and policy-makers. Generally, we found that individuals cycled between work and welfare over the course of their lives, and the reason for this was the temporary and insecure nature of the work available. Our general conclusion was that the channelling of job seekers into, or the offer of, growing precarious work – insecure, low-waged and of poor quality – kept people in poverty, undermining the purpose of welfare and delaying wider prosperity in areas like Teesside.

Steve: How did you find your participants?

Colin: Our experience of conducting the studies became a preoccupation with accessing people who were poor, living on Teesside's estates, and were hard to reach. We did this by contacting local welfare and employment agencies, advertising in shop windows, job centres, housing offices, community centres, youth clubs and even local prisons. We then asked participants if they knew anyone living in the same situation and place as them, extending our reach. We limited finding and contacting people who were willing to be interviewed to the poorest areas where experiences of poverty were most likely. Once we established our research sample of 186 individuals, we returned to them again and again, although refining the sample to somewhat fewer individuals who best exemplified the most important themes and issues that emerged from the first studies, and who we wished to study further and in more depth. Overall, we were surprised and gladdened by the extent to which participants joined the research study, trusted the researchers and were willing to speak. In this author's view, cooperation was helped by the very positive image we as members of the university had in the local area, as the university was a main source of local employment, investment and opportunity. We also offered a small monetary incentive to cover participants' time and effort.

Steve: What would you say were your most important findings regarding how to explain youth offending?

Colin: As the study was primarily about transitions from teenage years into young adulthood among people living in poor conditions and places, the Teesside Studies were not primarily about criminality. We examined the different aspects and dimensions of these transitions including school-to-work (e.g. training, jobs, unemployment); family (e.g. becoming a parent, partnerships); housing (e.g. leaving home, independent living); leisure (e.g. peer associations, identities); criminal (e.g. offending, desistance); and drug-using careers (e.g. recreational to dependent use).

As far as criminal and drug-taking activities were concerned, we found that the people we spoke to – those involved in crime and drug use as well as those having no involvement – shared very similar sorts of conditions and risks associated with economic marginality that might lead to criminal and drug-taking 'solutions' to poverty, stress, depression and boredom. The reason some individuals chose criminal and drug-taking activity while others did not was in part because of unpredictable, immediate personal crises and opportunities that had life-changing consequences. But more than this was the prolongation of persistent truancy and falling into street-based socialising, lacking structure or purpose, into late teenage and beyond; and most of all, the dramatic new impact of a local heroin market in the mid-1990s, as many in the studies progressed through to their mid-teens. This poverty-driven dependent drug use, as well as relieving troubled young lives, drove increasingly frequent, desperate and chaotic acquisitive offending. The consequences of addiction were long-term and conjured criminal careers in which individuals struggled to stop heroin use and the criminality used to fuel it.

Theoretically, the main factors discouraging criminal activity were separating from peer groups that had directed and encouraged criminality; employment, partnerships and parenting providing purposeful activity; personal crises and unpredictable turning points that could turn people away from, just as they had turned individuals towards, crime and drug careers. Reflecting critically about the research, the main contributions to knowledge and understanding of youth offending and how to respond to it through youth justice measures, are the strong links that perhaps sudden, then deep and persistent, generational poverty, concentrated in particular places, have with drug use and crime. Whether criminal and drug-taking 'careers' actually emerge will depend on the sorts of individual events and contingencies in individual lives, under these adverse conditions and circumstances of poverty, in these places.

Steve: What do the Teesside Studies tell us about how we should respond to youth offending?

Colin: Youth justice responses need to support youth transitions in the round, consistently over time, in the actual lives of young people in respect of schooling, training, jobs, unemployment and underemployment; becoming a parent and partnerships; leaving home and independent living; in respect of peer associations and identities; and most of all recognising the impossibility of young people living independently and positively in conditions of the systematic impoverishment of the lives of working-class children and 16- to 25-year-olds over three decades of adverse youth policy. If we are left with the single most important conclusion from these studies, it is that despite adversity born from recurrent poverty, reinforced by the low-paid, insecure work offered in the area to the people we studied, against Charles Murray's claim that people didn't want to work, we found an enduring and resilient commitment to work, and hatred of welfare dependency, among all the people we spoke to.

So, what do constructivist pathways theories contribute in explanatory terms?

Constructivist pathways theories have employed narrative, interpretivist methodologies to explain young people's pathways into and out of youth offending as shaped by experiences of risks as dynamic and complex processes (not deterministic, predictive 'factors') operating at social, contextual and political levels. Constructivist explanations focus on how young people (including previously marginalised groups such as black and ethnic minorities [BAME]) understand, construct and make meaning of their risk experiences as they travel along developmental pathways over the life course and how societal access routes to opportunities can help or hinder the negotiation of risk (see France and Homel 2006, 2007; see also Ungar 2004). Constructivist pathways theories have avoided the artefactual obsession with attempting to control risk variables and have largely rejected the notion of causal and predictive risk factors. Constructivist understandings of risk, therefore, offer a different perspective on risk and offending – a concerted effort to interpret and understand the dynamic and negotiated nature of risk (factors) and the relationship of risk with offending for individual young people along *processes* and *pathways*. Constructivists have attempted to *explain* the relationship between risk and offending, rather than simply to identify statistical links between the two and then claim these represent predictive relationships. The innovative focus on pathways *out of* crime (i.e. processes of desistance from offending and resilience to risk) has encouraged more investigation of the extent and nature of protective factors and their influential interactions with risk factors and offending. Constructivist pathways theories have also introduced more consideration of the neglected roles of (bounded) *agency* and *structure*, moving traditional risk factor theories away from their reductionist psychosocial biases by incorporating more examination of subjectivity, power and socio-political influence (France and Homel 2007). These foci progress risk factor explanations towards seeing risk as constructed in the present day through interactions between subjective/agency factors and social/environmental factors. Indeed, Kemshall *et al.* (2006) suggest that constructivism progresses risk factor explanations 'beyond traditional risk factors by giving appropriate attention to socio-structural factors, social processes and social context'.

5 EASY PIECES

5 Constructivist pathways risk factor theories

1   *Constructing risk*: constructivist pathways theories explore young people's ability to construct, make meaning of, negotiate and resist their exposure to risk and how this ability shapes their pathways into and out of offending.

2   *Different levels of constructivism*: weak constructivism considers agency and immediate social context as essential influences; moderate constructivism identifies interactions between agency and structure (e.g. power relations) as central; strong constructivism asserts that risk is a socio-historical and political product, thus social structure is the key influence on young offending.

3   *Pathways into/out of offending*: the *Pathways Into and Out of Crime* partnership explored how personal constructions, social processes and demographic characteristics mediate young people's experiences of, and resilience to, risk factors in the current lives.

4   *Lived realities*: the Teesside Studies conducted biographical interviews to examine the influence of social exclusion on the lived realities of young people in a socially disadvantaged neighbourhood, concluding that social capital, unpredictable critical moments and socio-historical context can influence offending pathways.

5   *Challenging artefactual explanations*: constructivist pathways theories attack the determinism and reductionism of developmental, artefactual risk factor theories, expanding the explanatory focus to consider the roles of socio-structural context and individual constructions of risk on shaping dynamic pathways and processes into and out of offending.

EXPLAINING YOUTH OFFENDING WITH RISK FACTOR THEORIES: SO, WHAT DO WE KNOW?

The body of risk factor theories explored in this chapter have offered alternative explanations to traditional classical and positivist theories while retaining several of their central principles (e.g. determinism), particularly the more artefactual and developmental forms of risk factor theory. There has been a clear chronological evolution in the explanatory breadth and depth of risk factor theories (within and between groups of theories), as illustrated in the summary table provided in Appendix 2.

The majority of risk factors theories have been quasi-positivist and developmental/life course in orientation, privileging the deterministic, predictive influence of psychosocial 'risk factors' on later offending. More recent theories have incorporated an additional focus on ecological, socio-structural factors and situational/contextual influences on decision-making. Indeed, contemporary constructivist variants of risk factor theories (and the interactional developmental theory produced by the Edinburgh Study) have incorporated ideas from critical theories, such as considering the effects of labelling, criminogenic social interactions and young people's reactions to the exposure to risk. Contemporary constructivist pathways theories have extended the explanatory utility still further by considering the young person's capacity to construct, negotiate and resist their experiences of risk (factors and processes) and how these constructions may shape pathways/trajectories into and out of offending over the life course. So where does this leave us? The majority of risk factor theories of history have been inherently (quasi-)positivist and artefactual in methodology and **epistemology** – belief in the nature of knowledge, in this case, that (quasi-)positivist methods can generate knowledge of quantitative, controllable factors that are causal or predictive of offending. But is this artefactual hegemony justified or even beneficial? In Table 3.2, you are presented with five 'not-so-easy' controversies for consideration which relate to the alleged advantages/disadvantages of quasi-positivism and the developmental, artefactual risk factor theories it has produced. What do you think of each point?

The arguments from Table 3.2 suggest that (artefactual) risk factor theories have evolved an increasingly broad explanatory framework that has produced a widely replicated and practical evidence base. However, methodological and explanatory reductionism remain. Although constructivist pathways theories have emerged to challenge the reductionism of artefactual, developmental approaches, a challenge initiated by the life course theories of Sampson and Laub, the theories critical of artefactual approaches have been slow to acknowledge their similarities with these same theories, particularly in relation to developmentalism and psychosocial bias. Constructivist pathways theories, for example, have grown in largely developmental ways (see Lawrence 2007), measuring young people's ability to negotiate and respond to risk at different developmental stages in their lives. Such developmentalism has continued to assign significance across the life course to the psychosocial, childhood-based risk factors of artefactual, developmental theories, albeit providing for young people's capacity to construct and negotiate these risk factors. Furthermore, by adopting a bias towards psychosocial risk factors as their normative touchstone (the accepted standard/basis to which they keep returning), constructivist pathways theories have (to an extent) privileged the conclusions of earlier developmental theories (e.g. the criminal careers model of the Cambridge Study) that childhood exposure to risk factors is somehow predictive of offending in adolescence. The logical follow-on from this assumption is that psychosocial risk factors should form a key component of any explanatory model of the active, current influence of risk factors on the offending of much older age groups of young people.

A key conclusion from this chapter is that the evolution of risk factor theories has provided explanations of youth offending that are integrated yet predominantly developmental, deterministic and psychosocial/individualised in nature. The obvious exception here are constructivist pathways theories, which are more faithful in their explanations to notions of the social construction of 'youth offending' (see also Chapter 1). For quasi-positivist risk factor theories, the most significant departure from the hegemonic positivist theories that came before them has been their prospective focus on risk factors as predictive of future youth offending, as opposed to the retrospective identification of the causes of past offending. As such, risk factors theories have provided a clear, reliable and practical explanatory framework for linking academic explanations of youth offending to the responses of youth justice organisations and professionals (see for example Chapter 5). It is to the chronological and conceptual development of youth justice responses that we now turn.

TABLE 3.2 RISK FACTOR THEORIES – FIVE NOT-SO-EASY CONTROVERSIES

1 Explanatory utility

Integration	Determinism
Quasi-positivist, developmental, artefactual risk factor theories have always retained an integrated element to their explanations. This integration has taken the form of a fusion of biological, psychological and sociological factors or the integration of biopsychosocial factors with broader socio-structural, situational/contextual and agentic factors. Such integration has expanded the explanatory utility of theories beyond that of the traditionally dominant single factor/theory positivist explanations (see Chapter 2).	As a group, artefactual risk factor theories have been subject to criticism for the alleged excessive determinism and overconfidence of their conclusions regarding the predictive influence of risk factors on offending. This determinism appears to contradict the general lack of definitive understanding of the nature of the risk factor–offending relationship and the precise influence of risk factors (e.g. causal, predictive, symptomatic, interactional, no influence) on offending.

2 Practicality

Necessary reductionism	Reductionist oversimplification
The reduction of 'risk' to a static, quantifiable 'factor' enables easy statistical manipulation and analysis, producing clear, understandable findings. It is these very 'risk factors', identified as statistically related to offending, that practitioners can use as dynamic targets for evidence-based and effective preventative interventions. As such, reductionism is a necessary, practical tool that enables the prevention of youth offending. It provides definitive measures of risk as an agreed fact/reality, rather than as an ethereal, overly complex construction of no practical value. As Laub and Sampson (2003: 277) assert, 'the challenge is to find a middle ground between naïve reductionism and a wholism that does not allow for any precise explanation'.	Lack of conclusive evidence regarding the nature of the risk factor–offending relationship is a product of the reductionism that pervades artefactual risk factor theories, particularly the oversimplification of 'risk' into quantifiable, objective factors for the purposes of easy statistical analysis. Critics accuse artefactual explanations of artificially reducing the potential complexity of risk and young people's ability to experience and negotiate it, which questions the ecological validity of any real-world responses to measured risk (see Case and Haines 2009). It is this very determinism and reductionism that constructivist approaches have challenged by offering more complex, qualitative, sensitive and nuanced explanations of how the risk factor–offending relationship can be constructed and negotiated (more akin to critical rather than positivist theories).

3 Individualisation

Necessary individualisation	Psychosocial bias
The majority of risk factor studies have identified factors situated within the individual (e.g. psychological, emotional, attitudinal) and their immediate social environment (e.g. family, school, peer group, neighbourhood) as the key predictive influences on later offending.	The more qualitative, interpretivist and ethnographic approach of constructivist pathways theories has evolved risk factor explanations beyond their typically reductionist psychosocial bias into a consideration of broader socio-structural factors and social interactions/experiences (see Kemshall 2008). However, the extent

TABLE 3.2 continued

These individualised, psychosocial risk factors have been consistently replicated in studies across time, place and a sample group since risk factor theories became popular explanations of youth offending in the 1990s (see Farrington 2007). Therefore, it is sensible, evidence-based practice for academics, policy-makers and practitioners to examine and target individual risk factors as priority.

of this progression is debatable. Arguably, all risk factor theories have a significant element of psychosocial bias that inevitably individualises explanations of youth offending by prioritising risk factors within the young person, including agency/choice and the effects of socio-structural factors and interactions on these individualised, psychosocial factors.

4 Replicability

Replicability

Incomparability

Artefactual risk factor studies have produced a large, replicable evidence base that has consistently identified the same group of psychosocial risk factors as predictive of youth offending. Arguably, artefactual risk factor theories are therefore underpinned by the largest and most reliable evidence base of any explanatory theory of youth offending, albeit evidence largely generated since the 1990s. This replicable evidence base has supported arguments about artefactual risk factor theories that constitute a cohesive, **homogenous** (comparable, uniform) theoretical and explanatory framework for understanding youth offending (YJB 2003).

The chronological development of risk factor theories has produced a body of similar but always evolving and clearly **heterogeneous** (diverse, varied) explanations. On this basis, the explanations of youth offending from risk factor theories have not been strictly replicable over time and place, nor have they been necessarily generated using identical or equivalent methodologies or sample groups. Where replicability is evident, accusations of a self-fulfilling prophecy are possible. Critics assert that measuring and analysing the same restricted group of risk factors in the same ways over time and place will inevitably produce some degree of replicability, because 'if you do what you've always done, you get what you've always got' (Case 2007: 92).

5 Explanatory development

Evolves explanations

Devolves explanations

Risk factor theories have evolved understandings of youth offending beyond their traditional positivist, single factor/theory limitations by establishing an integrated explanatory component. Integrated explanations have developed to consider an ever-broader range of influences and interactions between psychosocial factors, socio-structural and contextual factors, situational contexts and individual constructions. The simplistic and common-sense nature of these integrated explanations has facilitated ready links between explanation and response, thus evolving academic theories/explanations into the area of practical utility (see Chapters 4 and 5).

Despite their integrated nature, most risk factor theories (except constructivist pathways) continue to individualise the causes and predictors of youth offending and to responsibilise young people for failing to resist the criminogenic influence of risk factors. An oversimplified, individualised, psychosocial bias and developmental determinism underpins the most dominant developmental, artefactual risk factor theories. In explanatory terms, these reductionist biases downplay the potentially criminogenic role of socio-structural factors, context and interactions with the Youth Justice System, along with neglecting the potential for young people to be active constructors of their own life experiences.

5 EASY PIECES

Recommended further reading

The explanatory theories outlined in this chapter are discussed and evaluated in more detail in *Understanding Youth Offending: Risk Factor Research, Policy and Practice* by Stephen Case and Kevin Haines (2009). The book evaluates the evidence base for risk factor theories, exploring their methodologies, analytical techniques, conclusions and application in youth justice practice across the industrialised Western world. *Understanding Youth Offending* is essential reading for anybody wishing to understand risk factor explanations of crime, contemporary youth justice policy and responses to offending behaviour.

For a general overview of the central principles, methodologies and explanations of artefactual risk factor theories from their most influential proponent, students are directed towards the chapter 'Childhood Risk Factors and Risk-Focused Prevention' by David Farrington in the fourth edition of the *Oxford Handbook of Criminology* (Maguire *et al.* 2007). Farrington presents his arguments clearly, confidently and logically, so engaging with this chapter will leave you in no doubt as to the main elements of artefactual risk factor theories.

If you can track it down, the edited text *Taking Stock of Delinquency* by Terence Thornberry and Marvin Krohn (2003) makes fascinating reading. It covers the key integrated developmental risk factor theories and studies, including the Cambridge Study, the social development model and the Causes and Correlates studies (plus others not covered in this chapter) in methodological, evidential and explanatory detail.

Both *Crime in the Making* by Robert Sampson and John Laub (1993) and *Shared Beginnings, Divergent Lives* by Laub and Sampson (2003) are highly recommended. It could be argued that the age-graded theory of informal social control set out in these texts constitutes a middle ground between artefactual and constructivist risk factor theories. Furthermore, both texts outline an innovative and stimulating piece of research in a dynamic, clear and well-structured manner.

Finally, the best resource for a gaining a deeper understanding of constructivist pathways explanations is the edited text *Pathways and Crime Prevention: Theory, Policy and Practice* by Alan France and Ross Homel (2007). The central concepts, studies and explanatory theories of constructivism are discussed in depth by a range of talented researchers and scholars in this book. As such, it provides an ideal counterpoint to the hegemonic arguments of artefactual risk factor theories.

APPENDIX 2

THE EVOLUTION OF RISK FACTOR THEORY EXPLANATIONS

Theory	Explanation	Progression
Biopsychosocial developmental (Glueck and Glueck 1930, 1950; Cabot 1940; West and Farrington 1973).	Exposure to biopsychosocial risk factors in early life predicts later offending.	Identifies the predictors of future offending (for intervention purposes), not the causes of past/current offending.
Integrated developmental (Hawkins and Weis 1985; Catalano and Hawkins 1996; Wikstrom and Loeber 2000; Farrington 2005; Wikstrom 2008).	Interactions between biopsychosocial risk factors, rational choice, socio-structural factors and context in early life predict later offending.	Integrates rational choice and structural/contextual considerations.
Interactional developmental (Thornberry and Krohn 2003; Smith and McVie 2003).	Reciprocal interactions between risk factors and offending and criminogenic interactions between the young person and the YJS can lead to offending.	Explores the criminogenic influences of offending behaviour in its own right and system contact.
Age-graded life course (Sampson and Laub 1993; Laub and Sampson 2003).	Interactions between psychosocial risk factors, structural context, informal social controls and agency over the life course produce offending.	Extends developmental understandings across the life course, considers the influence of informal social controls and accounts for stability and change in offending behaviour.
Constructivist pathways (Kemshall 2003; Hine 2005; Macdonald and Marsh 2005).	Young people are able to actively construct, negotiate and resist their exposure to risk factors/processes, which shapes their pathways into and out of offending.	Expands artefactual theories by considering the influence of the individual's constructions of risk on their offending and desistance pathways/trajectories.

Responding to youth offending

The social construction of youth justice

4

The previous chapters have explored the social constructions of 'youth offending' through changing definitions and explanations over time, citing a recurring theme/ dichotomy of conflict and ambivalence surrounding how to understand and respond to young people who offend. We have journeyed through the socially constructed definitions of 'children' as simultaneously innocent/vulnerable and dangerous/threatening, leading into the social distinction between innocent children and threatening adolescents, which essentially provided a route into the social construction of 'youth offending' (see Chapter 1). Confusion and debate has been exacerbated by differing explanations of youth offending (see Chapters 2 and 3) by **key stakeholders** (participants in youth justice processes with a vested interest in them) in different historical periods. Traditional classicism versus positivism debates have wrestled with explanations of youth offending as the product of chance or predetermined factors, which in turn favour deterrent/controlling or rehabilitative/therapeutic (youth justice) responses. Similarly, positivist theories have struggled internally to resolve the aetiological (causal) dichotomies of nature–nurture, deprivation–depravation and personal–social; each of which recommends different forms of (youth justice) response (see Chapter 2). Critical theories have viewed youth offending as a socially constructed product of power and criminalisation processes (e.g. labelling). However, realist theories have undermined these critical perspectives by casting them as idealistic and impractical. The contemporary resolution to explanatory conflict and ambivalence has been the rise of quasi-positivist, developmental and artefactual risk factor theories (see Chapter 3), which offer simplistic, common-sense explanations of youth offending to inform practical, effective youth justice methods – clearly linking explanations to responses.

RESPONSES: TRIANGULATING THE 'TRIAD OF YOUTH JUSTICE'

The socially constructed definitions and explanations of youth offending have informed and shaped official 'youth justice' responses to youth offending. The social construction of 'youth justice' has been animated by the creation of bespoke, distinct *responses*[1] in the form of *philosophies* (e.g. welfare versus justice), *structures* (e.g. reformatory schools) and *systems* (e.g. bespoke juvenile/youth justice systems) to house and animate the youth justice *policies/strategies* (e.g. government laws and legislation) and *practices* (e.g. risk management, multi-agency working). The aim of this chapter is to present, explore and evaluate the nature of youth justice over history, particularly the nature of change in its socially constructed components and the role of key stakeholders (e.g. politicians, academics, media) in their (re)construction. Broadly speaking, these conflicting and ambivalent socio-cultural and political constructions of children and youth over history have informed similarly conflicting and ambivalent responses to youth offending and guiding philosophies for youth justice systems. Academics and politicians have broadly categorised this perennial ambivalence as the 'welfare versus justice debate' (cf. Smith 2005): the battle between prioritising the welfare, care and reform of children who offend as opposed to responding primarily in terms of executing justice, control and punishment. This debate/dichotomy has also been characterised as 'care versus control', 'reform versus punishment' and 'needs versus deeds'. However constructed, the debate/dichotomy concerns whether youth justice should prioritise responding to the offender/offence or the child/young person. The dichotomies have been played out in responses that variously save/rescue neglected and abused children from abusive adults and then educate and train these children to achieve positive outcomes, or save/rescue society (adults) from dangerous and threatening children by removing these children from their families and deporting, incarcerating or otherwise separating them (Shore 2011). In line with the 'triad of youth justice', interactions and overlaps between different elements of youth justice (e.g. philosophies, structures, strategies, practices) have contributed to the social (re)construction (e.g. creation, consolidation, perpetuation, exaggeration) of youth offending in terms of its perceived extent (amount) and nature (type).

In line with the established structure across the book, Chapter 4 adopts a five-stage approach, distinguishing five broad chronological periods[2] to enable the exploration and categorisation of significant youth justice developments. The five chronological stages by which responses are categorised are intended to map directly onto the five stages from the definitions chapter and more broadly onto the periods of theoretical development outlined in the explanations chapters (especially Chapter 2), ensuring a consistent focus on the 'triad of youth justice' that shapes this book. Accordingly, there is a degree of necessary, useful overlap with and consolidation of information presented in Chapter 1. This is inevitable when analysing the 'triad of youth justice', wherein definitions and responses can be inextricably linked in certain historical periods.

The chapter begins by exploring the widespread use of punitive custody for children in the first half of the nineteenth century and how this exemplified a punitive, justice-based response to (the as-yet untitled/unlabelled) behaviour of 'youth offending'. Discussion will move to the growing criticism of the appropriateness of custody for children and the subsequent introduction of welfare-orientated reforms in the mid-nineteenth century, most notably those from the Youthful Offenders Act 1854, which effectively formalised the welfare versus justice debate. What follows is a discussion of the formalisation of justice-based responses to youth offending from the start of the twentieth century through legislation introducing key youth justice structures – the juvenile court and borstals. The penultimate section focuses on the growing welfare versus justice conflict in the second half of the twentieth century, which was reflected in contrasting legislation and practices such as Intermediate Treatment (more welfare based) in the 1970s and an emphasis on diversion (more justice based) in the 1980s. The final section provides an overview of the 'punitive turn' in youth justice since the 1990s and the increasing emphasis on managerialism reflected in risk management approaches, which is contrasted with the growing children's rights movement reflected by 'child-friendly justice'.

5 EASY PIECES

Responding to youth offending: the social construction of youth justice

1   *The social construction of youth justice (pre-1850)* explores the early social construction of bespoke responses to offending by children in an era of control and custody, most notably the creation of youth justice *structures* (e.g. prison statistics, Parkhurst Prison) and an emerging *philosophy* that custody was harmful and inappropriate for children.

2   *Addressing the innocent–dangerous child dichotomy through welfare (1850–1900)*
    examines the steady move away from punitive custodial responses and towards
    differentiated (youth justice) responses to children who offended (e.g. the
    reformatory school) and to children perceived as neglected, in need and 'pre-
    criminal' (e.g. the industrial school).

3   *Addressing the innocent–dangerous child dichotomy through justice (1900–1950)*
    discusses the continuation of the welfare versus justice debate into the twentieth
    century with the legislative creation of 'new youth justice' structures (e.g. juve-
    nile courts, borstals, professional social work departments for troubled children)
    that pursued bifurcated (twin-track) welfare–justice objectives such as simultane-
    ous education and correction.

4   *Creating a distinct 'youth justice': welfare versus justice (1950–1990)* outlines a
    period of youth justice development that epitomised the conflict and ambiva-
    lence of welfare versus justice through contradictory legislation, strategies and
    practices (e.g. Intermediate Treatment, systems management, diversion) that
    were constructed and implemented in ambiguous ways.

5   *Punitive, practical, protective: the punitive turn, risk management and child-friendly
    justice (1990 onwards)* traces the development of contemporary models of youth
    justice beyond welfare—justice to incorporate neo-liberalism, minimal interven-
    tion and restorative justice, before setting out three discernible modern youth
    justice movements: *punitive* approaches based on the 'punitive turn' towards
    control, correction and custody; *practical* approaches grounded in risk manage-
    ment; and *protective* approaches coalescing into a positive, rights-compliant
    'child-friendly justice'.

1 THE SOCIAL CONSTRUCTION OF YOUTH JUSTICE (PRE-1850)

It is argued in our opening chapter that responses to children who offended prior
to the mid-nineteenth century were typically punitive (see Ariès 1962; see Smith
[2011] and Pollock [1983] for critiques of this position) and equivalent to the criminal justice responses aimed at adult offenders (e.g. deportation, imprisonment in
adult institutions). Children were treated like adults in society, with no distinct
legal or socio-political rights, largely because the category of 'childhood' had yet to
be socially constructed. As such, children were not yet subjected to **adulterisation**
(treatment as if they were adults; see also Chapters 1 and 5), because to all intents
and purposes, children *were* (little) adults. In the first half of the nineteenth century,
control in the form of custody was the preferred response to crime, with deportation
being phased out for political reasons (e.g. its lack of popularity in the colonies), and
there was little differentiation between children and adults in terms of punishment
and justice (May 1973). In explanatory terms, rational choice theories, with their
rejection of the causes of offending and the potential for rehabilitation/treatment,
were dominating criminological thinking and their explanations linked neatly with
the deterrence and incapacitation principles that underpinned the use of custody

as a preferred punishment. As discussed in Chapter 1, the historical period from 1820 to 1850 was particularly significant in the social construction of the child as distinct from the adult. Most notably, the creation of prison statistics during this period highlighted that although prisoners tended to be distinguished by offence seriousness, they were rarely segregated by age, leading to free association between relatively innocent children and mature, hardened, career criminals (see May 1973). Such a toxic mix of prisoners ran the risk of damaging and further criminalising children in custody. Added to this, the rapidly expanding prison population was encouraging politicians and **penal** (relating to the punishment of offenders via the legal system) reformers throughout the 1830s and 1840s to look towards the classification and segregation of prisoners by age – citing the success of such methods in the US (Henriques 1972). These arguments and findings led social reformers, politicians and academics to question the appropriateness of imprisonment for children (see also Chapter 1).

RTA = ECONOMIC/POLITICAL POLICY DRIVERS OF PROGRESSION

Penal policies may be motivated more by economic concerns and political expedience than principled responses to child welfare or critical reflection on evidence and academic theory. For a more contemporary example, see the progressive changes to post-2010 youth justice in the form of revised out-of-court and assessment-intervention frameworks (see Chapter 6).

A major step towards the segregation and special treatment of children who offended was the creation of Parkhurst Prison, which opened in 1838 with the objective of training young male offenders prior to their transportation to penal colonies. The social construction of this 'new youth justice' *structure* for children who offended reduced prisoner numbers and thus reduced 'mass contamination' in other custodial institutions (May 1973). The knock-on effect was that once again, children who offended became more visible in society (see also Chapter 1 discussion of the Industrial Revolution) and the need for them to receive special attention and special treatment entered the public and political consciousness. In this case, a reformation movement swept across prisons in the 1830s and 1840s, with a new breed of prison governors and prison chaplains keen to promote innovative methods of reforming the children in their care. This move towards reform over punishment and care over control indicates a change in the philosophy of youth justice responses at the time – a move towards prioritising the welfare of the child over exacting justice for the offence. However, new reform objectives were hampered by the increasing criminalisation of children in society, which led to exponential increases in the number of child offenders in custody.

RTA = CRIMINALISATION AND RESPONSIBILISATION

The counter-intuitive and counterproductive criminalisation and harming of children through responsibilising criminal (youth) justice responses that fail to meet their psychological and physical needs. Such harmful and damaging responses are commonly described as iatrogenic/harmful (see McAra and McVie 2007).

This dichotomy of increasing faith in reform simultaneous to the increasing criminalisation of children led the Surveyor-General of Prisons, Joshua Jebb, to assert that he did 'not think that the present prisons are at all adapted to juveniles' (Select Committee on Prison Discipline 1850, in Shore 2011). This would be the first shot in a long-standing debate as to the suitability of custody as a response to offending by children (see my 'Conversation' with Dr Tim Bateman in Chapter 6). Penal reformers began to criticise prisons for their corruption of the young specifically, rather than for the corruption of all inmates. The central thesis was that imprisonment was especially damaging (e.g. psychologically, emotionally, physically) for children in the short term and stigmatising and damaging their life chances (e.g. education, employment, relationship building) in the long term – thus custody was inappropriate for children.

5 EASY PIECES

1 The social construction of youth justice (pre-1850)

1 *Custodial control*: in the first half of the nineteenth century, control of offenders in the form of custody was the preferred response to crime (deportation was being phased out) and there was little differentiation between children and adults in terms of punishment and justice.
2 *Prison statistics*: the creation of prison statistics during 1820–1850 highlighted the lack of segregation by age in custodial institutions and the potential for a toxic mix between innocent children and hardened adult offenders.
3 *The first youth prison*: Parkhurst Prison was opened in 1838 as a bespoke youth justice structure to respond to the need for the segregation and special treatment of child offenders in custody.
4 *Punitiveness, criminalisation and responsibilisation*: the excessive use of punitive custody and lack of recognition of children as distinct from adults introduced the recurrent themes of criminalising and responsibilising youth justice responses into the analysis of the social construction of youth justice.
5 *Custody as inappropriate for children*: towards the end of the first half of the nineteenth century, socio-political attitudes towards custody had changed and it became increasingly viewed as inappropriate for children, signifying a move away from punitive, justice-based responses to children who offended.

2 ADDRESSING THE INNOCENT–DANGEROUS CHILD DICHOTOMY THROUGH WELFARE (1850–1900)

The crisis of confidence regarding imprisoning children in the first half of the nineteenth century reflected the conflict and ambivalence in society regarding offending as a threatening, dangerous behaviour committed by otherwise innocent and vulnerable children. A penal by-product was the inconsistent, uncertain use of court sentencing by magistrates and judges, who struggled to reconcile the view of innocent children in need of care (e.g. welfare and reform responses) with the social construction of 'juvenile delinquency' as requiring control through justice and punishment responses more suited to the adult-orientated sentences available to them. Systemic uncertainty and social ambivalence were exacerbated by the differing views of the moral and cognitive capacity of juvenile delinquents that were given to the Select Committee of 1852–1853. Expert opinion varied widely regarding the capacity of children who broke the law to distinguish between right and wrong, ranging from 10 to 16 years old. These estimates were all higher than the age of criminal responsibility at that time (7 years old), and they offered dramatically differing understandings of children's moral and cognitive capacity – furthering ambivalence about how best to understand and respond to children who offended.

The Youthful Offenders Act 1854: reformatory schools

The dichotomy of the innocent child (from the 'perishing classes') versus threatening child (from the 'dangerous classes') was met with a legislative compromise in the form of the Youthful Offenders Act 1854. The Act was inspired by the proposals of social reformer Mary Carpenter, who had identified the perishing–dangerous classes dichotomy. It legislated for official responses to children who offended to be differentiated from criminal justice responses to adult offenders through the creation of the reformatory school. The Act also foregrounded a bespoke response to neglected, needy, 'precriminal' children in the form of the industrial school (formally introduced by the Industrial Schools Act 1857). The most significant youth justice development within this legislation was the creation of distinct *structures* for children in need compared to children convicted due to offending behaviour (an early welfare–justice distinction). The overarching emphasis of the Act was on reform over punishment as the guiding *philosophy* for responding to children who offended. Children in reformatory schools (also known as 'reformatories') were to receive correctional and rehabilitative training to compensate for defective parenting and damaging neighbourhood experiences while preparing them for a life of labour. They were treated more as wards of the State than as labelled offenders deserving of punishment. Despite the welfare focus of reformatory schools, the use of custody for children was not entirely abolished. Reformatory school entry was preceded by imprisonment of up to two weeks as a concession to critics who felt that the measure would lack a sufficiently punitive element without it (May 1973). Reformatory schools animated the principle of parens patriae (Arthur 2016), where the monarch or other authority such as the State is regarded as the legal protector of citizens unable to protect themselves (e.g. vulnerable and neglected children). According to Burfeind and Bartusch (2006), the social construction of youth offending is the product of three main influences: the invention of childhood and adolescence (see Chapter 1), positivism (see Chapter 2) and parens patriae (see later in this chapter).

RTA = RESPONSIBILISING PARENTS

The reformatory schools and industrial schools of the mid-nineteenth century were structures created to animate middle-class standards of parenting and to use legislation to enforce these standards upon working-class parents. Parents were increasingly held responsible (through processes of responsibilisation) for the upbringing (moral, psychological, physical), behaviour and reform of their child. If they were seen to be failing and neglectful in this duty and raising their child 'in such a way as to almost secure his becoming a criminal' (Select Committee on Criminal and Destitute Juveniles 1852: 119, in Shore 2011), then legislation allowed for the parents to be punished and the child to be formally removed from the family in order to protect the child's welfare. The responsibilisation of parents was intended to be a method of incentivising them to improve their parenting approaches and to keep their children off the streets, thus reducing youth offending.

In the second half of the nineteenth century, the desire to punish children if they offended was diminishing. Previous punitive methods such as imprisonment, whipping and transportation were being replaced by new structures of institutional surveillance and control, including reformatory schools and industrial schools, which set out 'to treat these children not by way of punishing them – which is no remedy – but with a view to their reformation' (Lord Advocate 1908, in Pinchbeck and Hewitt 1981). The late nineteenth century heralded the establishment of a separate *system* for responding to children who offended (although it is debatable as to whether there was an officially labelled 'youth justice system' until 1998), wherein 'the experience of the industrial and reformatory school system, surely created the environment in which the behaviour and psychologies of working-class children became so important' (Shore 2011: 110). These early Victorian debates about reformatory practice were crucial to the social construction of the 'juvenile delinquent' (Rush 1992). The legislative, governmental establishment of reformatory and industrial schools marked a radical change in penal policy, recognising juvenile delinquency as a distinct behavioural category and recognising the State's responsibility to both young people who offended and children who required care and protection. Children coming before the courts were no longer regarded as little adults (May 1973). Consequently, the punitive imprisonment of children decreased dramatically until the end of the nineteenth century and a move towards welfare and away from punitive forms of justice-based approaches can be discerned – although the perennial welfare–justice tensions remained. Furthermore, the construction of the reformatory school extended the care–control dichotomy in youth justice into one of support–control for young people who had offended (see also Chapter 5) through its dual focus on reform/education (support) and correction/custody (control); while the industrial school retained more of a care–control focus when working with non-offenders.

5 EASY PIECES

2 Addressing the innocent–dangerous child dichotomy through welfare (1850–1900)

1 *Conflict and ambivalence*: in the second half of the nineteenth century, criminal justice professionals were struggling to resolve the innocent–dangerous child dichotomy (which can be seen as a paradox) in their responses to children who offended.
2 *Age of criminal responsibility*: conflict and ambivalence regarding appropriate youth justice responses were exacerbated by divergence in expert opinion regarding the appropriate age of criminal responsibility.
3 *Legislating for youth justice*: the Youthful Offenders Act 1854 was a legislative compromise that allowed for differentiated (youth justice) responses to children who offended, namely reformatory schools. Pre-offending, problematic and neglected children were sent to the industrial schools created through the Industrial Schools Act in 1857.
4 *Reform*: children in reformatory schools received corrective and educational training and reform to compensate for defective parenting and harmful experiences in their local neighbourhoods; an early incarnation of the support–control dichotomy (an extension of care–control) in youth justice.
5 *Moving away from punishment*: the desire to punish children who offended diminished from 1850 to 1900 and a separate, welfare-led, reform-based system of juvenile justice began to emerge.

3 ADDRESSING THE INNOCENT–DANGEROUS CHILD DICHOTOMY THROUGH JUSTICE (1900–1950)

The Youth Offenders Act 1854 legislated for changes in structural responses to children/young people demonstrating problems through offending behaviour; encouraging new ideas about how children/young people should be treated by the State. The tentative differentiation of the treatment of children/young people was further supported by emerging positivist academic theories that explained offending as the product of biological and psychological factors, which could be particularly influential during the developmental stage of adolescence (see Chapter 2). From the 1880s onwards, social reformers began to call for the introduction of new *structures* for responding to youth offending, for example, a special court to handle cases of offending involving children and young people (Behlmer 1998). The first half of the twentieth century ushered in more use of justice-based, offender-focused responses to offending by children, reflecting the ongoing tensions between welfare and justice as to which was the most appropriate philosophy to underpin youth justice. The Children Act 1908 formalised a new 'juvenile court' in Great Britain as part of a broader consolidation of existing legislation, such as refining the roles of **reformatory** schools and industrial schools (Hendrick 1994). The introduction of the juvenile court in Great Britain in 1908 (similar courts had already been established in Western

Australia in 1895 and Colorado and Chicago in the US in 1899: Platt 2009; Pruin, in Dunkel *et al*. 2010) marked the first step towards a piecemeal introduction of a formal and distinct, fully bespoke juvenile/youth justice *system* (Case and Haines 2010).

The second significant legislative development under the Children Act 1908 was the formal introduction of **borstals** as education-focused custodial institutions/wings for youths aged 16–21 years old who offended. As discussed in Chapter 1, the dual purpose of borstals was to instruct/socialise and to reform/treat. The Gladstone Committee (1895) had initially proposed the borstal as means of separating youths from adult offenders in adult prisons. The first borstal was established in 1902 at Borstal Prison near Rochester in Kent, England. Formalising borstals under the Children Act 1908 meant introducing a bespoke, youth-focused *structure* and *process* designed to be 'educational rather than punitive' (ostensibly more welfare-orientated) and also focused on rehabilitation, in accordance with the potential for individual reform supported by emerging (biopsychological) positivist theories at that time. At the same time, borstals were intended to be highly regulated (ostensibly more justice-orientated) and concerned with providing regular work, routine, discipline and authority (Arthur 2016). As such, borstals offered a further illustration of the support–control dichotomy in youth justice, simultaneously providing supportive intervention to young people who had offended, while controlling their behaviour and movements within a highly regulated custodial environment. Borstal sentences were indeterminate (a common criticism of welfare approaches), with young people kept in custody until they were considered to be properly socialised or too old to be socialised (i.e. they had become adults). Borstals were not officially abolished until the Criminal Justice Act 1982. By that time, they were seen as outdated and no longer seen as fit for purpose, so were replaced with youth custody centres.

RTA = THE TWENTIETH-CENTURY PARENTING CRISIS

The family is in 'crisis', and/or the parents are 'failing', comprises a cyclical phenomenon with a very long history.

(Day-Sclater and Piper 2000)

The responsibilisation of parents, holding them primarily responsible (fairly or excessively) for the offending behaviour of their child, is a recurring theme in the sociohistorical construction of youth offending and one we return to throughout this book. As is clear from the discussions thus far, the social construction of a troublesome developmental stage known as 'adolescence' was fused with a focus on inadequate parenting from the nineteenth century onwards to produce a responsibilising discourse (i.e. a narrative discussion assigning responsibility) explaining juvenile delinquency as a result of flaws and deficits in the child, the family and relationships between the two. We have seen, for example, how the 1816 Alarming Increases Committee identified a series of parenting deficits concluded to be the main causes of juvenile delinquency (see Chapter 1): 'improper conduct of parents', 'neglect of parental authority', 'permitting absence from school', 'laxity of morals' and 'weakness' being the main flaws (Goldson and Jamieson 2002: 83).

Across the first half of the twentieth century, the key explanation for juvenile delinquency was a lack of responsibility, morality and discipline on the part of adolescents, exacerbated by similar weaknesses in 'dysfunctional' parents. This perspective was given academic credibility by the biopsychological explanations of Cyril Burt (1925), which focused on the damaging influence of defective family relationships and discipline, consolidating the public view that inadequate parenting combined with the adolescent developmental stage to create juvenile delinquency.

The 1925 Home Office Departmental Committee on the Treatment of Young Offenders (the 'Molony Committee') and its successor, the Children and Young Persons Act 1933, established the courtroom as 'a site for adjudicating on matters of family socialisation and parental behaviour' (Muncie 1984: 45). The 1933 Act cemented the view of children as vulnerable and innocent victims of social disadvantage, raising the age of criminal responsibility from 7 to 8 years old and stating that 'there is little or no difference in character and needs between the delinquent and neglected child' (cited in Hendrick 1994: 182). The legislation further cemented the growing hegemony of child welfare approaches (e.g. probation, approved schools, boarding schools) over punishment and justice-based methods, hinting at another recurring theme in our responses to youth offending – welfare versus justice as the primary concern for youth justice. The 1933 legislation constitutes a watershed in youth justice policy – the formalisation of parental responsibility for youth offending. In a political climate where the needs and vulnerabilities of children were gaining importance, parents were being held incrementally responsible if their children offended, as this behaviour was perceived as a failure of socialisation and effective parenting.

The responsibilisation of parents has not been confined to the UK; it is a recurring theme of youth justice that has been reflected internationally. For example, the importance of parenting as a control against youth offending was the most significant feature of the juvenile court system in the US from its inception in 1899 until the 1960s. For the majority of the twentieth century, the juvenile court in the US worked to a civil-therapeutic model rather than a criminal-punitive model, identifying young people's problems and acting in loco parentis to offer them the guidance, care and supervision required to become mature, responsible adults (Bishop and Feld 2012; Zimring 2000).

The structural youth justice developments of the period 1900–1950, namely juvenile courts and borstals, were extended (legislatively) by increasing the age of criminal responsibility from 7 to 8 years old under the Children and Young Persons Act 1933. Consequently, the first half of the twentieth century was characterised by structural and legal changes that socially reconstructed youth justice towards more justice-led approaches than had been adopted in the previous (welfare-orientated) century. However, conflict and ambivalence regarding how to most appropriately respond to young people who offended did not disappear, and welfare-justice tensions remained. Indeed, as the half century came to a close, the Children and Young Persons Act 1948 established the first professional social workers to be allocated to work with troubled children, signifying a return to prominence for welfare-based responses to youth offending.

5 EASY PIECES

3 Addressing the innocent–dangerous child dichotomy through justice (1900–1950)

1   *The juvenile court*: the Children Act 1908 formalised the juvenile court in Great Britain, a legislative and structural development that was informed by foregoing legislation (e.g. the Youthful Offenders Act 1854), developments in social science (especially positivism) and similar structural approaches internationally.
2   *A nascent system of youth justice*: juvenile courts can be seen as a first step towards establishing a separate, formal system of youth justice in Great Britain.
3   *Borstals*: the Children Act 1908 also introduced borstals as custodial schools for correction, education and training for 16- to 21-year-old young offenders.
4   *Education, rehabilitation and reform*: borstals represented a distinct move away from the punishment of young offenders and towards educational, rehabilitative and reform approaches to delivering youth justice, thus illustrating the ongoing care–control, support–control and reform–punishment dichotomies in youth justice.
5   *Professional social workers*: the Children and Young Persons Act 1948 introduced the first professional social workers for troubled children, signifying a re-emergence of welfare within youth justice and exemplifying the conflict and ambivalence that has characterised the social construction of youth justice historically.

4 CREATING A DISTINCT 'YOUTH JUSTICE': WELFARE VERSUS JUSTICE (1950–1990)

Throughout the twentieth century until the beginning of the 1970s, there was a notable positive turn away from the punishment and control of children and young people who offended towards responses based on care and welfare measures. For example, the Children and Young Persons Act 1948 advanced the social agenda further through raising the age of criminal responsibility to 10, while the acts of the same name in 1963 and 1969 promoted a focus on responding to offending through social work-based therapeutic relationship building (1963) and by proposing a further extension of the age of criminal responsibility to 14, alongside giving more discretion to social services over criminal justice agencies (1969). As we learned from the opening chapter, however, a 1970 change of government meant that the Children and Young Persons Act 1969 was not fully implemented, nor was its intention of raising the age of criminal responsibility and abolishing borstals and detention centres. That said, a range of new welfare-based sentences for young offenders and children in need were introduced (e.g. care orders and supervision orders), as were residential homes with an educational emphasis and a new form of *practice* response known as 'Intermediate Treatment'. The zenith of welfare-based responses to youth offending promised by the 1969 Act was never fully realised, but welfare remained an important philosophy to guide youth justice responses. However, justice-based, punitive responses (e.g. custody) were equally high profile (particularly for adolescents), reflected in the structural and organisational tensions between newly created social services departments (armed with a host of welfarist interventions) and the juvenile/youth court with its range of justice-based, punitive sentencing options – classic welfare versus justice (Haines and Drakeford 1998).

Intermediate treatment: British youth justice in the 1970s

The term 'Intermediate Treatment' first appeared in a **Government White Paper** (a policy document setting out proposals for future legislation) released in 1968 and called *Children in Trouble*. This document preceded the Children and Young Persons Act 1969, which had proposed to raise the age of criminal responsibility to 14 years old and to give more discretion to social services regarding the nature of responses to young people who offended (see earlier in this chapter and also Chapter 1). **Intermediate Treatment** (commonly known as IT) referred to working with children who were considered 'at risk' of offending and other problematic outcomes in a way that was 'intermediate' between work in the family context and work with children once they had been removed from home and placed in a childcare institution.

IT typically consisted of face-to-face work with children, although the precise nature of this work was never clearly defined or understood by policy-makers or practitioners. The youth justice responses associated with IT were diverse, and much of the work social workers and probation officers conducted with children considered to be 'in trouble' was labelled IT. The professional social workers working in the newly created local authority social services departments (established by the 1969 Act) worked with (mainly disadvantaged) 'at-risk' children who were presenting problem behaviours or experiencing problems caused by others (typically adults). As such, the term 'at risk' was as loose and ill-defined as the concept of IT.

Philosophically, despite the catch-all nature of its label and method of implementation, IT was always intended to provide *welfare-* and *needs-focused* intervention and to be made available to a broader range of children in trouble (not just offenders) on a voluntary basis or as part of a formal Supervision Order made by the courts (Haines 1996). For most children and young people identified as 'at risk', social workers and the local social services department were the main service providers, whereas young people (aged 14 and over) appearing in the juvenile court received their interventions from probation offices and the probation service, except where they were already known to social services. This exception paved the way for the gradually diminishing role of the probation service in the juvenile court and in work with young offenders. As stated, the prevailing philosophy of IT across the 1970s was that of a welfare-based, needs-led youth justice response promoting positive intervention with children. As a consequence, social workers actively sought to work with increasing numbers of children in ways that promoted their 'best interests'. In practice, local areas developed IT in different ways, but there were common overarching themes to interventions, typically cohering around activities that were community-based, group work-focused, outward bounds–oriented and educational (Haines 1996).

RTA = LOCAL MEDIATION OF CENTRALISED PRACTICE REQUIREMENTS

IT illustrates how the centralised (government) practice requirements of legislation/policy can be mediated and moderated locally by policy-makers and practitioners in response to local context and the expertise, discretion, resources and objectives of local organisations and individuals.

The welfare-based intentions of the Children and Young Persons Act 1969 were only partially implemented in the 1970s following an immediate change of government in the UK. Consequently, the juvenile court continued to exist, with its own range of sentencing options (e.g. custody) that both complemented and ostensibly conflicted with IT. However, the potential for conflict between welfare and justice approaches at that time was *not* always realised in practice:

> While there has indeed been a great deal of conflict at the ideological level . . . this simply has not happened in practice. The two systems [welfare and justice] have, in effect, become vertically integrated, and an additional population of customer-clients has been identified in order to ensure that they both have plenty of work to do.
>
> (Thorpe *et al.* 1980: 22–23)

Conflict and ambivalence in youth justice responses were apparent, however, in the increasing rates of youth custody (ostensibly demonstrating a justice response) and increasing rates of residential care for children and young people (ostensibly demonstrating a welfare response) – on the basis that care was not punishment but was supportive. However, the increasing numbers of children/young people entering care at an early stage in the YJS as a consequence of welfarist interventions did nothing to reduce the problem of increasing numbers in penal custody at a later stage in the YJS, so it appeared that both welfare and justice responses to youth offending were failing in practice in the 1970s. The main explanations for 'failing' youth justice at the time were aimed at *poor decision-making*, most notably reflected in the report writing of social workers and probation officers. Morris *et al.* (1980: 42) summarised this critique:

> Because we do not understand the significance of much juvenile 'misconduct', the various reports presented to decision-makers contain value judgments and unfounded assumptions. As a general rule, we do not know with certainty which factors refer to, or which situations indicate which form of treatment. . . . As such, these reports are useless guides to choosing dispositions, but these 'facts' then justify the form and content of intervention.

Thorpe *et al.* (1980: 3) were even more direct in their critique, stating that 'cumulatively, these disparate bodies of professionals made the wrong decisions about the role children at the wrong time'. A notable example of these so-called wrong decisions was Thorpe *et al.*'s finding that social workers (ostensibly welfare-oriented in their professional culture) were significantly more likely to recommend custody for young people than were probation officers. Simultaneous to this critique of professional decision-making, there was a dramatic loss of faith in the utility of rehabilitation and treatment across the 1970s – the 'collapse of the rehabilitative ideal' (Allen 1991). The claim that 'nothing works' in terms of programmes to rehabilitate offenders (Martinson 1974) gained popularity internationally in the criminal justice field and was used to justify intervention (sometimes excessive interventionism) in the lives of young people who offended during this period (Haines 1996).

A return to justice: the 1980s revolution

At the end of the 1970s and into the early 1980s, the vociferous debate continued as to whether responses to/interventions with so-called children in trouble should prioritise their welfare or more justice-based considerations. Welfare responses were largely reserved for children and young people who came to the attention of social workers for their offending (or other issues that placed them 'at risk' of problematic behaviours and outcomes), with interventions typically focused on the individual's needs and methods to improve their social functioning (Hendrick 1994). Conversely, justice-based responses focused more on identified offenders and adopted interventions proportionate to the seriousness of the offending behaviour (the principle of **proportionality**), in opposition to the discretionary and indeterminate nature of welfare approaches. In the early 1980s, the probation service was falling into disrepair due to the collapse of the 'rehabilitative ideal', yet social work with young people experiencing problems appeared to be growing in strength and popularity (Haines 1996). Evaluations of the ways that youth justice was being delivered and developed focused increasingly on *decision-making* by youth justice professionals (e.g. magistrates, judges, police officers, social workers, probation officers). The prevailing belief was that a more focused and tightly managed approach to youth justice was required, based on a series of common criticisms, helpfully caricatured by one of my favourite youth justice academics, the witty and outspoken John Pitts:

- Youth crime is not a serious problem.
- Politicians and policy-makers make consistent 'idiotic' mistakes when formulating and implementing policy, which further criminalises young people.
- Professionals seeking to help in reality can be a major hindrance to young offenders.
- Residential and custodial care for young offenders is damaging.
- Community-based interventions for young offenders are far preferable.
- **Radical non-intervention** is the most desirable youth justice response – leaving young offenders alone to grow out of crime and not be damaged by intervention.
- Welfare considerations should be excluded from the juvenile court and dealt with elsewhere.

(Pitts 1988)

The overriding emphasis in youth justice during the 1980s was that improved decision-making processes would lead to more appropriate, proportionate and determinate justice-based responses to young offenders – an approach that became known as **new orthodoxy thinking** (Jones 1984). This new approach was simultaneously a set of *beliefs* about responding to youth offending (e.g. advocating the utility of diversion) and a set of *management techniques* for controlling youth justice decisions made about children and young people – the latter element becoming known as **systems management** (Tutt and Giller 1987). The criticisms/beliefs (articulated by Pitts 1988) around the exaggeration of youth offending and the criminalising influence of formal youth justice responses were not new, but the emphasis on systems management was certainly a new strategy for shaping youth justice responses (Case 2008).

The systems management element of new orthodoxy thinking recognised that youth justice interventions are 'made on an individual basis and the courts take time to change the decisions. . . . But it is the aggregated or cumulative effect of individual decision-making over time that produces overall change in sentencing patterns' (Bell and Haines 1991: 122). The rationale for an increasing emphasis upon systems management in the youth justice process was that the arrest, processing and sentencing of young offenders placed them on a trajectory that could be influenced by targeting specific decision-making points in the youth justice process – points where the outcome for young people may be changed. In other words, a young person's progress and trajectory through youth justice processes can be altered at key stages and should not be seen as inevitable or fixed.

Diversion: a justice-based approach to avoid formal justice?

A direct consequence of the re-emerging justice focus in the 1980s (in the guise of systems management) was the increased use of **diversion** – redirecting young people who offend away from formal youth justice processes through the increased use of cautioning, diversion from court and community sentences. Diversion had two key interlinked, evidence-based rationales, both of which have overtones of social constructionism:

1 *Exaggerated youth offending*: youth offending was considered to be an exaggerated phenomenon in both extent and nature, as was the need for widespread and intensive responsive interventions. Many children will simply grow out of crime due to natural processes of maturation (see Chapter 3; Glueck and Glueck 1930; see also Rutherford 2002).
2 *Iatrogenic youth justice*: formal youth justice intervention was considered damaging and counterproductive, leading to labelling (see Chapter 2; Becker 1963; Lemert 1951), net-widening (see this chapter; see also Shelden 1999) and further criminalisation (Haines and Case 2015).

Support for diversion with young people who had offended appeared to be at odds with the tough talking, more punitive public policy of the Conservative Government in the 1980s, but nevertheless, practitioners were encouraged to pursue this approach.

RTA = RHETORIC VERSUS REALITY

Contradictions between public, political **rhetoric** (claims, exaggerated speech) and espoused strategy (e.g. regarding punitiveness) and the private, practice reality, such as the use of more liberal, diversionary approaches. Sometimes, political rhetoric can be converted into practice reality through another RTA – local mediation of centralised practice **prescription** (instruction, strong guidance).

Diversion from increasingly formalised youth justice processes (e.g. the courts) throughout the 1980s was seen to represent the peak of the justice movement (Allen

1991), despite the approach actively avoiding *formal* justice-based sentencing and intervention. As such, diversion was, in essence, an *informal* youth justice strategy and practice shaped by new orthodoxy/systems management principles and led by formal youth justice organisations and practitioners. Diversionary and anti-custody responses aimed to prevent the damaging consequences of formal youth justice processes, such as unnecessary acceleration through increasingly serious sanctions for repeated (minor) offences ('up-tariffing') and the brutalising, harmful experience of custody, particularly shared custody with more serious youth offenders and adult offenders (the 'mass contamination' and the 'schools of crime' principles). During the 1980s boom in diversion, there were significant reductions nationally in the numbers of **first-time entrants** (FTEs) into the YJS (Haines 1996), there was no evidence of an increase in reoffending rates and the number of young offenders in custody was reduced from 8,000 in 1980 to under 1,500 by the end of the decade. The impressive statistical outcomes across this 'decade of diversion', led some to characterise the 1980s as the 'successful revolution' in youth justice (Allen 1991). Diversion was widely supported as a 'hugely beneficial way of dealing with the mass of young people who become peripherally involved in crime' (Haines and Drakeford 1998: 105). However, the popularity of new orthodoxy thinking and systems management had only a limited basis in justice concerns according to some critics. For example, John Pratt argued that

> the 'new orthodoxy' (Jones 1984) of the emergent 'justice model' took policy off at a different tangent and reversed many of the previous taken-for-granted assumptions about 'the way forward' . . . the welfare-justice dichotomy should not be seen as forming the analytical parameters of juvenile justice debate. Instead, this simply laid the foundation stones on which a third model – that of corporatism – has been built.
>
> (Pratt 1989: 237–238)

Pratt (1989) asserted that new orthodoxy thinking and systems management actively contravened some of the prerequisites of the justice model (e.g. certainty, due process, visibility, accountability) by prioritising administrative decision-making, sentencing diversity, the centralisation of policy, multi-agency partnership working and high levels of control in determining and managing sentencing programmes – a strategy labelled **corporatism**. This corporatism could be seen as reflecting centralised policy catching up with and reinforcing pre-existing discretionary practice at the local level, rather than necessarily the local mediation of centralised prescriptions. If this were indeed the case, then it adds a further stage to the RTA of 'local mediation of centralised policy', wherein local mediation/moderation processes (animated by practitioner discretion) motivate further changes in policy to reflect the nature of local mediation and moderation.

The 1950–1990 period of youth justice development illustrated the historical conflict and ambivalence in the social construction of youth offending and youth justice by encapsulating the welfare versus justice debate. Throughout this period, there was a discernible tension between welfare-based approaches, such as raising the age of criminal responsibility in welfare-based legislation (e.g. the Children and Young Persons Act 1963/1969) and justice-based responses such as the allocation of more discretion to criminal justice practitioners (e.g. the Children and Young Persons Act

1970). This tension was furthered by the contemporaneous use of a twin track (bifurcated) welfare–justice approach in the 1970s (Intermediate Treatment and juvenile custody) and the 1980s (welfarist elements of diversion and new orthodoxy thinking). Consequently, from 1950 to 1990, the welfare versus justice debate reached its peak in philosophical and practical terms within youth justice in the UK and beyond (see also Arnull and Fox 2016).

5 EASY PIECES

4 Creating a distinct 'youth justice': welfare versus justice (1950–1990)

1 *Social work-led youth justice*: the 1960s was a period of progressive, welfare-orientated youth justice, illustrated by an emphasis on social work-based therapeutic relationship building (Children and Young Persons Act 1963) and the allocation of more practice discretion to social services over criminal justice agencies (Children and Young Persons Act 1969).
2 *Return to justice*: the Children and Young Persons Act 1970 marked a return to justice by reallocating the main responsibility for dealing with young people who offended to criminal justice agencies, reinstating an emphasis upon punitive custody and refusing to enact the recommendation to raise the age criminal responsibility to 14.
3 *Intermediate Treatment*: IT in the 1970s dealt with children at risk of offending in a welfare-based context that was intermediate between the family context and custody.
4 *Systems management and diversion*: diversion and anti-custody responses in the 1980s, guided by new orthodoxy thinking and systems management (e.g. focusing on key decision-making points in the youth justice process), evidenced a 'successful revolution' in youth justice, with statistical decreases in both custody and first-time entrants into the Criminal Justice System.
5 *Welfare versus justice*: the welfare–justice debate was intensified over the 1950–1990 period due to the conflict and ambivalence illustrated by different legislative changes (e.g. social services versus criminal justice agencies as the dominant respondent to youth offending), structural/practical developments (e.g. juvenile custody versus Intermediate Treatment) and systemic constructions (e.g. diversion and systems management versus custody and corporatism).

5 PUNITIVE, PRACTICAL, PROTECTIVE: THE 'PUNITIVE TURN', RISK MANAGEMENT AND CHILD-FRIENDLY JUSTICE (1990 ONWARDS)

At the beginning of the 1990s, new legislation impacted upon the structural and systemic nature of youth justice in the UK, while philosophically moving closer to a justice-based model for responding to youth offending. Prior to this, the Children Act 1989 had removed all child welfare cases from the (criminal) juvenile court and moved them to a newly created family proceedings court. This legislation was followed by the Criminal Justice Act 1991, which reinforced the justice principle that sentencing should be based on the seriousness of the offence (proportionality). In October 1992, the juvenile court was renamed the 'youth court', which exists to this day. The Government extended the remit of the youth court to incorporate 17-year-olds for the first time, reflecting the increasing exclusion of younger offenders through the use of diversion in the 1980s. Despite its justice orientation, the youth court was also required to have regard for the welfare of the young person.

Notwithstanding the vociferous debates that had characterised the history of youth justice to that point, the 1980s were notable for a broad consensus among key stakeholders (e.g. politicians, academics, practitioners) that pro-diversion and anti-custody measures were working (Department of Health 1994; see also Haines 1996). However, the successes of the 1980s were not mirrored in the 1990s, a period characterised by the decreasing use of diversion and cautioning along with increasing levels of prosecution and custody for young people who offended. From the early 1990s, diversion began to suffer sustained attacks from prominent, influential individuals such as Home Secretary Michael Howard, who accused local authorities of 'bringing cautioning into disrepute' (Home Office 1994: paragraph 7). Howard's attacks reflected a recurring theme in youth justice – the constant desire for new and existing governments to socially (re)construct every element of the 'triad of youth justice' (definitions–explanations–responses) in order to be seen to be doing something about youth offending.

RTA = DOING SOMETHING ABOUT YOUTH CRIME

Governments need to be seen to be doing something about social problems (youth crime being an excellent example) and often feel that this 'something' should be new and different from the actions of their predecessors (including previous governments formed by their own political party), whether the actions worked or not and regardless of the actual extent or nature of the youth crime problem they are addressing. This particular RTA illustrates how political agendas and influences on the social construction of youth offending and youth justice can dominate other influences, such as those from academia, practice and the media.

In the mid-1990s, the incumbent Conservative Government commissioned a review youth justice on the eve of the 1997 General Election. The resultant report from the Audit Commission in 1996 was titled *Misspent Youth: Young People and Crime*, more commonly known as *Misspent Youth*. On the basis of unsubstantiated claims that youth offending was increasing at that time, the *Misspent Youth* authors stated that the systems and structures for delivering youth justice were not working. The report was highly critical of previous diversionary and non-interventionist approaches to youth justice. The Audit Commission privileged the criminal careers model explanation of David Farrington (Farrington 1996; see Chapter 3) to argue for an offence- and offender-focused model of youth justice founded on the prevention and management of risk factors associated with offending. *Misspent Youth* went on to characterise current youth justice processes as ineffective, inefficient and uneconomical, recommending instead that a new corporatist (e.g. centralised, multiagency, closely managed) system should be constructed based on the performance management of youth justice agencies and processes. The central features of the new risk-based, preventative and tightly managed approach recommended in the report formed the basis of the statutory requirements of the subsequent Crime and Disorder Act 1998; an approach that introduced the 'new youth justice' (Goldson 2000). We will explore the strategies of the 'new youth justice' in detail in the following chapter. At this stage, however, we will take a step back from the England/Wales context to examine broader developments in youth justice responses internationally since the 1990s and their relationship with the central welfare versus justice debate that had underpinned the social construction of youth justice to that point.

International youth justice: punitive, practical, protective

Youth justice globally has wrestled with the conflict and ambivalence around how to understand children (who offend) as simultaneously vulnerable and threatening (Smith and Ecob 2007; McAra and McVie 2010). According to McAra (2010), conflict and ambivalence surrounding appropriate youth justice responses has both encouraged and been exacerbated by competing system objectives for youth justice, which can be dichotomised as

1   To help troubled young people to change, develop and overcome their problems;
2   To deliver a firm, prompt and appropriate response to youth offending that protects the public.

(McAra 2010: 288)

It is evident that these dual objectives embody (in broad terms) the welfare-justice debate. The pursuit of these objectives has been animated by youth justice philosophies and strategies in different countries, which themselves have been mobilised within different youth justice structures. The foundations of international *strategies* are the systems and structures within which they are delivered, so our evaluation should start here.

CONTROVERSIES AND DEBATES

Differences in youth justice systems and structures

Youth justice *systems* across the world have developed different *structures* (e.g. institutions, organisations, processes) with which to animate the requirements of legislation, conventions, national philosophies and strategies for youth justice. Leslie McAra refers to these structures as the 'architecture of youth justice' (in Smith 2010). It is possible, for example, to distinguish between the following:

- *System types*: youth justice structures may be part of 'generic systems' that respond to children who offend and those considered in need of care and protection (e.g.

as in England and Wales for long periods until the Crime and Disorder Act 1998). Conversely, youth justice services may be part of 'specialist systems' dealing only with offenders and those at risk of offending (e.g. the current YJS of England and Wales; see Chapter 5) or be embedded within adult criminal justice systems.
- *Sentencing structures*: some international youth justice systems have a *court-based* structure for dealing with youth crime (e.g. youth courts in England and Wales), which may operate inquisitorial, participatory or adversarial procedures. Others have *non-judicial bodies* leading the decision-making for young offenders (e.g. the Children's Hearing System in Scotland), which may vary in terms of the inclusion and distribution of (trained) lay members of the public and experts along with the involvement of victims and families in decision-making processes.

There are logical relationships between certain structures and philosophies/models of youth justice, such as the indeterminate nature of welfare interventions being decided by non-judicial bodies or determinate justice-based sentences being better suited to court structures. However, the structures–philosophies relationship can be a flexible, mix-and-match affair, such that 'there is no necessary *causal* relationship between principle and architecture' (McAra 2010: 290). There is an important distinction to be made here between the structures within which youth justice decision-making is situated and the nature of the sentences (also known as 'disposals') and interventions themselves, which are less dependent on structure (McAra 2010). For example, the restorative justice measure of family group conferencing lends itself to non-judicial decision-making structures but can be easily integrated within court-based structures through statutory sentences with restorative elements, such as Referral Orders in England and Wales (Crawford and Newburn 2003; see also Chapter 5).

As you engage with the arguments throughout this chapter and our book, remember to Always Be Critical (ABC) by considering the extent and nature of the relationships (if any) between the specific responses to youth offending (structural, systemic, legislative, practical) and the philosophies of youth justice that have been alleged to inform our responses to youth offending at key points in history.

Following a detailed review of international models of youth justice, Neil Hazel (2008) concluded that it is possible to identify system 'models' that serve as 'ideal types' for youth justice, albeit models that are all traceable in some way to the welfare versus justice debate. Attendant to the local and national mediation of youth justice policies, Hazel cautioned that these models are not replicated exactly internationally and do not necessarily determine policy formation locally/nationally, but should be viewed as broad, fluctuating philosophical approaches and/or cumulative patterns arising from the competing pressures on youth justice (e.g. Government legislation, children's rights instruments). Hazel (2008) asserted that every identifiable model of youth justice globally, no matter how **hybridised** (a mixture of different types and influences) and complex, has emerged from and can be linked to either welfare or justice approaches; models that he defined as:

- *Welfare*: emphasises **paternalism** – those in authority restricting the freedom of and taking responsibility for others in their own interests (cf. the parens patriae principle – Burfeind and Bartusch 2006) and protection (cf. the United Nations Convention on the Rights of the Child [UNCRC] and child-friendly justice; see later in this chapter), encouraging treatment responses rather than formal justice and punishment. Children should not be viewed as rational or self-determining agents (as classicist explanations suggest), but rather as subject to and products of the environment within which they live (as positivist explanations suggest). Consequently, youth justice should identify, treat and cure the underlying social causes of offending, rather than inflicting punishment for the offence itself (Alder and Wundersitz 1994). In developmental terms, the child is situated at the heart of the supportive family and the family situated at the heart of the supportive community (McAra and McVie 2010). The focus of the welfare model is on the needs of the dependent child, diagnosis and treatment, informal processes and indeterminate (not fixed) sentences. The model has been perhaps most evident in the youth justice practice of Norway, Sweden, France, Germany and Japan (Cavadino and Dignan 2006).

- *Justice*: emphasises legal rights (e.g. due process) and accountability for crimes, favouring formal justice and proportionality in sentencing and favouring the deterrent aims of punishment in youth justice responses (McAra 2010). The model is most evident in the youth justice approaches adopted by different states of the US post-1960 (Cavadino and Dignan 2006). In direct contrast to the welfare perspective, all individuals (children included) are seen as rational agents who are fully responsible for their actions and so should be held accountable before the law (the classicist view). Therefore, they should also have full rights to due process and state powers must be constrained, predictable and determinate (Alder and Wundersitz 1994: 3), with the punishment fitting the crime (i.e. proportionality).

Underpinning his review, Hazel reasserted the caveat that the identified welfare–justice models are only ideal types. He argued that no individual country conforms exactly to every characteristic of either model at any point. They will tend to oscillate between the two poles (welfare and justice) over time, a phenomenon exemplified globally (Hagell and Hazel 2001) and specifically in England and Wales in the 1960s and 1970s (Harris 1985) and in South Australia (Wundersitz 1996). Hazel (2008) concluded his global review of youth justice by highlighting the growing complexity and diversity of international models. Other researchers and critical commentators have supported this perspective of increasing complexity and hybridity in youth justice responses globally (cf. Goldson 2014). For example, Dunkel (2006, 2014) reviewed youth justice models employed across Europe and identified three 'trends' that extend and move youth justice beyond traditional welfare and justice concerns:

- *Neo-liberalism*: especially influential in England and Wales (see Chapter 5) and the Netherlands, neo-liberalism promotes the individual's freedom of choice and places more emphasis on individual, family and community responsibility than on the social contexts of crime and state protection/intervention as responses to it (Rose 2000; Garland 2001). This model has given rise to the term **neo-liberal responsibilisation** (Garland 1996; Muncie 2009), which refers to governments placing increasing primary responsibility on individuals/families/communities to respond to and ameliorate the influences on youth offending, rather than the State taking primary responsibility. As such, the model is closely linked to an additional model, **neo-correctionalism** (Cavadino and Dignan 2006), wherein youth justice strategies and practices are based on the correction of perceived deficiencies (e.g. positivist causes, risk factors) in the individual.

- *Minimum intervention*: a challenge to the responsibilisation and increasing, excessive use of intervention (interventionism) promoted by neo-liberalism (Cavadino and Dignan 2006), the ethos of minimal (necessary) intervention is evident in diversion and education (e.g. in Germany) or welfare-based approaches with minimal use of justice-based interventions (e.g. the Children's Hearings System in Scotland; see 'Conversation' with Professor Bill Whyte). A growing body of international comparative longitudinal research suggests that any contact with a youth justice system (regardless of its principles/philosophies and structures) can result in increased risk of offending (cf. Sherman *et al.* 1998), which further suggests that formal youth justice contact can be labelling, stigmatising and criminalising and so should be minimised or avoided (McAra and McVie 2007; see also discussion of diversion in Section 4 of this chapter). Strong supportive evidence comes from a comparative study of youth justice in Bremen, Germany (lenient, diversion-focused system) and Denver, US (more punitive, limited diversion), which discovered that arrests and sanctions/sentences only had a limited impact on future offending and then only if previous offending had generated more severe sanctions (Huizinga *et al.* 2003, Denver Youth Study; see Chapter 3). These findings were corroborated by the Edinburgh Study of Youth Transitions (McAra and McVie 2005, 2007; see Chapter 3), which found that youth justice processes could produce selection and referral effects, which meant that certain categories of young people – the 'usual suspects' – were propelled into a 'repeat cycle' of referral into the Children's Hearing System. Therefore, the further into the system a young person was pushed, the less likely that they could desist, leading to the conclusion that youth justice intervention should prioritise diversion and less formal and stigmatising responses (McAra 2010).
- *Restorative justice*: demonstrated by practices such as the use of family group conferencing (e.g. in Belgium and Canada; see Arnull and Fox 2016), a restorative model of youth justice sees the young person as shaped by the community and cultural context (Zehr and Mika 1998). Children are understood as having rights but also as calculating, rational individuals who should take responsibility for their actions, acknowledge the harms that they have caused by offending, repair the damage and attempt to restore the broken links between them, their victim and the community (McAra 2010). Therefore, the focus of restorative justice is on individual accountability reparation, reintegration and mediation for victims, foci that can be facilitated by diversionary approaches (Cavadino and Dignan 2006).

I spoke to an international expert on restorative justice, Professor Dave O'Mahony from Durham University, regarding its theoretical and practical evolution into a major youth justice practice model. For reasons of space and coherence, the interview is presented in Appendix 3.

The five identified models (otherwise known as 'typologies') of youth justice (welfare, justice, neo-liberalism, minimal intervention, restorative justice) are ideal types (Hazel 2008) outlining broad trends that overlap and conflict within and between countries to create a complex, hybrid picture of international youth justice (Dunkel

2014). For our purposes, these models/trends can help to frame discussion of contemporary youth justice development since 1990, while we remain attendant to their inherent complexity and hybridity. Three broad philosophical and strategic 'movements' can be discerned from these post-1990s models/trends in youth justice. It is possible to characterise these varied movements as punitive, practical and protective, although an equally suitable alliteration could be retributive, risk and rights. Exploring each of these movements in turn allows a deeper understanding of the nature of youth justice developments in the contemporary Western world.

Punitive youth justice: the 'punitive turn'

According to a host of critical commentators (e.g. Goldson 2014; Pratt and Eriksson 2012; Wacquant 2009; Garland 2001), the 1990s onwards has witnessed a 'new punitiveness' in westernised youth justice – a 'punitive turn' (Muncie 2008) away from welfare-orientated and diversionary youth justice and a move towards more punitive, neo-liberal and neo-correctionalist justice-based approaches grounded in principles of proportionality and just deserts (themselves influenced by the 'punitive turn'). In England and Wales, for example, the Criminal Justice Act 1991 required a balanced, proportionate consideration of offence severity alongside the influence of offender demographics (e.g. age, maturity, attitude) to inform the selection of an appropriate sentence from a **tariff** (scale of increasing severity) of sentencing options (Haines and Drakeford 1998). Professor Barry Goldson (2014) has argued that rapid globalisation, dramatic socio-economic transformations, increasing insecurities (see Beck's 1992 'risk society' thesis – Chapter 3) and neo-liberal politics have combined to produce this new punitiveness and a growing **penal populism** – a political and social/public preference for more punitive forms of justice. Goldson's frequent writing partner John Muncie (2008, 2014) has identified a series of features associated with this punitive turn in youth justice:

- *Repenalisation*: a move towards more punishment-focused justice responses with retributive, deterrent and custodial inclinations.
- *Neo-liberalism*: placing less emphasis on social contexts, state protection and rehabilitation and more on prescriptions of individual responsibility (see also Dunkel 2014), an active citizenship and governments governing at a distance.
- *Responsibilisation*: allocating the primary responsibility for the prevention of youth offending to young people, families, communities and local authorities rather than the state.
- *Adulterisation*: the increasing treatment of children who offend as though they are adults in terms of maturity, capability and responsibility, reflected in punitive youth justice responses to offending.

Goldson (2014) outlines a dystopian vision (an imagined state of unpleasantness) for twenty-first-century youth justice that he believes has been perpetuated by the 1990s punitive turn and the 'culture of control' (Garland 2001) over young people's behaviour that it was used to justify. What he means by 'dystopian' is a vision of a dehumanising, undesirable and unpleasant YJS and set of youth justice practices. Goldson notes a retreat from the needs- and protection-focused welfare model that characterised European youth justice for the vast majority of the twentieth century (Bailleau and Cartuyvels 2002), arguing that the special protected status of children and young people has diminished as a result. Critics assert that the responsibilisation and adulterisation of children and young people who offend has become the norm and breaches of their human/children's rights have become commonplace. This aggressive exclusion and othering of young people who offend, this constant pushing to the outer limits of society, has been dubbed 'advanced marginality' (Wacquant 2008). The alleged dystopian 'punitive turn' in youth justice has been demonstrated by

> a decline in rehabilitative ideals, harsher prison conditions, more emotional and expressive forms of punishment emphasising shaming and degradation.
>
> (Snacken and Dumortier 2012: 2–3)

Loic Wacquant (2009: 1) observed that this 'new punitive common sense' (not limited to *youth* justice) was born in the US and exported internationally, then evidenced through vertical expansion (e.g. burgeoning prison populations) and horizontal expansion (e.g. the proliferation and diversification of technologies of regulation, control and surveillance). Let us stop for a moment to broaden our focus out to the expansion of the punitive turn across the Western world.

STOP AND THINK

Punitive juvenile justice systems in the industrialised Western world

By the late twentieth century, welfare had been largely subsumed by approaches favouring justice, punishment and the characteristics of the punitive turn in juvenile/youth justice systems across the industrialised Western world. Of course, the emerging hegemony of punitive youth justice and the relative marginalisation of welfare was animated differently based on national and local youth justice contexts (**RTA = the local mediation of centralised youth justice policy**), but punitive elements of youth justice approaches were becoming more discernible internationally (Muncie and Goldson 2006). Can you identify cogent evidence of punitive youth justice in each of the national systems described below?

US: the US has been criticised for promoting the most explicitly adulterising and punitive set of youth justice approaches in the Western world (Krisberg 2006). Many states have abolished the special youth courts that protected children from formal youth justice systems and processes, have expanded the range of offences for which children can be tried as adults and have lowered the age at which this can occur. Indeed, the age of criminal responsibility in some states is now as low as 6 or 7 years old – the lowest in the Western world (Krisberg 2006). Additionally, the US remains the only nation state yet to ratify the United Nations Convention on the Rights of the Child (see later in this chapter).

Scotland: the juvenile court was abolished in 1968 and replaced with a welfare-based children's hearings system (see 'Conversation' with Bill Whyte) for most young people under 16 years old. However, the resultant lack of legal safeguards for those aged 16 and over, alongside the re-establishment of youth courts for 16- to

17-year-olds in 2003, led some critics to argue that children were receiving excessively severe punishments for their offending (McAra 2006).

Belgium: the label of 'most deliberately welfare-orientated of all' youth justice
systems is alleged to belong to Belgium, with very few punishments available for
young people under 18 and an education- and protection-focused youth justice
model (Put and Walgrave 2006). However, the youth court can order reprimand,
supervision and custody for the purposes of observation and education, making it
possible to criticise the Belgian welfare approach as 'not justice without punishment,
but punishment without guaranteed justice' (Put and Walgrave 2006).

Allied to these nation-based examples, specific elements of the punitive turn are
evident across the globe (Muncie 2008), including:

Adulterisation: failing to effectively separate units from adults in custody and in
other youth justice processes (e.g. in Finland, Denmark, Switzerland, Austria, Ireland,
UK, Germany, Portugal).

Punitive restrictions on behaviour: zero-tolerance policing (e.g. France, Belgium,
Netherlands, Australia), parental sanctions (e.g. Japan, Canada, New Zealand), curfews (e.g. Belgium, France, Scotland), electronic monitoring (e.g. Netherlands, Scotland, France, Sweden), naming and shaming (e.g. Japan, Canada) and risk prediction
(England and Wales, Netherlands, Australia, Canada; see risk management discussion later in this chapter).

Punitive discrimination: 'some of the most punitive elements of juvenile justice do
appear to be increasingly used/reserved for the punitive control of primarily immi-
grant populations' (Muncie 2008: 113).

I chatted with Bill Whyte, a professor of social work at Edinburgh University, about
the historical and conceptual development of youth justice in Scotland, the immediate
neighbour of England and Wales – the main focus of this book. Bill is a leading expert
on youth justice and social work in Scotland and has written widely on the subject (see
Whyte 2009, 2014), so his insight is invaluable for the purposes of our book.

CONVERSATIONS

Youth justice in Scotland

**Steve: What have been the guiding philosophies of Scottish youth justice
historically?**

Bill Whyte: The Kilbrandon Committee report of 1964 provides the founding principles of Scotland's system for dealing with youth crime. It included no clear theoretical
exposition or any precise definitions of its founding principles. Nonetheless, the proposals were based on key assumptions recognisable in current theoretical debates. The
report contended that the 'similarities in the underlying situation' of young people
who offend and those in need of care and protection 'far outweigh the differences'

(Committee on Children and Young Persons 1964, para. 15). In many ways, Kilbrandon was a crucible of ideas and influences of its time and the subsequent structural developments could be described as part of a 'cultural project' on the nature of Scottish society. It is not a coincidence that Lord Kilbrandon also chaired a Royal Commission on the constitution in 1969, established in response to growing demands for Scottish independence. The committee viewed young people's criminality as only one aspect of life experience, associated with failures in their upbringing, particularly in the home, the local neighbourhood environment and in the school. While it was never argued in any simplistic way that social adversity caused or fully explained offending, it drew on developments in the social sciences at the time, which suggested that social and emotional deprivation associated with disorganised neighbourhoods, family disruption, separation and poor parenting would have a major impact on the subsequent behaviour of the young. The importance of positive schooling and the crucial role of parental supervision in preventing delinquency were strongly emphasised.

Steve: How have these philosophies been reflected in distinct structures, systems and practices for working with young people who break the law?

Bill: The Social Work (Scotland) Act 1968, which introduced the system, it was argued, launched a distinctive approach to youth justice in Scotland in 1971 which has lasted for over 50 years (Lockyer and Stone 1998). Scottish youth courts were disbanded and replaced by lay decision-making tribunals (considered a distinctively Scottish device) called Children's Hearings to deal with children at risk of abuse and neglect and children who offend, within a unified welfare system. A general principled duty of promoting well-being, individual and collective, was incorporated within the 1968 Act (s12). In regard to young people in trouble with the law, Kilbrandon recommended an extrajudicial system of Children's Hearings (with the intention of decriminalising young people) alongside the reorganisation of social services (originally to be social education departments) under the umbrella of all-purpose integrated departments with responsibility for child care and protection and youth justice as well as responsibilities previously undertaken by the national probation service, which was also disbanded. Commentators described the proposed changes not simply as a reorganisation of provision but as paradigmatic change (Bruce 1985).

Kilbrandon took the view that the criminal justice paradigm was unsuccessful in its attempts to compromise between crime, individual responsibility and punishment on one hand and the best interests of the young person and shared responsibility on the other, and that a new approach or paradigm was needed. It viewed the criminal process as having two fundamental functions: the adjudication of the legal facts – whether or not an offence had been established beyond reasonable doubt – requiring the skills of a professional judge, and decisions concerning disposal once the facts had been established, for which criminal judges, it suggested, had no particular claim on expertise. Accordingly, in what Lord Hope was later to describe as the 'genius of Kilbrandon', the new Scottish system separated adjudication from disposal – the former continued as the responsibility of criminal courts and the latter the responsibility of the welfare tribunal of trained community representatives (panel members). If the young person and their family accept the grounds (i.e. that an offence has been committed), there is no need for legal adjudication. Consequently, acceptance of the offence at the opening of a hearing allows it to deal with the disposal – the 'What should we do about it?' part – as a welfare tribunal geared to acting in the best interests of the young person, on the assumption that this is in the best interests of the community as a whole. As a consequence, a children's hearing has no power to determine questions of innocence or guilt. The ambition of decriminalising children and young people through the system resulted in a low age threshold for entry for offence reasons at age 8.

The promotion of social education – better known as social pedagogy in Northern Europe – as a new paradigm for practice was considered to draw directly from Scotland's European traditions and connectedness. This is also reflective of a very clear cultural dimension and a determination to do something 'different', something Scottish, where youth courts and probation departments were considered Anglo-American institutions, and the search was on for Scottish solutions. Kilbrandon did not suggest that children and young people should be seen to have no responsibility for their actions and its consequences, for themselves or others, nor that they should avoid being held to account as if they had no moral reasoning. It simply argued that responsibility for the behaviour of children has to be a matter of partnership between the young person, their parents and the State – in other words, child upbringing as a collective social responsibility – and failure in upbringing, represented by criminality, as a collective and not an individual failure.

The social education approach, often described as visionary, was certainly well ahead of its time in public policy in the UK, and in many respects it was a forerunner to the provisions of the UNCRC 1989 and its associated guidance, which focus, among other things, on well-being as a paramount consideration – extra-judicial solutions and socio-educational rather than punitive interventions. Nonetheless, this attempt at a paradigmatic shift was dealt a major blow from the outset. The proposal to establish a social education department was shelved in favour of social work departments as distinct and separate from education. More damaging in relation to the philosophy regarding young people in conflict with the law was that within a matter of a few years of the system's introduction, a key principle at the heart of the approach was undermined by UK legislation, the 1974 Rehabilitation of Offenders Act, which introduced a provision that offence grounds accepted at a children's hearing for the purpose of the Act would be treated as a criminal conviction (RoO 1974 section 3), when a founding principle was the decriminalisation of children.

It was really only in the punitive and risk-averse world of the 1990s, with its growth in demand for police checks, that many adults discovered they had recorded previous convictions, some from as young as age 8, when they had understood they had no criminal record. This marked not simply the undermining of but the beginning of the end of the cultural project and the influence of a 'punitive turn' in the UK as a whole. The evidence for this might lie with the Children (Scotland) Act 1995 which was introduced by a Conservative administration to bring Scotland closer in line with UNCRC. The fact that the Scottish system based on Kilbrandon principles needed to be brought closer in line with UNCRC highlights the major drift from those founding principles, particularly in the 1990s.

Steve: Has Scottish youth justice changed in nature since devolution?

Bill: Developments in international standards under UNCRC (1989) and the subsequent guidance promotes almost a replica, 25 years later, of the Kilbrandon agenda, through a social education practice paradigm, and have influenced changes in the Scottish system. From the re-establishment of the Scottish Parliament in 1997, support for the system as distinctively Scottish has been strong. However, few changes were introduced. By 2002, following a review of the Children's Hearing system, the Scottish 'New Labour' administration reintroduced criminal youth courts and made provision for antisocial behaviour orders (ASBOs) and criminal antisocial behaviour orders (CRASBOs) for children, compulsory parenting orders, and opened consultation on re-establishing a national probation service. While the principles espoused by Kilbrandon and the 1968 Social Work Scotland Act continued to hold some sway over the policy discourse alongside claims of a distinctive Scottish approach to young people in trouble with the law, this was not matched by reality and was more often rhetorical than substantive. By 2006 Scotland had gained an unenviable international reputation as having one of the lowest ages of criminal responsibility in the world and among the highest detention rates for young people under 18 in Europe. It was a country that locked female children in secure accommodation because of their risky, but not necessarily criminal, behaviour and routinely prosecuted young people from the age of 15 in adult criminal proceedings.

The establishment of an SNP Government in 2007 has seen changes introduced into legislation to restore the system to Kilbrandon's principles (e.g. decriminalisation), but the legislation passed to do this has still to be implemented. Youth courts have disappeared quietly and a whole system approach based on child care principles – Getting It Right for Every Child – has influenced practice and resulted in fewer young people under 18 prosecuted in criminal systems or detained in custody. The system no longer allows for the prosecution of under-12s in adult courts but still retains an age of criminal responsibility of 8.

The 1990s, particularly in the first half of the decade, witnessed a 'punitive turn' in youth justice – a move away from traditional welfare versus justice concerns and towards more punitive forms of justice such as surveillance, control and custody. The period from the 1990s into the twenty-first century evidenced a dystopian evolution of this punitive turn – a further collapse of faith in rehabilitation, the onset of harsher prison conditions for young people and more expressive forms of punishment, control and targeting of young offenders. Later in the decade, a risk management movement developed (see also Chapter 3) that was more practical and (slightly) less punitive in strategic terms compared to punitive approaches, albeit a movement retaining significant elements of neo-liberalism and neo-correctionalism.

Practical youth justice: risk management

In the 1990s, a new way of thinking about and delivering youth justice entered the political sphere, one concerned more with pragmatism than principles or philosophies.

The 'risk management' approach channelled elements of the 'punitive turn', neo-correctionism (Cavadino and Dignan 2006), neo-liberal responsibilisation (Dunkel 2014) and **managerialism** (the close control, management and prescription or practice) into a model that prioritised the identification and targeting of risk factors – very much informed by the findings and conclusions of developmental, artefactual risk factor theories (see Chapter 3). Risk management in youth justice has its origins in the conception of the 'risk society' (the 'risk' part of risk management) and in the increasing implementation of systems management and methods of **actuarial justice** – managing responses to offending based on the individual's predicted risk of reoffending (the 'management' part of risk management). In the early 1990s, there was a growing view in the Western world that we live in a 'risk society' – a world full of social, economic, political and physical risks resulting from rapid, widespread social changes, increasing processes of globalisation (e.g. the diversification and spread of technology) and socio-economic uncertainty (see Chapter 3). Risk became a buzzword for insecurity and anxiety, presented by politicians, the media and academics as denoting a threat or harm to be managed or mitigated (n.b. not a positive pursuit as in risk-taking and sensation-seeking; Katz 1988). The growing perception of risk among the general public offered an ideal political vehicle to drive the social reconstruction of youth offending – lending itself neatly to representing young people as potential threats to themselves and others (see Case 2006; Goldson 2005). Indeed, the 'respectable fears' of successive generations of adults have manifested themselves in populist portrayals of 'risk' and 'young people', with both tending to be socially constructed as uncertain, unpredictable, uncontrollable and unwelcome (Pearson 1983; see also Chapter 1).

At the same time as the risk society thesis was gaining popularity, governments in the Western world were expressing concerns regarding the perceived exponential rise in youth offending, deep-rooted failures of deterrent approaches, the escalating costs of youth custody and the urgent need for public protection (Kemshall 2007). Westernised criminal justice systems began to place more emphasis on the effective, efficient and economical management of populations and resources in the late twentieth century, especially the actuarialist 'new technologies to identify and classify risk' (Feeley and Simon 1992: 454–455). Actuarialist technologies such as risk assessment/prediction instruments and advanced statistical tests enabled new approaches to the management and control of young people. For example, young people began to be categorised into subgroups based on their shared characteristics and shared levels of quantified 'risk' (Porteous 2007). This illustrates actuarial justice – the statistical identification of high- and low-risk groups for the purposes of planning interventions and allocating criminal sanctions (see Feeley and Simon 1994). Proponents of risk assessment have argued that the techniques of actuarial justice have rendered decision-making more accurate and consistent by grounding decisions in a rigorously empirical framework based on data from a potentially wide range of information sources (see, for example, Grove and Meehl 1996). Actuarial justice has engendered a shift away from clinical or subjective judgements based on ideology or professional expertise, which are implicitly seen as either poorly applied or flawed. Viewed positively, actuarial justice is a constructive way of standardising and raising the level of effectiveness of youth justice systems and practices. Viewed critically, actuarial justice is one element of a broader exercise in managerialism intent of exerting increasing levels of centralised control over youth justice systems

and, ultimately, the political management/manipulation of 'youth' as a social problem (see, for example, Smith 2011, 2014). Managing the risk presented by young
'offenders' through an actuarial justice agenda has received significant support from
the burgeoning explanatory evidence base of risk factor theories (see Chapter 3).
There has been an explosion in the popularity of developmental, artefactual risk
factor theories that seek to identify the factors in childhood predicting/increasing
the risk of offending in later life (see Burnett 2007). As two of the leading life course
risk factor researchers the US have noted:

> The risk-factor and prediction paradigms have taken hold of criminology, espe-
> cially for those interested in crime prevention and crime control policies.
>
> (Laub and Sampson 2003: 289)

Risk management approaches in youth justice have been mobilised by the 'risk
factor prevention paradigm' (Hawkins and Catalano 1992), a model of developmental crime prevention that sets out a clear, common sense and practical approach to
responding to youth offending.

> The basic idea . . . is very simple: Identify the key risk factors for offending and
> implement prevention methods designed to counteract them. There is often a
> related attempt to identify key protective factors against offending and to imple-
> ment prevention methods designed to enhance them.
>
> (Farrington 2007: 606)

The risk factor prevention paradigm (RFPP) was imported into criminal justice
from the fields of medicine and public health, where it had been used to identify
'risk factors' for physical illnesses (e.g. a high-cholesterol diet and lack of exercise
as risk factors for heart disease) and 'protective factors' that mediated against these
illnesses (e.g. a healthy, low-cholesterol diet and regular exercise to protect against
the onset and exacerbation of heart disease). Identified risk and protective factors
were then targeted by preventative interventions (e.g. health promotion) administered to 'high-risk' or 'at-risk groups – those scoring high in exposure risk factors and
low in exposure to protective factors. The alleged capability of the RFPP to identify
and reduce risk in a clinical, evidence-based manner offered a common-sense, practical and readily understandable approach that proved irresistible to some politicians, policy-makers, practitioners and researchers working in the youth offending
field. The RFPP has had particular appeal to youth justice policy-makers and practitioners working in a risk-averse political climate of increasing managerialism, audit
focus, accountability, transparency, defensible practice and cost-effectiveness (see
Chapter 5). It has provided a paradigm/model to enable the collection of actuarial,
quantitative and empirical 'evidence', underpinned by developmental and life course
risk factor theories, to drive policy and practice that is therefore evidence based and
defensible (Stephenson *et al*. 2007; Bateman and Pitts 2005). Farrington confidently
proclaimed that

> a key advantage of the risk factor prevention paradigm is that it links explanation
> and prevention, fundamental and applied research, and scholars and practition-
> ers. Importantly, the paradigm is easy to understand and to communicate, and it

is readily accepted by policy makers, practitioners, and the general public. Both risk factors and interventions are based on empirical research rather than theories. The paradigm avoids difficult theoretical questions about which risk factors have causal effects.

(Farrington 2000: 7)

Risk management using the RFPP has become a dominant model of contemporary youth justice in the industrialised Western world (e.g. England and Wales, Australasia, North America) as a means of exploring the development of youth offending and for informing 'interventions designed to prevent the development of criminal potential' (Farrington 2000: 3). The international body of research underpinning risk management/RFPP has found favour with politicians, policy-makers and practitioners due to its generation of evidence through ostensibly value-free, objective, 'scientific', positivist, empirical methods such as observation and experimentation that quantify complex elements of human behaviour into risk factors/variables. In other words, risk management explicitly and logically links explanation to responses in the 'triad of youth justice'. Politicians and policy-makers have been attracted by the large, replicable, generalisable evidence base generated by developmental, artefactual risk factor research and the RFPP in particular. The identification of a small group of replicable risk factors with a proven statistical relationship to offending has encouraged Western governments to promote an evidence-based approach to youth justice with three clear benefits:

1   Providing a rationale for distancing youth justice policy and practice from previously held beliefs about the causes and subsequent treatments of juvenile delinquency.
2   Offering a 'third way' alternative to traditional preoccupations with welfare or justice.
3   Implementing a mechanism for building a youth justice system capable of managing the youth 'problem'.

(France 2008: 3)

The risk management approach, therefore, targets risk factors in order to reduce youth offending in a demonstrable and defensible context of 'what works' interventions and 'evidence-based practice' (Mason and Prior 2008; Prior and Paris 2005): providing governments with a rationale for offering increasing levels of supportive, yet invasive intervention (**RTA = simultaneous support and control**). The exponential popularity of risk-focused, evidence-based practice in youth justice systems across the Western world (manifested particularly in England and Wales; see Chapter 5) has addressed the uncertainties of the risk society and the increasingly invasive government-led managerialism of public sector (e.g. youth justice) services (Case and Haines 2009). Evidence-based risk management has offered an

ostensibly neat and coherent approach to the messy and ill-defined complexities of practice. . . [that] promises a consistent risk management methodology resting on a platform of knowledge . . . a cautious and defensive response to the challenges of modern society.

(Stephenson *et al.* 2007: 3–4)

TELLING IT LIKE IT IS

A subjective critique of the risk factor prevention paradigm

In the chapter discussion thus far, I have tried hard to provide a balanced evaluation of the emergence of risk management as a dominant paradigm for delivering youth justice. However, it is important to acknowledge my own position as a long-term vociferous critic of risk management, particularly its animation in the Youth Justice System of England and Wales through the RFPP (see Chapter 5 for more discussion). In addition to critical articles published in *Youth Justice: An International Journal* (cf. Case 2006, 2007; Haines and Case 2008, 2012), I have provided critical chapters on risk management to edited texts such as *Youth Crime and Justice* (Goldson and Muncie 2015) and the *Youth Justice Handbook* (Taylor *et al.* 2010), and I have written an entire book dedicated to a thorough dissection of the RFPP and its underpinning research and evidence base (Case and Haines 2009; see Chapter 3). Let me summarise my main criticisms here (which will be expanded upon in the following chapter) and you can decide for yourself as to their validity:

- *Factorisation*: the risk assessment processes used to inform and guide the RFPP have oversimplified the complexity of risk by converting it to quantifiable factors. This factorisation process reduces potentially dynamic, multifaceted and interacting experiences, characteristics, individual meanings (constructions), circumstances and behaviours into crude, meaningless statistics that wash away the quality and validity of the outcomes measured.
- *Developmental bias*: the theoretical basis for the RFPP is developmental risk factor theory, which leads to an emphasis upon assessing psychosocial risk factors in the family, school, neighbourhood and personal life of a young person, on the basis that these predict future offending. However, this developmental/psychosocial bias neglects to consider the potentially criminogenic influence of broader socio-structural or contextual factors such as 'socio-economic status, local area . . . cultural, political or historical context' (Case 2007: 93). In other words, the RFPP measures and responds to certain significant 'determinants' of the development of youth offending but practically ignores others.
- *Determinism*: an evaluation of the relevant literature suggests that the evidence base underpinning the RFPP is far too confident in its conclusion that risk factors exert a quasi-positivist, deterministic influence on future offending and the consequent conclusion that this makes them ideal targets for preventative intervention. In reality, the precise nature of the risk factor–offending relationship has never been conclusively identified. There is much debate within and between studies as to whether risk factors function as determinants, causes, predictors or indicators of offending, with some suggestions that they may even be symptoms of offending or simply correlates with offending (therefore, not risk factors in any predictive sense).
- *Technicisation*: in contrast to arguments that processes of risk management provide practitioners with structured and reliable evidence to support their decision-making and to inform intervention (Baker 2005), my view is that the RFPP

(particularly in the form of risk assessment interviews) has been animated in overly technical, rigid and impersonal ways. Factorising risk assessment has become a mechanical and bureaucratic tick box process that robs practitioners of the ability to fully employ their expertise, knowledge and discretion in assessment and intervention processes (see Chapter 5; see also Pitts 2001; Souhami 2007).

- *Predictive futility*: the ability of risk assessment instruments to predict future offending by young people is a major benefit of the RFPP, according to its advocates (cf. Baker 2005). However, these levels of prediction rarely rise above two-thirds accuracy, which leaves one-third of the population of young offenders with incorrectly predicted outcomes. They may be 'false positives' who are predicted to offend but don't, and therefore receive a disproportionately high level of intervention, which may label and criminalise them. In contrast, they may be 'false negatives', who are predicted not to offend but do, and therefore receive a disproportionately low level of intervention relative to their need for support.
- *Adult centric*: risk management processes such as the completion of risk assessment instruments and the decisions relating to intervention planning are typically adult led. Consequently, young people's constructions (perspectives, voices, meanings, experiences, lived realities) are often marginalised and neglected. This being the case, the key stakeholder in the youth justice process who may have the best understanding of the (risk factor) influences on offending behaviour is relatively ignored, and resultant interventions may be crucially limited in their validity and practicality.

Locate and read through the references I've cited above and make your own decision. The most important question to answer as you journey through this book and engage with its key arguments and debates is 'What do you think?'

In an era of modernisation, managerialism, audit culture and quality assurance in the public sector (see Chapter 5), risk management through the RFPP has been employed as an 'effective', defensible and transparent approach to constructing youth justice with an ostensibly robust empirical evidence base (see Brown 2005; Bateman and Pitts 2005). The explanations from artefactual risk factor theories (see Chapter 3), animated in practice by variations of the RFPP, have provided researchers, politicians, policy-makers and practitioners with an expedient method of controlling and managing risk in an age where uncertainty and anxiety rule (Case 2010). The focus of this contemporary youth justice model, therefore, is the practical prevention and reduction of exposure to risk factors and the risk of future offending, rather than the punishment of previous offending behaviour, any emphasis on welfare or justice principles or the protection of children's rights (see next section).

Protective youth justice: child-friendly justice

A youth justice movement emerged in the late 1990s that directly contrasted with and challenged the punitive (retributivist) and practical (risk-based) nature of other youth justice movements. Child-friendly justice has emphasised the protection of young people who offend and rejected the necessity for punitive measures, thus reflecting ambiguity and contradiction over whether to respond to children and young people who offend as

> vulnerable *becomings* in need of protection, help, guidance and support, or as undisciplined and dangerous *beings* necessitating correction, regulation, control and punishment, is central to such uncertainty and flux.
>
> (Goldson and Muncie 2009: vii)

The becomings–beings distinction offers a new dichotomy to add to our growing list (e.g. innocent–dangerous, needy–risky, care–control), linking neatly into a dichotomy suggested earlier in this chapter: punitive–positive youth justice responses. The punitive model we have just discussed is only one vision of youth justice past, present and future – a dystopian, negative vision. In direct contrast, Goldson (2014) has also identified an evolving utopian, positive, protective vision of child-friendly justice that prioritises the protection of the universal human rights of children who offend when they are subject to youth responses.

The development of youth justice responses across nation states in the Western world can be understood in the context of a series of international children's rights instruments that provide the foundations for a 'globalised' human rights–compliant and 'child-friendly' youth justice (Goldson and Muncie 2012). Just as local areas have attempted to mediate and adapt centralised policy and practice prescriptions from their national governments, so national governments have needed to mediate the requirements of international children's rights instruments and their implications for the delivery of youth justice. The emerging global children's rights movement has led Goldson (2014) to identify the potential for a child-friendly, positive form of youth justice that prioritises the best interests of the child and employs correctional intervention (particularly custody) as a last resort.

Any discussion of child-friendly, rights-focused youth justice must be placed in the context and significance of the United Nations Convention on the Rights of the Child 1989 (UNCRC). The UNCRC established a baseline for constructing children's rights and for implementing rights-compliant responses through 54 articles focused on the protection, provision and participation of children – with 'child' defined as any young person below the age of 18 (UNICEF 1989). The UNCRC is a legally binding international agreement setting out the civil, political, economic, social and cultural rights of every child, regardless of their race, religion or abilities – and establishing how governments should work together to make these rights available to *all* children. Every country in the world has ratified this international treaty (except for the US), which makes explicit that the common, principal aim of youth justice should be to act in the best interests of the child – not to punish, correct or even prevent (as in England and Wales). The UNCRC sets out a positive view of children and it seeks to promote and protect the place of children in society and the value and status of children as citizens (Haines and Case 2015). Muncie (2010: 201) asserts that the principles of the UNCRC are 'a vital first step for governments. . . [to] move towards child-centred and rights-compliance systems of youth and juvenile justice'. The relevant provisions of the UNCRC in relation to youth justice are:

● Article 3 (best interests of the child) – establishes the primacy of the best interests of the child in all decisions affecting them, notably in terms of budgets, policy and lawmaking;

- Article 4 (protection of rights) – asserts that governments should respect, protect and fulfil children's rights;
- Article 12 (respect for the views of the child) – sets out the right of children to express their views and have them taken into account on all matters affecting them, with children's participation appropriate to their level of maturity;
- Article 13 (freedom of expression) – outlines the child's right to receive and share information that is not damaging to themselves or others;
- Article 17 (access to information) – establishes that children have the right to information that is important to their health and well-being;
- Article 37 (custody as a last resort) – stresses that the detention or imprisonment of a child shall be used only as a measure of last resort and for the shortest appropriate period of time;
- Article 40 (juvenile justice) – provides that children who are accused of breaking the law have the right to legal help and fair treatment in a justice system that respects their rights.

(UNICEF 1989)

Implementation of the UNCRC in individual countries is monitored by the Committee on the Rights of the Child, a body of 18 independent experts. Every five years, countries submit a report to the Committee on their implementation of the UNCRC and the Committee responds with 'Concluding Observations'. The objective of this exercise is, in part, to assess the extent of any discrepancies between (political) rhetoric and (practice) reality in the implementation of youth justice measures (**RTA: rhetoric vs reality**) – the disconnect between political claims to adhere to the UNCRC and the realities of youth justice policy and practice on the ground. Unfortunately, as legally binding as the UNCRC claims to be, nation states regularly contravene its articles, and the Committee on the Rights of the Child has no sanctioning powers to respond officially to breaches, instead having to 'rely on persuasion and admonishment rather than enforcement' (Muncie 2010: 202).

The youth justice–focused articles of the UNCRC have been consolidated by specific guidelines in other children's rights instruments from the United Nations General Assembly, including:

- United Nations Standard Minimum Rules for the Administration of Juvenile Justice (the Beijing Rules; United Nations General Assembly 1985) – provide guidance for the protection of the human rights of children and young people in the development of separate and specialist youth justice systems.
- United Nations Guidelines on the Prevention of Delinquency (the Riyadh Guidelines; United Nations General Assembly 1990a) – the prevention of juvenile delinquency should be prioritised by youth justice systems and should be pursued through progressive diversionary and other non-punitive measures.
- United Nations Rules for the Protection of Juveniles Deprived of their Liberty (the Havana Rules; United Nations General Assembly 1990b) – deprivation of liberty for a child who offends should be a disposition of last resort and used only 'for the minimum necessary period'.

Critics have noted that children's rights conventions create conflict and ambivalence when applied in the youth justice context, most notably through the introduction of tensions between welfare and justice imperatives (Put and Walgrave 2006). Using the example of the Beijing Rules for the administration of juvenile justice, McAra (2010) explains that youth justice systems are presented with the simultaneous requirement to meet the needs of the child (welfare), protect their rights (children's rights) and meet/ protect the needs of society (justice). The Beijing Rules require children's rights to be met through minimum intervention (itself an identified model of youth justice; see Dunkel 2014; Cavadino and Dignan 2006), prevention, diversion, community sentences and the use of custody as a last resort. However, intervention must also be proportionate to offence seriousness (justice-based) and offender (welfare-inclined) circumstances (e.g. the use of care, protection, education and vocational training). Very limited guidance is given regarding how to balance and reconcile these competing imperatives (McAra 2010). Furthermore, analyses of the Committee's Concluding Observations have discovered a general lack of implementation of the UNCRC principles across youth justice systems globally. For example, Abramson's (2000) meta-analysis of 141 countries concluded that there was a widespread absence of 'sympathetic understanding' of UNCRC principles in juvenile justice approaches, typified by punitive practices such as 'torture, inhumane treatment, lack of separation from adults, police brutality, poor conditions in detention facilities, overcrowding, lack of rehabilitation . . . and the improper use of the juvenile justice system to tackle other social problems' (Abramson, in Muncie 2010: 202). Current criticisms (all features of the punitive turn) are evident in successive Concluding Observations from the Committee, particularly excessive criminalisation, adulterisation and a punitive ethos of 'offender first, child second' (CRC 2008: 32; see also the 'children-first' model of positive youth justice discussed in Chapter 6; Haines and Case 2015). Following an analysis of UNCRC compliance in 15 Western European countries, Muncie (2010: 203) observed that 'most of these European states [except Norway] appear to have failed to recognize the centrality of such issues as distinctive needs, dignity, humane treatment and so on as core to the realization of children's rights'.

Notwithstanding ongoing problems with adherence and implementation, several UNCRC principles have been reflected in the 'European Rules for Juvenile Offenders Subject to Sanctions or Measures: Basic Principles 2008' (Council of Europe 2008; see also Muncie and Goldson 2015), including the right to be respected, effective participation, minimum necessary intervention, deprivation of liberty as a last resort and non-discrimination. The children's rights–informed models of youth justice supported and encouraged by United Nations instruments have been consolidated by more recent, formally adopted Council of Europe guidelines for 'child-friendly justice' (Council of Europe 2010). These guidelines state that any young person under the age of 18 should be regarded as a 'child' (cf. UNCRC) and that the work of youth justice systems should prioritise the child's right to participation in criminal justice proceedings, their best interests, dignity and protection from discrimination through adhering to the rule of law. The guidelines must apply to 'all ways in which children are likely to be, for whatever reason and in whatever capacity, brought into contact with . . . bodies and services involved in implementing criminal, civil or administrative law' (Council of Europe, sec. I, para. 2).

Contemporary 'child-friendly justice' embodies a positive approach to working with young people who offend by seeking to protect their rights (established under the UNCRC and European rules for juvenile offenders), acknowledging their inherent states as children, promoting their best interests and actively rejecting punitive, negative approaches such as custody and excessive intervention. However, despite the legally binding status of the UNCRC principles, reviews consistently identify a lack of compliance with and recognition of these principles across nation states, indicating that much work is still needed to realise the rhetoric of rights in the realities of youth justice responses internationally.

5 EASY PIECES

5 Punitive, practical, protective: the punitive turn, risk management and child-friendly justice (1990 onwards)

1 *Youth justice movements*: the development of youth justice from 1990 into the twenty-first century was exemplified by (at least) three movements: a 'punitive turn' towards surveillance, control, expressive punishment and custody; a practical risk management approach animated by the risk factor prevention paradigm; and a protective, child-friendly justice grounded in the UNCRC.

2 *The 'punitive turn'*: a 'dystopian' youth justice was encouraged by the 'punitive turn' of the 1990s away from welfare and justice approaches (guided by the proportionality principle) and towards more punitive-focused justice approaches (e.g. re-penalisation), an increased focus on individual, family and community responsibility (e.g. neo-liberal responsibilisation) and responding to offending children based on adult standards (e.g. adulterisation).

3 *Practical risk management*: a practical risk management approach utilising the risk factor prevention paradigm came to prominence in the late 1990s, identifying risk factors for offending through the use of risk assessment instruments and 'actuarial' statistical probability testing, then targeting these risk factors through risk-focused intervention in order to reduce and prevent future offending.

4 *Protective child-friendly justice*: a model of 'child-friendly justice' has emerged to challenge the punitive and practical movements. The model is underpinned by the **universal** (applicable to everyone, everywhere at all times) principles of children's rights instruments such as the UNCRC (e.g. non-discrimination, deprivation of liberty as a last resort, minimum necessary intervention), although recognition of and adherence to these principles has been inconsistent and incomplete internationally.

5 *Conflict and ambivalence*: the post-1990 era of youth justice has demonstrated conflict and ambivalence regarding how best to construct and respond to young people who offend. Dominant responses have ranged from the punitive (justice-based, negative) to the practical (no discernible principles) to the protective (rights-based, welfare-focused, positive) to the positive new frontiers of youth justice that will be discussed in Chapter 6.

RESPONDING TO YOUTH CRIME: SO, WHAT DO WE KNOW?

Discourses of child protection, restoration, punishment, public protection, responsibility, justice, rehabilitation, welfare, retribution, diversion, human rights, and so on, intersect and circulate in a perpetually uneasy and contradictory motion.

(Goldson and Muncie 2009: vii)

Goldson and Muncie's conclusion neatly encapsulates the inherent complexities and hybridity in the formation and delivery of youth justice. Chapter 5 has demonstrated the complexity and hybridity of contemporary international youth justice models, following a long history of conflict and ambivalence in the form of dynamic, contingent and contested philosophical, systemic, structural, strategic and practical constructions of youth justice responses to youth offending. As we have seen, numerous dichotomies have shaped youth justice historically, exemplified by welfare–justice and extended in this chapter through discussions of punitive and child-friendly visions for youth justice. However, it is crucial to reiterate that these are generalisations drawn to aid our analysis and understanding of overarching trends and trajectories – a foundation for understanding the intricacies of international models of youth justice as dynamic social constructions rather than definitive, factual and fixed models. The traditional welfare–justice debate and the more contemporary models of youth justice internationally are, by necessity, only 'ideal types' (Hazel 2008), albeit ideal types that can enhance our understanding of the 'myriad principles' that shape youth justice policy in Western world and that produce youth justice systems with 'complex architectural phenomena . . . with a multiplicity of processes, procedures and programmes' (McAra 2010: 287). Much more nuanced analysis of individual contexts is needed in order to be sensitive to the precise, multifaceted nature of youth justice constructions within and between nations (McAra 2010; Goldson and Hughes 2010). For example, one of our frequent RTAs has been the local mediation of centralised, generalised youth justice philosophies, strategies, objectives and practices – mediation that has been dependent on socio-historic, political, economic, cultural, judicial and organisational contexts – often resulting in hybridised models of youth justice (Goldson 2014). Mediation processes in these different contexts are further influenced by professional values, principles, cultures and discretion when interpreting, adapting and implementing centralised policies (cf. Souhami 2007). Sensitive analyses of the nature of youth justice in any given location must account for such local mediation (similar to social reconstruction) and the influences upon it.

In summary, this chapter has highlighted the complex hybridity to the construction of youth justice through different philosophies/principles, structures, systems, strategy/policies and practices across history and within and between countries. The throughgoing welfare versus justice debate and the range of twenty-first-century models and movements of youth justice identified in this chapter indicate that responses to youth offending have been as dynamic, contingent and contested as the socially constructed definitions and explanations of youth offending that have (to some degree) influenced these responses over history within the 'triad of youth justice'.

5 EASY PIECES

Recommended further reading

An appropriate starting point for expanding upon the arguments in this chapter is the edited text *Comparative Youth Justice* by John Muncie and Barry Goldson (2006). This was the first book to critically reflect on contemporary youth justice reform across a range of Western jurisdictions, identifying similarities and differences and how global trends have been translated at the local level. John and Barry are two of the most respected and knowledgeable scholars in the youth justice field and they consistently present arguments that inform, stimulate and challenge the reader.

Despite being a little dated now, the superb edited text *Youth Justice: Critical Issues* by John Muncie *et al.* (2002) remains essential reading for those interested in the key themes, debates and controversies that have shaped the construction and implementation of youth justice internationally and historically.

Additional evidence and rationale for the identified 'models' of youth justice can be found in Neal Hazel's report: 'Cross-National Comparison of Youth Justice' (2008). This clearly structured and concise comparative analysis explores the overall approaches taken by Western youth justice systems, their structures and procedures for administering youth justice and the associated interventions, including a detailed examination of relative ages of criminal responsibility internationally.

For a more up-to-date discussion of contemporary international youth justice, I would recommend the journal article 'Juvenile Justice Systems in Europe: Reform Developments between Justice, Welfare and "New Punitiveness"' by Frieder Dunkel (2014). The article evaluates youth justice policies and practices across Europe from a comparative perspective, focusing on tendencies towards certain forms of legislation, sentencing practices and the influence of the welfare–justice debate. Dunkel writes in a direct and accessible style reflective of the content and style of the current chapter.

In order to address the ethnocentric bias towards Western youth justice systems in the current chapter, you are directed towards *Delinquency and Juvenile Justice Systems in the Non-Western World* by Paul Friday and Xiu Ren (2006). This book offers a welcome and much-needed focus on the youth justice systems of 11 non-Western countries (India, Pakistan, Nigeria, South Africa, Turkey, Saudi Arabia, Japan, China, Thailand, Macao and the Philippines) in terms of their legal traditions, underpinning principles and compliance with the UNCRC. This is a descriptive text with little comparison between the countries, but it is nonetheless valuable reading for broadening understandings of global youth justice.

NOTES

1 To reiterate a crucial point from Chapter 1, youth justice is not only concerned with responding to offending; it also focuses on bringing justice into the lives of young people who offend. Historically, these young people are disproportionately likely to have a background of social adversity, victimisation, social exclusion, experience of being in care and be members of disadvantaged social groups such as the working class and black and minority ethnic (BAME) populations. There is insufficient space within this book, however, to provide a detailed analysis of the social construction of youth offending and youth justice in relation to these disadvantaged groups specifically.

2 Please remember that these chronological periods have been drawn in a generalised, approximated way to provide you with a framework for understanding and to render the information more coherent, accessible and digestible. Consequently, they are subjective 'constructions', not universally agreed historical 'facts', and there is a necessary degree of overlap between them.

APPENDIX 3

CONVERSATIONS

Restorative justice internationally

Steve: What are the origins of restorative justice in the Western world?

Dave O'Mahony: It's been argued that restorative justice (RJ) has its roots in ancient forms of dispute settlement. Indeed, there are tribal methods of bringing wrong-doers and victims together, overseen by elders, to resolve conflicts and repair the harms caused. However, many of the current practices of RJ, particularly as used in criminal justice, are fairly recent developments. Schemes really began to develop in earnest from around the 1970s, particularly in North America. Since then, we have seen RJ rapidly expand, taking on a wide variety of differing forms within criminal justice. For example, at the pre-prosecution stage, they are often used by the police as restorative types of cautions, at the sentencing stage, restorative youth conferenc-ing is used in Northern Ireland to agree outcomes that form court sentences, and at the post-conviction stage, we have examples of restorative work that takes place within prisons.

Steve: Does RJ have an identifiable theoretical basis and set of underlying principles or strategies?

Dave: Yes it does, though there are differing views and opinions. This is understand-able, given the wide variety of practices that take place globally. But, explanations of RJ usually centre on those that define the practice, or those that give theoretical accounts as to how it works. Looking at the work that defines RJ – the most com-monly accepted definition is provided by Marshall (1999: 5), who describes it as 'a process whereby parties with a stake in a specific offence collectively resolve how to deal with the aftermath of the offence and its implications for the future'. This definition captures many of the crucial elements that make up RJ. Similarly, Zehr and Mika (1998) have highlighted how RJ is underpinned by three core assumptions. Firstly, crime is seen as a violation of relationships, particularly between the offender, victim and wider community interests. Secondly, such violations create obligations and liabilities between these parties. Thirdly, RJ seeks to heal and put right wrongs. This is achieved through dialogue, consent and reconciliation. Thus, RJ is achieved through a process that is inclusive and non-coercive and which actively encourages participation on how the offence should be dealt with.

On the other hand, there are theoretical explanations that unpack how and why RJ works. For example, Braithwaite (2002) argues that RJ can be understood as a pro-cess in which 'reintegrative shaming' is used to encourage offenders to reflect on the consequences of their actions, giving them opportunities to make amends for their wrongdoing. Thus, it allows offenders to reintegrate back into the moral community. His work focuses on the importance of shame for the offender. But, rather than blam-ing and denouncing the offender, as is common in criminal justice, the wrongfulness of the offence is emphasised over the wrongfulness of the individual. As such, the process allows offenders to make amends and move forward from their offending, rather than simply being punished and labelled as criminals.

In our recent book *Reimagining Restorative Justice*, Jonathan Doak and I (O'Mahony and Doak 2017) contend that RJ is usefully understood, from a theoretical perspective, as a process and set of outcomes that seek to re-empower those impacted by crime. We argue that crime disempowers victims and criminal justice but can also be disempowering for all of those drawn into its process. The potential of RJ, theoretically and practically, is realised through its capacity to re-empower those impacted by crime, and this is achieved through our positive goals of 'agency' and 'accountability'. Agency is achieved when participants are given opportunities to make effective choices and take ownership for the consequences of offending and its outcomes. It contrasts to the disempowering impacts that victims and offenders commonly experience in the criminal justice system. Similarly, accountability is the empowering goal that gives individuals the power to accept responsibility for their actions and to take responsibility towards others. Thus, it focuses on the importance of creating and accepting positive obligations and commitments between the parties, rather than having them imposed through a retributive focused sentencing process. Together our goals of agency and accountability provide a lens that helps us to critically reflect the empowering potential of RJ against disempowering impacts of crime and how this should play out practically at the individual and collective levels.

Steve: Are there differences in how RJ is delivered on the ground?

Dave: Yes, there are considerable differences, and as I mentioned there are considerable variations in how restorative programmes are delivered in practice. For example, much of what currently happens in England and Wales emerged as diversionary mechanisms, or alternative ways of dealing with young people who have offended. For instance, the Youth Restorative Disposal gives the police a diversionary 'restorative' method for dealing with offenders by way of a summary disposal, similar to a Caution, Reprimand or Final Warning. Similarly, the Referral Order in England and Wales was established as a 'restorative' programme for young people brought before the courts for the first time. It allows cases to be dealt with through a youth offender panel with a restorative focus, rather than the normal court process, and recently this has been widened in scope to include young people with previous convictions. Unfortunately, however, evidence has shown that these types of restorative programmes have limited engagement with the victims of crime. So, only a very small minority of Referral Orders involve victims, which greatly limits their ability to provide a truly restorative process. Similarly, for Youth Restorative Disposals there is little evidence that they provide victims a meaningful say in how the offence is dealt with. As such, they've been shown to have relatively limited restorative potential.

However, Northern Ireland has adopted a mainstreamed and more fully formed RJ programme for young offenders, similar in some respects to the conferencing model used in New Zealand. The restorative conferencing model brings offenders and victims (and their supporters) together, with a conference coordinator, to deal with the consequences of offence and decide how it is dealt with. It is used to devise a conference plan which will take into consideration the offence, the needs of the victim and the needs of the young person. The young person has to consent to process and the plan needs to be agreed among the participants. This plan can then be ratified by the court and effectively becomes the sentence.

Research examining the conferencing process has been positive. Restorative youth conferencing has considerably increased levels of participation in the justice process for offenders, victims and other parties. Victims have been shown to be generally willing to participate in the process, and their reasons for doing so seem to be based around wanting to understand why the offence happened and to explain how it impacted them. They have been shown to be able to engage in conferencing. It appears the forum is largely successful in providing an opportunity for participants to express their feelings and have a say. Research shows that generally victims appear to be satisfied that the young person was genuine and were happy that they got the opportunity to meet them and understand more about them and why they had been victimised. Interestingly, it's been found victims usually don't come to conferences to vent anger or seek retribution. Rather, most victims are more interested in moving on or putting the incident behind them and seeing something positive come out of it. Indeed, most victims say they would recommend conferencing to a victim in a similar situation to themselves.

For offenders, the conferencing process appears to hold them to account for their actions, particularly by having to explain to the conference group and victim why they offended. Offenders commonly say they wanted, and gave reasons such as wanting to make good for what they had done, to apologise to the victim, or to seek forgiveness. Only some offenders said they were initially not keen to attend. Indeed, many offenders appreciated the opportunity to interact with the victim. Though some offenders who participated in conferences said they did so to avoid going to court, most felt it provided them with the opportunity to take responsibility for their actions, seek forgiveness and put the offence behind them. The Youth Conferencing process is by no means an easy option, and most offenders said they found it very challenging. Offenders find the prospect of coming face-to-face with their victim the most difficult aspect of the process. Yet despite their nervousness, observations of the conferences revealed that they were usually able to engage in the restorative conferencing process and accept responsibility for what they had done. The offenders identified the most meaningful aspect of the conference as the opportunity to apologise to the victim. It is notable that accepting responsibility to the victim and apologising to them are features virtually absent from our traditional court process. Yet, these have been identified as the most meaningful, if sometimes difficult, parts of the process, underlining their importance to RJ and to the people involved.

Steve: Will RJ continue to expand into the future?

Dave: There is no doubt that RJ measures are becoming an important feature of criminal justice developments internationally. RJ's ability to provide a useful and effective method for dealing with crime has made it an attractive model for criminal justice reform. In particular, its ability to engage victims in a meaningful process and provide them some form reparation, as well as helping individuals to recover from the impacts of crime, are all highly desirable.

This is not to suggest RJ is some kind of cure-all for crime and how we deal with it. But, international research shows that RJ can deliver high levels of satisfaction from victims in terms of the process they go through and how they are dealt with as individuals. Research also shows them to be satisfied with the outcomes, as these usually attempt to directly address their needs. In relation to offenders, RJ measures can offer a process that holds them to account. It requires them to face up to the consequences of their actions and see the impact of their behaviour on others. It also gives offenders the opportunity to make amends and to help put things right. Thus, RJ can help to re-empower those who have been directly affected by crime, particularly when it involves direct interactions through a conferencing model, and it certainly contrasts favourably with our traditional model of criminal justice.

Responding to youth offending

New Labour and the 'new youth justice'

5

Chapter 4 explored the socio-historical construction of 'youth justice' in the UK and how youth justice responses have been influenced to different degrees at different times by socially constructed definitions and explanations of youth offending. The chapter outlined the different philosophies/principles, systems, structures, strategies and practices that constitute the 'youth justice' developed to tackle youth offending. The chapter focused on two specific dichotomies that have underpinned youth justice objectives historically: care versus control and welfare versus justice. The chapter concluded with discussion of the hybrid nature of models of youth justice since the 1990s, influenced to different degrees in different countries by punitive approaches (following the 'punitive turn'), practical risk management and protective 'child-friendly justice'.

This chapter will apply and extend our knowledge of youth justice by examining a revolutionary period of youth justice in England and Wales that occurred under the Labour Government from 1997 to 2010. During this time, a controversial 'new youth justice' was developed that departed dramatically from its predecessors (nationally and arguably internationally) in focus and form, most notably in terms of the strategies of responsibilisation, prevention, risk-focused early intervention and managerialism employed to respond to the modern social construction of the 'youth offender' as dangerous, risky and irresponsible (see Chapter 1). As always, discussion will be divided into '5 easy pieces' across the chapter and within each chapter section. The chapter begins by tracing the emergence of a new brand of Labour Party ('New Labour') in the first half of the 1990s, one espousing radically new policies that laid the foundations for a new model of youth justice. The second stage outlines the recommendations from the influential *Misspent Youth* review of the systems and structures of youth justice in England and Wales (Audit Commission 1996) and the subsequent *No More Excuses* **Government White Paper** (a document setting out policy and inviting opinion on it), which formalised the requirement for a set of strategies that would coalesce into the 'new youth justice'. The main section of the chapter offers an explanation of the youth justice structures, systems, strategies and practices introduced by the Crime and Disorder Act 1998 and how they cohered around the central aim of prevention to reconstruct youth justice. In the penultimate section, the success of the 'new youth justice' over the first decade of the New Labour administration will be evaluated in terms of its impact upon the Government's three priority outcomes for the revamped Youth Justice System: reductions in first-time entrants (into the system), reoffending and custody. There is a further evaluation of the key elements of the 'new youth justice' in terms of their rationale and impact upon the delivery of youth justice in England and Wales. The chapter concludes with an investigation of the significant youth justice developments during the short period from 2008 to 2010 following the first decade of the 'new youth justice' and immediately preceding the fall from power of New Labour as the Government of the UK. This conclusion section evaluates the extent to which these developments demonstrated a break from the 'new youth justice', an extension of its existing elements, or both.

5 EASY PIECES

Responding to youth offending: New Labour and the 'new youth justice'

1 *The birth of New Labour (1992–1997)* outlines the emergence of a new type of Labour Party promoting a new model of youth justice informed by realist explanations and based on strategies of communitarianism and responsibilisation.
2 Misspent Youth *and* No More Excuses *(1996–1997)* discusses the two pivotal reports that shaped the future of youth justice in England and Wales, both of which concluded that existing systems and structures were ineffective, inefficient and uneconomical.
3 *The Crime and Disorder Act 1998: formalising the 'new youth justice'* examines the most radical and influential piece of youth justice legislation in England and Wales for 150 years, which cohered around a series of modernising, responsibilising, practical and managerialist strategies offering a 'third way' of delivering youth justice within a formalised 'Youth Justice System' that was not wedded to welfare or justice priorities.
4 *Evaluating the 'new youth justice' (1997–2007)* evaluates the impact of the Crime and Disorder Act 1998 and associated legislation on the delivery of youth justice and the outcomes it recorded for young people in relation to arrests, first-time entry into the Youth Justice System, sentencing/disposals, reoffending and custody rates.
5 *The final years of the 'new youth justice' (2008–2010)* explores the shape of youth justice immediately prior to the change in Government during a period characterised by conflict and ambivalence, evidenced by the reversal of trends in criminalisation due to increased use of diversion and changing professional attitudes alongside the consolidation of 'new youth justice' strategies of responsibilisation and risk-focused early intervention.

1 THE BIRTH OF NEW LABOUR (1992–1995)

In 1992, the Shadow Home Secretary Tony Blair fired a significant shot in the Labour Party's campaign to seize power from the incumbent Conservative Government of the UK. In an audacious bid to become the 'party of law and order', traditionally the domain of the Conservative Party (e.g. see Chapter 1 discussion of the Children and Young Persons Act 1970), Blair famously announced that the new and improved Labour Party would be 'tough on crime and tough on the causes of crime'. This move towards the political centre/right from a traditionally more socialist, welfare-focused political agenda (e.g. see Chapter 1 discussion of the Children and Young Persons Act 1969) was part of a major rebranding exercise for the party from which emerged New Labour (Hopkins-Burke 2016). The idea of this rebranding was twofold: to modernise/update old-fashioned policy agendas and to make the party more attractive to the

voting public (Hopkins-Burke 2016; Solomon and Garside 2008; Pitts 2003). I interviewed Alun Michael (a key youth justice policy adviser to Tony Blair at the time)
specifically to inform our book, and he explained the New Labour thought process:

> There was a political imperative to be seen to be doing the things that will make a differ-
> ence to what the public is concerned about, but there's also the need to do it in a sensible
> way. That's why we had the slogan 'tough on crime and tough on the causes of crime'.
> (Alun Michael 2017, personal interview)

The youth justice policy developed by New Labour while in opposition to the Conservative Government was informed by three Es[1] (Smith 2014): political *expedience*,
research *evidence* and personal and professional *experience*. Political expedience came in
the form of seizing the law and order mantle from the Conservatives and rebranding
the party as New Labour, while research evidence came largely in the form of secondary
data analysis and scholarly arguments presented by realist criminologists (see Chapter 2).
However, the role of personal and professional experience should not be underestimated.
In 1994, Tony Blair became Labour Party leader and was replaced as Shadow Home Secretary by Jack Straw (who became Home Secretary in 1997). Straw worked closely with the
Shadow Home Affairs Minister Alun Michael (who became Minister of State for Home
Affairs in 1997) and Norman Warner (Straw's 'Special Adviser'). Both Straw and Michael
had professional experience of the relationship between socio-economic disadvantage
and high (youth) crime rates as Members of Parliament (MPs) for socially deprived con-
stituencies (Blackburn and Cardiff South, respectively). In particular, both MPs gained
first-hand experience of widespread public perceptions of the social disadvantage-youth
offending relationship in their local areas, which fuelled public opinion of a youth crime
'problem'. During an interview, Alun Michael (2017) told me:

> I spent an enormous amount of time going to local areas up and down the coun-
> try with a political agenda, accompanying local MPs or candidates in the next
> election. That gave me a real insight. Wherever he went, it would start with local
> residents talking about the problem of young people being out of control.

Alun Michael had further professional experience of the relationship between
social disadvantage and youth offending as a youth court magistrate in Cardiff in the
1970s and 1980s, while Norman Warner had a background working with vulnerable
and offending young people in local government social services. He told me:

> My background of working with young offenders and in the court has been very
> much saying 'you know what, a lot of kids we were involved with didn't need to
> be offending. There may have been circumstances in the area where it was unu-
> sual not to be involved in crime, but it does need to be like that'.
> (Alun Michael 2017, personal interview)

Jack Straw also had personal experience of growing up in relative poverty in Blackburn and being surrounded by youth offending, yet never committing crime himself.
Straw's experiences led him to develop a less than tolerant attitude to understanding
the problems faced by socially deprived young people who did offend, which laid
the foundations for a more realist and responsibilising political perspective on youth

offending. In 1995, he visited New York and became enamoured with crime prevention approaches based around **zero tolerance policing** and the **'broken windows thesis'** (Zimring 2011; Sousa and Kelling 2006) of responding to antisocial behaviour and community disintegration in a strict, non-discretionary, timely and intensive manner, which consolidated his preference for focusing on the manifestations of crime rather than its causes (Smith 2014). That same year, Labour produced the document *Safer Communities, Safer Britain: Labour's Proposals for Tough Action on Crime*, in which Straw asserted that effective youth justice policy should try to 'nip young offending in the bud' (Straw 1995: 1). With Straw, Michael and Warner working together, 'there was a coincidence of taking a similar view of what needed to be done and bringing different strands of experience together to support what Jack Straw wanted, which was to get the issues tackled' (Alun Michael 2017, personal interview). The responsibilisation agenda was now in full flow, with New Labour proclaiming that

> individuals must be held responsible for their own behaviour, and must be brought to justice and punished when they commit an offence.
>
> (Straw and Michael 1996: 6)

Furthermore, in a move that distanced New Labour from traditional welfare-based approaches to young people who offended, Straw and Michael went on to assert that

> the welfare needs of the young offender cannot outweigh the needs of the community to be protected from the adverse consequences of his or her offending behavior.
>
> (Straw and Michael 1996: 6)

A focal *policy/strategy* of New Labour, therefore, was to be the promotion of social responsibility and in particular the values of **communitarianism** – an ideology emphasising the responsibility of the individual to their community and the social importance of the family unit (cf. Etzioni 1995). New Labour wished to balance the rights afforded to the individual with their responsibilities to their community and to the State (e.g. their responsibility not to commit crime or to harm others). The politically attractive focus on dealing with the growing social 'problem' of youth offending (always a vote winner) was theoretically underpinned by the increasingly influential realist explanations of youth offending from the left and right of the political spectrum (see Chapter 3). Realists understood crime as a real problem with real impacts on real people, a problem that required urgent attention. Right realists explained this problem as the product of rational choice and immorality among the working classes (e.g. Wilson and Herrnstein 1985; Murray 1994), while left realists fused rational choice explanations with consideration of the socio-economic contexts in which offending takes place (e.g. Lea and Young 1984).

> The underlying principle was that it doesn't work to be soft on crime because crime has a victim and it's serious to the victim. Whatever the background, unless you look at the offence as well as the causes, you have more offences.
>
> (Alun Michael 2017, personal interview)

The realist emphasis upon rational choice influenced the New Labour strategy of **responsibilisation** that was to have a significant influence on their developing youth justice policy – assigning increasing levels of responsibility to young people (not to mention their families and local communities) for tackling the causes of their own offending behaviour. This strategy is also called **neo-liberal responsibilisation** (cf. Muncie 2014; Dunkel 2014; McAra 2010; see also Chapter 4), with 'neo-liberal' in this case referring to a strategy of placing less emphasis on the social contexts of behaviour and more on individual, family and community responsibility and accountability. Consequently, social problems such as crime were redefined in terms of individual rather than State responsibility (Arthur 2016), a strategy known as **individualisation**. Upon becoming the Labour leader in 1994, Tony Blair pronounced that 'we should never excuse the commission of criminal acts on the grounds of social conditions' (Blair 1994), having previously characterised youth offending as a descent into 'moral chaos' (Scraton and Haydon 2002). With regard to young people, the (left realist) New Labour view was that young people should take more personal responsibility for their behaviour and in return would receive community and Government support to reintegrate back into society (Smith 2014). New Labour planned to 'encourage' young people to accept more responsibility for addressing their (offending-related) problems and behaviours by adopting a strategy of early intervention. According to Straw and Michael (1996):

> Insufficient attention is given to changing behavior. . . . Too little is done to change youngsters' behaviour early in their offending career. . . . We have to start again . . . by prioritising early intervention to nip offending in the bud.

In summary, the rebranded New Labour Party began the 1990s by developing a policy response to youth offending based on communitarianism and responsibilisation strategies that cohered with political expediency (the need to be popular with the voting public), research evidence (particularly realist explanations) and the personal and professional experiences of key constructors/influencers of the new approach, particularly Jack Straw, Alun Michael and Norman Warner.

5 EASY PIECES

1 The birth of New Labour (1992–1997)

1   *New Labour*: in the early to mid-1990s, the Labour Party rebranded itself as New Labour, the modernised party of law and order that would be 'tough on crime and tough on the causes of crime'.
2   *Communitarianism and responsibilisation*: the key New Labour strategy of communitarianism emphasised the individual's social responsibility to their community as a way of making them eligible to access their right to support from the State. This strategy, along with support for realist explanations of youth offending, motivated the strategy of responsibilisation that was to underpin the subsequent 'new youth justice'.
3   *Realism*: New Labour favoured realist explanations that viewed youth offending as the product of rational choice, irresponsibility and immorality (right realist) among young people who are more likely to be suffering from social

> deprivation and social exclusion (left realist), which motivated a youth justice strategy based on responsibilisation and broader social policies focused on minimising social exclusion.
>
> 4 *Key individuals*: Jack Straw (Shadow Home Secretary), Alun Michael (Shadow Home Affairs Minister) and Norman Warner (Special Adviser to Jack Straw) shaped and drove the New Labour youth justice agenda based on their personal and professional experiences of youth offending in socially deprived areas.
>
> 5 *Expedience, evidence, experience*: the constructions of youth offending and youth justice that were to shape the 'new youth justice' introduced from the late 1990s were based on political expediency, academic evidence and personal/ professional experience.

2 *MISSPENT YOUTH* AND *NO MORE EXCUSES* (1996–1997)

The year before the 1997 General Election, the Audit Commission published a review of the Youth Justice System (YJS) of England and Wales; a review that had been requested by the outgoing Conservative Government. The results of this review were damning, with the Audit Commission (1996: 6) concluding that

> the present arrangements are failing young people – who are not being guided away from offending to constructive activities. . . . Resources need to be shifted from processing young offenders to dealing with their behaviour. At the same time, efforts to prevent offending behaviour by young people need to be coordinated between the different agencies involved.

Following a secondary data analysis of system outcomes and a consultation exercise with key stakeholders (e.g. policy-makers, practitioners, academics), the review authors Mark Perfect and Judy Renshaw concluded that the current YJS was ineffective, inefficient and uneconomical. The YJS was considered ineffective due to rising levels of youth offending, with Renshaw and Perfect (1997) claiming that 'a quarter of known offenders are under 18 and account for around seven million criminal offences every year'. The authors also claimed that annual decreases in youth offending rates were more apparent than real – the artefact of demographic changes, reclassification of offences and the increased use of cautioning. The YJS was considered inefficient because multiple agencies were very poor at working together to address youth offending in practical terms, resulting in the very slow processing of young people through the system. The YJS was considered uneconomical because it allegedly spent around £1 billion per year responding to youth offending (Audit Commission 1996). The review was titled *Misspent Youth*, a double entendre suggesting that huge amounts of money were being wasted on ineffective and inefficient approaches to youth offending/justice and that large numbers of young people were wasting (misspending) their adolescent years committing crime and damaging their communities.

The report authors put forward a series of recommendations to make the YJS more effective, efficient and economical – recommendations that would shape New Labour youth justice policy over the next ten years (Muncie 2014). It was recommended that co-ordinated *multi-agency partnerships* should be constructed to pursue agreed system objectives and strategies, which would enable young people who offended to be processed and dealt with more quickly, efficiently (e.g. through organisations sharing objectives) and economically. The organisations and staff within these partnerships should be subject to rigorous and consistent *performance management* to ensure that they were working effectively and efficiently. This introduced the strategy of **managerialism** – a set of techniques and practices (driven by the pursuit of effectiveness, efficiency and economy) that aimed to transform the structures and processes of youth and criminal justice through close, intensive management and control (Muncie 2008). The second radical recommendation for the YJS was that it should focus on one central objective: the prevention of youth offending. *Misspent Youth* had concluded that because formal youth justice responses (e.g. out-of-court cautioning, court sentences, custody) were ineffective, inefficient and expensive, it was therefore far preferable to prevent offending from occurring in the first place and, when offending occurred, to divert young people from the formal YJS in order to prevent further criminalisation and expense. Linking the managerialist and preventative objectives together was to call for all youth justice practice to be 'effective' and 'evidence based'. The evidence of effectiveness that the Audit Commission privileged was drawn largely from the artefactual risk factor theories that informed the risk factor prevention paradigm (RFPP) and that had come to dominate explanations of youth offending in the late twentieth century and risk management responses to it (see Chapters 3 and 4). Therefore, the main recommendation for reorientating youth justice practice was that it be (evidence) based in the assessment and targeting of risk factors (i.e. the RFPP) in order to prevent future offending. The advocacy of risk assessment chimed with support for early intervention practice with young people who could be identified as 'at risk' of offending for the first time or 'at risk' of reoffending once they had offended. As such, the review promoted an **interventionist** model of youth justice, wherein adults (e.g. in the form of the State, communities, local authorities, youth justice agencies) would increasingly intervene in the lives of young people in order to provide them with support, to control their behaviour and to pre-empt future problems. In summary, *Misspent Youth* offered a blueprint for a radically revised YJS, replacing the historical system-guiding philosophies/principles of welfare and justice (see Chapter 4) with recommendations for an overarching strategy of managerialism and an underpinning strategy of prevention.

 ## CONTROVERSIES AND DEBATES

The partiality of *Misspent Youth*

The validity (accuracy, comprehensiveness, honesty) of the *Misspent Youth* review has been subject to criticism due to its partiality, with 'partial' in this sense having a dual meaning: limited/incomplete and subjective/biased. The claims from the report were put under the microscope in an insightful article by Denis Jones (2001) titled 'Misjudged Youth'. Jones criticised the Audit Commission for its focus on performance management, which was a move away from its main area of expertise, that of reviewing financial efficiency. Such an expansion beyond its original remit was seen as evidence of the Audit Commission 'adapting new roles from bases of limited knowledge, or indeed ignorance' (McSweeney 1988). Jones was critical of what he perceived as the selective (partial, biased) use of evidence and analysis across the report by the authors Renshaw and Perfect, citing 'their use of their own surveys instead of more detailed research, when it seems to suit', combined with 'numerical sleight of hand' (Jones 2001: 3). In particular, the claim that 'a quarter of known offenders are under 18' (Renshaw and Perfect 1997) was based on very questionable assumptions and generalisations from adult offending figures, with no evidence that these extrapolations were valid. Similarly, the claim that 'public services spend around £1 billion a year processing and dealing with offending by young people' (Audit Commission 1996: 7) was presented uncritically. On closer inspection, two-thirds of this expenditure was by the police and there was a lack of evidence as to how this had been calculated, which gave 'serious cause for concern' (Jones 2001: 5). Finally, there was a misleading claim that recent decreases in youth offending rates were more apparent than real (the result of demographic change, reclassification of offences and the increased use of cautioning), which overlooked any tangible 'successful revolution' in offence-focused youth justice practice in the 1980s and early 1990s (Jones 1993; see also Chapter 4).

Further allegations of selectivity raised serious questions about the independence, comprehensiveness and appropriateness of the review's findings and recommendations. Although the review authors appear to have consulted with a range of academics and other key stakeholder groups (cf. Haines and Case 2015), some critics feel that the final recommendations were the product of significant political influence and the cherry-picking of evidence to support pre-formed policy priorities. Political influence shaping the nature of the reported findings and consequent recommendations was exerted by politicians from New Labour (who were on the brink of a landslide triumph in the 1997 General Election), particularly from Jack Straw (Shadow Home Secretary) and his soon-to-be official Senior Policy Adviser, Norman Warner (Kevin Haines 2017, personal interview). Like all potential new State leaders, New Labour were keen to dismiss previous policies as ineffective and even keener to offer new and progressive alternatives. The imminent Blair Government was seeking a 'third way' to move youth justice beyond the 'distractions' of welfare and justice (Alun Michael 2017, personal interview). Welfare in any form was not a viable option for a party looking to distance itself from universal provision, State support and notions of collective responsibility (Haines 1999) and keen to replace these with communitarian and responsibilising strategies. Similarly, justice was a non-starter for a political party who had committed to the view that previous approaches to tackling youth offending (notably the justice-informed practices of the 1980s) had done little to address the problem. Consequently, the recommended risk management approach of the 'psychologically oriented criminologists' (Case and Haines 2009), who we have come to know as artefactual risk factor theorists (see Chapter 3), offered the incoming New Labour their desired model of youth justice: evidence based, managerialist and practical. The fact that the 'evidence' privileged by the Audit Commission reviewers was highly selective, restricted and politically expedient was not acknowledged in the *Misspent Youth* report. New Labour had identified a common-sense and much-needed 'third way' for youth justice. Better still, *Misspent Youth* offered recommendations that promised to make the YJS more effective, efficient and economical.

So, what do you think of *Misspent Youth*? Were its recommendations effective and reflective, or selective and subjective?

No More Excuses: A New Approach to Tackling Youth Crime

Following the 1997 General Election, the 'New' Labour Party seized power in the UK, with Tony Blair as Prime Minister and Jack Straw as **Home Secretary** – the Government minister responsible for internal affairs in England and Wales, including all criminal justice matters. From that point, Straw worked closely with Alun Michael (now Home Affairs Minister/Deputy Home Secretary) and Norman Warner (now Senior Policy Adviser) to further develop the new Government's youth justice policy, which had been a key vote winner in the election. Indicative of the continued policy significance of youth offending/justice, one of the first acts of the new Government was to produce a White Paper that built on the recommendations of *Misspent Youth* by proposing a root-and-branch reform of the YJS of England and Wales. The resulting report, *No More Excuses: A New Approach to Tackling Youth Crime* (Home Office 1997), officially announced a new model of youth justice in order to 'draw a line under the past' (Home Office 1997: preface by Jack Straw). Two clear youth justice strategies were heavily favoured in *No More Excuses*: the *responsibilisation* of young people who offend and the *prevention* of further offending. It could be argued that this embodied a dual strategy of blaming/punishing young people who offended (see Section 1 of this chapter), in conjunction with providing support to help them to stop offending and to appease public anxieties regarding reoffending (**RTA = support–control**), reflecting 'the philosophy and approach that we had developed' (Alun Michael 2017, personal interview). Whether these dual foci were complementary and compatible or contradictory and conflicting remains debatable. Emphasising the break from the past and need to do something new and the commitment to realist explanations and the strategy of responsibilisation, Alun Michael (2017) told me during our interview:

> The welfare and justice debates got in the way of common sense. It takes us back to the 'tough on crime and tough on the causes of crime' slogan, because if somebody commits an offence and you can see causes and factors, this doesn't reduce the seriousness of the offence. Therefore, if you create an excuse culture such as they live in a community that's likely to encourage them to offend, then you almost create a self-fulfilling prophecy.

The new strategic emphasis on responsibilisation reflected in the document title was consolidated in the Home Secretary's preface, setting out the new Government's stance on youth offending:

> An excuse culture has developed within the youth justice system. It excuses itself for its inefficiency, and too often excuses the young offenders before it, implying that they cannot help their behaviour because of their social circumstances. Rarely are they confronted with their behaviour and helped to take more personal responsibility for their actions.

The prevention focus recommended in the *Misspent Youth* review was formalised with a sound bite that built upon a 1995 declaration by Jack Straw:

> There will be a new focus on nipping crime in the bud – stopping children at risk from getting involved in crime and preventing early criminal behaviour from escalating into persistent serious offending.

(Home Office 1997: 3)

The objective of nipping crime in the bud embodied a two-stage prevention process – preventing first-time offending and preventing reoffending by identified offenders. The vehicle to pursue prevention would be the identification and assessment of 'at-risk' young people (n.b. not the 'children' of Straw's rhetoric) and early intervention using evidence-based approaches to targeting criminogenic risk factors – in other words, risk management through the RFPP. While some commentators have portrayed the White Paper as reflecting New Labour's ideological commitment to punishment (cf. Arthur 2016), others have perceived an 'alarming' absence of philosophical basis replaced with an explicitly strategic and technical approach (cf. Case and Haines 2009). Taken together, *Misspent Youth* and *No More Excuses* formalised and mobilised a new risk-focused, preventative model of constructing and working with young people who offend that contrasted with the traditional dominance of welfare and/or justice when understanding youth offending and delivering youth justice. This new, modernised model of youth justice would be very closely managed as a way of ensuring efficiency and economy; distancing youth justice responses from the existing system that 'excuses itself for its inefficiency' (Home Office 1997: 3).

5 EASY PIECES

2 *Misspent Youth* and *No More Excuses* (1996–1997)

1 *Pre–'new youth justice'*: the origins of New Labour's 'new youth justice' approach are apparent in the recommendations of the Audit Commission's *Misspent Youth* review of the YJS and the Government's *No More Excuses* White Paper.
2 Misspent Youth *conclusions*: the Audit Commission review concluded that the YJS was ineffective, inefficient and uneconomical, so it required sweeping revisions to address these weaknesses.
3 Misspent Youth *recommendations*: the Audit Commission recommended that the YJS should implement a new model of youth justice based on a responsibilising strategy and central prevention agenda animated by risk-focused early intervention and driven by multi-agency partnership working.
4 *Criticisms of* Misspent Youth: the report was criticised for its selective use of evidence, its questionable interpretation of key evidence and for an alleged undue degree of political influence on its findings and recommendations.
5 *No More Excuses*: the Government formalised the *Misspent Youth* recommendations by proposing a root-and-branch reform of the YJS in the *No More Excuses* White Paper, which would be underpinned by New Labour strategies of responsibilisation and prevention through risk-focused early intervention.

3 THE CRIME AND DISORDER ACT 1998: FORMALISING THE 'NEW YOUTH JUSTICE'

It shall be the principal aim of the youth justice system to prevent offending by children and young persons.

(Home Office 1998: sec. 37.1)

The recommendations of *Misspent Youth* and the associated policy proposals in *No More Excuses* were legislated into existence by the Crime and Disorder Act 1998, the first substantive piece of legislation from the incumbent Labour Government. Although the Act also covered criminal justice responses to adult offending, it is best known for its radical, wholesale reform of the existing philosophies/principles, structures/systems, strategies/policies and processes/practices that constituted youth justice. In the first instance, 'youth justice' responses would now be located within an official Youth Justice System (YJS) – a fully formed, comprehensive and modernised structure, as opposed to the previous collection of piecemeal responses to offending by young people that were largely tacked onto the adult-focused Criminal Justice System (CJS). Although the Government retained control over the whole UK, the new YJS would have authority for England and Wales only – reflecting its position as a separate jurisdiction for criminal and youth justice for many years previously. By the end of the 1990s, policy-making responsibility for youth justice had been formally ceded to the recently (partially) devolved governments of Scotland (see Whyte 2009) and Northern Ireland (see Chapman and O'Mahony 2007). Rather than pursuing a central *philosophy* of either welfare or justice, like the youth justice legislation that had preceded it (see Chapters 1 and 4), the Crime and Disorder Act 1998 was driven by a central *aim* or *strategy* – the prevention of offending. Prevention was the focal point to encourage an effective, efficient and economical YJS. The prevention aim was to be facilitated by a series of youth justice strategies that would shape youth justice practice: managerialism, responsibilisation (which some may argue is an ideology more than it is a strategy) and interventionism. The revolutionary changes that resulted from the Crime and Disorder Act 1998 coalesced to form an approach that Barry Goldson (2000) labelled the 'new youth justice'. From that point, youth justice would be defined by 'new' systemic, structural, strategic and practical responses to youth offending. Let's take a closer look at these central elements of the 'new youth justice' and what exactly made them 'new'.

'New youth justice' structures: monitoring and multi-agency partnerships

The Crime and Disorder Act 1998 introduced new structures that would play major roles in modernising, shaping and delivering the new model of youth justice promoted by the Labour Government. Initially, every local authority area in England and Wales had a statutory obligation to form multi-agency Crime and Disorder Reduction Partnerships (called Community Safety Partnerships in Wales) consisting of representatives from the statutory agencies (police, local authority, probation health) and other relevant key professional stakeholders (e.g. voluntary services, charities, prison service, local businesses, academics). Each partnership was to conduct an audit of the extent and nature of crime in their local area, followed by a strategy highlighting the key issues and proposed responses to them. Perhaps unsurprisingly, given its history of social construction by key influencers (see Chapter 1), youth offending became a commonly identified issue in local strategies and many partnerships convened subgroups specifically to deal with the 'problem'. Through Crime and Disorder Reduction Partnerships and their associated audits and strategies, the Crime and Disorder Act 1998 had introduced statutory multi-agency partnership working into the criminal/youth justice domain. Furthermore, the Act legislated for localised criminal/youth justice structures to address local issues using local (and national) resources – a deliberate strategy of decentralisation and localisation of (youth) justice. The extent to which this local discretion was realised in practice will be discussed in our evaluation of the 'new youth justice' (see Section 4 of this chapter; see also Chapter 6).

Two structures specific to 'new youth justice' were created under the Crime and Disorder Act 1998 that would drive the 'new youth justice' forwards: the Youth Justice Board for England and Wales and multi-agency Youth Offending Teams (YOTs). The Youth Justice Board (YJB) was established as a non-departmental public body (NDPB; also known as a 'quango', or quasi-autonomous non-governmental organisation) to oversee the functioning of the YJS. The YJB was to adopt a dual role: the provision of 'independent' expert guidance to youth justice agencies (e.g. YOTs) and advice to the Government on the effective operation of the YJS (see Case 2014; Souhami 2011; Pitts 2001; this 'independence' will be evaluated in Chapter 6), while developing consistent standards and coherent approaches to youth justice (Haines and Case 2015). The YJB was charged with:

- Monitoring the operation of the youth justice system.
- Advising the secretary of state [Home Secretary] on the operation of the youth justice system and National Standards, and on how the aim of preventing offending by children and young people can most effectively be pursued.
- Identifying and disseminating effective practice across youth justice services.
- Making grants to YOTs and other organisations to support development and delivery of effective practice.
- Commissioning a distinct Secure Estate for young people.
- Placing young people in custody.

Note: the last two requirements of the YJB were not in the original statute, which is why it has been possible to remove them subsequently without legislative change (see Chapter 6).

The inaugural chair of the YJB was Norman Warner (previously Senior Policy Adviser to the Home Secretary) and the first chief executive was Mark Perfect (co-author of the *Misspent Youth* review). These appointments represented a degree of continuity and coherence with the development of New Labour youth justice policy but simultaneously raised concerns over the degree of 'independence' from Government in the first incarnation of the YJB, similar to the concerns raised regarding the *Misspent Youth* report. While the YJB was to take a strategic leadership role in monitoring and managing the YJS, the majority of day-to-day youth justice practice was to be located in new YOTs. Prior to 1998, dealing with young people who offended was the responsibility of Youth Justice Teams consisting largely of social workers from the local authority. Following the Act, YOTs became a statutory requirement in local authority areas in England and Wales – a new structure to work with young people who offended in order to pursue the statutory aim of the YJS to prevent offending. YOTs were required to be multi-agency in structure, consisting of representatives from the four statutory agencies – police, local authority (typically, their education and social services departments), probation and health – and also including voluntary, charitable and other third-sector partners where appropriate and available locally. The make-up of YOTs was further evidence of the Government affording discretion to local areas in how they allocated their resources to deal with youth offending. The number of representatives from each statutory agency was not prescribed by the centre (Government), neither was the type of staff member from each agency or the nature of the other key stakeholder groups represented. That said, typically most YOT staff were (and still are) social workers from the local authority social service department who had traditionally dealt with young people who offended (see Chapter 4 discussion of the Children and Young Persons Act 1948). It is important to note, however, that YOTs were (still are) only one group of practitioners in the YJS, albeit the majority group. The remit of YOTs under the Crime and Disorder Act 1998 was to work with young people entering/re-entering the YJS following arrest by the police (another practitioner group in the YJS), subject to formal sentences (community-based and custodial) from the youth court (containing other practitioner groups such as solicitors and magistrates) or given out-of-court disposals (more later). Young people given custodial sentences would also be dealt with by staff in the 'Secure Estate', which consisted of three specific structures: young offender institutions (YOIs), secure children's homes (SCHs; for young people under 15 years old) and secure training centres (STCs). (For more discussion of contemporary youth custody, see my 'Conversation' with Dr. Tim Bateman in Chapter 6.)

In summary, implementation of the prevention-focused 'new youth justice' of the Crime and Disorder Act 1998 would be monitored and managed by the YJB, who had oversight of the daily practice of both YOTs and the Secure Estate. The Crime and Disorder Act 1998 introduced new systems and structures to pursue its central aim of prevention and a series of new strategies to guide practice in these new systems and structures. At this point, therefore, it is instructive to discuss the strategies and practices of the 'new youth justice' together, as the strategies have been animated and illustrated by the practices introduced by the Act.

'New youth justice' strategies and practices: responsibilisation

An influential New Labour strategy predating the Crime and Disorder Act 1998 that significantly affected subsequent youth justice practice was the emphasis on responsibilisation – holding young people (and their families and communities) responsible and accountable for their offending behaviour and for ensuring the success of youth justice responses to it. This strategy abandoned the minimal intervention (diversionary) trends of the 1980s and early 1990s (e.g. Criminal Justice Act 1991), in favour of more punitive, retributive system objectives (Joyce 2017). The overarching strategy of responsibilisation was best illustrated by the abolition of doli incapax – the historical, legal presumption that young people aged 10–13 years old could not distinguish between right or wrong to the extent that they could be held responsible for criminal actions, unless this presumption could be refuted in court (see Chapter 1). Although the age of criminal responsibility had been 10 years old since the Children and Young Persons Act 1963 (when it was increased from 8 years old), the principle of doli incapax had served as a safeguard to effectively maintain the minimum age for a 'youth offender' at 14 years old. Its abolition in 1998 removed this safeguard. All young people aged 10 and above (up to the age of 17) were now considered to be criminally responsible for their offending behaviour and could be tried and sentenced as such – evidencing the Government's growing commitment to the responsibilisation of young people who offended by making all children from the age of 10 'unequivocally responsible and accountable for choices made and harm caused' (Bandalli 2000: 86–87). The abolition of doli incapax exerted a **net-widening** influence on youth justice practice – extending the remit of the YJS to a larger group of young people (including children) than would previously have been defined (socially constructed) and worked with as 'youth offenders'.

'New youth justice' strategies and practices: sentencing changes

The Crime and Disorder Act 1998 set out a range of 'new youth justice' processes and practices to be employed by staff in YOTs (to some extent, also by staff in the Secure Estate) to prevent offending by 10- to 17-year-olds. Initially, a commitment was made to dramatically improve the system effectiveness and efficiency by halving the time taken to process 'persistent young offenders' through the YJS from 144 days to 72 days, on the basis that

> when somebody offended, not very much happened. I'd found a real problem as a juvenile magistrate with having youngsters in front of the court who couldn't remember the offence because it was so long after the event. We very much believed that getting them before the court in a time that they could remember was going to make a big improvement to the outcomes.
>
> (Alun Michael 2017, personal interview)

This increased efficiency was pursued through the creation of multi-agency YOTs and closer partnership working between YOTs, police and the courts. Each stage of this reinvigorated youth justice process was revised, from out-of-court sentencing to court to custody to release. Previous pre-court processes, characterised by the discretionary and flexible use of police cautioning, were replaced with a new antisocial behaviour management process (see 'Early intervention: Antisocial Behaviour Management' section) and a new system of out-of-court sentencing. The Crime and Disorder Act 1998 legislation created a new, escalating out-of-court sentencing process that was more determinate and rigid than the cautioning system it replaced. It consisted of two new pre-court 'orders' administered to young people by the police if their offence was not considered serious enough in gravity to warrant immediate referral to court: 'Reprimands' for young people admitting a first offence, followed by 'Final Warnings' for those admitting a further offence – at which point there was to be a referral to the YOT for further assessment and preventative intervention. A young person receiving either a Reprimand or a Final Warning on first offence would count as a first-time entrant (FTE) into the YJS, as both measures were effectively classed as 'cautions'. Subsequent offending meant that the young person had to go to court for sentencing (classed as a 'conviction'). If a young person made a no comment interview, the police were obliged to prosecute. The young person, if convicted, was then precluded from receiving another out-of-court disposal. Goldson (2007: 8) argued that this more determinate out-of-court process 'essentially put an end to diversion (cautioning) and established instead a statutory, interventionist system'.

A variety of new court sentences were also made available, varying in their duration and the intensity and nature of YOT supervision required, but all offering a mixture of control over the young person's behaviour (through restrictions and prohibitions) and supportive intervention to address their psychosocial problems (see Chapters 2 and 3) and prevent future offending (**RTA = support-control**). The raft of new sentences reflected Government support for community alternatives and their apparent opposition to the criminogenic and expensive nature of custody (which didn't preclude a subsequent rise in custodial rates, however). The many and varied sentencing options made available (some of which had existed pre-1998) included Drug Treatment and Testing Orders, Reparation Orders, Supervision Orders, Action Plan Orders, Attendance Centre Orders and Community Punishment and Rehabilitation Orders (for 16- to 17-year-olds only). This enhanced range of sentences was, in part, an appeal to **penal populism** – the perceived public desire for clear, decisive and punitive responses to identified offences by young people (Pratt 2005).

The raft of community sentences was supplemented by two new additional disposals: Parenting Orders and Child Safety Orders. The new Parenting Order was created as a three-month programme of support and guidance to parents of young people committing antisocial behaviour or crime, on the basis that 'strong families are the centre of peaceful and safe communities. Parents have a critical role in teaching their child the difference between right and wrong' (Home Office 2003: 8). A YOT Parenting Coordinator was to work with parents in weekly support/guidance sessions designed to develop parenting skills and to enable better control of the child (Joyce 2017). It was made compulsory for parents to attend sessions for 'support and guidance', reflecting a conflict and ambivalence (**RTA**) between support and control/compulsion (**RTA**). Child Safety Orders could be administered to children under the age of criminal responsibility (below 10 years old) who had committed an act that would be considered an offence if they were 10 years old or over or who had committed 'antisocial behaviour' of some kind, thus demonstrating vulnerability and parental neglect. Child Safety Orders were administered by a family proceedings court following application by the local authority social care department and contained requirements for intervention and support by a local authority social worker and/or YOT worker.

The Youth Justice and Criminal Evidence Act 1999 introduced a new court sentence, the Referral Order, to be given to young people pleading guilty (to an offence not considered serious enough for custody) on their first visit to court. Upon receiving the Referral Order, a young person was to be referred to a Referral Order Panel (aka Youth Offender Panel) consisting of practitioner(s) from the police, the YOT and at least two lay members of the general public. The role of the panel was to agree on an appropriate intervention 'contract' with the young person, with the expectation that it would be grounded in restorative justice – encouraging the 'offender' to take responsibility for their actions (i.e. responsibilisation), to repair the harm they have caused and be reintegrated into the community/society (cf. Haines and O'Mahony 2006). All existing *custodial sentences* awarded by the Youth Court (the Crown Court retained authority to give custodial orders for grave crimes) were replaced by the Detention and Training Order (DTO). The DTO allowed for the young person to spend the first portion of their sentence in custody and the latter portion back in the community. Previous custodial sentences had involved elements of custody and community provision, so the change under DTOs was to a large degree cosmetic, although it loosened the criteria that had to be met before custody could be imposed on children aged 12–14. New Labour also implemented the Secure Training Order (legislated for by the previous Government and opposed by Labour in opposition), which reduced the minimum age at which custody could be imposed by the Youth Court from 15 to 12 years old.

In 2001, the Government reviewed the CJS in *Criminal Justice: The Way Ahead* (Home Office 2001). The most significant youth justice development in the review was the introduction of the Intensive Supervision and Surveillance Programme (ISSP) as a more restrictive and controlling community sentence for young people on the brink of custody. The ISSP was established 'to work with 50–60 hard core repeat young offenders a year' for at least six months each, by combining 'close surveillance by the police and other agencies with a highly structured intensive daily programme tackling the causes of offending' (Home Office 2001: 32). In addition to the ISSP, the Government committed to strengthening the YJS response to serious and repeat young offenders by making provision for more STC places and high-quality programmes for young people in custody.

'New youth justice' strategies and practices: managerialism through performance management

The statutory reforms of the Crime and Disorder Act 1998 reflected a modernising and risk-averse political agenda that required transparent, defensible, accountable and evidence-based practice, in direct contrast to what was perceived as the indeterminacy and excessive discretion of previous welfare approaches and the ineffectiveness of justice-based models. Establishing the YJB was crucial to these modernising goals by ensuring the close, consistent monitoring and management of the performance of the YJS, particularly the practice of YOTs and their staff. The Crime and Disorder Act 1998 progressed the Government's modernising and managerialist agenda for the YJS by introducing centralised control processes and more prescriptive, technical working practices justified by an ethos of performance management. Indeed, it seems that the YJB was created specifically to fulfil this purpose. The goal of prevention was to be driven centrally through the closer management of practice by the YJB and the management of risk by YOT practitioners (see next section). A central feature of the 'new youth justice', therefore, was a cultural change in the way that youth justice was to be delivered, neatly summarised by Anna Souhami (2007: 25) as

> a marked departure from the accustomed ethos of youth justice work. . . . The formation of YOTs demanded the development of new, multi-agency practice, new routines and ways of working.

In order to promote standardised, transparent and accountable practice that was effective, efficient and economical, the YJB formulated a series of performance guidelines and targets for YOTs and the individual practitioners working within them. The YJB created three main measures to allow them to guide, monitor and manage the daily performance of YOT staff:

- *National Standards*: a framework was established setting out 'the minimum expectations of staff and managers in the youth justice system' (YJB 2004: 19). National Standards relating to youth justice governance, planning, service delivery and performance management were established (by the Secretary of State for Justice and the Secretary of State for Children, Schools and Family, following advice from the YJB); with these standards focused on key areas of youth justice practice: preventing offending, out-of-court disposals, bail and management, assessment, planning and delivering interventions, court-related work, victim work and custodial work (YJB 2004).

- *Key Elements of Effective Practice* (*KEEPs*): to shape their delivery of 'the essential elements of practice with all children at all stages of the YJS' (YJB 2003: 6). A series of source documents (practice manuals) relating to KEEPs were produced subsequently edited and synthesised within the text *Effective Practice in Youth Justice* (Stephenson *et al.* 2007/2011). The source documents set out the evidence underpinning the KEEPs, which addressed 'effective' and 'evidence-based' practice in the areas of Education, Training and Employment, Mental Health, Substance Use, Young People who Sexually Abuse, Offending Behaviour Programmes, Parenting, Restorative Justice, Mentoring, Targeted Neighbourhood Prevention, Final Warning Interventions, Swift Administration of Justice, Intensive Supervision and Surveillance Programmes, Custody and Resettlement, and Assessment, Planning Interventions and Supervision (APIS).
- *Case Management Guidance*: in 2009, the YJB produced guidance to assist and support YOT case managers and operational managers in helping their staff to work through the key stages of a young person's case, from arrest to court to planning and managing post-sentence interventions (YJB 2009a). Created as part of the introduction of the Scaled Approach (see later in this chapter), Case Management Guidance constitutes a how-to guide for practitioners, covering a variety of practice areas such as out-of-court disposals, court work, bail and remand management, assessment, writing reports for court and the Youth Offender/Referral Order Panel, planning and delivering interventions (in the community and custody), resettlement into the community and transfer to secure hospital (cf. Haines and Case 2015).

At the organisational (YOT) level, the main set of performance/outcome targets were Key Performance Indicators (KPIs; formalised in October 2007) to be collected on a quarterly and annual basis from the Police National Computer (PNC) and the Youth Justice Management Information System (YJMIS). The three priority KPIs for YOTs in England and Wales (where they were called 'Youth Justice Indicators') were identified as annual reductions in:

- *First-time entrants* (*FTEs*): the number of young people receiving a pre-court disposal or court disposal (conviction) upon entering the YJS for the first time.
- *Reoffending*: the frequency of reoffending among a cohort of young people in each YOT area who had received a disposal.
- *Custody*: the number of custodial sentences per 1,000 young people aged 10–17 in each YOT area.

An additional set of KPIs were identified as targets for YOTs on the basis that they were protective against reoffending. These protective KPIs focused on increases (not reductions) in the number of 'youth offenders' receiving appropriate 'education, training and employment', placement in suitable 'accommodation' and timely 'substance use' assessment and treatment (Wales only). The additional KPIs initially applied in England as well as Wales but were subsequently dropped. They were retained in Wales after the Welsh Government lobbied to keep them.

A supplementary organisational performance management measure was introduced in the form of YOT inspections. The practice of YOTs was to be inspected by Her Majesty's Inspectorate of Probation every three years through a methodology of case studies and interviews with staff, young people and victims. The inspection criteria focused on three areas: assessment (risk of harm to others, likelihood of reoffending, safeguarding), intervention (cf. assessment) and outcomes (achieving and sustaining outcomes).

The performance management measures introduced in the Crime and Disorder Act 1998 enabled the YJB to monitor, manage and control the youth justice practice of YOTs and their staff as a means of pursuing the prevention goal and facilitating effective, efficient and economical working in the YJS. The emphasis on accountable, defensible and transparent practice that was also evidence based was indicative of a modernised, risk-averse system, while the emphasis on the micromanagement of YOT performance illustrated the Government's increasingly managerialist and centralised control over practice.

'New youth justice' strategies and practices: prevention

New Labour adopted a twin-track approach to their strategic emphasis on the prevention of youth offending, the new primary aim of the YJS. In accordance with their 'tough on crime and tough on the causes of crime' mantra and their support for realist explanations of crime, New Labour resolved to address both the individual (micro-level) and social (macro-level) causes of youth offending through preventative early intervention approaches, marking an interventionist shift away from the diversionary 'new orthodoxy' of the 1980s (Bateman 2016; see also Chapter 4). The individual (psychosocial) causes of youth offending (see Chapters 2 and 3) would be addressed through a series of preventative initiatives focused on young people identified as 'at risk' of either offending for the first time or of repeat offending (individualised crime prevention) and specific social groups and neighbourhoods identified to be at 'high risk' of offending (targeted crime prevention). Social (socio-structural) causes would be addressed through universal programmes to tackle the manifestations of social exclusion and disadvantage (often packaged as generalised or universal crime prevention); programmes typically located outside of the YJS and focused on areas such as youth provision, educational improvement, family tax credits and community development. The Crime and Disorder Act 1998 revisions to youth justice policy and practice, however, prioritised young people who were either in the YJS or at risk of entering it, so the focus was inherently on individualised crime prevention (Smith 2014) with far less emphasis on universal prevention.

Individualised crime prevention was to be guided by the RFPP, a risk-focused early intervention approach to youth offending that was common sense and practical. As discussed in Chapter 4, the basis of the RFPP is to

> identify the key risk factors for offending and implement prevention methods designed to counteract them. There is often a related attempt to identify key protective factors against offending and to implement prevention methods designed to enhance them.
>
> (Farrington 2007: 606)

The RFPP came highly recommended by the *Misspent Youth* report (Audit Commission 1996). It chimed with the 'new youth justice' strategy of responsibilisation and informed recommendations for early intervention, which was to be risk-focused and grounded in closely managed, 'evidence-based' practice. The objective of the RFPP in the YJS was to link standardised (risk) assessment procedures with interventions that had been demonstrated to be what works in terms of effective practice in preventing youth offending (cf. Sherman *et al.* 1998). Once again, this model chimed with the New Labour/YJB emphasis on assessment and intervention as a KEEP, if not the central KEEP (called APIS), to guide and shape the prevention work of YOT staff (YJB 2003; Case and Haines 2009).

The main tool for risk-based early intervention practice was a bespoke risk assessment instrument called 'Asset' (unusually for the new YJS, this title was not an acronym for anything). Asset was developed for the YJB by Colin Roberts and Kerry Baker of the Probation Studies Unit at the Oxford Centre for Criminology for the explicit purpose of identifying the individualised, psychosocial (risk) factors that should be targeted in order to prevent youth offending. As of April 2000, when YOTs became official, all young people entering the YJS were to be subject to this new 'structured needs assessment' that was 'designed to identify the risk factors associated with offending behaviour and to inform effective intervention programmes' (*National Standards for Youth Justice Services*, YJB 2004: 27). A requirement was placed on YOTs by the YJB to assess all young people in the YJS using Asset. This was not a statutory requirement, but rather one enforced financially by the YJB via the YOT grant allocation. Asset provided a direct challenge to the perceived inconsistent, indeterminate and discretionary nature of previous youth justice practice. According to the YJB (2003: 5; see also Baker 2005), Asset introduced

> a common approach to the process of assessment [that] can assist practitioners in planning their work, gathering appropriate and relevant information and analysing that information. . . [as] the basis for arriving at judgements and making decisions which are clearly rooted in assessment outcomes and transparent to young people, their parents/carers and professional alike.

STOP AND THINK

The validity of Asset risk assessment

Asset required YOT staff to rate a young person's likelihood of reoffending – more accurately, their risk of reconviction – by their (current or recent) exposure to psychosocial 'risk factors' (see Chapter 3) in 12 domains of life: living arrangements, family and personal relationships, education, training and employment, neighbourhood, lifestyle, substance use, physical health, emotional and mental health, perception of self and others, thinking and behaviour, attitudes to offending and motivation to change (YJB 2000). The risk factor sections were supplemented by individual sections measuring the influence of positive (protective) factors, indicators of vulnerability, indicators of risk of serious harm to others and a self-assessment 'What Do You Think?' section. Each Asset section consisted of a series of risk-based statements regarding the presence or absence of that risk factor in the young person's life, which YOT staff had to rate yes/no/don't know. For example, the 'neighbourhood' section asked practitioners to 'indicate whether any of the following is a problem in the neighbourhood' (YJB 2000: 45):

- Obvious signs of drug dealing and/or usage.
- Isolated locality/lack of accessible transport.
- Lack of age-appropriate facilities.
- Racial or ethnic tensions.
- Other problems (e.g. lack of amenities).

Practitioners then quantified the extent to which they felt that the risks in each domain (when taken together) were associated with 'the likelihood of further offending' by the young person: 0 = no association, 1 = slight or limited indirect association, 2 = moderate direct or indirect association, 3 = quite strong association, normally direct, 4 = very strong, clear and direct association. These quantitative judgements were supplemented with qualitative, narrative explanations in a small, summative 'evidence box' at the end of each section, which enabled practitioners to explain how they felt the risk factors in each domain were related to past offending (cf. Case and Haines 2009).

So, what do you think about the content and structure of Asset as a means of explaining and responding to the influences on youth offending? Here are five not-so-easy questions to consider:

1 Is the risk factor focus of Asset the most appropriate theoretical basis for explaining youth offending?
2 What are the potential strengths of risk assessment in practical terms?
3 What explanatory factors and influences might the Asset tool neglect?
4 How might this limited explanatory focus affect the validity of the assessment and its subsequent recommendations for intervention?
5 How comprehensive and valid can information on a young person's life possibly be when elicited from a 5-point quantitative ratings scale that is largely completed by practitioners?

The YJB's intention was for the Asset risk assessment process to underpin practice with all people entering and spending time in the YJS, thus underpinning National Standards, Case Management Guidance and the delivery of all other KEEPs. The introduction of Asset demonstrates at least three central features of the 'new youth justice: an emphasis on *prevention* through *risk management* processes that are explicitly *managerialist* in nature. The Government/YJB commitment to Asset risk assessment and risk-focused 'what works' interventions (cf. Stephenson *et al.* 2011; Case and Haines 2015a) led one critic to quip that 'New Labour would be tough on risk and tough on the causes of risk' (Porteus 2007: 260).

'New youth justice' strategies and practices: early intervention

In the immediate aftermath of the Crime and Disorder Act 1998, the YJB expanded its commitment to the RFPP as the driver of preventative youth justice practice (not to mention its commitment to an endless stream of acronyms) by introducing a new antisocial behaviour management process and two new early intervention pro-grammes for young people 'at risk' of entering the YJS: Youth Inclusion Programmes and Youth Inclusion and Support Panels. The early intervention strategy consolidated existing elements of the 'new youth justice' (prevention, risk focus), while illustrating at least two additional characteristics:

- *Net-widening*: expanding the remit and scope of the YJS in order to 'capture' increasing numbers of young people committing an increasing range of behav-iours considered to be problematic (but not necessarily criminal), with the ration-ale of offering support.
- *Interventionism*: justifying increasing levels of intervention in the lives of young people and their families on the basis of assessed 'risk' of future problems and an espoused desire to offer pre-emptive support.

Early intervention: antisocial behaviour management

As part of the New Labour approach to youth justice, a new category of 'anti-social behaviour' (ASB) was socially constructed. Although it was defined and operationalised in various ways by different legislation and organisations, the general objective was to construct a catch-all category to facilitate early interven-tion by identifying individuals (typically young people or problem families) whose behaviour was borderline criminal or otherwise problematic (annoying, nuisance, threatening, causing harassment) to communities and/or persons not in their household. In a sense, ASB represented the 'disorder' in the Crime and Disorder Act 1998. Young people whose behaviour was identified (e.g. by police, neighbours, landlords) as troublesome and problematic, but not necessarily criminal or in need of referral to the formal YJS, could be subject to an escalating scale of ASB man-agement measures, led by local police, YOTs or newly formed Antisocial Behaviour Units. The first stage of the escalating, tiered ASB management process was to be a formal warning letter to the young person, often followed up with a home visit. Failure to curb ASB could then result in the young person being required to sign an Antisocial Behaviour Contract (ABC) outlining rules and prohibitions regarding their future conduct (originally a local initiative developed in Islington). The final stage of the ASB management process was to be the infamous Antisocial Behaviour Order (ASBO), which set further rules and prohibitions/restrictions for behaviour. Ironically, although the ASBO was a civil order (not a court order) given for behav-iour that was antisocial (not criminal), breaching the order would be a criminal offence that could even lead to custody (**RTA = the criminalisation of young people**). It would also be possible to administer an ASBO on conviction following a criminal offence – a lesser used response that became known as the Criminal ASBO (CRASBO). From the perspective of Alun Michael (2017, personal interview), a key influencer of how youth justice policy/strategy was socially constructed at that time:

> The idea was that using the civil burden of proof would increase the likelihood of being able to succeed with the process. It was entirely about saying that if you continue with this activity then you put yourself at risk of a criminal record so stop it now.

Initially, Government guidance didn't favour a staged approach to ASB management, preferring to assign discretion to local areas in how to respond to ASB, which actually prompted Home Secretary Jack Straw to write to local authorities complaining about their limited use of ASBOs. Research published by the YJB indicated that some areas were moving straight to ASBO following ASB by young people or adults, while others had a more graduated response (Solanki *et al*. 2006), so staged ASB management was by no means a national strategy.

It should also be noted that young people below the age of criminal responsibility (i.e. under 10 years old) who were identified as having committed ASB could be given a 'Child Safety Order' by the court, with attendant requirements, restrictions and supportive interventions. If the ASB management process was exhausted for a young person or their behaviour was considered more criminal than antisocial in nature, they could enter the new out-of-court system/process. The ASB management process was intended to support a strategy of preventative early intervention that diverted young people from the formal YJS. Alun Michael (2017) told me:

> I take quite a lot of personal responsibility for the way we approached antisocial behaviour. Where you have a lot of low-level activity going on, it can escalate to the point of offending and the young person can go into the Youth Justice System. However, if you're able to deal with the behaviour early then you can prevent the young person from getting to this stage. That's the whole point of early intervention.

Early intervention: identifying 'at risk' young people

The Government supplemented the ASB management process with the creation of two new early intervention programmes intended for young people who had yet to offend (officially), including those as young as 8 years old who were therefore below the age of criminal responsibility. Youth Inclusion Programmes (YIPs) were established by the YJB in 2000 in response to the recommendations of the *Misspent Youth* report and the New Labour commitment to further investment in targeted preventative activity with young people living in 'high-risk' neighbourhoods (see Audit Commission 1996; Straw and Michael 1996; Home Office 1997). YIPs were created as risk-based early intervention/prevention programmes for 8- to 17-year-olds living in 114 neighbourhoods in England and Wales, neighbourhoods that were considered to be at 'high risk' of experiencing youth offending due to their high levels of social disadvantage and existing crime (YJB 2006). The key objective for YIPs was to prevent offending and reoffending by conducting risk assessment with the top 50 'at-risk' young people in each neighbourhood and then targeting identified risks through intervention at the individual, family and community levels. As such, YIPs were a targeted crime prevention initiative informed by the RFPP. Referral to a YIP was the responsibility of any agency working with children and young people, notably the statutory agencies of police, education (local authority), social services (local authority) and health. These stakeholders were instructed to 'identify not only those who are offending, but also those at risk of future offending, social and educational exclusion' (Morgan Harris Burrows 2003).

Youth Inclusion and Support Panels (YISPs) were established in April 2003 as multiagency committees consisting of representatives from different agencies working with young people (the same agencies as those referring to YIPs) in 13 pilot areas in England and Wales. The objectives of YISPs are to prevent offending and antisocial behaviour by 8- to 13-year-olds (or 14- to 18-year-olds in the case of the YISP+ programme) who had been identified by referring agencies as 'at risk' of offending and to ensure that these young people and their families could access mainstream services at the earliest possible stage. In summary:

> Using a matrix of the risk and protective factors which may lead young people into, or protect them from, crime, the YISPs were tasked with constructing a personally tailored package of support and interventions, summarised in an integrated support plan (ISP) designed to facilitate the kind of provision which will prevent the young person moving further towards crime.
>
> (Walker *et al.* 2007: ix)

As YIPs and YISPs were risk-based early intervention programmes, they required a bespoke risk assessment instrument to enable practitioners to identify young people for referral based on their status as 'at risk' of offending. Consequently, the 'Onset' tool was created (by the authors of Asset) to measure young people's exposure to risk factors for first-time offending (i.e. the 'onset' of offending), rather than for reoffending or reconviction (as with Asset). The Onset form was divided into risk domains/ sections equivalent to those in Asset: living and family arrangements, statutory education, neighbourhood and friends, substance misuse, emotional and mental health, perception of self and others, thinking, behaviour and attitudes, positive factors, vulnerability and risk of harm by young person (see Case and Haines 2009). Each section required the practitioner to assess 'the extent to which you think the following factors are associated with the young person's likelihood of offending or serious anti-social behaviour in the future' (YJB 2006: 3), and ratings mirrored the Asset scale of 0–4: 'not associated', 'slight/indirect association', 'moderate but definite association', 'quite strong association' and 'very strong association'. For example, the 'living and family arrangements' section asked practitioners to assess the presence of risk factors relating to whether the young person:

- Is separated from either or both of his or her parents;
- Lives in a deprived household;
- Experiences inconsistent supervision at home;
- Experiences harsh discipline in the home;
- Family is known to be involved in crime/anti-social behaviour;
- Is currently experiencing unstable accommodation.

                                                                                    (YJB 2006: 3)

Like Asset, practitioners provided further explanation of their ratings in a qualitative evidence box at the end of each section/risk factor domain. Practitioners were given equivalent guidance to those completing Asset (see YJB 2006) regarding the questions that they should ask themselves when rating evidence of risk (e.g. Was the factor linked to past behaviour? Is the link to offending direct or indirect? Does the risk factor lead to offending on its own or in the presence of other factors?). The practitioner-completed sections were supplemented by an optional (for the practitioner) 'Over to you' section to be completed by the young person, which corresponded to the 'What do you think?' element of Asset. 'Over to you' asked young people for their responses on a 4-point scale ('not like me', 'a bit like me', 'a lot like me', or 'just like me') to a series of questions regarding:

- Your family and where you live (e.g. I never stay away from home without asking);
- School (e.g. I need help with reading and writing);
- Where you live and about your friends (e.g. I live in areas where there is not much to do);
- Smoking, drinking and drugs (e.g. I have family or friends who use drugs);
- Your health (e.g. I worry about something that might happen in the future);
- How you think and behave (e.g. I rush into things without thinking).

(YJB 2006: 1–3)

At the end of the Onset form, practitioners set out their reasons for referral of the young person to the YIP or YISP by highlighting the aspects of behaviour that they were most concerned about (typically those sections rated 3 or 4) and their assessed impact on current behaviour (cf. Case and Haines 2009).

Early intervention: expanding antisocial behaviour management

Widening the remit of the YJS to incorporate assessment-intervention relating to 'pre-offending' behaviour by 'at-risk' young people, including those below the age of criminal responsibility, offered a further example of the YJB's faith in (interventionist) risk management as its central approach to prevention. Indeed, a more accurate description of the prevention approach taken might be risk-focused early intervention (i.e. the RFPP), typically in the form of individualised and targeted crime prevention (cf. Smith 2014). The net-widening, interventionist approach was expanded still further in 2003 through a beefing-up of antisocial behaviour management legislation to include a more explicit emphasis upon the responsibilisation of young people. The Home Secretary at that time, David Blunkett, expressed increasing frustration and intolerance regarding young people who offended, portraying them as 'young offenders who believe that their age makes them untouchable, who flout the law [and] laugh at the police' (Blunkett, Labour Party Election Broadcast 2003). The responsibilising, right realist rhetoric of Blunkett and the Labour Party translated into amendments to ASB legislation and policy, with a conspicuous target being 'youths who hang around street corners intimidating the elderly' (Blunkett 2003: 2). Consequently, the Government produced a White Paper titled *Respect and Responsibility: Taking a Stand against Antisocial Behaviour* (HM Government 2003), which officially kick-started their responsibilising, moralising 'Respect' agenda. The recommendations from the White Paper were manifested in the Antisocial Behaviour Act 2003, which gave local authorities and the police broader and more flexible powers to address nuisance crime and low-level incivility. The Act widened the use of ASBOs, enabling local authorities, and registered social landlords and the British Transport Police to apply for them. Furthermore, 'Dispersal Orders' were introduced, which allowed police and police community support officers to disperse groups of two or more people from designated areas if the group's behaviour was 'perceived' as likely to cause harassment, alarm or distress to members of the public. Unsurprisingly, like ASBOs, the use of Dispersal Orders fell disproportionately on young people as they were more likely to be on the streets in groups and behaving in 'visible' ways (**RTA = responding to the visible**

behaviour of street children as if it were problematic) – taking us back to the street children of the Industrial Revolution period (see Chapter 1). The Antisocial Behaviour Act 2003 also broadened the availability of Parenting Orders, making them applicable to parents of children who had truanted or been excluded from school, rather than being restricted to parents of children who had offended (HM Government 2003). The broadening of ASB powers expanded the net-widening and interventionist influence of the YJS by drawing in children and young people who had not offended and subjecting them to formal intervention (e.g. ASBOs, notices to disperse, Parenting Orders), on the basis that ASB was indicative of irresponsibility (thus necessitating a responsibilisation approach) *and* was a demonstrable risk factor for offending that needed to be prevented (thus justifying early interventionism).

Early intervention: social crime prevention

It is clear that the 'new youth justice' was driven by a largely individualised approach to prevention the targeted psychosocial risk factors (see also Chapters 3 and 4), rather than fully considering potential socio-structural influences on youth offending. However, there was an explicit element of **social crime prevention** – dealing with the social and economic conditions that can lead to crime. This approach addressed the left realist explanation that offending was a product of interactions between the individual's rational choice and social problems/disadvantage. When analysing New Labour's social crime prevention policy, Turnbull and Spence (2011: 954) commented that

> larger social concerns such as disadvantage, poverty and racial inequality are also individualised in a similar way, with young people subject to interventions designed to shape their responses to these structural forces, irrespective of the limited agency of young people in such circumstances.

The social crime prevention made available universally to young people was located outside of the formal YJS. Managerialist youth justice responses were augmented by longer-term social reform programmes, which were made more palatable to the voting public by being presented as crime prevention initiatives (Joyce 2017). A £900 million Neighbourhood Renewal Fund was created and linked to a *National Strategy for Neighbourhood Renewal* (Social Exclusion Unit 2001) to prevent social problems such as youth crime, ASB and educational failure. New Labour implemented a series of universal crime prevention initiatives, typically located within broader strategies to address social exclusion and the risk factors associated with it (many of which were also related to youth crime), which included truancy and school exclusion, teenage pregnancy, substance use, unemployment and being in care (Social Exclusion Unit 2001). Universal prevention initiatives included family support, community development and education, training and employment schemes (see Smith 2014). Ultimately, however, even these 'universal' social exclusion prevention programmes prioritised the psychosocial risk factors typical of individualised and targeted youth crime prevention programmes, which (perhaps inadvertently) fuelled the New Labour agenda of responsibilisation by individualising the causes of crime. The individualised aspect of universal crime prevention was arguably a product of New Labour's faith in left realist explanations of youth offending as a combination of rational choice and irresponsibility being exacerbated by social disadvantage – thus focusing on the symptoms of socio-structural problems rather than their specific influence on offending (Pitts 2003).

In summary, the Crime and Disorder Act 1998 and its associated legislation radically reorientated the YJS of England and Wales through a series of systemic, structural, strategic and practical changes to modernise responses to youth offending and to make them more effective, efficient and economical. Structurally, new multiagency partnerships (Crime and Disorder Reduction Partnerships, Youth Offending Teams) were formed to pursue an explicit prevention aim, with their practice (along with that of the Secure Estate) monitored, guided and managed by the YJB, who would also advise the Government on the development of youth justice policy. The new strategies that would shape the 'new youth justice' delivered by the YJS were formalisations of the strategies of responsibilisation (of young people, parents, local areas), risk-focused early intervention(ism) and managerialism recommended by the *Misspent Youth* review and the *No More Excuses* White Paper.

5 EASY PIECES

3 The Crime and Disorder Act 1998: Formalising the 'new youth justice'

1 *The 'new youth justice'*: the Crime and Disorder Act 1998 and subsequent legislation established a 'new youth justice' – a new set of responses to youth offending that prioritised prevention through new strategies of responsibilisation, risk-based early intervention(ism), net-widening and managerialism and new practices of risk assessment and community sentencing.
2 *Philosophy*: the 'new youth justice' was largely devoid of philosophy (e.g. welfare, justice), although it did introduce an ideological focus on responsibilisation – increasingly holding young people, families and communities to account for dealing with youth offending (e.g. through abolishing doli incapax and implementing Referral and Parenting Orders).
3 *Prevention*: under the Crime and Disorder Act 1998, the primary aim of the YJS became the prevention of offending as a means of making the delivery of youth justice more effective, efficient and economical. All ideologies, strategies and practices of the 'new youth justice' were linked to this overarching objective.
4 *Strategies*: the Crime and Disorder Act 1998 abolished the legal presumption of doli incapax (promoting responsibilisation, net-widening), broadened the remit of the YJS to incorporate antisocial behaviour management and early intervention with 'pre-offenders' (encouraging net-widening, interventionism), prioritised risk management (supporting interventionism) and embedded multi-agency partnership working and performance management as models to shape practice (enabling managerialism).
5 *Practices*: the prevention aim of the 'new youth justice' was pursued through risk-focused assessment and intervention (i.e. the RFPP) with young people inside and on the cusp of the YJS – an ostensibly evidence-based, transparent and defensible practice model that fit with the modernising and managerialist ethos of New Labour.

4 EVALUATING THE 'NEW YOUTH JUSTICE' (1997–2007)

Reflecting on the first decade of the 'new youth justice', critical debate in the youth justice field has been polarised. A large body of academic literature has been highly critical of the neo-liberal, neo-correctionalist and managerialist approach, contrasting starkly with a partial, almost promotional literature from the YJB (as you might expect) and the work of a supportive academics. Over this first decade, the YJB and critical academics rarely engaged in a constructive dialogue for the purposes of developing understandings of youth offending or identifying and evaluating the most appropriate youth justice policy/practice responses. The polarised literature available to students and practitioners of youth justice has precluded balanced debate being made available in the literature – an issue that this book is intended to address. That said, students should continue to engage with the critiques of key academics such as John Muncie, John Pitts, Barry Goldson, Roger Smith, Jo Phoenix, Leslie McAra, Roger Hopkins Burke, Kevin Haines and Tim Bateman – all of whom have greatly influenced my own scholarship. To ignore this literature would be to deprive yourselves of engaging with a body of incisive, invigorating and challenging arguments that will develop your critical thinking. Similarly, students of youth justice are urged to read the relevant YJB publications (e.g. YJB 2000, 2003, 2008, 2009a) and associated supportive/ less 'critical' academic texts from Kerry Baker (Baker 2005; Baker *et al.* 2002, 2005), David J. Smith (2010) and Stephenson *et al.* (2007/2011). Indeed, the general advice is to Always Be Critical (ABC) of everything that you read from both camps, to critically consider the issues and to draw your own conclusions.

With the battle lines drawn between the YJB and critical scholars, the two sides rarely engaged in debate over the first decade of the 'new youth justice' and something of a cold war ensued. Politicians and YJB staff tended to view critical academics as unconstructive, presenting exaggerated critique and failing to give appropriate credit for system successes (see, for example, my 'Conversation' in Chapter 6 with John Drew, the former chief executive of the YJB). For their part, critical academics have perceived the 'new youth justice' as perpetuating negative perceptions of young people who offend and as promoting punitive, dehumanising and overly mechanical youth justice responses. Academics have also criticised the YJB for their failure to engage in debate and meaningful critical reflection on the state of youth justice (John Drew reinforces this claim in Chapter 6), which was seen as a double standard from such a strong proponent of critical reflection as a vehicle for improving youth justice practice. It is vital to evaluate the 'new youth justice' in as balanced a way as possible, acknowledging, comparing and contrasting the polarised and equivalently one-dimensional arguments from each side in order to draw conclusions as to the 'effectiveness' of the new model for delivering youth justice. The impact of the 'new youth justice' merits detailed evaluation, both on its own terms (i.e. in relation to what the Government was trying to achieve) and in terms of the key elements of the approach, which have been either lauded or lambasted depending on which side of the youth justice divide the argument emanates from. The forthcoming evaluation has two clear strands: a discussion of the independent audit of New Labour's youth justice reforms from 1907 to 2007 and an evaluation of the central characteristics (mainly strategies) of the 'new youth justice' that were formalised by the Crime and Disorder Act 1998 and progressed in subsequent legislation.

In 2008, the Centre for Crime and Justice Studies published *Ten Years of Labour's Youth Justice Reforms: An Independent Audit* (Solomon and Garside 2008). The Centre reviewed the success of youth justice from 1997 to 2007 based on the Government's own targets and stated objectives for improving the effectiveness, efficiency and economy of the YJS in terms of offending levels, processing, spending and meeting young people's needs. The report was largely critical of the new YJS, drawing the conclusion that the 'new' YJS was *not* effective, efficient or economical:

> Overall, most of the targets have been missed and success in achieving the desired outcomes has been far more elusive than the government claims. In reality, the record on youth justice reform is at best mixed. Despite the huge investment, self-reported youth offending has not declined.
>
> (Solomon and Garside 2008: 11)

(In)effective

Annual decreases in the numbers of young people convicted of an offence from 1997 to 2007 indicated that the YJS had become more effective in preventing youth offending. However, the Centre for Crime and Justice Studies authors challenged this assumption by suggesting that decreases were likely to have been an extension of previous downward trends in youth offending, combined with decreases in the numbers of young offenders being reported to the police. The argument that decreases in youth offending were more apparent than real (coincidentally, an argument first employed in *Misspent Youth* to justify the need for system change) was supported by the stability of self-reported offending levels over the same period, suggesting that actual levels of offending were stable and it was more likely to have been levels of reporting that had fluctuated. Therefore, the review

> places in some doubt confident claims that the falls in youth convictions for these offences are related to recent government reforms.
>
> (Solomon and Garside 2008: 37)

In relation to the three KPI measures of system effectiveness that were rolled out in 2007, the review suggested that the 'new youth justice' of 1997–2007 had only been moderately successful in achieving one (reducing reoffending). Even then, the report queried the extent to which system changes were responsible for this outcome. The report also queried the methodological robustness of Government claims to have reduced reoffending, suggesting that there had been a lack of clarity over the nature of the reoffending outcome measured (i.e. a lack of validity) and a constant revision of how the target outcome had been operationalised (i.e. a lack of reliability) – a criticism supported by John Drew (see Chapter 6), who took over as chief executive of the YJB the year following the report. The authors concluded that very little progress had actually been made in reducing reoffending over the decade of the review.

A lack of effectiveness in reducing FTEs and custody levels was clear from the audit. The authors discovered that from 2003 to 2006, the annual number of FTEs had actually increased (although there was no FTE target during this period) – an outcome that was largely attributed to the Government target introduced in 2002 for increasing the number of 'Offences Brought to Justice' by the police (Home Office 2002; see also next section). Targets for the identification and processing of (young) people who had offended placed considerable pressure on police to increase their arrest numbers and so were considered contradictory to the preventative aim of the YJS (Solomon and Garside 2008). From May 2000 to May 2008, the average youth custody population rose from 2,804 to 2,898 (Ministry of Justice 2012) and the population had increased by 8 per cent since March 2003, despite a YJB target to reduce it by 10 per cent. Not only had the Government/YJB failed to meet its own system targets for reducing custody, but the introduction of the ISSP in 2001 also appeared to have been ineffective in leading to the desired reductions in custody.

(In)efficient

Reviewing system efficiency, the audit authors concluded that the 'new' YJS was

> a considerable advance over the previous arrangements for the delivery of health, education, substance misuse and mental health services to young people who are convicted.
>
> (Solomon and Garside 2008: 64)

The authors noted that the Government/YJB had easily and swiftly met its original target to halve the processing time for persistent young offenders from 144 to 72 days and that it had placed over two-thirds of young people into suitable education, training and employment (what classed as 'suitable' was left to the discretion of local YOTs). However, targets for young people who offend to be placed into 'suitable accommodation' (again, subject to YOT discretion) had not been met, neither had targets for the timely assessment and intervention of young people who presented with substance use or mental health needs. The concluding view was of a largely inefficient YJS struggling to meet the welfare needs of young people who offended and struggling to co-ordinate specialist support for these young people, despite the systemic expectation for multi-agency partnership working (see Smith 2014).

(Un)economical

The report asserted that the Government objective to make the YJS more economical had failed. Youth justice spending had increased by 45 per cent from 2001 to 2007, despite annual decreases in the numbers of young people offending and entering the YJS for the first time. There was a particular increase in spending on custody. The authors conceded, however, that increased expenditure could be, in part, the result of more young people entering the YJS who would have previously been dealt with by the ever-shrinking welfare system. Consequently, a large percentage of youth justice expenditure was now being financed by local authority social services departments. Therefore, increased expenditure and a lack of economy was not necessarily the product of system ineffectiveness or inefficiency and was, if anything, more indicative of the changing role of the YJS within a broader social work context for young people experiencing problems (Solomon and Garside 2008; see also Chapter 6).

The 10-year review of the YJS and its conclusions regarding the system's (lack of) success in meeting Government and YJB targets was both critical and pessimistic. Elsewhere during the evaluation period, however, there had been more positive reflections on the 'new youth justice', in particular, in the Audit Commission's fol-lowup to *Misspent Youth*, titled *Youth Justice 2004: A Review of the Reformed Youth Justice System* (Audit Commission 2004). *Youth Justice 2004* concluded that 'the new system is a considerable improvement on the old one' (Audit Commission 2004: 2). Young peo-ple who offended were, by that time, dealt with more efficiently (e.g. processing time had been halved), were more likely to receive an intervention and were more likely to offer reparation for their offending. The review commended YOT practice, particu-larly in terms of co-ordinating multi-agency work with young people and in working effectively with local magistrates, also commending the role of the YJB in establishing and monitoring a clear national framework with minimum performance standards. For *Youth Justice 2004*, the YJS *had* become effective, efficient and economical.

Other key stakeholders were more critical, in a similar vein to the Centre for Crime and Justice Studies review. Perhaps most damningly, the outgoing chair of the YJB, Professor Rod Morgan, at the time of his resignation in 2007 accused the YJS of 'gratuitous criminalisation' of young people (Morgan 2007: 5). Morgan claimed that criminalisation had become an inevitable by-product of the escalating severity of YJS processes (i.e. ASB management, out-of-court sentencing, court disposals) and the Offences Brought to Justice police targets that brought increasing numbers of young people into the system (see next section). Morgan and other critics (e.g. Fergus-son 2007; Muncie 2004) identified the ambiguous approaches to youth offending at play within the 'new youth justice', illustrated by contradictions between the suppos-edly diversion-influenced prevention agenda and the criminalising and net-widening nature of ASB management measures (as early intervention) and the Offences Brought to Justice target. The Government's insistence on micromanaging the YJS was also viewed as counterproductive, as overriding practitioner discretion with an excessively prescriptive, inflexible and graduated (escalating) approach that 'risks undermining efforts to divert large numbers of young people from the youth justice system' (White-head and Arthur 2011: 476).

Commentary on the impact of the 'new youth justice' in its first decade was mixed, although the weight of evaluation was largely negative and unsupportive. With this in mind, it is important to examine in more detail the central (strategic) characteristics of the 'new youth justice' in order to evaluate how and why they may have impacted upon the YJS in England and Wales from 1997 to 2007. As discussed above, the 'new youth justice' was characterised by strategies for responding to youth offending in effective, efficient and economical ways. It is to these strategies that we now turn, because they best illustrate the polarisation of opinion regarding the 'new youth justice': promoted by supporters (e.g. the YJB) as modernising and successful, while challenged by critics (e.g. critical youth justice academics) as harmful and mis-guided. Let us now consider the main strategic elements of the 'new youth justice' and the impact that they have had on the social (re)construction of youth offending and youth justice in England and Wales.

Responsibilisation

A central feature of early New Labour policy and the 'new youth justice' of the Crime and Disorder Act 1998 was the strategy of responsibilisation – increasing the degree to which young people, their families and local communities were held responsible for dealing with the influences upon youth offending. The Crime and Disorder Act 1998 built on the review recommendations of *Misspent Youth* (Audit Commission 1996) and the policy proposals of the *No More Excuses* White Paper (Home Office 1997) to broaden the extent to which young people and their families were made accountable for offending and other problem behaviours (e.g. ASB). The abolition of doli incapax fit with this responsibilising agenda by lowering the age at which young people were considered legally and morally responsible for their offending behaviour and moving away from what Labour saw as an excuse culture for young(er) offenders. Effectively lowering the age of criminal responsibility from 14 to 10 years old also broadened the reach of the YJS (net-widening) and the numbers of young people it could support, manage and control through 'effective' early intervention and youth justice sentences (interventionism). A focus on parental responsibility (**RTA**) was reintroduced through the introduction of Parenting Orders. Here we can discern an additional RTA/ dichotomy created by the responsibilisation strategy – the responsible–irresponsible young person. Under New Labour, young people from the age of 10 were viewed as fully responsible for their offending behaviour (channelling communitarianism and responsibilisation), and youth offending was constructed as a product of rational choice and immorality (channelling right realism). However, the social (re)construction of young people who offended as dangerous and threatening also portrayed them as irresponsible (again, channelling right realism), and young people were seen as incapable of resisting criminogenic influences (channelling positivism and risk factor theories) without adult intervention. Therefore, children/young people considered irresponsible and undeserving of responsibility in all other areas of their lives (e.g. the right to leave school, vote, get married) were assigned full responsibility when they offended – although not the capacity to desist from offending. Such contradiction and double standards move beyond conflict and ambivalence and are indicative of political influence on the construction of youth offending and youth justice.

It has been argued that the abolition of doli incapax demonstrates a creeping punitiveness and excessive interventionism in youth justice policy in England and Wales, leading to the criminalisation of a new group of young people (10- to 13-year-olds) who were not previously classed as 'youth offenders' (Bateman 2016). The extension of the age range for 'youth offending' illustrates how the category is subject to constant social reconstruction (see Chapter 1). It also introduces the associated critical theme of **adulterisation** into the discussion – the perception and treatment of children and young people as having the cognitive capacity of adults when they offend (similar to the little adults of pre-Victorian times), but not in any other areas of their lives. The very low age of criminal responsibility relative to other Western countries runs counter to the progressive principles of 'child-friendly justice' (Goldson and Muncie 2012; see Chapter 4) and offers further evidence of the responsible–irresponsible dichotomy. Following the Crime and Disorder Act 1998, young people who could be more accurately described as pre-teen children (aged 10–12) and youths (teenagers/adolescents) aged 13–17 years old were considered fully responsible for offending behaviour yet not mature enough to be allocated other social responsibilities (especially below the age of 16). Critics have argued that this dichotomy demonstrates a selective form of responsibilisation that unfairly punishes and criminalises young people for offending behaviour (Haines and Case 2015; Kemshall 2008). Furthermore, the full legal responsibilisation of young people aged 10–13 and indeed the adulterisation of all young people who offended was not 'evidence based' – a central tenet of Government youth justice policy. The strategy contradicted evidence from cognitive psychology and neuroscience of children's delayed moral development (cf. Piaget 1932; Kohlberg 1958, 1984), their lack of brain maturation (cf. Beckman 2004; see also Chapter 2) and their associated lack of culpability, reduced capacity for abstract thought and inability to adopt a future-time perspective (cf. Bateman 2016; Lipscombe 2012; Royal Society 2011). Therefore, it is possible to conclude that the responsibilisation strategy was indicative of a political agenda to reconstruct youth offending and youth justice in the service of political expedience and professional experience rather than academic evidence.

Prevention

Under the 'new youth justice', prevention became the primary aim of the YJS. Prevention ticked a number of boxes for New Labour: it offered an alternative goal to ostensibly ineffective welfare and justice models, it was 'evidence based' and 'effective' when animated by the RFPP (Stephenson *et al.* 2007/2011) and it offered an efficient and economical means of 'nipping offending in the bud' (Straw 1995). New Labour truly believed in the effectiveness of prevention as *the* new priority for youth justice, basing this commitment on expedience, evidence and experience. Prevention as better than cure was a simple, common-sense aim to sell to the voting public and YOT staff on the grounds of effectiveness, efficiency and economy. Most importantly, with every element of YOT practice having prevention as its touchstone, the multi-agency working of staff seconded from diverse statutory agencies could cohere around an agreed aim (Home Office 1998). This coherence was a cultural revolution for the previously piecemeal and fragmented YJS (see Souhami 2007).

Perhaps the most relevant criticism to make here for the purposes of this book is that prevention as the primary aim of the new YJS was constructed and operationalised in an ambiguous way. The 'prevention' outlined in the Crime and Disorder Act 1998 was constructed as a catch-all term to signify the prevention of first-time *re*offending (cf. the reduction of FTEs, Onset risk assessment and YIP/YISP programmes), but also the prevention of reoffending (cf. the objective of Asset and most court sentences and YOT interventions). There was further confusion over the difference between prevention and early intervention. The terms were regularly employed interchangeably in the YJS (e.g. in relation to YIPs/YISPs), despite early intervention being only one particular form of prevention, typically with individuals identified as 'at risk' of offending (Case and Haines 2015b). This slippage and ambiguity around how key concepts have been constructed and operationalised is problematic for prevention practice in youth justice. Even if we are to accept that prevention can cover all of the bases outlined above, the manner in which prevention goals have been pursued has come under increasing criticism. In particular, the individualisation of explanations of youth offending by privileging individualised and targeted crime prevention methods (e.g. the RFPP) has been a considerable source of concern (see Bateman 2011; Case and Haines 2009; France 2008; O'Mahony 2009; Pitts 2003). The Government/ YJB approach to the prevention of youth offending has been seen by critics as encouraging negative understandings of young people as risky, dangerous and threatening (see also Chapter 1) and negative, excessively responsibilising approaches to dealing with their offending (e.g. through control, punishment and excessive interventionism), which could foster the further labelling and criminalisation of these young people (Bateman 2016).

CONTROVERSIES AND DEBATES

Youth justice in Wales

Following partial devolution from the UK Government in 1999, the Welsh Assembly Government was given policy-making powers in several areas related to youth justice, including education, social services, health and housing. However, youth and criminal justice remained non-devolved policy areas, and decisions regarding the YJS of England and Wales were made in Westminster, England. At the same time, social policy for children and young people in Wales began to take a form that was distinct from England, being more focused on collective responsibility (compared to individual responsibility), social inclusion (compared to preventing social exclusion) and universal rights/entitlements to services, guidance and opportunities (compared to rights being by demonstrating responsibility). Here, 'entitlements' differ from and extend the concept of 'rights', in that they promote the achievement of maximum outcomes for young people rather than the pursuit of minimum standards (Haines and Case 2011). During interview, Professor Kevin Haines (an influential Welsh academic in the youth justice field) explained the entitlements–rights focus of developing Welsh social policy as it related to (non-devolved) youth justice:

> The Welsh representative on the Youth Justice Board (Howard Williamson) was a former youth worker and architect of Extending Entitlement, so believed strongly that young people entering the Youth Justice System should be able to access their rights and not be treated punitively like they were in England.
> (Kevin Haines 2017, personal interview)

Following the Crime and Disorder Act 1998, a tension emerged in Wales regarding the need to reconcile the (arguably positive) Welsh social policy agenda with the (arguably negative) 'new youth justice' agenda prescribed by the UK-based Government, a tension that emerged when dealing with young people who offended.

> When the YJB was created, Norman Warner [Chair of the YJB] came to Wales to tell us how to run youth justice and was slapped down by Edwina Hart, the Minister for Social Justice. She felt that Welsh politicians should decide the shape of Welsh youth justice because so many relevant services were devolved to the Welsh Assembly Government. This was the beginning of Wales-specific youth justice.
> (Kevin Haines 2017, personal interview)

Accordingly, the Welsh Assembly Government (now the Welsh Government) and the YJB produced a co-ordinated policy document in 2004, the *All Wales Youth Offending Strategy* (Welsh Assembly Government and Youth Justice Board 2004), which provided a 'national framework for preventing offending and reoffending among children and young people in Wales' (Welsh Assembly Government and Youth Justice Board 2004: 1). The *All Wales Youth Offending Strategy* (AWYOS) echoed the prevention focus of the Crime and Disorder Act 1998 by asserting that 'whenever we can prevent offending there is benefit for us all . . . the best way to stop offending is to prevent it from happening in the first place' (Welsh Assembly Government and Youth Justice Board 2004). Notable in the strategy, however, was the commitment to responding to young people who offended in line with Welsh social policy principles by treating them as 'children first and offenders second' (Welsh Assembly Government and Youth Justice Board 2004: 3), which directly challenged the offender-first, risk-focused, responsibilising 'new youth justice' (Haines and Case 2015; see also Chapter 6). Additionally, there was a clear attempt to balance 'new youth justice' strategies of 'early intervention, restorative justice measures, appropriate punishment and supported rehabilitation' with Welsh social policy principles of prevention through 'promoting the welfare of children and young people' (Welsh Assembly Government and Youth Justice Board 2004: 3).

The AWYOS officially marked a point of divergence from the UK Government/ English approach to youth justice, as it introduced a set of principles to supplement prescribed youth justice strategies. The Welsh principles of 'children first and offenders second', rights-based and entitlements-based working and the promotion of social inclusion and positive behaviours/outcomes contrasted with the ostensibly more punitive, responsibilising and risk-based strategies of the 'new youth justice' (see Haines and Case 2015; Muncie 2008). However, the extent to which these principles have been understood and actualised in practice in Wales is debatable, as is the degree of divergence between youth justice *practice* in England and Wales, despite divergence in policy. The extent of disconnect between policy rhetoric and practice reality (**RTA**) within local areas in Wales and England due to local mediation processes (**RTA**) will be explored in more detail in Chapter 6.

Interventionism

The 'new youth justice' agenda expanded the remit of the YJS (i.e. net-widening) to facilitate a project of interventionism, animated by a continuum of ASB management and early intervention through to a new out-of-court sentencing system to a new spectrum of community sentences (informed by risk assessment) to new custodial sentences. The (left realist) rationale for increased intervention was to enable adult experts to provide demonstrable, measurable, standardised and monitored 'effective' and 'evidence-based' support, treatment, rehabilitation and control/surveillance for otherwise irresponsible, helpless and deprived children and young people (**RTA = support and control**). Goldson (2007: 8) observed that interventionism reflected how 'discourses of intervention switch interchangeably between benign child-centredness and tough punitiveness'. Such interventionism contrasted sharply with the 1980s period of new orthodoxy/systems management-inspired 'minimum necessary intervention' and diversion (see Chapter 4), which had become viewed (politically) as too lenient, too prone to practitioner discretion and manipulation and encouraging an excuse culture, whereby young people were not compelled to take responsibility for their actions. Consequently, the Crime and Disorder Act 1998 evidenced a move away from diversion/minimum intervention and towards more interventionism, shaped by the right realist responsibilisation agenda. During our interview in 2017, Alun Michael (one of the architects of the Crime and Disorder Act 1998) told me:

> I query the suggestion that it is an objective to stop people getting into the Youth Justice System. The right language is to enable young people to sort out their lives and to stop them offending. This means that you're dealing with the offender, stopping people becoming victims and stopping the damage done to the young person's own family and community. It's not just about the offender, it's about the impacts as well. But you can't say that you won't do anything because that would be almost like giving a licence to offend.

However, criticisms have been raised regarding the criminalising and net-widening potential of early intervention(ism). A particular focus has been the tiered, escalating nature of the 'support' systems introduced following the Crime and Disorder Act 1998: ASB management (from warning letter to Acceptable Behaviour Contract [ABC] to ASBO to conviction), the revised out-of-court sentencing process (from Reprimand to Final Warning to Referral Order in court) to court-based community and custodial sentencing (from Referral Order to other community sentences to ISSP and DTO to custody). Critics have argued that these tiered systems were inflexible and functioned more like escalators that young people could not get off once they had got on, thus encouraging (inadvertent) strategies of criminalisation (e.g. the breach of an ASBO being a criminal offence), not to mention labelling and stigmatisation (Bateman 2016) – in direct contradiction of Government objectives to prevent youth offending through diversion from formal youth justice processes. In particular, ASBOs had become disproportionately targeted on young people (their original target was meant to be 'problem' families/neighbours), primarily negative in focus and lacking in the provision of appropriate levels of support (Bateman 2016: Solanki *et al.* 2006). Goldson (2007: 8) has been particularly scathing about the widespread use of early intervention and the resultant increase in the number of young people labelled as 'offenders', arguing that the YJS 'has become bloated and obese, as an inevitable consequence of a policy obsession with early intervention'. He cites the labelling theories of Lemert, Becker and Matza (see Chapter 2), asserting that contact with the formal YJS (e.g. prosecution processes, court appearances) can criminalise young people by establishing 'delinquent identities' and going on to claim that 'early intervention encourages child criminalisation as distinct from crime prevention' (Goldson 2007: 9). Goldson's conclusion reiterates Matza's view that youth justice interventions can be 'self-defeating' because 'the very effort to prevent, intervene, arrest and 'cure' persons. . . [can] precipitate or seriously aggravate the tendency society wishes to guards against' (Matza 1969: 80).

Further issues have been raised regarding the Government's interventionism project being misplaced; prioritising and targeting the wrong areas in which to offer support and treatment (Smith 2014). The focus on individualised psychosocial risk factors, for example, was seen as dealing only with superficial manifestations of poverty (considered one of the major neglected influences upon youth offending) and unlikely to provide real or lasting solutions to the 'structural, economic and political problems at the heart of social exclusion' (Pitts 2001: 147). Therefore, the 'new youth justice' could be criticised as a limited interventionist approach that primarily targeted the symptoms ('tough on crime') rather than tackling the causes of social deprivation and crime ('tough on the causes of crime'). Universal social crime prevention programmes that were created to address social exclusion tended to become opera-tionalised (constructed) as individualised/targeted programmes designed to manage and eradicate only its visible representations (e.g. poor parenting, substance use, tru-ancy, homelessness) – in other words, psychosocial risk factors (Smith 2014) – illus-trating the individualisation of the youth crime 'problem'.

Risk-focused early intervention

The chosen vehicle for driving New Labour's prevention and interventionism agenda was risk-focused early intervention using the RFPP, an evidence-based and 'effective' approach reflecting the modern dominance of risk factor theories of youth offending (see Chapter 3) and risk management models of youth justice (see Chapter 4). The combination of a large, growing evidence base and practical simplicity underpinned the roll-out of the risk-focused early intervention strategy across the YJS and the expan-sion of the approach to at-risk and 'antisocial' non-offenders as a means of deliber-ate and strategic net-widening. The YJB's faith in the 'evidence-based' utility of the RFPP was reinforced by ostensibly successful evaluations of the high predictive validity (69 per cent after two years) and the practitioner-friendly nature of Asset (Baker *et al.* 2002, 2005) as a standardised and transparent assessment tool to inform preventative intervention with identified offenders. Results from the original evaluation of YIPs for the at-risk young people considered 'pre-offenders' (Morgan Harris Burrows 2003) were inconsistent, however, identifying general reductions in arrests and school exclu-sions in YIP areas but large increases in truancy rates and recorded youth crime. The evaluators cited a lack of consistent implementation of the programme across areas, a finding that was repeated in the evaluation of the Scaled Approach to assessment and intervention (see next section). The initial evaluation of YISPs (also employed with at-risk young people) was hampered by restrictions in the amount, completeness and representativeness of qualitative data collected through Onset assessment (Walker *et al.* 2007). Drawing mainly on the quantitative interview data, the evaluators made con-clusions that YISPs had an *indirect* impact on youth offending, in that

> some of the changes in circumstances may well have been facilitated by the fact that the child had been referred to YISP and members of the multi-agency panel had been able to commit resources to affecting change in the family's life.
>
> (Walker *et al.* 2007: 23)

Notwithstanding the inconsistent and incomplete evaluations of YIPs and YISPs, the main criticism of the risk-focused early intervention agenda has been reserved for the Asset risk assessment tool. Claims that Asset has been effective (at predicting likeli-hood of reoffending) and practical (for YOT staff) have been questioned. Firstly, ambi-guity surrounding what constitutes prevention is illustrated by Asset's claims to predict the likelihood of reoffending when it actually predicts the likelihood of *reconviction* (Case 2007). Although reoffending and reconviction are broadly similar outcomes, they are also subtly different and not necessarily equivalent in terms of the experiences of young people who reoffend (who may not be caught or convicted) and compared to young people who are reconvicted (who then experience interactions and outcomes that may exacerbate existing risk factors or create new ones). Furthermore, the finding that Asset correctly predicts reoffending outcomes (i.e. whether young people do or do not reoffend) in over two-thirds of cases has been attacked by critics (e.g. Bateman 2011; Case and Haines 2009). They argue that this outcome is unconvincing, neglecting to explain what happens to the one-third of young people who are incorrectly predicted to reoffend (so receive intervention that they may not actually need) or who are predicted not to reoffend (so receive no/insufficient intervention to meet their needs).

More generally, critical youth justice academics have raised a series of concerns with the 'negative youth justice' (Case and Haines 2015b) perpetuated by the interventionist RFPP. Arguments have focused on how young people who offend have been socially constructed as dangerous, threatening and problematic (not innocent and vulnerable) by risk assessment and intervention approaches, and as presenting risks to themselves and others that must be nipped in the bud by adult intervention. Therefore, the risk assessed young person is constructed as deserving of control and punishment more than in need of care and support, while increasing levels of criminalisation, surveillance and regulatory control have been rationalised as preventative and diversionary support mechanisms (Goldson 2007). A significant by-product of this perspective is that young people have been judged and responded to on the basis of what they are predicted to do in the future, not what they have done, which is anathema to legal principles such as due process and burden of proof (Goldson 2007), anathema to 'child-friendly justice' (see Chapter 4) and contrary to the notion of 'evidence-based practice' – as it relies on evidence that is not yet available and that may never exist. Furthermore, the negative and individualising nature of risk-focused early intervention has promoted a **neo-correctionalist** approach to youth justice – responding to youth offending by attempting to correct assessed 'deficits' in young people, rather than by supporting and nurturing young people (Muncie 2014). The implication of neo-correctionism is that young people who offend are somehow flawed (as opposed to troubled, victimised, vulnerable), which justifies punitive and interventionist responses that reinforce the individualisation and responsibilisation strategies of the 'new youth justice'. The individualising, psychosocial bias of the RFPP could limit the validity of youth justice responses by neglecting the influence of socio-structural, contextual and interpersonal factors in the young person's life (Goddard and Myers 2017; Case 2007). This individualising approach fosters a culture of responsibilisation and interventionism at the individual level, which is arguably invalid and disproportionate as it unfairly blames young people for the criminogenic influence of factors beyond their control (Case and Haines 2009; see also Chapter 3).

CONTROVERSIES AND DEBATES

The 'new youth justice' and the UNCRC

A long-standing criticism of the strategies that have animated the 'new youth justice' is that they contravene or at least undermine state adherence to the principles of the United Nations Convention on the Rights of the Child (UNCRC), largely due to their criminalising nature. As discussed in Chapter 4, the UNCRC established a baseline for treating children in trouble with regard to their rights and for prioritising their protection, provision and participation (UNICEF 1989). However, periodic inspections of State compliance with the UNCRC have frequently criticised the UK Government for ignoring its requirements, particularly when working with young people who have offended. For example, the 2002 inspection expressed concerns that UNCRC provisions and principles 'have not yet been incorporated into domestic law, nor is there any formal process to ensure that new legislation fully complies with the Convention' (Committee on the Rights of the Child 2002), while in 2008 the Committee expressed concern 'at the general climate of intolerance and negative public attitudes towards children which appears to exist in the State party, including the media, and may often be the underlying cause of further infringements of their rights'. John Muncie (2008) has offered an incisive synthesis of the key UN Committee criticisms as they relate to specific, criminalising elements of the 'new youth justice'. Muncie outlines three central criticisms of the lack of rights compliance within the 'new youth justice', as identified in the UN Committee inspections of 2002 and 2008:

1   *Criminalisation*: the continued use of ASBOs (including their encouragement of 'naming and shaming' by the media), failure to use custody as a last resort (contravening Article 37b) and the generally intolerant public climate – socially constructing children and young people who offend as dangerous and threatening.
2   *Adulterisation*: the very low age of criminal responsibility (contravening Article 40) in Scotland (8 years old, now 12 years old), England and Wales, and Northern Ireland (both 10 years old) compared to every other country in Western Europe (except for Switzerland – also 10 years old), where ages range from 12 to 18 years old.
3   *Inhumane treatment*: the use of physical restraint and strip searching in custody, poor custodial conditions (contravening Articles 37a and 39), the 'degrading' use of risk assessment practices that are 'inimical to their [children's] rights and possibly their welfare interests' (Morgan 2009: 15).

Explicit reference to the UNCRC in Labour's youth justice policy was rare; entirely absent from the Crime and Disorder Act 1998 and the Youth Crime Action Plan 2008 (see next section), for example (Bateman 2016). Successive UN Committee reports (2002, 2008) recommended that the YJS of England and Wales increase the age of criminal responsibility, abolish the use of ASBOs with children and curtail the use of youth custody. During the 1997–2010 governance of New Labour, these recommendations were neither acknowledged nor implemented and the central strategies of the 'new youth justice' continued to contravene the provisions and principles of the UNCRC and associate notions of 'child-friendly justice' (see Chapter 4).

Managerialism

The overarching strategy employed to implement and monitor the 'new youth justice' was one of managerialism. The revised and reorientated YJS of England and Wales was more tightly monitored and managed than ever before through the creation of the YJB to oversee YOTs' pursuit of KPIs and adherence to National Standards, Case Management Guidance and Key Elements of Effective Practice (KEEPs), in addition to the regular inspection of YOT practice by HMI Probation. Embedding a managerialist approach was a deliberate attempt to encourage the YJS to become more effective, efficient and economical by speeding up justice, cohering the practice of multiple agencies towards efficient and evidenced approaches, removing the (perceived) excessive, unchecked discretion and indeterminism of welfare responses to youth offending and ensuring greater use of proven 'evidence-based' responses to improve upon failing justice-based responses. The end game was, of course, increased system effectiveness, efficiency and economy through a more transparent, accountable, defensible and reflective YJS and a set of modernised, fit-for-purpose youth justice processes and practices.

A common critique of managerialism and its associated performance management was largely inevitable: prescriptiveness. Key stakeholders felt that YOT practitioners were being deprived of the opportunity to exercise their expert judgement and discretion, based on utilising their experience and developing close, meaningful relationships with young people in the YJS, in favour of an overly prescriptive model that instructed and restricted rather than guiding and empowering them (as the YJB claimed it did). A no-holds-barred outline of this critique was offered by the acerbic John Pitts in his journal article *Korrectional Karaoke: New Labour and the Zombification of Youth Justice* (Pitts 2001). He argued that the practice of the 'new youth justice' had become 'deprofessionalised', 'routinised' and 'technicised' by excessive performance management, prescription and an obsession with statistical outcomes. Pitts observed that youth justice practice had regressed into 'korrectional karaoke', with practitioners being compelled to adopt a heavily prescribed, off-the-shelf approach to targeting a restricted group of psychosocial risk factors using the limited and biased methods dictated by the YJB. His article really is a must-read for anyone interested in hard-hitting (if selective, one-sided and hyperbolic) critique of managerialism in youth justice. Reflecting on the growing YJB prescriptiveness post-2000, Professor Kevin Haines told me that

> people were entering YOTs to work with no previous experience of youth justice and were just doing what Asset told them to do. Experienced YOT workers were being constrained by the Key Elements of Effective Practice. Movement away from this prescriptive working culture was difficult, very much against the flow of the stream.

A counterpoint to the criticism of managerialist automation of youth justice practice is, of course, local mediation. It was likely that practitioners were still able to exercise a degree of discretion when interpreting and implementing centralised guidance, such as risk assessment processes (cf. Briggs 2013; Kemshall 2008) – linking to the RTA of local mediation of centralised prescriptions through practitioner and organisational (re)constructions and expertise.

Further criticism has taken issue with the extent to which the centre (Government, YJB) retained control over the nature of youth justice practice and how this was to be evaluated, despite espousing an approach that alleged decentralised control and empowered local authority areas to deal with their own social issues in their own ways. The extent of decentralisation and capacity for localised discretion in the YJS was clearly limited by the extent of centralised performance management and practice prescriptions. A cynic could view this simultaneous centralised–decentralised approach as the Government/State responsibilising local areas for the success of centralised youth justice measures, while only accepting any responsibility itself if and when such measures proved successful.

5 EASY PIECES

4 Evaluating the 'new youth justice'

1   *Effective, efficient, economical*: reviews of the first decade of the 'new youth justice' were polarised in their conclusions as to whether it had achieved its objectives, with the Audit Commission (2004) indicating successes, yet the Centre for Crime and Justice Studies and other critics claiming inconsistent to negative results.

2   *Responsibilisation*: the underpinning strategy of making young people (at increasingly younger ages), parents and local communities primarily responsible for dealing with youth offending (e.g. by reducing the age of criminal responsibility) was based on political expedience and personal/professional experience rather than research evidence. It has been criticised for its negative, net-widening, interventionist and adulterising impact and a lack of justifying evidence base.

3   *Risk-focused prevention and early intervention*: the prevention agenda offered a common-sense, practical touchstone for multi-agency youth justice practice, animated by the RFPP as an evidence-based and similarly practical approach. However, the RFPP evidence base is unconvincing and its construction has been inconsistent in terms of what outcomes are being prevented, including ambiguity over the difference between prevention and early intervention. There are further concerns that the RFPP is neo-correctionalist and individualising.

4   *Interventionism*: youth justice processes were revised to enable adults to offer more support to supposedly irresponsible, helpless and deprived young people once they offended. However, the inflexible, tiered approach to intervention has been accused of escalating young people's progress into formal youth justice processes and thus potentially accelerating their criminalisation, rather than preventing offending.

5   *Managerialism*: the YJB tightly managed the performance of the YJS in order to improve its effectiveness, efficiency and economy. Critics have argued that this amounted to micromanagement that neutered practitioners and robbed them of their ability to use discretion and expertise, while responsibilising local areas and absolving the Government of responsibility if their youth justice prescriptions did not demonstrate success.

5 THE FINAL YEARS OF THE 'NEW YOUTH JUSTICE'? (2008–2010)

Following a decade of 'new youth justice', Tony Blair was replaced as Prime Minister by Gordon Brown in June 2007. The final years of the New Labour Government (2008–2010) evidenced an emerging ambiguity in relation to youth justice policy and practice (**RTA = conflict and ambivalence**). On the one hand, the strategies of the 'new youth justice' were consolidated and extrapolated. On the other hand, there was evidence of a shift away from punitive, responsibilising, interventionist and criminalising youth justice and towards more progressive approaches (Smith

2014). The 2008–2010 period was notable for two key developments in relation to youth justice:

1 *(Re)constructing targets*: the abolition of the Offences Brought to Justice target for police and the imposition of KPIs for YOTs, which preceded a period of significant decreases in FTEs into the YJS and falling custody rates.
2 *More 'new youth justice'*: a reassertion of the main strategies of the 'new youth justice' in the Youth Crime Action Plan 2008 and the Scaled Approach to assessment and intervention.

(Re)constructing targets: Offences Brought to Justice

A major review of policing practice in 2007–2008 concluded that the Offences Brought to Justice (OBTJ) target (aka 'sanction detections') had served as a perverse incentive that encouraged police to formally process excessive numbers of low-level offences and incivilities that would previously not have warranted arrest or conviction (Smith 2014). The report asserted that

> an emphasis on sanction detection levels has undoubtedly to a degree produced the unintended effect of [police] officers spending time investigating crimes with a view to obtaining a detection even when that is clearly not in the public interest. An example of such would be a low-level playground assault.
>
> (Flanagan 2008: 10)

The previous section introduced the complaints of Rod Morgan and others that OBTJ targets had led to unnecessarily criminalisation by increasing the numbers of young people 'ending up in the youth court when magistrates complained many cases do not warrant their attention' (Morgan 2007; see also Bateman 2008). This criminalisation process was more likely to occur because young people's behaviour was more visible than that of adults (**RTA = criminalising the visible street behaviour of street children**) and so they were easier targets for police activity – what Morgan (2007) called 'low-hanging fruit'. The Government responded to the police review by revising its approach to processing offences and thus effectively abolishing the OBTJ target measure as of April 2008 (cf. Solomon and Garside 2008). The police response to this abolition was supportive, urging their leadership to 'ensure that these OBTJ targets are not reinstated' (Flanagan 2008: 56). The impact of the change on KPIs from 2008 to 2010 was significant, with FTEs falling by 55 per cent (likely because fewer young people were being arrested at the first stage of the youth justice process), reoffending falling by 29 per cent and custody rates falling by 30 per cent (Youth Justice Board and Ministry of Justice (MoJ) 2012). The use of pre-court disposals (Reprimands and Final Warnings) also decreased by 62 per cent from its 2006–2007 peak (Youth Justice Board and Ministry of Justice 2012).

An issue emerges here, however, as to what extent the reductions across the three main KPIs from 2008 onwards can be attributed to the abolition of the OBTJ targets. For example, to what extent were these decreases the result of the more effective systems management and decision-making in the YJS (e.g. due to the abolition of OBTJ) as opposed to the strategies of the 'new youth justice' coming to fruition after a decade, regardless of or in addition to the abolition of OBTJ? Understanding these trends in youth justice outcomes is of crucial importance for any balanced evaluation of the 'new youth justice'. The Government's perspective was that systemic changes to the 'new' youth justice machinery since 2008 had accelerated existing longer-term trends (themselves seen as a product of the 'new youth justice'), notably declines in FTEs (50 per cent) and custody (49 per cent) over the period 2000–2001 to 2010–2011 (Youth Justice Board and Ministry of Justice 2012). However, even the Government concluded that reduced use of formal youth justice processes could not be explained by one single factor (e.g. the abolition of the OBTJ target) or any specific strategy of the 'new youth justice'. This more balanced and tentative conclusion was reasserted by Tim Bateman (2012) following his detailed critical analysis of youth justice trends since 2000. Bateman echoed the view that post-OBTJ outcomes had accelerated existing downward trajectories in KPI outcomes, especially in terms of decreasing FTEs (along with decreases in recorded youth offending), while qualifying that custody rates had fallen dramatically only since 2008, having remained largely stable since 2000. Bateman perceived a growing momentum in 'depenalisation' (moves away from official, punitive responses) at all stages of the YJS, in stark contrast to trends in the adult CJS. This momentum had directly affected youth justice processes and had exerted a subtler impact on the 'climate of opinion' regarding the fair and proportionate treatment of young people, particularly among youth justice practitioners (see also Smith 2014). According to Bateman (2012: 45):

> In addition to channelling literally tens of thousands of children away from formal criminal justice responses . . . harsh responses for children who broke the law were no longer de rigueur – alternatives were available and should be used.

The combination of enhanced systems management and changing professional attitudes to appropriate youth justice, therefore, can be seen as a possible explanation for the discrepancy between post-2007/OBTJ developments in youth justice and the lack of success in reducing youth custody in the first ten years of the 'new youth justice'. Writing in 2011, Rob Allen suggested that a range of dynamic structural and systemic factors should be considered as explanatory of the sharp change in direction in youth justice practice and outcomes since 2008. He observed the growing frustration of enforcement agencies (e.g. police, courts) in having to deal formally with minor offences committed by young people. He argued that this frustration motivated

> a greater engagement between the Youth Justice Board and Youth Offending Teams on the one hand and courts on the other, which may have developed a shared view that custody should be a last resort.
>
> (Allen 2011: 4)

Furthermore, structural relationships within Government were changing around the time that the OBTJ ceased, with youth justice policy responsibility transferred from the Home Office to the Ministry of Justice and the Department for Children, Schools and Families (jointly). Allen viewed this transfer of responsibility as encouraging a more liberal perspective on youth justice, cohering with Bateman's (2012) view that professional attitudes were motivating changes in youth justice outcomes, rather than any particular change in public mood or 'overt political enthusiasm' (Allen 2011: 9). This begs the question as to what may have motivated changes in professional attitudes? Structural and systemic changes in the delivery of youth justice may well have been more strategic than principled on the part of youth justice agencies; instrumental changes in order to pursue the newly introduced KPIs from 2007 (Evidence to House of Commons Justice Committee, 21 June 2012). It appeared that YOTs were now 'taking a more systemic and targeted approach to the provision of alternatives to custody, while also working to improve their credibility with the courts' (Allen 2011: 20). There are clear similarities here with the new orthodoxy thinking and systems management of the 1980s (see Chapter 4), where practitioner decision-making processes stimulated decreases in recorded youth offending and custodial sentencing (see Haines and Drakeford 1998). Bateman (2012: 46) observed that punitiveness remained the dominant ethos for youth justice policy, but that it was mediated by various 'institutional frameworks, cultural constructions, national dynamics and local political or economic considerations'. The possibility of local mediation of centralised policy prescriptions (**RTA**) becomes especially significant here. It was increasingly evident that local areas (e.g. represented by YOTs) were mediating and moderating centralised youth justice policy and practice prescriptions to suit their own contexts and circumstances, either in collaboration with the YJB and/or conducted by innovative practitioners and progressive managers under the radar of centralised monitoring processes (cf. Morgan 2009). A certain degree of local mediation was accepted and even expected by the centre (i.e. Government, YJB) as indicative of their empowerment and responsibilisation of local areas; some mediation was not necessarily condoned nor desired. However, there was a sense that it would be tolerated if it did not diminish KPI outcomes and could be demonstrated as 'effective' practice (e.g. the case of Swansea YOT; Haines and Case 2015).

More 'new youth justice'

Despite apparent structural, systemic, cultural and attitudinal changes, Government youth justice policy remained highly contradictory, as usual (see Smith 2014). This contradiction was best illustrated by the subsequent policy statement, the Youth Crime Action Plan 2008 (HM Government 2008) and the extension of risk-focused early intervention practice through the Scaled Approach (YJB 2010). Both of these youth justice developments contrasted with the diversionary, less punitive youth justice context that was emerging post-2007, by virtue of their reinforcing central strategies of the 'new youth justice'. Indeed, several academics have been critical of the ambiguous and contradictory nature of youth justice in the final period of New Labour power (e.g. Smith 2014; Muncie 2008), as illustrated by the purported successes in meeting KPIs through progressive practice, balanced against the rolling-out of punitiveness and the 'new youth justice' in the form of the Youth Crime Action Plan 2008 and the RFPP. Bateman (2012) identified a longer term 'direction of travel' shaped by the 'new youth justice' that had been subverted and overridden in the short term by a host of contingent factors such as revised targets, restricted budgets, changes in governmental structures, and policy and practitioner innovation. In other words, short-term successes in reducing FTEs, reoffending and custody and even the amount of intervention delivered were more likely to be the result of pragmatic decisions influenced by resource and financial concerns (Smith 2014), rather than a consequence of a fundamental cultural shift away from the risk-focused interventionism – a situation that was to play out further after the 2012 change of government (see Chapter 6).

Youth Crime Action Plan 2008

The Youth Crime Action Plan (YCAP) 2008 outlined New Labour's strategy for moving youth justice forwards and tackling youth crime. The YCAP 2008 outlined a 'triple-track' approach of 'enforcement and punishment where behaviour is unacceptable, non-negotiable support and challenge where it is most needed, and better and earlier prevention' (HM Government 2008: 1). The YCAP 2008 committed the Government to reducing FTEs by 20 per cent by 2020 (Bateman 2016). A notable distinction was made between vulnerable young people in need of support and those who were apparently more threatening and irresponsible (**RTA**), illustrated by the assertion that 'for those who are struggling we will offer more support; and those who do not take their responsibility seriously we will challenge them to do so' (HM Government 2008: 5; see also the support–control dichotomy). The more punitive, enforcement-led and 'non-negotiable' elements of youth justice were acknowledged as essential to the Government's preventative aim, thus giving the act a 'veneer of toughness' (Smith 2014). There was also an increased emphasis on public protection as a goal of youth crime prevention and on community responsibilisation as a strategy to pursue it. Specifically, the reaffirmation of 'new youth justice' strategies (**RTA = support–control**) evidenced in the YCAP 2008 would focus on:

1 *Enforcement and punishment*: setting clear boundaries for acceptable behaviour and clear consequences for failing to meet them (e.g. custody).
2 *Prevention*: tackling the root causes of youth offending by improving universal services and committing to further (risk-focused) early intervention to identify vulnerable young people and families.
3 *Support*: non-negotiable intervention with young people and families at risk of offending, to include extra funding and a re-emphasis on individual parental responsibility.

The YCAP 2008 re-emphasised the Government's faith in 'new youth justice' strategies of punitive responsibilisation and early intervention through net-widening as a way to appear tough on youth crime to the voting public (i.e. political expedience). Consequently, the YCAP 2008 appeared to contradict the positive intentions of the abolition of OBTJ targets and their diversionary move away from criminalising young people who offended.

The Scaled Approach

The Government's recommitment to 'new youth justice' peaked in 2009 with the introduction of the Scaled Approach to assessment and intervention. The Government and YJB had long-standing concerns that YOTs and the staff were making insufficient attempts to link the results from Asset risk assessment to subsequent interventions. Indeed, the *Youth Justice 2004* report (Audit Commission 2004: 142), the follow-up to *Misspent Youth*, recommended that

YOTs should make better use of Asset to determine the amount as well as the nature of interventions with individuals using a scaled approach.

In response to this recommendation, the YJB produced the Scaled Approach assessment and intervention framework, which effectively formalised the existing APIS KEEP guidance (YJB 2008). The Scaled Approach formalised the assessment–intervention link by requiring YOT practitioners to tailor or scale the frequency, duration and intensity of planned interventions to the level of risk assessed using Asset (YJB 2009a). The introduction of this framework was planned to coincide with the introduction of the Youth Rehabilitation Order, a new generic court sentence that would replace the host of existing community sentences available to courts should the Referral Order (which remained on the books) not be considered appropriate. Asset scores were to be categorised into three indicators of future offending: low, medium and high risk. These risk categories were then linked to the frequency and intensity of intervention: low standard, medium enhanced and high intensive. Despite a highly questionable evidence base for the utility of risk-focused early intervention (see Case and Haines 2009, 2015b, for a detailed critique), the Government fully committed to the Scaled Approach as the updated animation of the RFPP as a tool for shaping effective youth justice practice. It was clear that the model had been embraced conceptually and strategically (i.e. politically) long before its introduction; it was only the method of its implementation that required testing. Consequently, the Scaled Approach underwent a process (not outcome) evaluation from December 2006 to June 2007 in four pilot YOTs in England and Wales, which were compared with four control YOTs from the same geographical areas but not implementing the Scaled Approach (YJB 2010). The aims of the evaluation were to:

- Explore the practice requirements of the risk-based approach to interventions;
- Compare the different elements of the risk-based approaches adopted by the four pilot YOTs;
- Identify a set of working procedures that can be used when adopting a risk-based approach;
- Identify the differences between the pilot and comparison YOTs in tailoring and targeting of interventions.

(YJB 2010: 7)

The evaluation collected empirical data from risk assessment and intervention planning processes conducted with 1,133 young people, which included Black and Minority Ethnic (BAME) and female booster groups. Qualitative data was collected from interviews with key stakeholders, including YOT staff, judges/magistrates and Referral Order Panel members in the pilot and control areas. Evaluators identified variations in Scaled Approach practice between the pilot areas in relation to central elements of the assessment–intervention process: how young people were allocated to risk categories, pre-sentence report recommendations to courts regarding suitable interventions, and the way Asset scores were linked to intervention. However, the evaluation team also identified four shared 'effective' principles for implementing the Scaled Approach across the pilot areas: accurate and consistent assessment, intervention plans appropriate to risk, case reviews that monitor and respond to changes in risk, and enforcement of breach (YJB 2010: 14). The pilot YOTs were more likely than the control YOTs to provide information to courts and Referral Order Panels related to the risk (of reoffending, serious harm, vulnerability) presented by a young person, and they were more likely to have their recommendations followed by the courts. The conclusion was that there was a 'broad and clearly defined consensus among the practitioners in the four pilot YOTs that the risk-based approach results in better outcomes for children' (YJB 2010: 15; see also Sutherland 2009).

However, the Scaled Approach evaluation suffered from at least two significant methodological weaknesses that raise serious doubts over the validity and reliability of its findings and recommendations (Haines and Case 2012, 2015). Firstly, there were significant variations across the pilot YOTs in the ways in which the Scaled Approach was implemented in terms of assessment, decision-making and intervention practice. Therefore, the outcomes in each pilot area did not necessarily relate to the equivalent implementation of the assessment and intervention framework and so cannot necessarily be considered to be reliable (consistent, replicable). Secondly, the outcomes measured were rather narrow, with no data collected on outcomes such as reconviction or cost-effectiveness. These limitations forced the YJB (2010: 14) to concede that 'the lack of this information is a constraint in making objective assessments of the variety of practices that were adopted by the YOTs' (see also Sutherland 2009). It is important to critically consider these methodological weaknesses (remember your ABC: Always Be Critical) and the lack of conclusive evidence of success/effectiveness in light of the subsequent, definitive (uncritical, policy-led) decision to roll out the Scaled Approach nationally.

As you would imagine in such a polarised context where critical academics drove much of the debate (such as it was), the Scaled Approach received a swathe of additional criticism. The most common and vociferous issue raised was the potential for the model to encourage disproportionate intervention (see also our earlier discussion of Asset), in line with the tendency of the 'new youth justice' for interventionism (see Muncie 2008; Squires and Stephen 2005). Young people committing similar offences could be subject to different levels of intervention under the new framework based solely on differences in their risk profiles, with these interventions having the potential to be disproportionate to the young person's offence and circumstances (Bateman 2011; Paylor 2010). For example, a young person assessed as at high risk of reoffending who actually does *not* go on to reoffend (known as a 'false positive') could receive excessive intervention that they never really needed. Conversely, a young person assessed as low risk of reoffending who *does* go on to reoffend (known as a 'false negative') could receive insufficient intervention when in reality it was needed. This disproportionality occurs because a young person is receiving intervention based on their risk of future reoffending, rather than based on their current circumstances, needs or any actual, demonstrable behaviour. Critics have argued that there was a potential under the Scaled Approach for practitioners to deal with disproportionality by using their discretion, such that 'the link between the Asset score and the number of contacts required by the "evidence-base" is sufficiently loose to allow alteration at will' (Bateman 2011: 178). This potential for manipulation could 'widen the net of influence exerted by the state and the YJS' (Paylor 2010: 31). Of course, there is the converse potential that risk categories could be manipulated upwards in favour of the young person so that they can be provided with much-needed support even though they have received a low risk rating, which would be simultaneously supportive of, and in breach of, Scaled Approach principles!

CONTROVERSIES AND DEBATES

My experience of the Scaled Approach

I'd like to share my professional experiences of the development of the Scaled Approach, which will indicate (my view of) the degree to which the framework was a political project, rather than the evidence-based practice enhancement it was claimed to be. The first of these experiences was more academic/scholarship; the second more academic/practical.

In 2009, I released the book *Understanding Youth Offending: Risk Factor Research, Policy and Practice* (co-authored with Professor Kevin Haines), a detailed critical evaluation of risk factor theories and associated research (see Chapter 3) and its application in the YJS. As part of our research, we examined the theoretical and evidential bases of the RFPP and made an alarming discovery. Despite claims that the Scaled Approach was 'evidence based' (YJB 2009a) and grounded in a long-standing, reliable and validated body of empirical research (see also Loeber *et al.* 2003), there was a paucity of evidence that risk-focused intervention actually worked in practice (Haines and Case 2008; Goldson 2005). In reality, much of the developmental and life course research that influenced the RFPP (e.g. Glueck and Glueck 1930, 1950; West and Farrington 1973; Sampson and Laub 1993) did not even attempt interventions to reduce/prevent risk factors. The original risk factor research study in criminology (Glueck and Glueck 1930) did not look at intervention at all; neither did the Cambridge Study in Delinquent Development (West and Farrington 1973) that shaped Asset. Indeed, Glueck and Glueck concluded that maturation had the greatest influence upon desistance from youth offending, which presents itself as a cogent argument for minimal/non-intervention with young people who offend. The original application of the risk factor theories to the prevention of offending, the Cambridge-Somerville Youth Study (Cabot 1940) had discovered that risk-focused intervention was often ineffective and could be actively harmful (McCord and McCord 1959; McCord 1978). Other studies that evaluated the impact of long-term, risk-focused interventions with young people demonstrated very limited and inconsistent evidence of success (e.g. the Causes and Correlates studies in the US ([Thornberry and Krohn 2003] and *Criminals Coming of Age* [Bottoms and McClintock 1973]) and evidence of the deleterious consequences of risk-focused preventative intervention when delivered through contact with the YJS (e.g. Edinburgh Study; McAra and McVie 2007). Consequently, the evidence base for the Scaled Approach was seriously questionable, as was the claim that risk-focused early intervention is effective. However, this contradictory evidence base did not deter the Government from supporting the Scaled Approach, indicating a pre-formed political project being rolled out regardless of academic evidence.

The suspicion that the Scaled Approach roll-out was a project of political expediency, rather than being evidence based (see also Goddard and Myers 2017), was compounded by professional experience of the development of the model (2008–2009) prior to its inception. I worked as part of an Open University consultancy team developing YJB-funded training materials for YOT managers preparing to implement the Scaled Approach. These materials consisted of a series of modules unpacking the RFPP – its origins and evidence base, how it should be implemented and how practitioners should critically reflect on risk-based practice. My role was to encourage critical reflection by practitioners through evaluating the methodology, analysis, evidence, conclusions and ethics of the framework, how it could be adapted and whether it was appropriate based on its (lack of) validity and reliability – a critical point that was rather off message for the YJB! The reaction to my course materials was one of outrage from the YJB and from the external training provider contracted to produce the materials. I had allegedly caricatured youth justice practice and been unnecessarily negative regarding the key elements of the RFPP, to the point that practitioners may find the approach impractical and inappropriate. I disagreed, as did the Open University consultancy team manager and the external reviewer (a respected critical youth justice academic), who argued that I was 'encouraging practitioners to reflect critically on their practice in a challenging way, very much in the spirit of reflective practice and quality academic scholarship'. Such reflection was, of course, in accordance with YJB requirements for YOT practice, but apparently not so welcome if it were targeted at the evidential basis of youth justice policy and practice! My impression from this process was that the Government/YJB commitment to the RFPP/Scaled Approach was fixed, so any reflection must be focused on how to implement it effectively, not whether to implement it at all. The emphasis seemed to be on generating policy-based evidence rather than evidence-based policy. My view was soon reinforced when attending a conference presentation to youth justice practitioners – a critique of the Scaled Approach by two critical academics. A senior policy adviser from the YJB gatecrashed the session and proceeded to interrupt the post-presentation critical question-and-answer panel by informing practitioners in the audience that 'you will be doing this', regardless of their expressed concerns. Once again, the Scaled Approach was being presented (in this case by senior policy-makers) as a done deal and practitioners were being browbeaten into its implementation. They had, after all, been through a consultation exercise regarding the new framework. However, this consultation had taken the form of a prescriptive and prejudged reflection exercise along the lines of 'this is what you will be doing, so how can you make sure that it works?'. In my experience, this has been an all-too-common approach to 'consultation' with practitioners in the YJS – key stakeholders from the centre (Government, YJB) presenting a pre-formed and politically agreed policy/practice proposal and expecting YOT staff to accept it and make it work (with YJB support, of course). The implementation of the Scaled Approach appeared to me to exemplify such an unreflective process, which I have characterised elsewhere as 'a prescription without a consultation' (Case 2007: 174).

To summarise, the final years of the New Labour Government (2008–2010) were characterised by ambiguity surrounding the shape and direction of youth justice policy and practice (**RTA = conflict and ambivalence**). Progressive, positive moves towards reduced criminalisation and increased diversion were largely overshadowed by elaborations of 'new youth justice' strategies reflected in policy (Youth Crime Action Plan, Home Office 2008) and practice (the Scaled Approach). Notwithstanding ambiguity and contradiction in youth justice policy and practice, the suggestion throughout this period has been of a Government convinced that its 'new youth justice' approach had been successful on its own terms and that same Government being resistant to critical reflection on the potential weaknesses of the approach and the potential for other influences to have impacted upon the successful delivery of youth justice.

5 EASY PIECES

5 The final years of the 'new youth justice' (2008–2010)

1   *Ambiguity*: the final three years of the New Labour Government evidenced con-fusion, ambivalence and ambiguity in how youth justice was to be constructed and delivered, with conflict between diversionary practice and extensions of the 'new youth justice' strategies of responsibilisation and risk-focused early interventionism.
2   *Reversing criminalisation*: the abolition of the Offences Brought to Justice target in 2008 accelerated existing declines in FTEs, reoffending rates and custody levels, ostensibly reversing worrying trends in criminalisation of young people by the police (largely the product of pressure to meet these targets by making arrests) through the more effective systems management of police decision-making processes.
3   *Changing professional attitudes*: reviews of the YJS attributed successes in reduc-ing youth justice outcomes to the abolition of the Offences Brought to Justice target in combination with changing professional attitudes, which encouraged police, YOTs, court and others to work more closely together to pursue less crim-inalising and more diversionary responses to young people who offended.
4   *A new, ambiguous youth justice*: the Youth Crime Action Plan 2008 was a con-fused, ambiguous combination of enforcement/punishment, prevention and 'non-negotiable' support that extended existing 'new youth justice' strategies and illustrated the support–control dichotomy in youth justice.
5   *Political (re)construction*: the new Scaled Approach assessment and intervention framework extended the Government's faith in the RFPP by implementing a preformed Government policy/strategy initiative without convincing practical or academic evidence of its effectiveness – indicative of the role of political influ-ence on the social (re)construction of youth justice.

NEW LABOUR AND THE 'NEW YOUTH JUSTICE': SO, WHAT DO WE KNOW?

The 'new youth justice' of the New Labour Government departed from traditional welfare versus justice concerns and radically reformed the YJS of England and Wales. This new model of youth justice was informed by three Es: political *expedience*, aca-demic and other *evidence* and professional/personal *experience* of key policy influenc-ers. The 'new youth justice' attempted to circumvent the welfare versus justice debate by introducing a new system priority – prevention – which formed the touchstone of the Crime and Disorder Act 1998. Prevention would be the priority for the new, fully formed YJS (no longer a set of piecemeal, ad hoc youth justice responses), which would prioritise three different Es: *effectiveness, efficiency* and *economy*. The YJS would henceforth be overseen by the newly created YJB, who would closely manage the performance of new multi-agency YOTs in each local area (i.e. managerialism). The youth justice practice of YOT staff was to be heavily influenced/shaped by 'new youth justice' strategies of responsibilisation (of young people, families, local communities) and risk-focused intervention (the RFPP). The Crime and Disorder Act 1998 formalised the prevention aim and the new strategic foci of responsibilisation (e.g. by abolishing doli incapax, by encouraging restorative justice) and risk-focused intervention, for example, by introducing a new ASB management process, new early intervention programmes and a new/revised out-of-court sentencing system. In addition, a series of new community sentences were introduced as alternatives to custody, whilst custodial options were also strengthened. Revisions to court sentencing indicated a twin track (bifurcated) approach that emphasised prevention with all but the most serious and persistent offenders, who would receive more punitive, intensive and controlling responses (**RTA = simultaneous support and control**). This approach illustrates the 'new penology' (Feeley and Simon 1992) of progressive minimalism (e.g. diversionary out-of-court sentencing) and corporatism (e.g. multi-agency working) as a means of cost-effective youth justice, alongside interventionism for high-risk and persistent offenders (Joyce 2017; Pitts 2003). An overarching goal of the 'new youth justice' was to modernise the YJS, moving past traditional (philosophical) welfare-justice concerns and creating an 'evidence-based' and (cost-)effective set of practical responses that were transparent, accountable and defensible.

The Labour Government and the YJB claimed success for the practical, common-sense strategies of 'new youth justice' in terms of annual reductions in FTEs, reoffending and custody. Accordingly, the approach was expanded through the YCAP 2008 and the Scaled Approach to assessment and intervention. Critics have argued that any success has been exaggerated (at least to a degree) through the selective misrepresentation of evidence (which can be traced back to the *Misspent Youth* rationale for system changes), the constant manipulation of youth justice targets and a failure to acknowledge external influences such as the abolition of police OBTJ targets, the role of change of professional attitudes and the potential for localised, innovative, under-the-radar practice by YOT staff. There has also been significant criticism of 'new youth justice' strategies for encouraging overly negative, labelling, criminalising and stigmatising perceptions of young people who offend, which may lead to further criminalisation and neglect of children's rights.

The big picture here is one of conflict and ambivalence, particularly between support and control. Youth justice from 1997 to 2010 appears ambiguous – simultaneously supportive and punitive, diversionary and interventionist, preventative and criminalising, evidence based and evidence lacking. Reflective of the hybrid nature of contemporary youth justice and the non-linear translation of policy into practice (Goldson 2014), the 'new youth justice' was a mass of contradictions, constantly reconstructed in response to political priorities, the selective collection and interpretation of evidence, and media misrepresentations fuelling a youth crime 'problem' and perception of young people who offend as 'dangerous'. This mass of contradictions is perhaps the biggest RTA of all – reflecting the climate of youth justice since it was first socially constructed. The constant ambiguity, reconstruction and myriad of key stakeholder influences is not 'new' to youth justice. What is most 'new' about the 'new youth justice' is the absence of *principles*, abandoned in favour of the structures, strategies and practices that modernised the YJS into a tightly managed focus on mechanised processes and statistical outcomes – a world away from the care--control and welfare–justice considerations of youth justice past.

5 EASY PIECES

Recommended further reading

For more detail in relation to the origins of the 'new youth justice', you should obtain a copy of the Audit Commission report *Misspent Youth: Young People and Crime* (1996). Until you have read through this straightforward and concise report, you will not be in a position to conduct a valid analysis of its central claims and the criticisms that have resulted. It is crucial that you locate source material such as this and decide for yourself how you feel about its contribution to youth justice.

In much the same spirit of engaging with literature that is supportive of the 'new youth justice' in order to balance the wealth of critical materials, I would advise you to read *Effective Practice in Youth Justice* by Martin Stephenson *et al.* (2011). This book is a synthesis of the main KEEP guidance documents and has been employed as the 'academic' core text on training courses for YOT practitioners. It maintains a standardised structure across its chapters and the 'evidence-based' arguments presented are somewhat partial (biased and selective) to support YJB prescriptions for practice. That said, such bias offers a valuable balance and counterpoint to the critical bias of much other youth justice literature. As such, this text is essential reading for the ABC learner.

A more comprehensive and critical perspective on many of the topics in the Stephenson *et al.* book is provided in the *Youth Justice Handbook: Theory, Policy and Practice* by Wayne Taylor *et al.* (2010). This edited text is an accessible review of contemporary youth justice practice in five key areas: contexts of childhood and youth; research, knowledge and evidence; policy, possibilities and penal realities; reflective practice; and widening contexts. This was to be the source book for the YJB-sponsored 'Foundation Degree in Youth Justice', but it was rejected due to its perceived overly critical nature. Again, essential reading.

For students keen to learn more about the origins of the 'new youth justice' in the context of the practical realities that faced the construction of multi-agency YOTs, I would highly recommend *Transforming Youth Justice: Occupational Identity and Cultural Change* by Anna Souhami (2007). Anna's ethnographic study traces the formation of a YOT and the lived experiences of practitioners from different agencies when attempting to make the YOT work and to reconcile their often-conflicting professional objectives. The discussion is lively, dynamic and engaging, telling an enthralling story of the messy and complex realities of practice as it tries to make sense of policy.

Last but most definitely not least, *Doing Justice to Young People: Youth Crime and Social Justice* by Roger Smith (2011) is a must-read for those of you seeking to build on your understanding of the 'new youth justice' in the broader context of the socially constructed definitions and explanations of youth offending explored throughout the current book. Roger's book is an ideal complement to mine in both content and tone. His arguments are insightful, considered, balanced and coherent, building logically as the text progresses. Furthermore, he consistently challenges the reader to evaluate the constructed realities of youth justice. Adopt your ABC mindset and engage with this book.

NOTE

1   Not to be confused with the 3 Es of effectiveness, efficiency and economy that shaped system change under the Crime and Disorder Act 1998.

Responding to youth offending

A newer 'new youth justice'

6

CHAPTER OUTLINE

Chapter 5 examined the revolution in youth justice policy and practice under the Labour Government of 1997–2010. Following the Crime and Disorder Act 1998, the historically piecemeal approach to youth justice cohered into a comprehensive Youth Justice System with the central objective of preventing offending. We explored how this prevention agenda was pursued through a 'new youth justice' that replaced traditional care–control and welfare–justice principles for responding to youth offending with strategies of responsibilisation and prevention through risk-focused early intervention(ism), which themselves promoted net-widening, adulterisation and a degree of criminalisation. The strategies of 'new youth justice' were animated by a new multi-agency structure (e.g. the Youth Offending Teams), whose practice was tightly performance managed by a new monitoring body (the Youth Justice Board) in order to ensure systemic responses that were effective, efficient and economical. The result was a hybridised, confused youth justice that incorporated elements of welfare, justice, diversion prevention, restorative justice, neo-liberal correctionalism, education and so on (see Chapter 4) within a modernised system that prioritised the *how* of youth justice (strategies, processes, practices) over the *why* of youth justice (principles, theories).

Our final chapter brings youth justice up to date by examining contemporary developments in youth justice in England and Wales since the fall of New Labour in 2010, evaluating the extent that they have reflected trends in the socio-historical (re) construction of youth offending and youth justice, compared to being more akin to extensions of the 'new youth justice' of the early twenty-first century. We have previously updated our discussion of explanations of youth offending (see Chapters 2 and 3), concluding that artefactual risk factor theories provide the hegemonic explanatory framework in the Western world. This conclusion was consolidated by an up-to-date discussion of the dominant contemporary youth justice responses to youth offending internationally (see Chapter 4), which are variously based on punitiveness, practical risk management (linked to risk factor theories) and protective child-friendly justice. In this chapter, contemporary youth justice is updated in '5 easy pieces'. We start by investigating the youth justice developments in the period of Coalition Government (2010–2015) immediately post–New Labour. During this significant period, Prime Minister David Cameron introduced the 'Big Society' idea and his Coalition Government produced the *Breaking the Cycle* Green Paper (2010) and the Legal Aid, Sentencing and Punishment of Offenders Act (2012), each heralding important progressions in youth justice policy and practice. Government policy developments regarding youth justice occurred at the same time as the release of an influential review of youth justice: the Independent Commission on Youth Crime and Antisocial Behaviour *Time for a Fresh Start* report (2010). The final notable Coalition development discussed will be the evolution of the 'AssetPlus' assessment and intervention framework, which attempted to address long-standing criticisms of the 'risk factor prevention paradigm' and its animation through Asset and the Scaled Approach. Section 2 of the chapter evaluates Coalition youth justice in terms of its statistical outcomes, the strategies that it pursued (e.g. interventionist diversion, the use of custody, local devolution) and its recommendations for abolishing the Youth Justice Board (YJB), leading into a focused evaluation on the role of the YJB in contemporary youth justice. There follows a detailed discussion of youth justice developments under the Conservative Government that came to power in 2015, in particular the commissioning of a thorough review of the Youth Justice System and the recommendations that stemmed from it

5 EASY PIECES

Responding to youth offending: a newer 'new youth justice'

1 *Developing Coalition youth justice (2010–2015)* outlines the developments in youth justice policy and practice introduced by the Coalition Government, most notably the revised out-of-court sentencing process and the AssetPlus assessment and intervention framework.
2 *Evaluating Coalition youth justice (2010–2015)* explores the impact of post-Labour youth justice policy developments and independent reviews on the shape of ('new') youth justice.
3 *Conservative Government youth justice (2015–present): ambiguity and inertia?* discusses early youth justice developments under the Conservative Government since 2015, including the YJB *Participation Strategy* and the outcomes of the recent Taylor Review of the Youth Justice System.
4 *Welsh youth justice (2000 onwards): dragonised or anglicised?* explores the special case of youth justice in Wales by examining its structural, strategic and (allegedly) practical distinctions from and similarities to youth justice in England.
5 *Children-first positive youth justice: a new frontier* broadens the scope of our investigation of contemporary youth justice by considering new frontiers in national/international responses to youth offending, specifically positive constructions of youth justice grounded in children-first, child-friendly, normalising, promotional, participatory and rights-based partnerships. The chapter ends by bringing youth justice up to date with an evaluation of the YJB Strategic Plan 2019–2022, which commits to a 'child-first' national youth justice strategy for England and Wales.

(Taylor 2016) and the continued significance of the youth custody debate. The penultimate section explores the special case of youth justice in Wales and evaluates the extent to which a distinct 'dragonised' youth justice (the dragon being the national symbol of Wales) has emerged structurally, strategically and in practice. Finally, there is an examination of new frontiers in youth justice nationally and internationally, paying special attention to conceptual, principled and practical developments in relation to the 'children-first' model of 'positive youth justice'.

1 DEVELOPING COALITION YOUTH JUSTICE (2010–2015)

The New Labour Government of the UK was replaced in 2010 by a Coalition Government (the 'Coalition') led by the majority Conservative Party (whose leader, David Cameron, became Prime Minister) and supported by the minority Liberal Party (whose leader, Nick Clegg, became Deputy Prime Minister). The Coalition inherited a nation beset by socio-economic uncertainty during a period of widespread globalised economic austerity. They also inherited a legacy of decreasing levels of youth offending and the decreasing use of formal youth justice responses to deal with this behaviour, in no small part the result of economic austerity and its associated cost-cutting pressures to keep young people out of the formal Youth Justice System (YJS). For the new Government, this was a time of high anxiety about the future of the nation – often the catalyst for making significant changes to youth and criminal justice as political and public outlets for these anxieties. However, the perennial desire for new Government to enact change (**RTA**), in this case change to youth justice, was hampered by the two key issues identified: economic austerity (lacking the money to affect change, at least in an interventionist sense) and recent trajectories of effectiveness in terms of the Key Performance Indicators for youth justice (reductions in first-time entrants, reoffending and custody). Therefore, socially (re)constructing youth justice was not a high-priority issue for the incoming Government. However, broader social change was high up on their agenda.

Prime Minister David Cameron outlined his vision of a 'Big Society' (Cabinet Office 2010) – a bigger and stronger society that would mend 'societally Broken Britain'. The causes of crime in this supposedly broken society were 'family breakdown, welfare dependency, debt, drugs, alcohol abuse, inadequate housing and failing schools' (Cameron 2008: 2, 2011: 3) and the source of these criminogenic problems was the 'choices that people make' (Cameron 2011: 4). The Big Society mantra emphasised individual action and nurturing people's sense of community, citizenship and civic duty (Evans 2011). Shades of New Labour's communitarianism strategy were readily apparent. Cameron and his Coalition argued that the State promoted 'selfishness and individualism' rather than social solidarity, so the Government would empower and enable individuals, families and communities 'to take control of their lives so we create avenues through which responsibility and opportunity can develop' (Cameron 2009: 2). In particular, there was to be a focus on 'enabling individuals to make their own moral choices and enforcing the individual responsibility of young people and their parents' (Bell 2011: 122). Shades of New Labour's responsibilisation strategy were readily apparent. The responsibilisation ethos of the Big Society movement encouraged individuals to take responsibility for their own welfare needs (Kisby 2010: 486) and placed primary responsibility for society's problems with communities (not Government), justifying the empowerment of these communities to solve social problems.

The Big Society empowerment-responsibilisation strategy translated seamlessly into the arena of crime through an enhanced emphasis on localisation (a key strategy of the 'new youth justice') and an associated withdrawal of the State – devolving power to local areas to produce local criteria to suit local circumstances and focus on local priorities (**RTA = simultaneous centralisation and decentralisation of Government control and responsibility**). For example, from 2012, each local authority area in England and Wales was to have its own directly elected Police and Crime Commissioner, an independent authority figure to ensure that police forces were more accountable to the communities they served and that they policed in as effective and efficient a manner as possible. Early political statements relating to youth offending were encouraging. Home Secretary Theresa May maintained that the Big Society would tackle 'the root causes of poverty and criminality' (May 2010: 2) and that the Government would 'move away from an approach that has unnecessarily criminalised people, particularly young people' (Home Office 2011: 10). She also called for an approach to dealing with youth offending that was 'rehabilitating and restorative rather than criminalising and coercive' (May 2010: 2), indicating a possible departure from previous (more punitive) strategies for tackling youth crime and antisocial behaviour (Hopkins-Burke 2016).

Breaking the Cycle: Effective Punishment, Rehabilitation and Sentencing of Offenders (2010)

In 2010, the Ministry of Justice published the first criminal justice **Green Paper** (a consultation document outlining proposed policy) of the new Coalition Government, titled *Breaking the Cycle: Effective Punishment, Rehabilitation and Sentencing of Offenders* (Ministry of Justice 2010). The *Breaking the Cycle* Green Paper was critical of the rigid and inflexible approach to out-of-court sentencing promoted by the 'new youth justice', which necessitated automatic escalation to more intensive disposals regardless of the nature of the offence (see also Chapter 5). *Breaking the Cycle* presented this approach as both criminalising and depriving youth justice practitioners of their ability to exercise discretion. The Government recommended more systemic discretion generally (by extension, less prescription from the centre), suggesting that 'an informal intervention could be more effective' (Ministry of Justice (MoJ) 2010: 68) than a formal disposal and that 'trust in the professionals who are working with young people on the ground' should be encouraged in order to 'determine the most appropriate response, depending on the severity of the offence and circumstances of the young offender' (Ministry of Justice (MoJ) 2010: 69). *Breaking the Cycle* outlined five key objectives for improving the YJS:

1 Prevent more young people from offending[1] and divert them from entering into a life of crime, including by simplifying out-of-court disposals;
2 Protect the public and ensure that more is done to make young offenders pay back to their victims and communities;
3 Ensure the effective use of sentencing for young offenders;
4 Incentivise local partners to reduce youth offending and re-offending using payment by results models;
5 Develop more effective governance by abolishing the Youth Justice Board[2] and its freedoms and flexibilities for local areas.

(Ministry of Justice (MoJ) 2010: 67)

Several themes/strategies emerged in *Breaking the Cycle* that reflected and built on New Labour strategy, thus representing a newer version of the 'new youth justice'. Most notably, the Green Paper reaffirmed the Government commitment to *prevention* through risk-based early intervention and to *responsibilisation* through encouraging parental responsibility (through YOT parenting work and enforcing more Parenting Orders), promoting restorative justice as an 'informal intervention' and allowing more local discretion in delivering youth justice. The prevention agenda was consolidated through funding: in 2010–2011, the YJB gave £31 million to Youth Offending Teams (YOTs) for targeted youth crime prevention work, of which £10 million was allocated to Youth Inclusion Programmes, £11 million to Youth Inclusion and Support Panels and £4 million to parenting services. However, the focus on local discretion went beyond the more prescriptive and performance managed empowerment of the 'new youth justice' era through recommendations to allow police, prosecutors and YOTs much more discretion to administer out-of-court/pre-court diversionary disposals. Further still, the Green Paper recommended localising the funding and governance of youth justice, including incentivising local authorities/YOTs to reduce demand on the YJS through a 'payment by results' model. The paper extended its localisation/decentralisation (withdrawal of the State) agenda with a recommendation to abolish the YJB, a recommendation reiterated in the Taylor Review in 2016 (see Section 3 of this chapter).

The Independent Commission on Youth Crime and Antisocial Behaviour (2010)

In the same year as *Breaking the Cycle* was released, a report was published that purported to offer the YJS 'a blueprint for reform . . . a fresh start in responding to youth crime because of intractable and deep-rooted problems that current systems can't reform' (D.J. Smith 2010: 1). The report, titled *Time for a Fresh Start*, was produced by the Independent Commission on Youth Crime and Antisocial Behaviour (hereinafter the 'Independent Commission') and was sponsored by the Nuffield Foundation. The Independent Commission was led by Anthony Salz (executive vice chairman of the Rothschild banking organisation), who was supported by John Graham (director of the Police Foundation) and David Utting (an independent analyst). The objectives of the Independent Commission were:

- To identify a set of principles for responding fairly, effectively and proportionately to antisocial behaviour and offending by children and young people and reduce the harms caused by these behaviours;
- To evaluate existing responses to antisocial behaviour and offending through evidence gathering, consultation with key stakeholders and local visits;
- To investigate and identify alternative approaches;
- To devise a blueprint for an effective, just, humane and coherent response to children and young people's antisocial behaviour and offending;
- To propose sustainable and evidence-based reform of services;
- To influence policy through a report and an academic text.

(ICYCAB 2010: 2)

The Independent Commission's report *Time for a Fresh Start* heavily criticised the YJS of England and Wales for the 'questionable nature' of its underpinning youth justice policy and its unimpressive record of 'deep-rooted failings' (ICYCAB 2010: 17). Contemporary ('new') youth justice responses were castigated for their 'lack of coherence', 'adultifying' tendencies (treating children/young people as adults), the discriminatory targeting and criminalisation of young people from deprived backgrounds, the 'inflated use of penal custody' and wasting money on 'expensive and ineffective and probably harmful' youth justice responses (ICYCAB 2010: 23). The report concluded with a series of recommendations for reform based on prioritising prevention, early intervention, restorative justice and reintegrating young offenders into mainstream society (e.g. by limiting the use of ASBOs and custodial sentences).

The extent to which these recommendations represented 'reform' in relation to existing ('new') youth justice strategies was debatable. In a thorough analysis of the report, Barry Goldson (2011) argued that it had failed to provide the promised degree of critique: existing social constructions (definitions) of 'crime' and 'antisocial behaviour' had been accepted and adopted uncritically, as had the social construction of 'young offenders' as 10 years old and above and the assumption that children and young people present harm to themselves and others, as opposed to being harmed themselves by system contact and labelling. Furthermore, the so-called reform recommendations remained wedded to risk-based targeted early intervention, reflected in the conclusion that 'an understanding of "risk" and "protective" (or "promotive") factors provides a valuable basis for planning and implementing prevention strategies' (ICYCAB 2010: 39). The report also favoured the 'new youth justice' strategy of responsibilisation, expressing faith in restorative justice (with its 'unconvincing' evidence base) over broader considerations of universal prevention and children's rights agendas (Goldson 2011). Despite incorporating the (much-neglected) views of critical academics, non-government organisations, progressive practitioners and children's rights organisations, the *Time for a Fresh Start* recommendations for reform retained faith in much 'conventional youth justice apparatus' (Goldson 2011: 7). Consequently, the Independent Commission produced a somewhat confused and disparate set of well-rehearsed criticisms (of the 'new youth justice') and recommendations (based on the same 'new youth justice'), ultimately settling on recommending a slightly modified version of the YJS. Therefore, rather than the promised 'blueprint for reform', the Independent Commission recommendations were at best illustrative of a conflict and ambivalence in how to construct youth justice and at worst simply extrapolations of existing strategies of 'new youth justice'. An edited academic text titled *A New Response to Youth Crime* (D.J. Smith 2010) was released contemporaneously to accompany the *Time for a Fresh Start* report. The book attempted to provide the 'frame-work of evidence and detailed analysis that supports the Commission's proposals' (D.J. Smith 2010: 6) through a series of invited chapters reviewing literature, evaluating research evidence and outlining current thinking in the field. The key youth justice themes addressed included patterns of youth (David Smith), causes of youth crime and antisocial behaviour (Michael Rutter), responding to youth crime and antisocial behaviour (John Graham), preventing youth crime (David Hawkins, Brandon Welsh and David Utting), family and parenting (Barbara Maughan and Francis Gardner), models of youth justice (Leslie McAra) and public opinion (Trevor Jones). Smith concluded this edited text by setting out a number of recommendations for reform that reflected the key themes of the invited contributions and the three key reform principles established in the *Time for a Fresh Start* report: prevention, restoration and integration.

Author's note: I reviewed this text for Youth Justice Journal (Case 2011: 106–108). My review was extremely critical, to the point of being scathing and overly subjective. As such, the review does not model the type of balanced, open-minded and fully informed (ABC) discussion and evaluation encouraged throughout this book. However, it is still of value, and so it is reproduced in Appendix 4 to encourage you to engage critically with the book and the *Time for a Fresh Start* report (which I call the *Report* in my review), to evaluate the subjective views of the review author (me) and to consider your own opinion on the contents of both the review and the book itself.

In the first two years of Coalition Government, the *Breaking the Cycle* Green Paper and Independent Commission recommendations for improving the YJS were packaged as 'reforms' when in essence, they were often more similar to consolidations of established strategic trajectories from the 'new youth justice' – support for responsibilisation (e.g. the low age of criminal responsibility, prioritising restorative justice), prevention through risk-focused early intervention(ism) and local discretion, albeit with a diminishing emphasis on centralised performance management. However, in 2012, there was a significant deviation from this apparent newer 'new youth justice' through the reintroduction of *diversion* (see also Chapter 4).

The Legal Aid, Sentencing and Punishment of Offenders Act 2012

In 2012, the Coalition Government released the Legal Aid, Sentencing and Punishment of Offenders Act 2012 (hereinafter the 'LASPO Act 2012'), the basis of which was a critique of the formulaic and inflexible approach to out-of-court sentencing introduced by the Crime and Disorder Act 1998. The LASPO Act 2012 represented a step change from the *Breaking the Cycle* Green Paper and the *Time for a Fresh Start* review by attacking the escalator-like, criminalising out-of-court process of Reprimand to Final Warning to court/Referral Order and replacing it with a new pre-court process underpinned by diversionary principles (similar to those of the cautioning approach adopted in the 1980s; see Chapter 4). The new pre-court disposals would be:

- *Community Resolution*: a police-administered first-stage response requiring the young person's agreement to participate, which takes victims' perspectives into account and typically adopts a restorative emphasis. The disposal has assumed various labels in different local areas, but its purpose remains the same – a first-stage, diversionary out-of-court response that is not a 'criminal' disposal, so the recipient does not receive a criminal record and is not classed as a first-time entrant (FTE) into the YJS.
- *Youth Caution*: a second-stage disposal, typically determined locally in partnership between the police and the YOT, which requires assessment and intervention by the YOT. The Youth Caution does assign an official criminal record to the young person and they are counted as an FTE due to receiving a caution (FTE status can be assigned following caution or conviction).
- *Youth Conditional Caution*: a third-stage, pre-court disposal (assigning a criminal record and FTE status) with proportionate rehabilitative, punitive and reparative conditions, seen as an alternative to prosecution. YOTs are charged with monitoring compliance, and non-compliance can result in prosecution for the original offence.

A crucial distinction between the out-of-court systems introduced by the LASPO Act 2012 and the Crime and Disorder Act 1998 was *flexibility*. The contemporary system would be more flexible and discretionary, with young people able to move up and down the scale/tariff, receive the same disposal on multiple occasions and even move back into the out-of-court process following a previous court sentence, so they were no longer fixed on a criminalising escalator into court once a first offence had been committed. Indeed, some local areas have built on the flexibility of the new system by adding further diversionary alternatives such as supplementing the 'No Further Action' response (available prior to Community Resolution) with referral to a supportive agency, or adding extra measures, such as Surrey's 'Youth Restorative Intervention' that sits between Community Resolution and Youth Caution (no criminal record, no FTE status).

A further distinction between the 1998 and 2012 revisions to the out-of-court system was that the Community Resolution first-stage response (unlike the Reprimand that it replaced) would not be classed as a caution, so would not count as criminal or towards FTE statistics. Subsequently, annual numbers of FTEs continued to decrease, potentially as an artefact/direct product of reconstructing the definition and parameters of what constituted an FTE, consolidated by the increased use of the Community Resolution measure. Consequently, the LASPO Act 2012 prioritised out-of-court diversion to progress contemporary youth justice beyond the punitive and inflexible systemic responses fostered by the 'new youth justice' and towards non-criminalising, systems management-led responses (Haines and Case 2015). Local discretion was required to determine the processes by which these diversionary disposals would be administered. Local authority areas (represented by police, courts and YOTs) were given a statutory obligation to implement the new out-of-court system, to formulate localised structures and decision-making processes to deliver this diversion, and to accompany it with early support mechanisms and services in the absence of formalised interventions (Hart 2014; Bateman 2016).

The Coalition Government soon followed up their significant revisions to the out-of-court sentencing system with a radical change to the way that young people who entered the formal YJS would be subject to assessment and intervention. Following years of intense critique of risk management (see Chapter 4) and its animation through the risk factor prevention paradigm (RFPP) and Scaled Approach as central components of the 'new youth justice' (see Chapter 5), the YJB introduced AssetPlus, a revised framework that attempted to address many common criticisms.

AssetPlus (2013)

Soon after the 2009 introduction of the Scaled Approach to assessment and intervention, John Drew became the new chief executive of the YJB, a position he held until 2013. One of his first commitments was to tackle what he perceived as an unreflective and overly protective culture that had developed within the YJB as a defence mechanism against vociferous academic and practitioner critique of policy direction, most notably critical of the Scaled Approach itself. Drew believed that the YJB had become somewhat isolationist and prescriptive in its methods, avoiding debate with (unconstructive) critical academics (and other critics), for example, in case the results undermined the strategic trajectory to which the organisation had committed (see also Chapter 5, 'Controversies and debates: My experience of the Scaled Approach').

TELLING IT LIKE IT IS

Thawing the YJB–academia cold war

When planning this book, one of my top priorities was to secure an interview with John Drew in order to obtain a priceless insight into the workings (and thinkings) of the YJB during the period of Coalition Government rule that covered John's tenure as chief executive (2009–2013). I was particularly interested in exploring his rationale for addressing the polarisation of knowledge production in youth justice that had developed due to the YJB–academia relationship becoming one of disconnect and active hostility. John was characteristically accessible, honest, gracious and incisive with his recollections. He told me:

> One of my first objectives upon taking post in 2009 was to try to establish new relationships with academics. We [YJB] were already starting to build alliances

with practitioners, but we were very resistant to working with academics. When I arrived, our Communications people gave me a blacklist of academics who were *persona non grata* and my first question was why? They were the best thinkers in youth justice and having debates was critical to developing youth justice. But critical academics were seen as dangerous wild men from the left of the political spectrum. The YJB resisted such criticism. Critical criminologists had spent a lot of time and energy chastising the YJB, in many ways completely justifiably. At the same time, others from within Government were undermining the organisation (for example, due to the issue of child deaths in custody), so we were relatively friendless in 2009 and became immensely defensive. Many very good people had developed very thin skins. A good example of this was the critique of the first decade of 'new youth justice' by Solomon and Garside in 2008 [see also Chapter 5]. They raised completely legitimate comments about how targets were constantly changing and it was a good synopsis of the situation. YJB people talked about the report in the hushed tones, responding with a combative letter and receiving an equally combative response – it was not a sensible situation to be in. So, I immediately resolved to build relationships with these critical academics. You definitely want your best brains and biggest critics to get involved in youth justice to explain their criticisms and to develop new systems.

Under John Drew's leadership, the YJB initiated a consultation exercise with key stakeholder groups in the YJS (e.g. policy-makers, practitioners, academics, children and families). The objective was to evaluate the utility and appropriateness of the Scaled Approach, particularly in the light of ongoing criticisms regarding its risk-focused, negative portrayals of young people (e.g. Case and Haines 2009), its encouragement of disproportionate, stigmatising and potentially criminalising interventionism (e.g. Bateman 2011), its neglect of the voices of children (e.g. Case 2006, 2007) and its capacity to deprofessionalise practitioners (e.g. Pitts 2001). This was to be a genuine, open-minded consultation exercise, unlike certain other examples of 'consultation' where the YJB effectively presented pre-formed policy to practitioners and required them to discuss the best ways to operationalise it in the real world. The academic group consultation in 2010 held at YJB headquarters in London brought together a highly critical collection of academics (should it be a 'critique' or 'complaint' of academics?) who had previously been blacklisted or marginalised by the YJB and prevented from entering into a constructive dialogue in relation to improving the YJS, admittedly on the basis that these critics had seldom offered constructive alternatives themselves. As John Drew recollected in his interview with me, 'I asked my staff to produce the list of academics and they were all good people, but there were so many names missing. I added a series of names and was met with concerned faces'. The academic consultation group included John Pitts, Tim Bateman, Barry Goldson, Jo Phoenix, Kevin Haines, Roger Smith and me, sharing a room with senior YJB strategic and operational managers and the creators of the Asset risk assessment instrument.

The consultation exercise with key stakeholder groups in 2010 had the overarching objective of revising and refining the Scaled Approach, not just with regards to

TELLING IT LIKE IT IS

The Scaled Approach academic consultation

My recollection of the consultation exercise was that it consisted of three hours of detailed criticism of the theoretical, methodological, ethical and practical weaknesses of the Scaled Approach, all welcomed by Chief Executive John Drew, who embraced critical and reflective dialogue. However, the response from other YJB staff and the YJB-friendly researchers in the room was a mixture of intrigue, shock and anxiety! I also recall that certain senior YJB staff expressed deeply held, sincere support for the widely published damning critique of the RFPP and much enthusiasm for identifying a replacement assessment and intervention framework. Such high levels of support appeared incongruent with long-standing and firmly held YJB resistance to critique of policy and reluctance to engage with critical academics to that point. However, a cynic (maybe a realist?) could argue that such a 180-degree shift exemplified the realities of politics – that senior policy-makers were acutely aware of the prevailing socio-economic, political and institutional climates (which included an appetite for policy and practice change) and were taking ownership of the processes of change by socially reconstructing their explanations of and responses to youth offending – a common theme across this book. This was the political expedience typified by the development of New Labour youth justice policy. The new-found openness to radical new ideas, change and system improvement among previously intransigent senior staff (whose tenure predated that of John Drew) also coincided with recent *Breaking the Cycle* recommendations for abolishing the YJB and so may have been motivated (entirely justifiably) by a degree of self-preservation and the desire to carve out a new sense of value in the eyes of Government (see also Appendix 5 interview with Anna Souhami). A lesson that I learned from this exercise was that while the political and policy stakeholders who influence the social (re)construction of youth offending explanations and youth justice responses will inevitably change over time in a 'between-individuals' way (e.g. key individuals may leave an organisation and be replaced), they may also change in a 'within-individuals' way (e.g. the expressed policy and practice views of key individuals may change dramatically). That said, politically experienced and critically reflective stakeholders are perfectly within their rights to change their views, as exemplified in academia by the great Professor Jock Young (who developed realist theory from the perceived weaknesses of his own critical criminology) and even by myself in the years following a pro-RFPP doctoral thesis!

academic critique but also in the context of contemporary developments in assessment practice, theoretical debates around 'risk' and the perceptions and experiences of both practitioners and young people who offended (YJB 2012). The outcome of the consultation with youth justice stakeholders was a revised assessment and intervention framework for young people subject to statutory court orders in the YJS, AssetPlus, which was to replace the Scaled Approach from 2013. Guidance documentation explained that the new framework would enhance the current assessment and intervention process by addressing several of the weaknesses of the Scaled Approach (YJB 2013). According to John Drew, from the YJB perspective at the time:

> I had inherited this [scaled] approach, which had gained credibility in central Government as it was seen as a much more scientific approach to youth justice – there was a huge appetite for some science. However, it was clearly problematic. It had a heavy focus on risk and looked much more at the negatives than the positives of young people's lives. It also encouraged a tick box approach to what is much more than that and ignored the importance of relationships. I had it, I couldn't cancel it, but it was clearly something we needed to roll-back from, so we adopted a 'softly softly' approach with YOTs to coming away from the Scaled Approach, primarily by deciding to reform Asset to create AssetPlus.
>
> (John Drew 2017, personal interview)

AssetPlus was presented as a more holistic, contextualised and dynamic method of assessment and planning interventions when compared to the Scaled Approach. It promised more emphasis on accessing young people's *voices* (not neglecting their input and allowing adults to dominate the assessment process), identifying their *strengths* (not prioritising negative characteristics such as risk factors), assessing *interactions* between different elements of young people's lives (not focusing on the deterministic influence of individual risk factors) and *promoting positive behaviours and outcomes* (not prioritising the prevention of negative behaviours and outcomes). The intention was to enable a greater *focus on needs over risks*, more scope for *practitioner discretion/expertise* and improved *self-assessment* for young people and parents/carers (YJB 2013). The proposed enhancements to the assessment and intervention process reflected a culture shift and paradigm shift[3] away from the negative, deficit-based and backward-facing RFPP and towards more holistic, prospective, appreciative and optimistic understandings of young people's lives that incorporated their potential for desistance, positive behaviour and making meaningful contributions to the assessment process by helping to construct understandings of their offending behaviour (Haines and Case 2015).

The AssetPlus framework provided to YOT staff currently comprises an ongoing assessment–intervention cycle across the YJS, which is animated by practitioners completing a tripartite 'Core Record' for each young person they work with: Information Gathering and Description, Explanations and Conclusions, Pathways and Planning (see Figure 6.1).

The 'Information Gathering and Description' section contains four quadrants:

1   *Personal, family and social factors*: assesses the young person's current life situation in relation to family and environmental factors (e.g. family history/functioning, wider family networks, living arrangements, housing, social and community/ neighbourhood factors, significant life events); parenting, care and supervision (e.g. their experiences as parents and carers); and the young person's (child) development (e.g. mental, emotional and physical health, speech, language and communication needs, lifestyle and behavioural development, substance use and peer associations, relationships and identity, education, training and employment). This section is intended to identify needs, problems and (desistance-promoting) strengths that can help practitioners (and the young person presumably) better understand and explain youth offending without blurring the boundaries between need and the risk of reoffending.

FIGURE 6.1 ASSETPLUS ASSESSMENT AND INTERVENTION FRAMEWORK (YJB 2013)

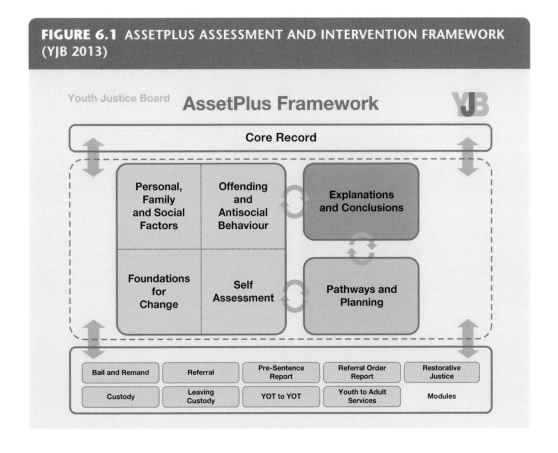

2   *Offending/antisocial behaviour*: describes characteristics and patterns of problematic behaviour, including details of current and previous offending, patterns of offending over time, attitudes to offending, 'other behaviour' indicative of future offending and a calculation of the likelihood of reoffending.

3   *Foundations for change*: explores aspects of the young person's life that promote or prevent behavioural change, such as resilience (e.g. when presented with opportunities to offend), goals, attitudes, engagement and participation. This section is intended to encourage practitioners to explore positive factors and the young person's willingness to change as a way of informing intervention plans that are underpinned by the promotion of strengths and positive pathways out of offending.

4   *Self-assessment*: completed by both the young person and their parents/carers in order to facilitate engagement and participation in the assessment and intervention planning process and to encourage critical reflection on behaviour, on future aspirations and on what is needed to promote desistance and positive outcomes (YJB 2013). The self-assessment section focuses on influential factors in the young person's life in the domains of family, home and relationships, smoking, drinking and drugs, health and how I feel, friends, school, college and work, offending, my future and working with the YOT. The young person rates their strength of agreement (yes, no, sometimes) with a series of statements in each section that are worded to indicate either the presence of risk (e.g. 'There are problems or arguments at home') or protection/resilience ('I know that my family care about me'). Certain sections include an extra open-ended question at the end (e.g. 'Who are

the most important people in your life?' 'What do your friends think of you?'), with restricted space for an extended answer.

(Adapted from Haines and Case 2015: 151–152)

The assessment ratings/measures used in the 'Information Gathering and Description' subsections of AssetPlus are not quantified, unlike in similar sections of the Asset risk assessment instrument, signifying a move away from previous methods of reductionism, most notably the oversimplistic quantification/factorisation of potentially complex life experiences (see Chapter 3; see also Haines and Case 2012). The culture shift away from the factorisation of a restricted group of risk factors as the means of explaining and responding to youth offending is extended in AssetPlus by expectations that practitioners conduct more holistic explorations/assessments of a broader range of behaviours, investigate foundations for change and place an increased emphasis on meaningful self-assessment by the young person. These changes reflect a progressive rationale – a departure from potentially less valid, adult-centric assessments and the consequent neglect of young people's voices/perspectives towards a greater emphasis on situating young people's views, experiences and aspirations at the centre of youth justice planning and intervention processes (Haines and Case 2015).

The second section of AssetPlus, 'Explanations and Conclusions', requires practitioners to utilise the information gathered in the previous section to explain the young person's offending behaviour in a supposedly more holistic and valid way than afforded by the Scaled Approach, because the information itself is intended to be more comprehensive and meaningful. YOT staff are encouraged to consider contextual information and time-sensitive interactions between influences in the young person's past and present life (not the stand-alone and one-off effects of separate risk factors), life events (not deterministic, individualised risk factors) and positive factors (YJB 2013). Following a full consideration of the influence of the information gathered in the previous section, practitioners provide a summary prediction of the young person's 'indicative' and 'final' likelihood of reoffending using a 3-point scale reminiscent of the Scaled Approach risk judgement: low, medium and high (YJB 2013).

The summative 'Pathways and Planning' section is intended to build on the 'Explanations and Conclusions' information to assist practitioners in designing appropriate interventions linked to assessment information (the intended basis of the Scaled Approach) that are not just preventative or offence focused but are also desistance focused, capacity building, needs led and promotional. Unlike its predecessor, AssetPlus emphasises engagement, participation and the promotion of positive behaviours in interventions that are appropriate to the young person's circumstances, experiences and perceptions (YJB 2013). As such, the 'Pathways and Planning' portion introduces a progression from traditional offence- and offender-focused youth justice intervention and towards a more young person/children first mindset for responding to youth offending.

Antisocial behaviour management

In the final full year of Coalition Government, the Anti-Social Behaviour, Crime and Policing Act 2014 finally abolished the infamous Antisocial Behaviour Order (ASBO), in line with successive United Nations Committee recommendations (see Chapter 5), replacing it with the new Crime Prevention Injunction (CPI). The Criminal Behaviour

Order (CBO) replaced the CRASBO (ASBO given on conviction of a criminal offence). The CPI was to be a civil order requested by local authorities against young people aged 10 and above in order to address low-level misbehaviour that fell short of offending. Breach of the CPI would need to be established on the criminal standard of proof but would not constitute a criminal offence or result in a criminal record (whereas breach of the CBO would be criminal), unlike the notoriously criminalising ASBO (see Hopkins-Burke 2016). The CPI differed from the ASBO in its inclusion of positive requirements for the young person to address the root cause of their offending (e.g. the requirement to attend appointments to address substance use issues), rather than privileging negative restrictions and prohibitions. However, at this early stage of implementation, the CPI appears to be very much a rebranded ASBO. It replicates many of the original mechanisms associated with the ASBO, most notably in its compulsory nature, which exacerbates the potential for breach (although breach is not a criminal offence; it constitutes contempt of court) and further criminalisation of the young person (Bateman 2016).

In summary, the major youth justice developments of the 2010–2015 period of Coalition Government were the empowering-responsibilising 'Big Society' agenda, the ostensibly diversionary emphases of the *Breaking the Cycle* Green Paper of 2010 (which also supported an enhanced focus on local devolution and discretion) and the LASPO Act of 2012 (both supported by the Independent Commission's *Time for a Fresh Start* review in 2010), the introduction of the revised AssetPlus assessment and intervention framework in 2013 (YJB 2013, 2014) and the abolition and replacement of ASBOs in 2014. Perhaps the most notable among these developments were the significant revisions to the out-of-court sentencing process introduced by the LASPO Act 2012 and the replacement of the risk-based Scaled Approach signified by AssetPlus. The extent to which these and other youth justice strategies of the Coalition Government constituted developments in youth justice as opposed to extensions of the existing 'new youth justice' will be evaluated in the following section.

5 EASY PIECES

1 Developing Coalition youth justice (2010–2015)

1   *Big Society*: Prime Minister David Cameron committed to fixing 'Broken Britain' through the Big Society ethos of empowering individuals, families and communities to mobilise and to take control of their lives, which linked closely to the communitarian and responsibilisation strategies of the 'new youth justice' when applied to the prevention of crime.
2   Breaking the Cycle: this Green Paper recommended a simplified out-of-court process, more public protection from young offenders, more effective sentencing and the increasing localisation of youth justice governance and funding. The aims were to be achieved through consolidated versions of 'new youth justice' strategies of prevention, risk-based early intervention, restorative justice and the responsibilisation of young people, parents and communities.

3   Time for a Fresh Start: the Independent Commission's 'blueprint for reform' crit-
    icised the incoherent, adulterising, criminalising and punitive strategies of the
    'new youth justice', essentially portraying the YJS as ineffective, inefficient and
    uneconomical. However, the proposed reform principles of prevention, risk-
    based intervention and restorative justice were arguably rehearsals of 'new youth
    justice' strategies.

4   *The LASPO Act 2012*: building on *Breaking the Cycle*, the LASPO Act introduced a
    new simplified, flexible and diversionary out-of-court process consisting of Com-
    munity Resolution–Youth Caution–Youth Conditional Caution to replace the
    escalatory, interventionist and potentially criminalising Reprimand–Final Warn-
    ing–court process under the 'new youth justice'. There was a lack of central
    guidance and an increased degree of local devolution/discretion in terms of how
    this new process would be implemented.

5   *AssetPlus*: the Coalition Government introduced the AssetPlus assessment and
    intervention framework, which addressed common criticisms of the Scaled
    Approach/RFPP through provisions for more input from young people, more
    practitioner discretion, a focus on strengths and foundations for change and
    more consideration of qualitative, contextualised interactions between different
    factors and life experiences.

2 EVALUATING COALITION YOUTH JUSTICE (2010–2015)

Youth justice under the Coalition Government has been presented as a success story, particularly in statistical terms. Under Coalition governance, there was a continuation (even acceleration in some areas) of previous downward trends in annual numbers of young offenders, arrests, official disposals and the three main KPIs of FTEs, reoffending (numbers, not rates) and custody. An examination of youth offending statistics and youth justice outcomes from March 2006 to March 2016 (Ministry of Justice (MoJ) and Youth Justice Board (YJB) 2017) identified clear statistical successes in relation to:

- *Young offenders*: the number of young people cautioned or convicted fell by 79 per cent between 2006 (218,100 proven offences) and 2016 (45,200 proven offences).
- *Arrests*: there was a 75 per cent decrease in the number of young people arrested for an offence between 2006 and 2016 and annual decreases year on year since arrest levels peaked in March 2007.
- *FTEs*: 83 per cent fewer young people entered the YJS for the first time in 2016 compared to 2006.
- *Disposals (cautions and convictions)*: compared to 2011, the number of young people subject to a disposal fell by 61 per cent.
- *Reoffending*: although the *number* of young people reoffending continued to fall year on year over the measurement period, the reoffending *rate* in 2015 (percentage reoffending amongst a selected cohort) rose by 4.3 per cent compared to 2006.
- *Custody*: there were 66 per cent fewer young people in the average custodial population 2016 (960 young people) compared to the population in 2006.

The Coalition Government have taken credit for the continuation of downward trajectories in youth justice outcomes, attributing these outcomes to their consolidation of existing good practice and implementation of new approaches to youth justice (Ministry of Justice (MoJ) and Youth Justice Board (YJB) 2017). For example, the revised out-of-court process, particularly the introduction of Community Resolutions, consolidated the downward trends in FTEs by offering a new, diversionary and non-criminalising measure that would not count towards FTE outcomes. Reflective of New Labour, the Coalition's claims to success have been politically motivated and partial (biased and limited), neglecting a full consideration of other potential influences such as *practitioner discretion* and *local innovation* outside/under the radar of centralised guidance and monitoring, *institutional culture shifts* in constructing youth offending/justice (e.g. more effective and child-friendly systems management), the possibility that youth offending levels were falling independently for *social, economic and cultural reasons* (e.g. less substance use, more time spent engaging with mobile technologies; Bateman 2017), and the influence of *economic austerity* on all of the above. In other words, whilst the statistical decreases in youth justice outcomes are 'fact', there is debate as to whether they are indicative of the success of a 'Coalition youth justice' (and if so, to what extent?), the continued success of the 'new youth justice' or the 'artefact' (social construction) of systemic and external influences unconnected to Government youth justice strategy. To their credit, the YJB has acknowledged the complexity involved in explaining youth justice outcomes.

CONVERSATIONS

Evaluating YJB successes

Steve: What was the major success story of the post-2009 YJB?

John Drew: When I became chief executive of the YJB, I had a central objective to reduce the numbers of children in custody. We [YJB] were going to talk about this issue wherever we could to whoever we could and we immediately put it at the forefront of our thinking. Reducing custody is one of the things the YJB was created to do and this is why we took responsibility for the Secure Estate in 2000. It meant building and rebuilding a series of alliances and new relationships with the police, magistrates, YOTs and the children's voluntary sector – organisations that were very critical of us in the past.

To my mind, the crowning achievement of the YJB since 2000 has been the reductions in custody. This is not an achievement of the YJB alone, but one that the YJB played a part in. The numbers were falling before the abolition of the Offences Brought to Justice target and the YJB contributed to this outcome. We built constructive alliances with YOTs and their managers reported that the pressure we inserted through best practice guidance and performance management, notably the KPI to reduce custody, had the biggest impact on their custody rates and encouraged them to use custody as a last resort. One of the tricks that we used, for example, was to create the impression of a link between the level of YOT Practice Grant we would award and the custody rates of individual YOTs. Of course, this was an illusion and we never intended to follow through on it, but it encouraged YOTs to target reductions in this area.

Steve: What were the major challenges to the YJB achieving their goals?

John: During my time in post and before that, we faced numerous challenges to our objectives to do good work for young people, for example, from Government and from academics. We exist in a complex dance with Government, and certain parties always wanted to run youth justice from the centre. The main challenge was to convince politicians that the YJB and local areas know what they're doing and can achieve what is needed, such as reductions in KPIs under New Labour and reduced expenditure under the Coalition Government. However, the civil service hates non-departmental public bodies (quangos) like the YJB because they have the freedom to say and do things that civil servants don't (possibly off message), so resentment comes to the surface. Anna Souhami's research shows this mentality clearly (Souhami 2007, 2011; see Appendix 5). Envy, distrust and suspicion from civil servants have always been a problem for the head of the YJB. The YJB has a confrontational nature if it's doing its job properly and so has inevitably roughed up a few people; people who have long memories. This created a climate where the YJB was not the easiest body to defend, so we had to build political and practical alliances that enabled us to survive.

Then we have critical criminologists. You guys were very slow to acknowledge falling custody numbers and over-grudging to attribute responsibility for it to the YJB, most likely because you had got yourselves into a mindset making it impossible to accept that New Labour machinery could deliver that kind of change. But let's also be honest, part of the change had been to recover from the mess created in the first place. And of course, critical academics and theorists feed on controversial arguments – that's how ideas get formed. So, another challenge during my time at the YJB was to build critical friendships with academics and to encourage more modest thinking by the YJB. In the 1970s, one of the most attractive aspects of working in youth justice was the partnership between academics and practice, which drove scholarship and drove practice. However, New Labour created a managerial infrastructure that sat on top of what otherwise could have been a partnership between practitioners and academics. Practitioners had to wear two hats and didn't know who to work with or learn from.

Author note: I also conducted a detailed 'Conversation' with Dr Anna Souhami regarding her ethnographic research into the challenges faced by the YJB when attempting to influence and implement youth justice policy. Due to the interview's length, it is presented in Appendix 5. It is highly recommended as it animates, reinforces and elaborates the arguments in this chapter (including those in the 'Conversation' with John Drew), with Anna offering an invaluable insight into her groundbreaking research study of the daily life of the YJB. Her findings and views of the research experience are essential reading.

     With the identified successes and challenges in mind, we can now consider in more detail the extent to which Coalition youth justice represented a distinct approach consolidated by practitioner discretion/innovation and institutional culture shifts or a rebranding and extension of 'new youth justice' strategies that may have then motivated practitioner discretion/innovation and institutional culture shifts as a direct challenge to it.

Big Society responsibilisation

As discussed in the previous section, soon after taking power, Prime Minister David Cameron introduced his notion of a 'Big Society' as a 'set of principles underpinning the Government's policy agenda' (House of Commons 2012: 4). The concept of Big Society was employed to cohere and direct new Coalition strategy, but for critics this offered nothing original. Some argued that the concept was merely a rehash and rebranding of New Labour's preoccupation with 'active citizenship' (Davies and Pill 2012); others went further by viewing it as an extension of the responsibilisation strategy that began under the Conservatives and that peaked under the 'new youth justice' of Blair, Straw and others (Bone 2012). The damning conclusion of critics, therefore, was that the so-called empowering Big Society agenda when applied to youth justice actually encouraged a blaming/responsibilising culture that did not adequately account for young people's circumstances or life experiences, unfairly constructed children as fully autonomous individuals and promoted ineffective, punitive sanctions (Smith 2014).

Coalition prevention: 'new youth justice' again?

The Coalition Government priority for youth justice was targeted prevention animated by risk-focused early intervention (consolidating the strategic driver of the 'new youth justice') over universal prevention and diversion (but see next section) as the most practically and financially 'effective' response to offending behaviour by young people. In 2011, UK Coalition Government Under-Secretary of State for Prisons and Youth Justice Crispin Blunt argued that most existing prevention programmes in England and Wales target children on the cusp of offending, justifying the need for more investment in early intervention (CYP Now 2011). In October 2012, Prime Minister David Cameron asserted that 'prevention is the cheapest and most effective way to deal with crime. Everything else is simply picking up the pieces of failure that has gone before' (Cameron 2011, speech to the Centre for Social Justice). However, as stated, the strategy of prevention has been pursued in a restricted manner through offender/offence-first, risk-focused early intervention (often with identified offenders, so more akin to crime reduction than prevention) and responsibilisation – all constructions of prevention that were elaborated from the 'new youth justice' inherited by the Coalition. With this argument in mind, it is informative to take a closer look at some of the key policy/strategy developments from 2010 to 2015 from a prevention perspective:

- *Breaking the Cycle: Effective Punishment, Rehabilitation and Sentencing of Offenders (2010)*: this Green Paper advocated for more emphasis on prevention work in the YJS, yet it was to be prevention through 'intervening early in the lives of children at risk. . . [is] our best chance to break the cycle of crime' (Ministry of Justice (MoJ) 2010: 68). *Breaking the Cycle* therefore consolidated the risk-based, targeted early intervention approach to prevention adopted by the 'new youth justice'. Its sister publication, *Prevention Matters*, followed suit by characterising the main KPI objectives (i.e. annual reductions in FTEs, reoffending rates and custody levels) as prevention goals rather than indicators of diversion. By conflating multiple objectives and outcomes (prevention, reduction, diversion), both *Breaking the Cycle* and *Prevention Matters* evidenced conflict and ambivalence (**RTA**) regarding the Coalition view of prevention; a loose, catch-all construction for a range of youth justice objectives and practices. Furthermore, *Breaking the Cycle* consolidated the responsibilising-supportive agenda (**RTA = simultaneous support control**) introduced by the Youth Crime Action Plan 2008 by promoting restorative justice as an 'informal intervention' to enable children to 'face up to the consequence of their crime, provide reparation and prevent further offending' and 'responsibilising parents who refuse to face up to their responsibilities' (Ministry of Justice (MoJ) 2010: 68) by enforcing more Parenting Orders alongside providing more parenting skills support.

- *Independent Commission on Youth Crime and Antisocial Behaviour (2010)*: the 'blueprint for reform' of the YJS provided by the *Time for a Fresh Start* report (ICYCAB 2010) heavily criticised the 'new youth justice' of the previous Labour Government for its 'adultifying' tendencies and for continuing to target and criminalise children in the name of supportive intervention (Haines and Case 2015). The report recommended more effective prevention as a central reform principle for the YJS. However, the Independent Commission view of prevention remained wedded to 'new youth justice' strategies of risk-based targeted early intervention and responsibilisation over broader considerations of universal prevention, diversion or children's rights agendas (Haines and Case 2011). Indeed, a key conclusion of the report was that 'an understanding of "risk" and "protective" (or "promotive") factors provides a valuable basis for planning and implementing prevention strategies' (ICYCAB 2010: 39).
- *Early Intervention Grant (2011)*: the Coalition Government's commitment to early intervention as prevention was formalised in 2010 by the establishment of the Independent Commission on Early Intervention. This new Government Independent Commission (not to be confused with the ICYCAB) was established to identify best practice models of early intervention which 'ensure that children at greatest risk of multiple disadvantage get the best start in life . . . to help fulfil their potential and break the cycle of underachievement' (Department for Education website, August 2010). The Independent Commission's recommendations for effective early intervention practice were supported by the Department for Education's Early Intervention Grant, a new funding stream (in England only; education remained a devolved policy area in Wales) to subsidise local authority provision of early intervention and preventative services and to replace funding streams for existing early intervention initiatives (e.g. Sure Start Children's Centres, Youth Opportunities Fund, Children's Fund, Positive Activities for Children). The Government allocated £2,222 million to the Early Intervention Grant initiative in 2011–2012, rising to £2,307 million in 2012–2013, but spending on the initiative decreased to £1,709 million in 2013–2014 and £1,600 million in 2014–2015, largely due to service funding cuts during the period of economic austerity. It was possible to use the Early Intervention Grant to fund universal programmes for children/young people and families. However, it has been used predominantly to fund targeted services for young people and families in need of

intensive support (e.g. Sure Start, targeted support for young people with multiple problems, targeted mental health provision in schools) – programmes that the National Audit Office (2008, in Haines and Case 2015) reported had suffered from implementation difficulties and a lack of evidence as to their effectiveness.

- *Legal Aid, Sentencing and Punishment of Offenders Act (2012)*: the LASPO Act 2012 (HM Government 2012) provided clear indications of the Coalition Government's intentions to improve the YJS, most specifically through an out-of-court disposal process created to replace the previous punitive and inflexible systemic response and usher in non-criminalising, systems management-led, diversionary responses (see next section). Although explicit reference to prevention was limited in the LASPO Act 2012, the reorientation of pre-court processes suggests a tentative progression from risk-led targeted early intervention (at least for first-time offenders) and towards the prevention of entry into the formal YJS (Haines and Case 2015). As such, the LASPO Act 2012 began a process of reconstructing diversionary practice to serve preventative goals – moving beyond diversion from contact with the YJS (grounded in minimal intervention – see Chapter 4) towards diversion (prevention) from offending through (risk-focused) intervention.

Coalition Government youth justice was underpinned by a commitment to the prevention agenda introduced by the 'new youth justice', characterised by a targeted, risk-focused, early intervention approach with identified offenders and 'pre-offenders' (Case and Haines 2015b) as opposed to universal, needs-led prevention and diversion work. The Coalition approached prevention in the neo-correctionalist way of the 'new youth justice', identifying and targeting 'risk factors' as individual deficits to correct in the young person, rather than as the products of relative immaturity, socio-structural disadvantage and criminogenic interactions with the YJS. The Coalition prevention agenda mirrored the neo-liberal responsibilisation strategy of the 'new youth justice', holding young people and their families responsible for failing to resist the criminogenic influence of risk factors and for engaging effectively with State-sponsored interventions to address these risk factors. Similarly, the Government's abolition of ASBOs simply made space for the Crime Prevention Injunction (a measure to prevent nuisance and annoyance) that was largely equivalent to its predecessor in the sense of being intrusive, prohibitive, punitive, criminalising and interventionist (Bateman 2016). The major piece of criminal justice legislation from the Coalition, the LASPO Act 2012 offered nothing explicit about the Government's approach to prevention, yet it introduced a new diversionary out-of-court process that said much (implicitly) about the Government's commitment to prevention as the guide to youth justice practice. It is to this supposedly diversionary development that we now turn.

Interventionist diversion

The Coalition Government ushered in a 'new era of diversion' (Creaney and Smith 2014: 83) for contemporary youth justice during their time in office (2010–2015), illustrated by a new, more flexible, non-escalating and non-criminalising out-of-court process. The new era was introduced by the *Breaking the Cycle* Green Paper (Ministry of Justice (MoJ) 2010), which shifted youth justice policy direction for youth justice towards a more nuanced approach where individual circumstances could be taken into account (NAYJ 2012), notably through the diversionary potential of a revised out-of-court system, to counter the criminalising nature of the current system where

> young offenders are automatically escalated to a more intensive disposal, regardless of the circumstances or severity of their offence.
>
> (Ministry of Justice (MoJ) 2010: 68)

Coalition diversion was, however, something of a curate's egg. On the one hand, it set out to replace the New Labour emphasis on diversion from crime (i.e. prevention) with a new approach to diversion from prosecution, linked to ideas that formal system contact could be labelling and criminogenic (see Chapter 4 discussion of diversion). On the other hand, the new diversionary focus of the pre-court system retained the interventionism of the 'new youth justice' to the extent that it has been dubbed 'interventionist diversion' (Kelly and Armitage 2015). For example, *Breaking the Cycle* outlined the Coalition's intention to simplify the existing out-of-court disposal framework by making it more flexible (e.g. curtailing the automatic, escalatory 'uptariffing' element) and offering more discretion to key stakeholder staff in the YJS (e.g. police, YOT workers, prosecutors) in relation to appropriate sentencing and intervention planning. Simultaneously, however, the Government prioritised the use of diversionary initiatives that had been piloted nationally under New Labour, including the Youth Restorative Disposal (the forerunner of the Community Resolution), the Youth Conditional Caution (part of the new out-of-court process), the Youth Justice Liaison and Diversion Scheme (Haines *et al.* 2012) and the Triage model (Home Office 2012). The prioritisation of diversionary initiatives represented a continued desire to retain an element of centralised control over local practice, couched as the empowerment of local areas (**RTA = simultaneous centralised prescription and decentralisation/local empowerment**). There were also clear variations in the nature and focus of these different diversionary schemes (**RTA = conflict and ambivalence**), with some programmes appearing more focused on increased efficiency in processing young people and utilising practitioner resources (e.g. Triage cf. Haines *et al.* 2013), some adopting a more interventionist reparative/restorative approach (e.g. Youth Restorative Disposal) and other programmes being more committed to addressing young people's support/welfare needs and children's rights (e.g. the Swansea Bureau – Haines *et al.* 2013). The outcome was further conflict and ambivalence around how out-of-court diversionary interventions should be implemented, what their focus should be and what structures, systems and processes young people should be diverted *away from* and diverted *into* (cf. Richards 2014).

There remains conflict and ambivalence over how local authorities should implement both out-of-court processes and AssetPlus. The **decentralisation** (removing power from the centre/government and transferring it to local authority areas) of responsibility for diversion, along with assessment and intervention, was couched as empowerment and local devolution, but it is possible to view this move as a withdrawal of the State. Decentralisation has introduced the potential for further practical ambiguity, ambivalence and confusion concerning how existing local arrangements will fit into the new out-of-court disposal system (Haines and Case 2015). Ongoing issues include how outside agencies will support police decision-making (the typical process within Triage), the appropriate relationship between police and YOT staff in planning and delivering diversionary interventions and the potential role for children and parents/carers in shaping diversionary processes (Haines *et al*. 2013). The overarching conflict and ambivalence at the strategic level relates to the nature of diversion – whether the appropriate focus for practice should be diversion from prosecution (e.g. avoiding system contact) or diversion from crime (i.e. prevention).

On the surface, the re-emergence of diversion as a central animator of youth justice practice in England and Wales appears to reflect its significance in international children's rights conventions (see Chapter 4). For example, the United Nations Guidelines for the Prevention of Juvenile Delinquency (the Riyadh Guidelines) assert that youth justice agencies should 'use, to the maximum extent possible, programs and referral possibilities for the division of young people from the justice system' (UN 1990a: para. 58), while the United Nations Standard Minimum Rules for the Administration of Juvenile Justice (the Beijing Rules) recommend 'dealing with juvenile offenders without formal trial . . . [and] without recourse to formal hearings' (UN 1985: para. 11.1–11.2). These children's rights conventions emphasise the iatrogenic nature of formal system contact as the key rationale for youth justice diversion (see Jordan and Farrell 2013; Wallace and Jacobsen 2012). The new pre-court system in England and Wales has employed diversion in order to avoid the criminalisation of young people through system contact (diversion from prosecution). However, an interventionist form of diversion has been preferred to a more hands-off, radical non-/minimum necessary intervention approach to diversion on the basis that limiting (supportive) intervention could actually increase offending and system contact in the future if young people were left to fend for themselves (cf. Weatherburn *et al*. 2012; Richards 2014). Such interventionism raises a dilemma, however, particular in terms of how to offer support via diversionary intervention without a young person acquiring a criminal label through its associated risk-based assessment and informal contact with youth justice agencies. Arguably, the revised out-of-court system in England and Wales has yet to address how to improve young people's lives using intervention and restorative approaches that could unintentionally compound their negative identity as a 'young offender' (NAYJ 2012).

Other diversionary rationales were evident during the Coalition's time in Government, such as welfare-based approaches to meeting young people's needs within and outside the YJS, indicating a multifaceted diversion strategy with multiple objectives. Indeed, diversionary practice in the YJS (indeed, across international youth justice systems) continues to experience an identity crisis in terms of precisely what young people should be diverted *from* (e.g. crime, prosecution, system contact) and diverted *into* (e.g. youth justice services, external support services, community reintegration processes), although the hegemonic objective in contemporary youth justice appears to be diversion (from crime) as a preventative tool (cf. Jordan and Farrell 2013). The LASPO Act 2012 provided the space for 'dialogue around costly, net widening, criminalising, counterproductive and damaging institutional practices' (Yates 2012: 5). However, the official guidance (such as it was) given to YOTs regarding the implementation of the new out-of-court system recommended that they prioritise existing diversionary programmes (MoJ and YJB 2013) and that assessments of young people in the out-of-court system should prioritise prevention, operationalised as preventing/reducing the risk of reoffending, self-harm and harm to the general public. The Coalition Government was so committed to the prevention (diversion from crime) agenda that the statutory self-assessment element of AssetPlus administered to young people in the court system was modified into a prevention tool for pre-court use (YJB 2014) simply by removing the term 'offending' from within it, indicating that Government/ YJB thinking around diversion had actually hardly moved from the interventionist prevention focus of the 'new youth justice'.

AssetPlus = Asset Lite?

The AssetPlus assessment and intervention framework could constitute a major shift in focus for contemporary youth justice. AssetPlus moves beyond the quantitative measurement of (psychosocial) risk factors as part of a preventative, risk-focused early intervention process (i.e. the Scaled Approach), towards a more clearly defined focus on needs in personal, family and social domains, strengths that promote desistance and change, and positive outcomes such as well-being, safety, engagement and participation. However, the ostensible explanatory reliance on assessing risk and protective factors (in the self-assessment section) and the risk/ likelihood of reoffending as a means of informing a one-size-fits-all scaled intervention appears contradictory to this paradigm shift and very much in line with the Scaled Approach. It can be argued, therefore, that these changes to the assessment and intervention framework have not yet gone far enough in reorientating contemporary youth justice towards positive, child-friendly and engaging processes and goals (Haines and Case 2015). The components of AssetPlus have been largely focused on amending and augmenting current assessment procedures (e.g. even the revised title remains wedded to Asset) and reframing assessment and intervention through an incorporation of more potential influences on children's behaviour and a greater scope for adult practitioners to identify and interpret these influences. While AssetPlus could offer a promising improvement on the inherent weaknesses and deleterious elements of the Scaled Approach (see Chapter 5), it does not (yet) offer a comprehensive overhaul of youth justice principles, policies and practices for the benefit of those young people who become embroiled in the YJS. For example, there remains only limited scope for the equitable participation of young people beyond vague proposals for 'improved self-assessment', with no accompanying explanation of its potential role or influence in the new assessment process. Indeed, the early practice materials (cf. YJB 2013) circulated around self-assessment were disappointing – indicative of a residual risk and resilience (resistance to risk) focus as opposed to any emphasis on strengths and future-orientation on promoting positive behaviours and outcomes.[4]

The potential success of AssetPlus could be hampered by the problems and limitations outlined. Like the Asset tool and APIS KEEP that preceded it (see Chapter 5), AssetPlus can be viewed as a youth justice technique without an overarching purpose or philosophy (see Haines and Drakeford 1998 for a broader discussion). Furthermore, the potential overemphasis of the information from the Personal, Family and Social Factors quadrant and the restricted, risk-focused summative judgement hints at a return to the reductionism and partiality of the Scaled Approach when explaining and responding to youth offending. There is a danger that practitioners will be encouraged to privilege psychological and immediate social (family, education, neighbourhood) influences, the foundations of artefactual risk factor theories (see Chapter 3) as explanatory influences on youth offending, to the neglect of socio-structural, socio-economic, political and systemic influences, leading to a reductionist, psychosocial bias. There is further potential for factorisation by stealth in the final tripartite judgement of 'likelihood of reoffending' (a risk prediction by any other name), which promotes the reduction of complex experiences and the holistic information gathered into a quantified, scaled category (Haines and Case 2015). In terms of the social construction of youth offending explanations and youth justice responses, therefore, AssetPlus runs the risk (pardon the pun) of starting off strong by gathering a wide range of information about young people's life experiences, but then fizzling out by using this information in a restricted way to inform limited and oversimplified (less valid, invalid) explanations of youth offending as a means of planning simple and practical responses.

5 EASY PIECES

2 Evaluating Coalition youth justice (2010–2015)

1   *Positive outcomes*: the period of Coalition Government consolidated and improved existing downward trajectories in KPIs for the YJS, evidencing annual decreases in the numbers of young people who offended, were arrested, entered the YJS for the first time, received disposals (cautions and convictions), reoffended (although reoffending rates remained stable) and were sent to custody.

2   *Big Society responsibilisation*: critics have portrayed the Big Society agenda as an extension of a governmental strategies of responsibilisation and communitarianism (couched as the empowerment of individuals and local areas) that built on the 'new youth justice' inherited from New Labour. This, it was argued, enabled the new Government to blame and punish young people who offended (along with their families and communities), under the guise of individual and community empowerment.

3   *Coalition prevention*: Coalition youth justice policy (e.g. *Breaking the Cycle, Prevention Matters*, LASPO) and funding (e.g. Early Intervention Grant) prioritised targeted prevention through risk-focused early intervention in a manner that built on the prevention strategy of the 'new youth justice'.

4   *Interventionist diversion*: a 'new era of diversion' was introduced by the Coalition Government and characterised by a more flexible, non-criminalising out-of-court sentencing system. Critics have argued that the new approach to diversion was excessively interventionist and more akin to New Labour's 'diversion from crime' (i.e. prevention) than 'diversion from system contact', so the approach retained the potential to label and criminalise young people.

5   *AssetPlus*: the revised assessment and intervention framework addressed several of the identified weaknesses of Asset and the Scaled Approach, particularly around reductionism, deficit-focus and the neglect of both young people's voices and practitioner discretion. However, AssetPlus currently remains wedded to the Scaled Approach weaknesses (to a degree) through its insistence on predicting the likelihood (risk) of reoffending based on psychosocial (risk) factors.

3 CONSERVATIVE GOVERNMENT YOUTH JUSTICE (2015–): AMBIGUITY AND INERTIA?

Following the General Election in May 2015, a Conservative Government was formed in the UK under Prime Minister David Cameron, taking over from the previous Conservative–Liberal Coalition. Just like the Coalition before it, the Conservatives assumed control of the UK at a time of heightened economic austerity and socio-political uncertainty. In the first two years of Conservative Government, levels of economic, social and political uncertainty increased and there were only limited developments in the youth justice context, including further withdrawal of the State from youth justice affairs locally. Perhaps the most notable socio-political development was the June 2016 referendum, in which the UK population voted to leave the European Union (a move dubbed Brexit). The fallout from Brexit resulted in the resignation of Prime Minister David Cameron (who had initiated the referendum) and his replacement by Theresa May (former Home Secretary), who herself was replaced as Home Secretary by Amber Rudd. In addition, Michael Gove (a high-profile Brexit supporter and subsequent contender for Prime Minister) was replaced as Justice Minister by Liz Truss. In a bid to rein in the chaos and uncertainty heightened by the fallout from Brexit (by establishing a larger political majority and so stronger policy-making powers), Prime Minister Theresa May called a snap General Election in June 2017. The outcome was a political disaster – a dramatically reduced majority and an enforced alliance with the Democratic Unionist Party of Northern Ireland. Following this latest election, Liz Truss was replaced as Justice Secretary by David Lidington.

The tumultuous, accelerated socio-political and socio-economic changes since 2015 overlapped with and shaped/constructed a period of 'development' characterised by confusion and uncertainty regarding the appropriate focus and objectives for youth justice (**RTA = conflict and ambivalence**). This situation was exacerbated by inertia, arguably paralysis, regarding policy and practice changes. In a period of such extreme political uncertainty and unpredictability, all that seemed certain and predictable was the constant political desire for change (**RTA**) – despite a political unwillingness to affect this change. At this point in our exploration of the socio-historical trajectory of youth justice, we will explore the nature of youth justice developments under the Conservative Government from 2015 onwards and the degree to which they evidence an updated form of the 'new youth justice' compared to a progressive movement of change. This section addresses the most significant of these developments, particularly the review of the YJS by Charlie Taylor and his subsequent recommendations for its improvement (Taylor 2016), along with the perennial issue of youth custody.

THE TAYLOR REVIEW 2016

In September 2015, then Justice Secretary Michael Gove commissioned a full-scale 'Review of the Youth Justice System in England and Wales' (hereinafter the 'Taylor Review'), which was led by Charlie Taylor, a former headteacher of a special school for children with behavioural difficulties (Taylor 2016). As has been noted, the contemporary youth justice context of England and Wales is one of ostensible successes, with long-term trajectories of annual decreases in arrests, FTEs and disposals (cautions and convictions), reoffending numbers and custody rates. The positive statistical trends inherited from the Coalition Government continued in the first year of Conservative Government (2015–2016)[5] (Ministry of Justice (MoJ) and Youth Justice Board (YJB) 2017), with annual decreases in arrests (7 per cent), FTEs (12 per cent), disposals (13 per cent) and custody (8 per cent). Indeed, Taylor acknowledged these encouraging statistical outcomes at an early stage by stressing that 'this review of the youth justice system in England and Wales presents an opportunity to build on considerable success' (Taylor, interim report 2016: 2). However, reoffending rates remained problematic. Although reoffending was diminishing in terms of the numbers of young people reoffending annually, rates of reoffending (the KPI employed by the YJB) had tended towards annual increases and at best stability in recent years (despite the 0.1 per cent drop in 2015–2016). The explicit Government/Gove rationale for the Taylor Review, therefore, was that reoffending remained a serious problem for the YJS, with the implicit rationale of maintaining and building on recent successes more cost-effectively and with fewer resources due to economic austerity. Although fewer young people were entering the system (Bateman 2017), those who did were disproportionately likely to present with personal and social disadvantages such as mental health problems, learning difficulties, multiple complex needs, a history of being in looked after care and coming from working-class and/or black and minority ethnic (BAME) groups (Taylor 2016). Justice Secretary Michael Gove extrapolated the stability in reoffending rates and the increase in young people with multiple complex needs and personal/social problems in the YJS (albeit an ever-decreasing cohort) into a cogent political rationale for a full review of the YJS, despite the long-term successes in other key youth justice outcomes. He argued that a small group of young people with highly complex problems continued to offend (current stakeholder jargon portrays this group as the 'thick soup') and to create victims and fear in their communities, so they needed to be held responsible for their actions and to be rehabilitated within an educational and transformative, 'better' YJS. At the practice level, traditional court-ordered responses to identified offending were viewed as having been unsuccessful, with 64 per cent of young people who received a Youth Rehabilitation Order and 69 per cent who received a custodial sentence going on to reoffend within a year (Ministry of Justice (MoJ) 2016; see also my 'Conversation' with Tim Bateman in the next section). This led Taylor to raise the question that would constitute his rationale for the review: 'with fewer young people requiring youth offending services, are the current arrangements for dealing with them the right ones?' (Taylor, interim report 2016: 2).

The Taylor Review: the findings

Charlie Taylor and his review team visited YOTs and secure establishments throughout England and Wales in order to inform their review, along with visiting youth justice organisations in neighbouring countries in the UK (Scotland and Northern Ireland) and Spain (for some reason), talking to key stakeholder staff (e.g. YOT workers, police, managers) and consulting with children. The Taylor Review set out a series of recommendations for building on the established trajectory of success in the YJS, while at the same time addressing the Government's explicit concerns regarding stubborn reoffending rates among young people and their implicit desire for a more economical approach to youth justice. The central recommendation was one of *principle* (not strategy), namely that a culture shift was needed in how central and local government conceive and construct youth justice. The review argued for a form of children-first youth justice where 'we see the child first and the offender second' (see also Section 5 of this chapter) and where 'education needs to be central to our response to youth offending' (Taylor 2016: 3). The other key recommendation was both structural and strategic, asserting that health, education, social care and other services should form part of a more integrated approach to multi-agency youth justice partnership working. The implication here was that stakeholder agencies should adopt a more holistic systemic response to the problems of young people who offend – one that does not other (label, marginalise, stigmatise) young people, does not compartmentalise youth offending as a stand-alone behaviour and does not silo or isolate/restrict work with young people who offend to (multi-agency) YOTs. The third recommendation was structural, strategic and procedural – that the centralised prescription and bureaucracy associated with the YJS should be stripped back through local devolution and more practitioner discretion in decision-making, assessment and planning and delivering youth justice interventions. Attached to this recommendation was the radical proposal that the YJB should be abolished (**RTA = proposed abolition of the YJB**) and replaced by a new Office of the Youth Justice Commissioner as an expert committee offering the Government 'independent advice and challenge on its approach to youth justice' (Taylor 2016: 55). Let us examine Taylor's three main recommendations in more detail.

- *Children-first youth justice*: the report encouraged the pursuit of a progressive and principled children-first approach to youth justice through a change in the language/narrative used to construct young people in the YJS, viewing them as 'children' rather than 'young offenders'. This changing construction brings us back to the chronological narrative of Chapter 1, which began by reconstructing children as children (not little adults) and ended with social construction of the distinct category of 'young offender'. The Taylor Review proposed two major structural innovations for youth justice: children's panels and secure schools. Children's panels were to consist of three specially trained magistrates working alongside the child, their parents/carers, local authority key workers, lawyer and other relevant professionals to investigate the causes of youth offending (with due consideration of welfare, health and educational issues) and to decide upon appropriate youth justice responses. Panels were recommended for young people receiving a sentence from the youth court, so they have prima facie similarities with existing referral order panels (minus a lay member of the public) and the more diversionary out-of-court sentencing panels formed in different local authority areas. Secure schools were intended to replace young offender institutions in the Secure Estate by functioning as education-focused custodial institutions prioritising qualifications, skills and knowledge development, commissioning support services (e.g. health, mental health, speech therapy) and essentially operating and being governed and inspected as schools.
- *Integrated service provision for young people who offend*: Taylor identified a series of innovative local structures and systems that would strengthen the relationships between youth justice and broader children's services in the areas of education, health and welfare. He drew attention to integrated models of youth justice

delivery wherein children who offend are given access to the same range of provision as children demonstrating other personal and social problems such as welfare needs, being NEET (not in education, employment or training) and being homeless. Some of the more integrated local authority models of youth justice identified had maintained YOTs in their original form, but co-located them within broader children's services (e.g. Newcastle, Stockport), some had essentially dissolved the YOT and integrated youth justice support within a whole system provision (e.g. Surrey Youth Support Service; see Section 5 of this chapter) and others had handed over youth justice responsibilities to non-statutory charitable organisations (e.g. Oldham Positive Steps). The rationale for more integrated service provision[6] was that a narrow youth justice response is insufficient for addressing offending as it neglects other relevant areas of children's lives, particularly welfare, education and health – in line with Drakeford's (2010) assertion that offending is only one part of the child's much broader identity and life experience. Taylor concluded the need for a more welfare-orientated approach to (integrated) youth justice, stating that 'our aim should be to create a twenty-first-century system that moves away from justice with some welfare, to a welfare system with justice' (Taylor 2016: 49).

- *Local devolution and discretion*: a major thrust of Taylor's recommendations to improve the YJS was to give local authorities more freedom to develop and innovate locally specific and progressive models (e.g. structures, strategies, practices) for the delivery of youth justice. Taylor argued that many of the centralised, statutory requirements placed upon YOTs should be removed as these were stifling creativity and ambition; in particular, that the Ministry of Justice (MoJ) should abolish their centralised, routine performance management of YOTs. Consequently, local authorities should be given the freedom to develop their own diversion schemes (a capacity now available almost by default due to lack of governmental guidance regarding out-of-court sentencing processes) and their own assessment systems for use with children who offend (e.g. the use of the needs-led Common Assessment Framework by Surrey Youth Support Service). Most importantly, local authorities should be freed up from the statutory requirement to operate a traditional YOT model; they should be free to form locally appropriate partnerships between statutory agencies to develop, deliver and oversee services for children who offend and they should have more financial freedom in how they employ their funding/ budgets to tackle youth offending.

To summarise, the Taylor Review made a number of recommendations to build on the success of the YJS and to improve its functioning, particularly when dealing with the high-profile and expensive yet diminishing cohort of reoffenders who are disproportionately likely to demonstrate multiple complex needs and other serious personal and social problems. The Taylor recommendations cohere around a three-point plan: to embed the principles of children first and education focus across all work with children who offend (e.g. through new structures such as children's panels and secure schools), to promote more structural and procedural integration of youth justice and other children's services and to facilitate structural and strategic advances in terms of local devolution and discretion when planning and delivering youth justice.

Taylor's emphasis on more child-focused, educational and integrated, holistic service responses for young people who offend has clear overlaps with the guiding principles of **social justice** – justice animated by the equitable distribution of wealth, opportunities and privileges in society. Dr Jess Urwin of De Montfort University has developed a social justice-based model of reconstructed youth justice, which she explained in an interview commissioned for this book.

CONVERSATIONS

Social youth justice

Steve: How did your social justice-based model of youth justice emerge?

Jess Urwin: My background is in psychology, and I am primarily interested in access to mental health support and services. As I began to carry out research into mental health services for young offenders, it became clear that there was a lack of fairness (equity) in the system; with some young people being able to access services and care that others could not. This idea of a system being 'fair' led to considerations of justice. Having initially considered institutional fairness as an aspect of distributive justice, I came to the view that because youth justice is a constructed, governmental organisation, with mandated aims and remits, the disparities in access could be a case of social injustice instead (Urwin 2015).

Social justice has a lot of different definitions; in my view, social justice is the rights and freedoms of citizens being upheld and promoted by a society. In terms of youth justice this would be allowing and supporting young people who offend to access the same opportunities that are guaranteed to all young people; such as education, health care, and housing. In the case of young people who offend, to achieve social justice they may need more support than others, due to disadvantages in their lives which might have contributed to their offending behaviour. Treating people the same is not necessarily social justice. This is why some individuals take issue with the concept of social justice; it inherently assumes disadvantage is present in society, and requires the State to intervene and restore balance.

Steve: What does your perspective contribute to the field of youth justice?

Jess: Viewing youth justice through a lens of social justice can be problematic, and potentially leads to aspects of criminal justice being overlooked. As formalised youth justice is a criminal justice institution, adopting an entirely social justice-based approach would be counterproductive. For both social and criminal justice to be achieved, they need to be in balance, or there needs to be at least some form of compromise between the competing aims of the two ideas needs to be reached. Some have questioned the need for social justice to be present in criminal justice organisations at all, however, this argument relies on very simplistic interpretations of society and overlooks some of the broader context. Young people who offend are often from underprivileged backgrounds, with reduced access to education, with greater mental health needs and with fewer opportunities for social mobility. These are issues that the State could remedy, but often do not, and so they contribute to a young person's propensity to offend. By promoting social justice within youth justice, some of these disadvantages can be addressed, and potentially, reoffending can be prevented.

For a long time, 'welfare versus justice' has been a key debate within youth justice. By reframing this as a question of how to find the balance between social and criminal justice instead, the emphasis is changed. As opposed to focusing on the work of frontline practitioners, the organisational structures and underlying principles are considered instead. Rather than debating if young people who offend should be punished or protected, considering social justice allows us to look at the aims of the system, and if our current approach to meeting those aims is fair. By looking at the system as a whole, change can be implemented that would benefit all young people, rather than localised areas of good (or bad) practice.

Steve: What do you think is the potential for your perspective to be accepted and integrated across contemporary youth justice systems?

Jess: The positive youth justice movement [see later in this chapter] shows elements of a social justice approach and the Charlie Taylor report focuses on rehabilitation working in tandem with punishment. The changes that are occurring within youth justice seem to reflect the desire for a balance between social and criminal justice. However, it often isn't discussed in these terms. By making the role and impact of social justice within youth justice explicit, a clear standard is given for practice, and youth justice as a whole can be evaluated against this concept as a marker of progress. Traditionally offending and reoffending rates are used as markers of improvement in youth justice practice, but what is an acceptable reduction in offending? It is unlikely to ever reach zero, and so using social justice as a standard in addition to this may be useful. If young people are being given opportunities for rehabilitation and desistance, youth justice could be said to be acting in a socially just way. This would also recognise that desistance is a process, and can take time for individuals. So, evaluating youth justice against what the *system* does, rather than what young people do may be more helpful. We can see that local youth justice initiatives that increase access to support services for young people who offend and integrate this support into already existing systems, rather than focusing on a separate YJS, are effective. Surrey and Pembrokeshire local authorities are particular examples of this. It is too soon to suggest what the long-term impacts of these approaches are for young people, but it seems likely that the future of youth justice is intertwined with social justice.

The Government response to the Taylor Review 2016

The Government response to Taylor's recommendations was inconsistent and lacking in enthusiasm, partly the product of the political and economic paralysis caused by Brexit and partly because the review had been commissioned by a previous incarnation of the Conservative Government led by David Cameron and Michael Gove (as Justice Secretary). Consequently, recommendations were published during a period of uncertainty, where the Government was not overly keen on political change, certainly not change essentially recommended by a previous Government (i.e. the same Government and political party, but with different key political influencers/ constructors). Inevitably, the Government acknowledged the successes of the YJS to that point (especially more recent successes that they could take some credit for – a standard political technique/construction), while also recognising the lack of systemic effectiveness in reducing reoffending following community and custodial sentencing, especially among the most complex and damaged children. Commitment to the recommendations of the review, however, was inconsistent and in some cases contrary. The Government response was partial, asserting that 'we will be implementing his [Taylor's] key recommendations by putting education at the heart of youth custody and improving the provision of healthcare to tackle the factors that increase the risk of offending' (Ministry of Justice (MoJ) 2016: 3). Consequently, the Government offered rhetorical support for enhancing the focus on education (and to a lesser extent health) across the YJS (particularly by creating secure schools), although very little was mentioned regarding mental health or welfare. There was also tentative support for local devolution and discretion through a vague commitment to exploring how local areas could be given greater flexibility to improve youth justice services, but no more definitive detail was provided.

Despite tentative, rhetorical support for more focus on education in the Secure Estate and a degree of local devolution, many of Taylor's recommendations were not responded to fully, contradicted or entirely ignored by the Government (Standing Committee for Youth Justice 2017). For example, the principle of responding to young people who offend as 'children first' was completely overlooked, as were proposals for children's panels, more local discretion around diversion schemes and the potential abolition of the YJB. In direct contrast to recommendations for more decentralisation and less centralised performance management of youth justice (consolidating an existing policy), the Government promised to work with the YJB review system to set clear, robust performance standards for youth justice practitioners. The main focus of the Government response appeared to be a reinforcement of the prevention agenda through early intervention and risk-focused strategies (cf. the 'new youth justice'). According to the Government response, the most effective way to reduce crime is 'to intervene early and to prevent children and young people from committing offences in the first place' (Ministry of Justice (MoJ) 2016: 4), while best practice in the area of prevention should be disseminated across the system. The prevention-early intervention objective would be facilitated by 'robust assessments which will enable interventions to be properly matched to the offending-related risks of individual young people' (Ministry of Justice (MoJ) 2016: 31). This assertion bears more than a passing resemblance to the discarded Scaled Approach, only a limited resemblance to the operating principles of AssetPlus and no resemblance whatsoever to Taylor's recommendations for a positive and empowering children-first, education-focused youth justice response.

However, just as key stakeholders were beginning to lose faith in the Government's commitment to improving the YJS in positive, principled and progressive ways (despite having commissioned the Taylor Review partly for this purpose), there was yet another twist to the tale. While the original draft of this chapter was being completed in April 2017, Charlie Taylor was appointed as the new chair of the YJB – the very organisation that his review had recommended should be abolished! Although it remains to be seen what role and influence the YJB can exert on the social construction of youth justice in the future under the leadership of Charlie Taylor and the extent to which the Conservative Government will acknowledge his existing and future recommendations (**RTA = youth justice as dynamic, fluid and contingent social construction**), there is some cause for optimism in the recent 'YJB Strategic

Plan 2019–2022' (YJB 2019a; see 'Bringing Youth Justice Up to Date' section at the end of this chapter), which outlines a commitment to child-first youth justice principles and practices.

Custody: the perennial problem in youth justice

Despite a recent trajectory of falling custody levels and claims from the YJB that these this indicated a legacy of success in reducing custody (see my 'Conversation' with John Drew), part of the Government rationale for the Taylor Review was that reoffending rates among young people who had been in custody remained stubbornly high (Ministry of Justice (MoJ) 2016). The implication was that custody remained an ineffective and inappropriate response to youth offending (taking us back to the care–custody dichotomy of Chapter 4). Successive reports from the Committee on the Rights of the Child (CRC 2002, 2008, 2016) have criticised the UK for failing to tackle the issue of youth custody due to it maintaining higher than (European) average custody rates (despite annual decreases), for failing to use custody as a last resort response to youth offending and for treating young people poorly while in custody (e.g. lack of educational provision, excessive use of restraint and other cruelty). I discussed the issue of youth custody with an international expert in the area, Dr Tim Bateman, deputy chair of the National Association for Youth Justice (NAYJ) and former youth justice policy adviser to the Office of the Children's Commissioner in England. Tim is commissioned by the NAYJ to produce their annual report on the *State of Youth Justice*. I urge you to access these reports on the NAYJ website (www.thenayj.org.uk).

CONVERSATIONS

The continuing problem of child imprisonment

Steve: What is the extent and nature of youth custody in England and Wales?

Tim Bateman: There are two rather different questions there. To take the first [extent], it is clear that the number of children who are locked up for offending fluctuates dramatically over time. So, for example, while the use of child incarceration fell sharply during the 1980s, the decade from 1992 onwards was characterised by a rapid increase: in 2001, the number of children sentenced to custody was 90 per cent higher than in 1992. Although there are genuine problems of comparison, it has been estimated that, at its peak, the proportion of the overall child population imprisoned in England and Wales was four times that in France, ten times that in Spain and 100 times that in Finland (Nacro 2003). More recently, the tide has turned again leading to a considerable decline in youth custody. In April 2016, the population of the child custodial estate was 70 per cent below that in April 2008 (Ministry of Justice (MoJ) and Youth Justice Board (YJB) 2017). This fall notwithstanding, the use of detention remains high by international standards, as the Committee on the Rights of the Child has recently noted (CRC 2016). Moreover, while the overall custodial population has contracted, the over-representation of children from minority ethnic communities has risen to account for 45 per cent of the total (Ministry of Justice (MoJ) and Youth Justice Board (YJB) 2017).

Turning to the second question [nature], custodial regimes are also subject to change over time (Hagel and Hazel 2001). Since 2000, the Secure Estate for children and young people has consisted of three distinct types of establishment: young offender institutions (YOIs) run by the Prison Service and closely resembling adult prisons, secure training centres (STCs) as privately managed custodial facilities for boys and girls aged 12–17 and secure children's homes (SCHs) managed by local authorities and operating with a child care/welfare ethos. Staff-to-child ratios vary considerably across the different sectors: from an average of 1 to 10 in YOIs to around 1 to 2 in SCHs (Children's Commissioner for England 2015). Children's experience of detention is determined largely by the nature of the establishment in which they are placed. Research conducted by the Her Majesty's Inspectorate of Prisons indicates that while less than a quarter of children in STCs report having felt unsafe at some point, one-third of children in YOIs do so; 97 per cent of children in STCs consider that staff treat them with respect compared with 70 per cent of children in YOIs; and a higher proportion (62 per cent) of children in STCs believe that they have done something while in custody that will reduce the likelihood of reoffending when they return to the community, compared to children in YOIs (52 per cent) (Redmond 2015). The survey does not encompass children in SCHs, and there are currently no equivalent figures for these establishments. But to the extent that the improved performance of STCs by comparison with YOIs is explained by establishment size and staffing ratios, one might reasonably anticipate better outcomes for children in that sector. Support for that assumption comes from data on isolation within the Secure Estate. Children are commonly isolated across each of the three sectors, but episodes are generally of a shorter duration in SCHs, such that on average children in YOIs spend eight times as long separated from their peers. These findings are explained by a variety of factors including culture, staff-to-child ratios and size of establishments (Children's Commissioner for England 2015). Children themselves agree that SCHs are better placed to provide an appropriate custodial environment. Almost two-thirds (65 per cent) of children in SCHs reported that, if they have to be in custody, the establishment they were currently in was the best for them; the equivalent figures for STCs and YOIs were 32 per cent and 28 per cent, respectively. It is deeply disappointing that the large majority of children in prison are locked up in facilities least suited to their needs. In April 2016, of the 906 children in custody, more than 71 per cent were placed in YOIs, 18 per cent were in STCs and just 11 per cent were accommodated in SCHs (Bateman 2017). It is hard to escape the conclusion that this configuration is driven by financial considerations: placement in a SCH costs more than three times in a YOI.

Steve: What are the reasons for our use of custody for young people who offend, from your perspective?

Tim: The common-sense view would suggest that child imprisonment reflects the extent and seriousness of children's offending. That suggestion is not borne out by the evidence. While the use of child incarceration has fluctuated considerably since the beginning of the 1980s, detected youth crime has fallen consistently over the whole of that period (Bateman 2012). Perhaps most significantly, from the current perspective, the explosion in custodial sentences imposed on children from 1992 onwards cannot be explained in terms of patterns of children's criminal behaviour, since youth offending declined by more than 20 per cent between 1992 and 2001 (Bateman 2015). Nor did youth crime become more serious during those years (Nacro 2003). A convincing explanation of custodial trends must look to other variables.

A number of commentators have highlighted similarities between the eras in which levels of incarceration dropped. Firstly, during the 1980s, diversion from court became increasingly prevalent through an increased use of police cautioning, which accounted for less than half of all substantive youth justice disposals in 1980, but for more than three-quarters by the end of the decade (Bateman 2012). Diversionary impulses, albeit expressed in a different form (an expansion in the use of informal alternatives to substantive disposals), are also characteristic of the more recent period of child **decarceration** (the process of removal from formal institutions such as prisons) from 2008 onwards, leading to a substantial decline in the number of children entering the YJS for the first time of almost 80 per cent by 2015 (Ministry of Justice (MoJ) and Youth Justice Board (YJB) 2016). The diversionary impetus was associated with a second feature of both periods: political administrations committed to reducing public expenditure in a climate of austerity in which youth offending became effectively depoliticised. The reduced political profile accorded to children's misbehaviour encouraged informal – and more cost-effective – mechanisms for dealing with youth crime, while simultaneously permitting the promotion of less punitive sanctions (Bateman 2014).

The cogency of this account is reinforced by the fact that the expansion in custody during the 1990s coincided with what has been referred to as a 'punitive turn'. Following the murder of 2-year-old James Bulger by two 10-year-old children in 1992, youth offending became highly politicised as mainstream parties strived to present themselves as tougher on children who broke the law than their rivals, leading to a reduced tolerance of children in trouble (Muncie 2014). The explosion in youth imprisonment in the subsequent years was in large part driven by the manner in which that punitiveness impacted on youth justice policy and practice. In particular, the rate of diversion (the proportion of all substantive youth justice disposals resulting in a pre-court outcome) fell from 73.4 per cent to 53.7 per cent in the decade following the murder, leading to a considerable increase in court throughput and the number of children liable to incarceration (Bateman 2015).

Explaining trends in the use of child incarceration over time, of course, sidesteps the broader question of why child imprisonment is used at all. A powerful case can after all be made for the abolition of such practice (Goldson 2005). The answer would appear to reside in the determination of successive governments to avoid appearing soft on youth crime and a wider societal assumption that retribution ought to underlie any response to youthful law breaking.

Steve: What are the implications of putting young people into custody?

Tim: The social costs of imprisoning children are enormous. Research indicates that children deprived of their liberty derive from the most disadvantaged communities and are among those with the highest levels of need and vulnerabilities. An analysis of the child custodial population published in 2010 established that more than half (51 per cent) lived in a deprived household and/or unsuitable accommodation, almost half (47 per cent) had run away from home at some point, and more than a quarter (27 per cent) had previously been in care. Twelve per cent had experienced the death of parents or siblings compared with 4 per cent in the general population. Almost half (48 per cent) had been excluded from school, one in five had self-harmed and 11 per cent had attempted suicide (Jacobson *et al.* 2010). In summary, 'around three-quarters of the sample are known to have three or more indicators of home/family disadvantage, and more than two-fifths to have five or more' (Jacobson *et al.* 2010: 52). As the number of children in custody has fallen, in the interim period, the extent of need within the Secure Estate has increased.

The glaring chasm between the welfare needs of children whose offending is sufficiently serious to result in deprivation of liberty and the ability of custody to deliver a service that meets those needs constitutes the tragedy of child imprisonment (Goldson 2005). Child prisons are places of violence and are deteriorating in this regard. Between 2010 and 2015, the number of assaults in custody rose from 9 per 100 detained children to 16.1; over the same period, the rate of physical restraint per 100 children increased from 17.6 to 28.2. In this context, it is perhaps unsurprising that episodes of recorded self-harm (presumably many lesser incidents go unrecorded) also expanded, from 5.3 to 7.7 per 100 (Ministry of Justice (MoJ) and Youth Justice Board (YJB) 2016). Sixteen children have died in custody since the YJB took over responsibility for the Secure Estate in 2000 (YJB 2014). Successive inspection reports demonstrate that provision of high-quality education, appropriate support within custody and on release is lacking (Bateman *et al.* 2013). The evidence that incarceration is criminogenic, increasing the risk of further offending, is clear with reconviction rates within a year of release standing at more than two-thirds. The lifelong barriers for children who have experienced imprisonment to reintegrating fully in society are considerable (Goldson 2005).

Steve: Can you suggest a way forward?

Tim: There are, it seems to me, two priorities. The first is to reduce substantially the number of children behind bars. The recent fall in youth imprisonment, while obviously welcome, is simply insufficient. It is, moreover, relatively easy to identify measures that would achieve this aim (although implementing them may prove more challenging). As outlined above, the use of child imprisonment is in part a product of the level of prosecution; further expansion of diversionary mechanisms would be likely to generate a contraction in custodial outcomes. Within the court arena itself, the existing custodial threshold for children is largely the same as that which applies to adults. It allows imprisonment for relatively minor, persistent property offending. Ensuring compliance with the UNCRC obligation that custody should be used only as a measure of last resort would require a tightening of the criteria that must be satisfied before a child can be imprisoned. Statutory provisions should mandate a non-custodial response other than in cases:

• Involving violent or sexual offending.
• Where the child poses a serious risk of harm to the public.
• Non-custodial options have been fully explored.

The second priority concerns the nature of custodial facilities themselves. Where incarceration is absolutely necessary, children should be accommodated in small child care establishments, with high staff-to-child ratios and a therapeutic environment. Taylor's review of youth justice has gone some way to recognising this ideal with a proposal that most existing custodial provision be replaced by a network of 'secure schools' that would be smaller than YOIs and would have a focus on education. While such a model would no doubt constitute an improvement over current arrangements, NAYJ has convincingly argued that the principle of: 'placement in a secure child care establishment with high quality education provided on the premises, rather than a school that provides secure accommodation . . . would better reflect the complexities of need experienced by this cohort of children and would reinforce the importance of healthy development and emotional support alongside education' (Bateman 2016: 3). SCHs would appear to fit the bill nicely. There would appear to be no need to reinvent the wheel.

The 'Conversation' with Tim Bateman indicates that youth custody is a continuing problem in the YJS of England and Wales, both in its extent (despite annual decreases) and its nature; including its seriously harmful consequences to those children who are imprisoned. In addition, continued use of the generic category of 'children and young people' perpetuates the (relative) neglect of girls when examining the impact of the YJS, in particular, the impact of custody on this marginalised population. To address this oversight, I invited Dr Pippa Goodfellow of the Standing Committee for Youth Justice to offer her evidenced views on the current custodial climate for girls in the YJS of England and Wales.

 ## TELLING IT LIKE IT IS

Girls and Custody (Dr Pippa Goodfellow)

If you can picture an average primary school class, you may be surprised to know that the total population of girls in custody across England and Wales today is a similar size. Over the past decade, the number of incarcerated girls has fallen by 90 per cent and has been around 30 in total at any time since 2017–2018. Girls are underrepresented in the Youth Justice System and make up only 3 per cent of all children in custody. Their diminishing minority has meant that girls have largely escaped the mainstream, androcentric attention of published data, research, policy and practice. This prompted me to undertake a study to shine a light on the imprisonment of girls, where I analysed data about all girls detained in custody over a two-year period. Despite the good news story about the fall in numbers, my research found that girls in custody have been left 'outnumbered, locked up and overlooked' and revealed a number of concerning issues:

A lack of national policy focus: While the Youth Justice System in England and Wales has been under a great deal of scrutiny in recent years, there has evidently been a lack of specific attention given to girls. Recent inspection reports have found inconsistent practice to meet the needs of girls in custody in the absence of a nationally co-ordinated strategy. Extensive changes to youth custody and the broader youth and criminal justice systems have been recommended in a number of reviews, but have not specifically addressed gender-specific needs or considered the implications for girls in custody. Proposed changes that are envisioned as gender-neutral may have unintended, gendered impacts for girls and inadvertently bring about counter-productive consequences.

Published figures disguise a bigger problem: Concerningly, the small number of girls in custody suggested by a 'snapshot' at a static point in time disguises the true picture of the number detained over a longer period, caused by a frequent flow of girls through custody for brief periods on short custodial sentences and periods of remand. The prevalence of short sentences imposed saw three-quarters of girls being sentenced to a custodial period of six months or less and 90 per cent of girls sentenced to a custodial period of 12 months or less. More than one-third of all Detention and Training Orders (DTOs) were just four months in length, spending only two months in custody.

Questions over the legitimacy of incarceration: Contrary to widespread perceptions, many girls in custody have not committed serious or violent offences. My analysis found that one-third of girls were sentenced to custody for non-violent offences and three-fifths were sentenced to custody for offences that were at the less serious end of the spectrum. I was particularly surprised to find that one-fifth of girls were sentenced to custody for primary offences that were neither violent nor serious. More than half girls who are imprisoned before their trial (on remand) do not subsequently receive a custodial sentence, which suggests that they possibly should not have been remanded in the first place. Nearly one-third of girls were remanded to custody for non-violent alleged offences. Many girls are experiencing the equivalent of serving a short custodial sentence prior to being acquitted or receiving a community-based disposal at court. These findings raise important questions over the necessity of the current use of custody for many girls in England and Wales.

The impact of custody on girls: Girls enter custody with a variety of complex pre-existing emotional problems, sometimes manifesting in volatile and challenging behaviour that is difficult to manage. Many have experienced abuse, exploitation and a lack of care from those responsible for their well-being. Shockingly, 60 per cent of girls admitted to custody (compared to 6 per cent of boys) are assessed as having sexual exploitation concerns. Inspections have repeatedly reported concerns about the treatment of girls in custody and found that as many as 80 per cent of girls in Secure Training Centres have felt unsafe. Attempts to manage behaviour through physical restraint, use of force and putting girls in isolation are deployed more frequently on females than males and at an increasing rate, which can bring about feelings of violation and re-traumatisation. Self-harm is a significant problem for many girls, with twice as many assessed as having concerns around suicide or self-harm as boys (63 per cent compared to 30 per cent). As the number of girls in custody has fallen, places have been decommissioned and the available placements are now more thinly spread across the country, with girls in England and Wales held on average 72 miles from home, compared to 49 miles for all children.

Black, Asian and Minority Ethnic (BAME) girls in custody: BAME girls are overrepresented in custody, with ethnic disproportionality significantly higher for remanded girls (36 per cent BAME) than in the sentenced population (28 per cent BAME). A higher proportion of BAME girls than white girls were placed in a Secure Training Centre (rather than a Secure Children's Home), potentially indicating that they are being assessed as less vulnerable. Investigation is needed to 'explain or reform' (Lammy 2017) why the disproportionality of girls in custody is so high, with specific consideration given to BAME girls and how gender intersects with their ethnicity to influence these outcomes.

In recent years, girls in custody appear to have paled into insignificance from a policy perspective, with the small numbers providing the justification for this over-sight. Instead, the very small population of girls currently in custody should be seen as presenting a timely opportunity to develop more innovative and appropriate responses to their needs and ensure that they are no longer overlooked.

For more detailed discussion of these issues, see my report *Girls in Custody: Outnumbered, Locked Up and Overlooked* (www.thegriffinssociety.org/outnumbered-locked-and-overlooked-use-penal-custody-girls-england-wales).

The personal, social and economic costs of imprisoning children and young people who offend, alongside its relative ineffectiveness as a youth justice strategy, suggest that alternatives to custody should be explored. It was the need for alternatives to both custody and other ineffective youth justice responses that the Taylor Review addressed in its recommendations for secure schools (to replace custodial institutions), children's panels (as a diversionary and restorative mechanism) and increased decentralisation, local devolution and discretion (permitted local mediation if you like) as a means of mobilising alternative, progressive approaches to youth justice. As noted, the Government has made supportive noises around creating recommended secure schools as a new structure for delivering youth justice. However, in early 2017, Justice Secretary Liz Truss announced that the YJB would no longer be responsible for commissioning and overseeing youth custody. A new structure, the Youth Custody Service, has now taken over the running of youth custody and function as a distinct arm of HM Prison and Probation Service, the new Government quango replacing the National Offender Management Service. Responsibility and accountability for commissioning youth custody services has been taken on by the Ministry of Justice. Initial responses to these proposed changes have been mixed and an air of uncertainty remains regarding the potential operation and influence of the Youth Custody Service, not helped by the departure of its first director in April 2018 after fewer than six months in charge. What is clear is that the Youth Custody Service will need to address the worryingly high levels of violence and bullying across the Secure Estate (in this case, Young Offender Institutions and Secure Training Centres) that were identified in a recent national assessment of secure institutions by HM Inspectorate of Prisons (2019, in Hampson 2020). In relation to the YJB, the Government has constructed the enforced reduction in their power as a positive that will enable the YJB

to build on its strong track-record and focus on its statutory function of providing vital independent advice on, and scrutiny of, the whole system, advising the government on what standards to set for the youth justice system and monitoring delivery of those standards. It will continue to work closely with youth offending teams to promote early intervention in the community and share best practice across the system.

(Liz Truss, Ministerial Statement, 24 February 2017)

It is not yet clear the extent to which the YJB will be given the power to provide advice on and scrutiny of the custodial aspect of the whole system. However, given that they have been stripped of commissioning and oversight responsibilities in this area (which surely include and overlap with scrutiny?), this power is likely to be restricted at best. The SCYJ, which represents more than 40 children's and justice organisations including Barnardo's and Catch 22, has described the move as a 'retrograde step', illustrating the YJB being 'broken up':

> The transfer of all youth custody responsibilities from the YJB . . . risks the development of an adult-centric and fragmented approach to children who offend. Charlie Taylor's recent review for the government called for a 'integrated, seamless and co-ordinated' response to the challenge of reducing offending by children. We agree. This announcement will make this harder.
>
> (Wigzell and SCYJ 2017)

5 EASY PIECES

3 Conservative Government youth justice (2015–): ambiguity and inertia?

1 *Ambiguity and inertia*: developments in youth justice under the Conservative Government thus far have been restricted due to their limited time in office and a context of heightened socio-economic and political uncertainty and upheaval, which has resulted in a change of Prime Minister, two changes of Justice Minister and the UK leaving the European Union.

2 *The Taylor Review*: the review by Charlie Taylor in 2016 concluded that an improved YJS should prioritise children first and education-focused principles, should enable broader service integration within and outside of the system and should facilitate more local devolution and discretion in the planning, funding and delivery of youth justice services.

3 *Government response to Taylor* (*progressive*): the governmental response to the Taylor Review supported the key recommendation for education-focused custodial services (i.e. secure schools) and offered tentative support for exploring more local devolution and discretion in the delivery of youth justice.

4 *Government response to Taylor* ('*new youth justice*'): the Government glossed over or largely ignored many of the other principled, structural, strategic and practical recommendations of the review, such as children's panels, local devolution and the abolition of the YJB. Instead, the crux of their response reinforced 'new youth justice' strategies of risk-focused early intervention and prevention. However, Charlie Taylor has now been appointed chair of the YJB, so the direction of future strategic developments is encouraging, as indicated by the YJB Strategic Plan 2019–2022.

5 *Custody*: the numbers of children/young people given custodial sentences for offending behaviour has decreased annually, yet the imprisonment of children/young people in custodial institutions poorly suited to their needs and social circumstances remains a systemic problem in England and Wales and a contravention of the UNCRC.

4 WELSH YOUTH JUSTICE (2000 ONWARDS): DRAGONISED OR ANGLICISED?

Chapter 5 introduced the possibility of a unique form of youth justice emerging in Wales, which contrasts with the more anglicised (English-centric) 'new youth justice' in significant ways. This so-called dragonised (Welsh-centric) youth justice (Haines 2010) attempts to reconcile the 'new' youth justice priorities and strategies dictated by the UK Government situated in Westminster, England with the distinct social policy context for young people in Wales,[7] which emphasises universal services over targeted provision, promoting children's rights/entitlements and positive outcomes over preventing negative outcomes, equality of outcome over equality of opportunity (Haines and Case 2011) and collective responsibility over individual responsibility (Case 2014). It was noted in the previous chapter that the Welsh Assembly Government (now Welsh Government) and the YJB collaborated to produce the *All Wales Youth Offending Strategy* (AWYOS; Welsh Government and Youth Justice Board 2004) to guide Welsh YOTs in delivering youth justice in a manner congruent with the risk-based early intervention and prevention focus of the Crime and Disorder Act 1998 ('prevention is better than cure') and the universalised, collectivist, rights-based principles of Welsh social policy ('children first and offenders second'). The debate emerging from this process concerns whether Welsh youth justice is/can be distinct in principle, structure, strategy and practice from that of England. The originator of this argument was Professor Kevin Haines, who has researched and written at length regarding the children-first Welsh approach to youth justice (Haines and Case 2015; Haines and Drakeford 1998). In particular, he has argued that the rights/entitlements basis of Welsh social policy and youth justice offers a more positive and promotional model of working with children who offend (a 'children first, offender second' model of 'positive youth justice'; see Section 5 of this chapter) when compared to the more responsibilising and punitive (risk-based) elements of youth justice and social policy pursued in England. Other key constructers of how youth justice in Wales, including Dusty Kennedy (head of the YJB in Wales [YJB Cymru]), are not as convinced as to the extent or even existence of this distinction. They argue that while Wales demonstrates certain structural and philosophical (arguably strategic) differences to England in how youth justice has been conceptualised and delivered, the extent to which these differences demonstrate a distinct practice has been overstated. I interviewed both Kevin and Dusty as a means of exploring the issue of Welsh youth justice and will incorporate their views into subsequent discussions. So, is a distinct Welsh youth justice (policy) rhetoric or (practice) reality? If dragonised youth justice exists, what can this tell us about the potential to construct progressive and positive forms of contemporary youth justice?

Towards the end of the New Labour reign, the Welsh Assembly Government and YJB published the *All Wales Youth Offending Strategy: Delivery Plan 2009–11*, which committed to 'mainstream and embedded consultation with and the participation of children and young people in the youth justice system' (Welsh Government and Youth Justice Board 2009: 10). The AWYOS Delivery Plan affirmed the Welsh Government's view that young people were entitled to express their views at every stage of the youth justice process, in line with the UNCRC (see Chapter 4). Six priority areas were identified in the Delivery Plan to facilitate implementation of the AWYOS, which mapped onto the Welsh Youth Justice Indicator Set (the Welsh equivalent of KPIs): reducing first-time entrants into the YJS, reducing reoffending, reducing custody rates, increasing engagement with education, training and employment, increasing access to suitable accommodation, and (Wales-specific) increasing access to appropriate substance use assessment and treatment (Welsh Government and Youth Justice Board 2009). While Welsh youth justice was distinct in certain respects (most notably the 'children first, offenders second' and participation principles), its strategies for pursuit of these principled objectives resembled the 'new youth justice' in key areas, particularly in terms of targeted (risk-based) prevention and early intervention focused on psychosocial domains of risk (e.g. family, school, community), restorative justice implemented by trained staff working in multi-agency partnerships and adherence to KPIs (Welsh Government and Youth Justice Board 2009). Let us examine the components of the alleged Welsh youth justice more closely.

Distinct youth justice structures in Wales

Despite clear similarities with 'new youth justice' *strategies* in its plans for delivery in practice, the AWYOS retains a children-first focus that is distinct from the risk-based prevention agenda in English youth justice and social policy (see Case and Haines 2015b). A series of bespoke *structures* have been created (socially constructed) to develop the youth justice agenda in Wales in accordance with this distinct Welsh social policy identity. For example, in 2011, the Wales Youth Justice Advisory Panel (WYJAP) was formed to provide expertise, challenge and scrutiny on a range of strategic, policy, practice and research issues relevant to youth justice in Wales. The primary purpose of the WYJAP[8] is 'to assist the Welsh Government and the YJB to implement policy that prevents offending and reoffending by children and young people in Wales' (Welsh Government and Youth Justice Board 2014: 1).

A further significant move towards constructing a distinct Welsh youth justice in structural terms was the formation of YJB Cymru in 2012 as a division of the YJB for England and Wales, to sit alongside its other divisions (Corporate Services, Effective Practice, Community and Secure Estate) on the YJB Executive Management Group. YJB Cymru monitors and manages the implementation of central Government/YJB policy in the Welsh context – acting as a mediator advising the UK Government, the YJB and the Welsh Government on Welsh youth justice policy matters and monitoring, supporting and advising the practice of Welsh YOTs (Youth Justice Board and Cymru 2012; Case 2014). The official role of YJB Cymru is set out in the document *Blueprint for Promoting Effective Practice and Improving Youth Justice Performance in Wales* (YJB 2012). In practice, the head of YJB Cymru (currently Dusty Kennedy) sits on the YJB Executive Management Group (EMG). A key part of his role (alongside other YJB Cymru representatives) is to provide expert advice to the group on Welsh youth justice matters, including contributions to the 'Issues for Wales' sections that are standing item within every Informational Decision Paper produced by the EMG (Case 2014). At ground level (structurally), a committee for the YOT managers across Wales, called YOT Managers Cymru, has been created/constructed to work with the YJB to consider the implications of legislation, government guidelines and youth justice policy for Welsh YOTs and to determine effective responses to youth offending in Wales (YOT Managers Cymru 2013; Case 2014).

A 'children-first' principled-strategic approach

Strategically, the Welsh Government has produced a Cabinet Briefing paper titled *Devolution of Youth Justice*, which established 'a vision for increasing Welsh

Government influence over the delivery of services to children and young people who are offending or at risk of offending' (Welsh Government 2011: 1). The Cabinet Briefing recommended a key philosophical distinction in how youth justice should be constructed and administrated administered in Wales, namely through an entitlement/rights-based approach to supporting children as 'children first' (not offenders first), grounded in the UNCRC:

> The principle is a focus on the needs of the children and young people, rather than on their offending behavior.
>
> (Welsh Government 2011: 4)

The philosophy/principle of dealing with young people who offended as 'children first, offenders second' was not new, of course (it was created by two Welsh academics, Haines and Drakeford, in 1998), but it was distinctively Welsh, having been introduced into policy by the AWYOS (see Chapter 5). The concept of 'children first' had been constructed as a direct challenge to the strategies that Haines and Drakeford correctly predicted would characterise New Labour's model of youth justice following the Crime and Disorder Act 1998. During interview, Kevin Haines recalled the philosophical origins of 'children first':

> There was a context of adulterisation, responsibilisation and a general hardening of attitudes to children in the lead up to the Crime and Disorder Act. Children first was a counterpoint to the punitive drift. All the evidence suggested that punitiveness was ineffective and that offence- and offender-focused work was ineffective and inappropriate, which leads us to looking at children as children. So, the idea came from the need for a guiding philosophy to shape and analyse youth justice. You can have a set of techniques for responding to children who break the law, but they need to serve a purpose.
>
> (Kevin Haines 2017, personal interview)

The year after the publication of the Cabinet Briefing, the Welsh Government published a Green Paper titled (deep breath . . .) *Proposals to Improve Services in Wales to Better Meet the Needs of Children and Young People Who Are at Risk of Entering, or Are Already in, the Youth Justice System* (Welsh Government 2012). The Green Paper progressed discussion regarding how the Welsh Government should employ its existing powers to develop a distinctive, rights- and entitlements-focused youth justice that benefited children in the YJS. It was consolidated by the recommendations of the Silk Commission on Devolution in Wales (2014); recommendations that were not fully supported by discussion or evidence. The Silk Commission advocated that key youth justice stakeholders in Wales (e.g. YJB Cymru) should be given more responsibility and influence over how Welsh youth justice was constructed and that youth justice decision-making powers should be devolved through a new Government of Wales Act.

THE *CHILDREN AND YOUNG PEOPLE FIRST* STRATEGY

In 2014, the Welsh Government and the YJB collaborated on an updated and improved version of the 2004 AWYOS, titled (another deep breath. . .) *Children and Young People*

First: Welsh Government/Youth Justice Board Joint Strategy to Improve Services for Young People from Wales at Risk of Becoming Involved in, or in, the Youth Justice System (Welsh Government and Youth Justice Board 2014), which became known as *Children and Young People First* for obvious reasons! The vision statement for *Children and Young People First* reflected its title, which was a commitment to a distinct children-first approach to youth justice in Wales:

> Children and young people at risk of entering, or who are in, the youth justice system must be treated as children first and offenders second in all interactions with services.
>
> (Welsh Government and Youth Justice Board 2014: 3)

This vision set out five priorities for youth justice practice, which broadly mirrored the approach favoured by the UK Government in England:

1   A well-designed partnership approach.
2   Early intervention, prevention and diversion.
3   Reducing reoffending.
4   Effective use of custody.
5   Resettlement and reintegration at the end of a sentence.

These five priorities were linked to specific children-first principles and objectives relating to the appropriate treatment of young people in the YJS, focused on: children-first practice and more engagement with children and young people in the YJS (including actively seeking children's voices), helping children to access their rights[9] (all distinctly Welsh forms of youth justice), along with emphasis on diversion, prevention and early intervention, challenging offending behaviours and enabling victim participation (e.g. through restorative justice) and delivering youth justice through accountable multi-agency partnership working (all strategies of the more anglicised 'new youth justice'). Therefore, the priorities and objectives of the *Children and Young People First* strategy can be mapped onto the guiding features and principles of a 'children first, offenders second' positive youth justice (discussed later in this chapter), which arguably constitute a distinct Welsh/dragonised youth justice.

Children and Young People First did not only differ in policy/strategic terms from the approach to youth justice adopted in England because of its principled children-first focus. There was also an emerging practice distinction in relation to its recommendations for a tiered and integrated approach to prevention, extending the more risk-focused targeted approach in England and predating the Taylor Review recommendations. The strategy clearly states that 'prevention in all its forms is the key to stopping young people coming into the justice system' (Welsh Government and Youth Justice Board 2014: 12). The tiered approach recommended moving along a preventative continuum from early intervention and prevention services (tier one) to targeted YOT prevention work (tier two) to alternatives to charging and diversion (tier three). Although still conflating the concepts of early intervention and prevention in a manner reflective of the 'new youth justice', the intention was principled – to promote a holistic and integrated approach to prevention work, especially with young people whose 'needs are too complex for easy integration into universal services . . .

in instances like these we believe targeted multi-agency prevention is appropriate' (Welsh Government and Youth Justice Board 2014: 14).

Youth justice in Wales: dragonised or anglicised?

> The political and organisational context in Wales, with partial devolution of relevant issues . . . and a distinctive policy orientation for young people (rights- and entitlements-focused), provides conceptual and practical space for progressive youth justice.
>
> (Case and Haines 2012: 40)

Despite the 'distinct, evidenced policy differences between England and Wales which support the argument that youth justice is dragonised' (Kevin Haines 2017, personal interview), a significant tension emerges when attempting to argue that youth justice is delivered in a distinctive way *in practice* in Wales. In another interview conducted to inform our book, Dusty Kennedy (Head of YJB Cymru) supported the view that youth justice in Wales was distinct from England in *policy/strategic* terms, largely due to the partially devolved nature of the Welsh Government:

> We designed legislation in Wales to bind together devolved and non-devolved functions when delivering youth justice. There was no way they were ever going to be delivered in the same way as England because of our devolved partners. Then we created a national strategy for youth justice. The strength you get from having such a national strategy that is avowedly rights-based and young person-focused is that you have a benchmark to judge staff against. The really important progressive thing here was that staff are given strategic permission to do the right thing.
>
> (Dusty Kennedy 2017, personal interview)

However, Dusty also conceded that 'you don't get this perfect translation of policy rhetoric and practice in reality' (Dusty Kennedy 2017, personal interview), a statement that highlights two recurring themes in the historical construction of youth justice: the perennial tension of transferring policy rhetoric into practice reality and the local mediation of centralised policy requirements in practice due to institutional and practitioner discretion. The presence of these recurring themes makes it difficult to argue definitively for a distinct youth justice in practice in Wales. While it is fair to say that 'Wales has always gone slightly its own way while operating within the legislative framework set in West-minster and some YOTs have exceeded in practice what is happening in England' (Kevin Haines 2017, personal interview), the policy-practice disconnect in Wales also suggests that the distinctions with England have been overstated (despite having a basis in reality):

> To be honest, when you sit down with YOT managers and talk about 'children first, offenders second', they all agree with you. I think people like to pat themselves on the back about children's rights. You still hear this English punitive, Welsh rights-led narrative, meaning that people envisage practice in Welsh YOTs to be different from in English YOTs. But when you go into a Welsh YOT and look at the practice, I don't think it's much different to England.
>
> (Dusty Kennedy 2017, personal interview)

However, there is a tentative agreement among key constructors of youth justice in Wales that there may be at least some differences in practice in Wales, seen largely as the product of a much smaller geography in Wales and a degree of charismatic leadership in specific YOTs. Claims that the delivery of youth justice practice in Wales is distinct from England were met with guarded agreement by the Head of YJB Cymru, who responded:

> I think yes to a certain extent in terms of consistency of approach. But that's not so much driven by strategy as having a smaller number of people to convince. Charismatic people with big ideas can move quickly in Wales because it doesn't take long to get around all of the YOTs. You can have a grassroots movement that can take hold.
>
> (Dusty Kennedy 2017, personal interview)

Kevin Haines agreed with this assessment of a consistency of approach across Wales, citing the influence of YJB Cymru in 'supporting YOTs and holding them to account, a process that does not happen in England. YJB Cymru is in touch, helping YOTs to identify and solve problems' (Kevin Haines 2017, personal interview). He also agreed that charismatic individuals can influence practice. While acknowledging that 'wide variations between local areas across YOTs can reflect local circumstances and so are appropriate and justifiable', he also cautioned that 'in other areas, variations reflect the personalities of YOT managers and so are more ideological driven and unjustified, although the same thing happens in England' (Kevin Haines 2017, personal interview). However, it appears that local and national differences in policy and practice terms have been superseded by the current climate of economic austerity, which adds a new layer of complexity onto the social construction of youth justice (in Wales).

Taken together, the perspectives of two of the major influencers/constructors of youth justice in Wales indicate that there is an overarching policy distinction that has not transferred seamlessly or consistently into practice. Social policy for children and young people in Wales has a distinct identity, promoting the principles of children's rights/entitlements, universalism and collective responsibility, compared to its English counterpart's tendency to prioritise risk reduction, conditional rights (e.g. no rights without responsibilities), targeted early intervention and individual responsibility (responsibilisation). The political and practical need to resolve the tensions between social policy and youth justice policy in Wales has fuelled the construction of a distinct form of Welsh youth justice. This distinction has been most evident in structural and policy terms through the creation of bespoke Welsh-centric youth justice bodies and children-first strategies to reconcile these policy tensions. However, there is a degree to which bespoke bodies (e.g. YJB Cymru), key individuals (e.g. the Welsh representative on the YJB) and Welsh youth justice strategy (e.g. *Children and Young People First*) have remained constricted in practice by the requirements of the Crime and Disorder Act 1998. Any distinctively Welsh youth justice may, in reality, be more of an add-on to mitigate some of the potential negatives of the 'new youth justice', informed variously by national strategy, local mediation and/or charismatic YOT managers, rather than functioning in practice as a stand-alone, distinct and consistent approach to delivering youth justice. Consequently, there is an ongoing debate regarding the extent to which has been truly dragonised as opposed to being Welsh centric, but constrained by the statutory requirements of the 'new youth justice'.

5 EASY PIECES

4 Welsh youth justice (2000 onwards): dragonised or anglicised?

1 *Partial devolution, significant tension*: youth justice is a non-devolved policy area in Wales, yet policy-making and service delivery responsibility for other areas relevant to the lives of children and young people (e.g. education, health, social services) is devolved to the Welsh Government, introducing competing priorities and approaches for working with young people who offend in Wales.

2 *Structural differences*: although England and Wales share a YJS, bespoke youth justice structures have been created to manage policy tensions and to implement a Welsh-centric youth justice strategy, most notably the Wales Youth Justice Advisory Panel and YJB Cymru becoming a separate division of the YJB.

3 *Strategic differences*: although YOTs in Wales must adhere to the ('new youth justice') requirements of the Crime and Disorder Act 1998, the Welsh Government and YJB (represented by their YJB Cymru division) have collaborated on the *All Wales Youth Offending Strategy* and subsequent *Children and Young People First* strategy in an attempt to reconcile English youth justice priorities (e.g. prevention, risk-focused intervention) with Welsh social policy principles and priorities (e.g. children first, children's rights/entitlements, universalism, collective responsibility).

4 *Potential devolution of youth justice*: ongoing debate regarding the possible devolution of youth justice responsibility to the Welsh Government has been inconclusive, but the prevailing view amongst politicians, policy-makers, operational managers and YOT staff appears to be one of staying with the current (non-devolved) arrangements and seeking ways of improving the delivery of youth justice to young people in Wales.

5 *Dragonised or anglicised*: there is an ongoing academic and political debate regarding the extent to which Welsh youth justice is distinct from youth justice in England in principled, structural, strategic and practical terms (i.e. dragonised), as opposed to being Welsh centric, yet being constrained by the strategies of the 'new youth justice' developed in England (i.e. anglicised).

5 CHILDREN-FIRST POSITIVE YOUTH JUSTICE: A NEW FRONTIER

In the final section of our final chapter, it is time to introduce a new frontier in the (re)construction of youth justice – a modern, progressive, evidence-based and child-friendly model of 'positive youth justice' (PYJ) developed over a 20-year period research partnership with children, families and other key stakeholders in the YJS (Haines and Case 2012, 2015; see also Case and Haines 2014, 2015a). As PYJ is my own construction (in partnership with Kevin Haines), you could read this section as if it were a subjective 'Telling it like it is' feature. PYJ was created to challenge established constructions of youth justice emerging from the welfare-justice debate and particularly as a deliberate, robust challenge to the negative excesses of the 'new youth justice'.

Despite its personalised and subjective nature, however, the PYJ model is firmly evidence based and reflective (see Haines and Case 2015). Furthermore, PYJ principles have gained traction in contemporary youth justice debates and have begun to influence the (re)construction of policy and practice recommendations. The 'children first, offenders second' basis of the model is supported and recommended within:

- *The Taylor Review*: 'I have described a new system in which young people are treated as children first and offenders second' (Taylor 2016: 48).
- *Children and Young People First*, the Welsh youth justice strategy: 'Children and young people at risk of entering, or who are in, the youth justice system must be treated as children first and offenders second in all interactions with services' (Youth Justice Board and Welsh Government 2015: 4).
- *National Strategy for the Policing of Children and Young People*: 'It is crucial that in all encounters with the police those below the age of 18 should be treated as children first' (NPCC 2015: 8).
- *Sentencing Children and Young People*: 'the approach to sentencing should be individualistic and focused on the child or young person, as opposed to offence focused' (Sentencing Council 2017: 4).

The PYJ model (Haines and Case 2015) constructs children who offend as part of the solution to youth offending, not part of the problem, and pursues this solution by embedding a set of principles within youth justice practice that are based broadly on notions of **normalisation**, inclusion and children's rights. These principles have been identified and developed through a long-term project of research in England and Wales; primary research with key stakeholders within the YJS and those receiving and delivering other children's services (see Case *et al.* 2005 – evaluation of the *Extending Entitlement* youth inclusion strategy), along with secondary analysis of other progressive work in the youth justice field nationally and internationally. The mutually reinforcing principles that contribute to the social construction of the PYJ model will be separated into five digestible (easy) pieces: child-friendly/appropriate treatment, diversion and systems management, promotion of positive behaviours and outcomes (including participation, engagement and legitimacy), evidence-based partnership and responsibilising adults (Haines and Case 2015).

Child-friendly/appropriate

The essence of the PYJ model is that responses to young people who offend should be constructed with the recipient's status as a 'child' at the forefront (i.e. children first). The rationale is that 'new youth justice' strategies of responsibilisation and risk-focused prevention have adulterised young people – treating them like little adults, rather than recognising their status and relative (lack of) development and capacity as a child in legal, (other) policy, cultural, social and psychological terms (see Sentencing Council 2017; Taylor 2016; Arthur 2016; see also Chapter 1). The children-first PYJ model deliberately rejects the 'new youth justice' practice of treating children who offend as mini-adults in a mini-criminal justice system (see also Muncie 2008; Fagan and Zimring 2000), because adulterisation overlooks children's inherent vulnerability and need for protection (see Chapter 1) and is contradictory to 'good youth justice' (Harding and Beecroft 2013) and 'child-friendly justice' (Goldson and Muncie 2015;

see Chapter 4). The co-creator of the children-first principle of youth justice, Professor Mark Drakeford (see Haines and Drakeford 1998), has asserted that offending by children is 'only one element of a much wider and more complex identity'and so should be responded to through a children-first approach that is 'embedded in a wider and more generic set of policy-making responses' (Drakeford 2010: 143). The children-first approach to youth justice avoids using the term 'offender' (Haines and Case 2015 opt for 'children in conflict with the law and the YJS') due to its potentially labelling and stigmatising effects on the recipient (see discussion of labelling theories in Chapter 2). Therefore, the children-first principle places the 'child' at the centre of its understandings and responses to youth offending (i.e. child-friendly); designing services and interventions that are fit for children (not targeted on 'offenders') and are child appropriate in the sense of being meaningful, understood, appreciated by and developed in participation with children. Child-friendly/appropriate youth justice engages with children in child-sensitive ways and responds to needs, problems and rights/ entitlements in all aspects of their lives in a holistic, whole child manner – in accordance with Principled Youth Justice[10] (Goldson and Muncie 2006), the characteristics of Good Youth Justice[11] (Harding and Beecroft 2013) and United Nations recommendations (OHCHR 2013). Consequently, all other principles of the PYJ are informed and underpinned by this central children-first principle of child-friendly/appropriate youth justice.

Diversion and systems management

The PYJ model supports the ethos of normalisation – understanding youth offending as an everyday, 'normal' aspect of childhood that children will most likely grow out of through maturation (see Glueck and Glueck 1930 – Chapter 3) and should be responded to accordingly through diversion and minimal necessary intervention (see 'Protective Youth Justice: Child-Friendly Justice' in Chapter 4). The model supports an approach to responding to children's offending (related) behaviour where possible (necessary) through normal child-rearing practices in the context of the family (see also Harding and Beecroft 2013). Where this process of normalisation does not or cannot occur and professional intervention is required, then its focus should be on promoting positive behaviours and outcomes for children (e.g. enabling their access to universal entitlements to services, activities, support and information) and children should be *worked with* in participatory ways to achieve these aims. This approach directly contrasts with the 'new youth justice' tendency to *do to* children by prioritising the prevention of negative behaviours and outcomes using correctionalist, punitive and interventionist methods. In this way, PYJ is not anti-intervention, but more opposed to unnecessary formal intervention, punitive intervention and interventionism.

The PYJ approach proposes that diversionary interventions for children who offend should be child-friendly/appropriate, rather than punitive or grounded in justice concerns. Formal interventions that are punitive and retributive (or at least experienced in that way by children) can have unintended consequences that exacerbate existing problems and offending trajectories (Kelly 2012), so are anathema to a children-first, positive approach to delivering youth justice. Similarly, the justice-based strategy of proportionality (matching the punishment to the seriousness of the offence) is inherently malleable and subject to a range of influences (e.g. political agenda, public opinion, practitioner discretion) that can encourage punitive responses

(Muncie 2008) such as increased accountability for children who offend (Hazel 2008), adulterised sentencing (Cavadino and Dignan 2006) and repressive crime control initiatives (Jepsen 2006). Arguably, some restorative justice has adopted these negative characteristics when applied to children who offend, prioritising the needs of the victim and the need for the 'offender' to restore and repair harm caused over the needs and status of the child (cf. Sherman and Strang 2007; Wilcox 2004).

Just as PYJ is not grounded in traditional justice-based models, neither is its diversionary emphasis underpinned by welfare. The welfare-based model of youth justice (needs over deeds, care over control; see Chapters 1 and 4) is guided by responding to the needs of the child (as constructed by adults) in order to provide a safety net which children must not be allowed to fall beneath (Hill *et al.* 2007). However, this needs-led, safety net focus is wedded to notions of treatment and correctionalism as opposed to the promotion of positive behaviours and outcomes by a more prospective and ambitious children-first approach. There are issues with welfare-based youth justice: the adult-centric approach taken can overlook the potential for children to contribute to service design and delivery as active constructors of their own futures and correctionalist welfare approaches may encourage interventionism, net-widening and indeterminism in the YJS. The children-first focus of PYJ addresses the adult-centrism and interventionism of welfarism by prioritising diversion into youth justice and broader interventions that promote positive behaviours and outcomes (see point 3).

The diversionary objectives of PYJ are animated by the strategy of **systems management** (see Tutt and Giller 1987), which holds that 'outcomes for individual children and the way in which the Youth Justice System as a whole works can be changed by managing processes and targeting specific decision-making points within the system itself' (Haines, in Goldson 2008: 349). Taking a systems management perspective, the YJS can be understood as an interconnected, mutually reinforcing series of decision-making points about children and young people, such as decisions to arrest, bail, remand, divert, punish, sentence/prosecute, imprison and release. Each decision has consequences for subsequent decisions, so targeting these decision-making points and encouraging children-first, diversionary and promotional practice at each stage should influence how individual children are treated in the YJS and should change the focus and shape of the YJS as a whole (Haines and Case 2015). Consequently, systems management is a principle with a clear philosophy (children first) and an explicit purpose (children as part of the solution to the problem, prevention is better than cure); challenging the unprincipled net-widening potential of the 'new youth justice'. As we will see below, systems management also seeks to enhance youth justice through principled goals (evidence-based partnership working, responsibilising adults) and outcomes (promoting positive behaviours and outcomes), thus giving clear direction to youth justice decision-making about children.

Promoting positive behaviours and outcomes

The previous chapter explored how prevention has become the principal aim of the modernised, 'new' YJS, encouraging an almost exclusive focus on preventing negative behaviours (e.g. offending, reoffending, substance use, antisocial behaviour) and negative outcomes (e.g. reconviction, exposure to risk factors). However, this negative and retrospective focus has been criticised for fostering punitive and criminalising youth justice responses that problematise (rather than normalise) offending by children and that socially exclude (rather than include) children when they offend by labelling and constructing them as 'young offenders'. Most prevention work is targeted (not universal) and takes place with identified offenders or children considered to be at risk of offending, which tends to draw these children further into the YJS. PYJ argues for a children-first response where intervention prioritises social inclusion, participation and engagement as drivers of the youth justice process and vehicles to promote positive behaviours and outcomes (e.g. access to universal services, rights and entitlements, diversion into child-focused services outside of the YJS, engagement with education, family cohesion, citizenship). This promotional approach is a central principle of the PYJ model, considered to be a progressive, normalising, valid and child-friendly/appropriate way of responding to children who offend and/or demonstrate associated problems (Case and Haines 2015a). This avoids the exclusionary potential of the prevention-obsessed, offender-first strategies of the 'new youth justice' (see Case and Haines 2009; see also Chapter 5).

An important positive behaviour/outcome for youth justice practice is children's *engagement*, which overarches other positive principles such as participation, legitimacy and relationship-building. Engagement encompasses children's meaningful involvement in and commitment to the decisions and outcomes at every stage of the youth justice process (e.g. assessment, sentencing, intervention planning; see also social development model – Chapter 3). As a principle of PYJ, engagement is crucial to effective systems management in the pursuit of child-friendly/appropriate, diversionary and positive youth justice responses. However, children's engagement in the YJS has been relatively overlooked in the construction of policy and practice guidelines. According to Williamson and Cairns (2005: 1):

> Principles are one thing; practice is another. Too often the aim of engaging young people is vitiated [made less effective] by existing structures of professional power and cultural attitudes.

A clear barrier to effective engagement with young people in the youth justice context is the underlying emphasis on enforcement and compliance, which can disengage children and hamper relationship-building between children and YOT staff (Case and Haines 2015a). The full and complete integration of young people's engagement with and participation in youth justice decision-making is a constant difficulty because YOT practitioners have a statutory obligation to enforce the non-negotiable rules and regulations and to ensure children's compliance with court orders (see CRC 2008). The enforcement-led nature of child–practitioner relationships in the YJS can reduce children's capacity, motivation, willingness and confidence to participate and to engage with youth justice services, while also reducing the capacity and willingness of practitioners and organisations to fully include and engage with young people. The limited body of engagement research and guidance that exists in the youth justice field has privileged the adult perspectives and skills development of practitioners at the expense of children's perspectives, despite successive children's rights conventions advocating that children have the right to be listened to regarding all decisions that affect them (Article 12 of the UNCRC). The neglect of children's voices in youth justice processes and the extent of centralised practice prescriptions, according to critics, has essentially rendered children's subjective experiences 'unknowable' (Phoenix and Kelly 2013). However, all is not lost.

A contemporary movement of academics and practitioners has championed the engagement of children in youth justice processes, for example, through 'maximizing the discretion of youth justice workers to hear and respond to young people's voices, and to 'rethink aspects of practice that impair what can be heard and acted upon' (Drake *et al*. 2014: 23). Contemporary research has indicated that enabling children's engagement with decision-making processes and with the design, implementation and evaluation of youth justice services can facilitate strategic planning, can enhance the meaningful and appropriate decision-making of practitioners and services, and can improve the quality of the child–adult relationships that influence intervention effectiveness (see also Nacro 2011; HMI Probation 2009). Indeed, Creaney and Smith (2014: 83) assert that

> in order to reconcile the lack of user-led engagement of offenders, and experiences of disempowerment, the priority should be, throughout the Youth Justice System, to involve young people in assessment and decision-making processes.

The PYJ model promotes children's engagement and participation in shaping youth justice services as having multiple potential benefits, such as improved understanding of youth justice processes and enhanced self-confidence among children, leading to a greater likelihood of both engagement and compliance with youth justice provision (see, for example, Hart and Thompson 2009; Nacro Cymru 2009[12]).

STOP AND THINK

YJB *Participation Strategy* (2016)

In 2016, the YJB published their *Participation Strategy: Giving Young People a Voice in Youth Justice* (YJB 2016), which was authored by Mark Cox of YJB Cymru (Senior Advisor, Oversight and Support), with input from various YJB departments and an editorial from Dusty Kennedy. The strategy committed to 'embedding young people's participation' at all stages of the YJS and giving young people much more say in youth justice decisions that affect them (cf. Article 12 of the UNCRC) and in the planning, delivery and evaluation of youth justice services (YJB 2016). According to the strategy, 'for children and young people, participation is an active, informed and voluntary process where they are able to express views and make decisions on issues that affect them' (YJB 2016: 3). Accordingly, the YJB established a set of core principles to underpin future participatory working with children and young people: voluntarism, inclusivity, hearing and respecting young people's voices, enabling young people to benefit from participation, communicating the outcomes of participation and improving services. A series of barriers to effective participation by young people were identified, including lack of confidence, communication problems, distrust of adults, unsatisfactory previous experiences, attendance difficulties and removal of choices through court sentencing. The strategy emphasised the significant practical benefits of enhancing young people's participation in youth justice services, including increased engagement, improved behaviour, respect and confidence, enhanced relationships between practitioners and young people, more inclusive decision-making and improved youth justice services based on need. While noting progressive participatory practice that already existed in the YJS (e.g. taking more account of young people's views through AssetPlus, ongoing consultation in policy development processes), the YJB acknowledged that effective participation is a work in progress and that continued efforts are needed in relation to communication, service commissioning, monitoring and development, effective practice and Government decision-making processes (YJB 2016).

So, what do YOU think? Have another look through Section 4 of this chapter and also read through the YJB *Participation Strategy* (it's not very long). Maybe even find time to read 'Children First, Offenders Second: The centrality of engagement in positive youth justice' by Case and Haines (2015a). You could then consider these five not-so-easy questions:

- What is the difference between engagement and participation?
- Does the YJB *Participation Strategy* have a sufficient focus on engagement?
- What are the similarities and differences between the YJB *Participation Strategy* and the central principles of PYJ?
- Could the YJB *Participation Strategy* have been influenced in any way by the 'distinct' policy context in which its author worked?
- How can the engagement and participation of young people be encouraged by YOT practitioners, by youth justice policies and by reconstructing the 'young offender'?

Another key element of engagement, **legitimacy**, directly challenges the potentially labelling and stigmatising effects of contact with the YJS. The concept of legitimacy refers to the maintenance of social order, suggesting that individuals are more likely to adhere to social norms and to obey the law if they view state authority and the discharge of authority by agents of the state as moral, just and fair (see Tyler 2006, 2007). In the criminal/youth justice context, the argument is that if interactions with and the behaviour of agencies and agents of law and order (e.g. police, courts) are perceived as moral, just and fair (i.e. legitimate), then individuals who break the law are more likely to perceive their treatment (even if it involves punishment) as legitimate and are more likely to obey the law in the future (cf. Tankebe 2008; Tyler 2006). In contrast, if treatment by criminal justice agencies and agents is perceived as illegitimate (e.g. immoral, unjust, unfair) then reoffending is more likely to occur. Research in the youth justice context has identified that perceptions of illegitimacy focus on treatment that is punitive, coercive, controlling and disproportionate (see Hawes 2013; Phoenix 2009; Jamieson 2006) and these perceptions can lead to resentment, disengagement and deviancy amplification (see also Chapter 2). As such, perceptions of legitimacy constitute a positive outcome for youth justice practice; the assertion being that they can be enhanced by child-friendly/appropriate, promotional, inclusive and engaging treatment within the YJS.

Evidence-based partnership

The PYJ model demands that its child-friendly/appropriate, diversionary and positive principles be turned into strategies through the mobilisation of *evidence*. The generation of meaningful evidence to inform youth justice strategy and practice should occur in *partnerships* between key stakeholders in the YJS, particularly, children, families, youth justice professionals (e.g. staff in YOTs and the Secure Estate, police, magistrates/judges, lawyers), policy-makers, politicians, civil servants and academic researchers. PYJ argues for the social construction of youth justice structures (partnerships) that implement a principled strategy (evidence-based policy and practice) in order to pursue the overarching principles of a children-first approach (Case and Haines 2014). Evidence-based partnership working should be integrated at strategic and practice levels and should emphasise the participation and engagement of children, rather than downplaying the potential contribution by pursuing more adult-centric 'trialogues' (three-way dialogues) between policy-makers, practitioners and researchers. Evidence-based partnership is, therefore, both a principle/strategy for practice development and an explicit challenge to the tendency of individual agencies to become excessively introspective and to over-rely on the simplistic, often risk-focused programmes and interventions marketed by the YJB as part of the KEEPs guidance (see Stephenson *et al.* 2011). The former chair of the YJB, Professor Rod Morgan, has been highly critical of the 'programme fetishism' of Government/YJB (Morgan 2002: 8); the privileging of pseudo-psychological, offender- and offence-focused (correctional), off-the-shelf programmes in guidance to youth justice practitioners. This limitation has been compounded by the YJB tendency to 'consult' with practitioners on how to effectively implement pre-formed policy/strategy (see also Edwards and Hughes 2009), rather than how to design and populate it in the first place, for example, during the implementation of the Scaled Approach to assessment and intervention (see Chapter 5). Therefore, evidence-based partnership between all key stakeholders in the youth justice process (including practitioners and children) underpins principled and progressive children-first understandings and responses to youth offending, while protecting against the reductionist, potentially criminalising and prescriptive programme fetishism promoted by the 'new youth justice' (Haines and Case 2015).

The principle of evidence-based partnership, particularly between practitioners and practice-focused academics, is not new, but it is experiencing a resurgence in popularity in contemporary youth justice as YOTs and the YJB come under increasing pressure to find alternative ways of working and doing more (or the same) with less due to economic austerity. The YJB has published an *Academic/YOT Partnership Working Guide* (YJB 2017) that provides practical advice for setting up and running evidence-based partnerships between universities and YOTs. The Working Guide also offers some limited case study examples and testimonies as to the benefits of these partnerships, which include: knowledge transfer, developing and sharing good practice, enhancing staff training and obtaining funding, with these benefits often achieved with the strategic use of student placements (YJB 2017).

The evidence-based Reflective Friend Research model of social science research (Case and Haines 2014) emphasises the *relational* aspects of meaningful, valid and context-specific knowledge development in the youth justice field (and beyond) through engagement with practitioner experience, expertise and discretion. Reflective Friend Research (RFR) evolves through five iterative, interrelated relational processes between the researcher and the researched (e.g. YOT staff, YJB, children, young people, families), with the researched parties reconstructed as active research partners, not passive recipients of research processes:

1   *Situated learning*: researchers actively immerse themselves in the everyday contexts
    of the research partners (e.g. the practice environments of YOT staff and children
    attending the YOT, including decision-making structures and processes), working
    with research partners to co-construct their learning, knowledge and understand-
    ing of the practical realities of the YJS. This can involve the co-development of
    research agendas, explanatory frameworks and the design, implementation and
    evaluation of youth justice services, disposals, assessments and interventions.

2   *Research partnerships*: situating research within the everyday contexts of partici-
    pants can foster the co-construction of knowledge and understanding through
    equitable and participative research partnerships. These reflective partnerships
    can resemble communities of practice (see Bredo 2005; Lave and Wenger 2002)
    that enable participants to contribute their expert knowledge, experiences, sub-
    jective interpretations and meanings to every aspect of the research (knowledge
    generation) process.

3   *Enhanced access*: situated research partnerships can facilitate researcher access
    to vital facets of the research process, which can include: research *participants/
    partners* (e.g. children, parents/carers, YOT staff, government ministers, policy-
    makers), key datasets locally and nationally, internal documentation and knowl-
    edge generation processes (meetings, steering groups, committees, advisory
    panels; see Case [2014] case study of YJB Cymru). This privileged access promotes
    more context-sensitive and detailed knowledge that is faithful to the expert per-
    spectives of research partners.

4   *Reflective engagement*: better understanding of the practice context and stakeholder
    experiences is facilitated by reflective, reciprocal feedback and constant dialogue
    between all research partners. Prioritising the relational aspects of applied research
    can promote 'dense relations of mutual engagement' (Wenger 1998: 74) between
    research partners that foster sense of mutual trust, confidence, openness, respect,
    interactivity and perceived competence (see also Cousin and Deepwell 2005).

5   *Critical friendship*: the relational aspect of critical friendship is vital if research
    partners are to avoid potentially invalidating influences born of friendship, prox-
    imity, loyalty, protectiveness and empathy (see Baskerville and Goldblatt 2009);
    influences such as bias, subjectivity, lack of independence, self-fulfilling practice
    and proselytising. It is crucial that the independence of all partners is maintained
    so that reflective engagement can be used as a tool to enhance the validity and
    appropriateness of research processes (e.g. evaluation of practice, explanation of
    behaviour) and the generation of knowledge and evidence.

The long-term, embedded partnership nature of these research relationships can
give them sufficient flexibility and resilience to withstand the inherent stress and
pressure of everyday youth justice practice, continued critical friendship and external
pressures, resulting in a strong connectivity that leaves partners more amenable and
receptive to new ideas and influence (cf. Losada and Heaphy 2004). The relational
nature of RFR is underpinned by these five research elements/principles, facilitating
the production of new information and understandings for participants as each element develops (see also Gittell 2003).

A contemporary illustration of evidence-based partnership principles has been
developed in Greater Manchester (England). I discussed the evolution of the Greater
Manchester Youth Justice–University Partnership (GMYJUP), a case study example in

the YJB Working Guide, with Anna-Christina Jones, the Partnership Research Associate, and Paul Axon, a founder member of GMYJUP and Director of Targeted Services for Oldham Positive Steps (the YOT substitute organisation).

CONVERSATIONS

Greater Manchester Youth Justice–University Partnership (GMYJUP)

Steve: What is the GMYJUP? How and why did it develop?

Anna-Christina Jones/Paul Axon: The GMYJUP is a collaboration between youth justice academics and practitioners, established to support Greater Manchester to become a beacon region for innovation and excellence in youth justice practice, while advancing strong outcomes for children, families and communities in our local area. Founded officially in 2014, the GMYJUP model took inspiration from the experience of academic-practitioner partnerships, for whom the formalisation of their collaboration had delivered enhanced mutual benefits. Our memorandum of understanding formalised an already-established alliance between academics from Manchester Metropolitan University (MMU), management and practitioners from the ten Greater Manchester youth justice services and representatives from the YJB.

All members of GMYJUP benefit reciprocally through the assistance of the partnership, generally without the need for financial contributions. Notably, youth justice practice in Greater Manchester has benefited from academic-led practitioner training on areas of criminological theory and the development of a research base to address local concerns through hosting student placements. In turn, the academic partner, MMU, has been able to offer both placement-based dissertation projects and guest lectures from youth justice practitioners to their students. These activities foster uniquely bidirectional practices of knowledge exchange between the forums of academia and practice, enabling each to influence the direction of the other.

Furthermore, in addition to supporting the operations of each of the partners through the skills and capabilities of the others, our multidisciplinary team now works collaboratively to identify progressive mutual aspirations, pursuing opportunities to improve youth justice practice in our region. One such initiative resulted in GMYJUP being awarded funding for a pioneering Knowledge Transfer Partnership (KTP) project, led on behalf of the Greater Manchester regions by Positive Steps in Oldham. The first in the field of youth justice, the KTP builds on the collaborative foundations established by the GMYJUP partnership by seconding of a staff member from MMU to the Greater Manchester Youth Justice Services on a full-time basis for two years.

Steve: Does the GMYJUP have key principles, structures, strategies and practices?

Anna-Christina/Paul: Our partnership shares a number of key principles and the KTP project has been established to distil these principles into enduring structures and strategies to be embedded in youth justice practice in the Greater Manchester region. Although the process of establishing the structures and strategies in practice is not yet complete, we are able to detail the key overarching principles that these will be based on.

Firstly, one of the primary principles of GMYJUP is to connect evidence and practice more meaningfully, using this coalition to explore the promotion of progressive youth justice. Consequently, we support strengths-based approaches to youth justice practice. We believe that desistance can be best encouraged through positive, strengths-based, self-directed and socially valuable activities (see Haines and Case 2015), so a key objective of our partnership is to support the implementation of 'what works' from desistance literature in practice.

Another key principle of GMYJUP is the importance of meaningful participation of young people in the youth justice system. It is the responsibility of the YJS to instigate and facilitate young people's right to express their opinions a meaningful way (Haines and Case 2008), and accordingly we seek to challenge the disempowering nature inherent in some elements of contemporary youth justice practice. We want to move away from tokenistic attempts at consultation, towards a more truly participatory and collaborative way of working with young people that makes relevant their identities, culture, experiences and perspectives and uses these to support their desistance journeys, pioneering the application of youth participatory action research (YPAR) in a youth justice setting.

Steve: In your view, what does the GMYJUP offer to progressive and positive youth justice?

Anna-Christina/Paul: The GMYJUP partnership has a lot to offer those seeking a more progressive, positive approach to youth justice. Firstly, the partnership itself provides an innovative and progressive model for the redevelopment of service delivery in the youth justice sector. Even in its most simple form, our partnership has demonstrated significant benefits, broadening knowledge in both academia and practice and enabling the disciplines to challenge one another. At its more ambitious, our partnership has also established initiatives which develop a more progressive, innovative youth justice service provision in a major region of England, making it more strengths focused, evidence led and young person centred. Secondly, in seeking to explore evidence-based approaches to youth justice, GMYJUP utilises theoretical concepts that align with PYJ, including the application of desistance approaches and the enhancement of participatory working with young people.

Furthermore, by piloting the application of YPAR approaches with a youth justice cohort, GMYJUP practically seeks to find ways to prioritise children's engagement over their enforced compliance, their participation over prescription and instruction, and their capacities and strengths over their deficits and differences to adults (see Haines and Case 2015). In doing this, we are valuing the expert contributions of young people and championing their right to help shape policy and practice (Haines and Case 2008).

Naturally, we suggest that GMYJUP lends a distinctly practical contribution, developing a practice-based progressive youth justice by implementing a strengths-based model based in both the PYJ model and the desistance paradigm. Output is co-developed, theoretically informed, strengths focused and youth led, offering an alternative framework of effective youth justice provision and making a unique contribution to the construction and development of contemporary youth justice.

An aspect of evidence-based partnership that has been much neglected in the construction of youth justice policy and practice is collaboration between academics and the State (e.g. national and local Government, politicians, YJB, civil servants). Youth justice is, in large part, a State-led activity and the scholarship and research of criminologists (particularly critical youth criminologists) often brings them into conflict with the State (cf. Hope and Walters 2008). Traditionally, academic criminologists have held a degree of distrust and scepticism regarding the legitimacy, credibility and transparency of the State when it deals with academia, researchers and research processes, findings and recommendations (see Hope 2005; Haines and Drakeford 1998). For their part, agents of the State have argued that criminology is anti-State, inherently negative and incapable of offering positive alternatives, which has led to resistance to soliciting academic perspectives and engaging with academic critique (see Section 1, 'Telling it like it is: Thawing the YJB–academia cold war').

The ongoing 'public criminology' debate focuses on tension for criminologists between providing policy- and practice-relevant scholarship and research on the one hand and academic rigour and critical reflection on the other (Loader and Sparks 2010) – a tension with clear similarities to the YJB position as a policy adviser to Government and practice mediator for YOTs. The PYJ position reflects that expressed by John Drew in his interview, namely that institutionalised distrust between academics and the State is an unhelpful obstacle to the development of critical and reflective youth justice policy, strategy and practice nationally and locally. Indeed, he went on to argue that addressing this distrust was an explicit objective during his time in post:

> I viewed the YJB as a bridge between different elements of the YJS to bring them into balance with one another, such as between policy-makers and academics. I wanted this to lead to more collaboration and less dogma, producing the sort of partnerships that we wanted.
>
> (John Drew 2017, personal interview)

Accordingly, the research that underpins the PYJ principles has been developed through a 20-year plus partnership of critical friendship between academic researchers, practitioners and representatives of the State nationally such as the Welsh Government (see Case et al. 2005), YJB Cymru (see Case 2014) and locally (e.g. local authorities and YOTs across Wales; see Haines and Case 2015; Case and Haines 2014; Haines et al. 2013).

Responsibilising adults

The final principle strategy that animates PYJ is that child-friendly, diversionary, positive and evidence-based practice must be supported and facilitated by responsibilised adults, in stark contrast to the legacy of responsibilising children and their families for the success or otherwise of youth justice sentences and interventions. PYJ argues that adults (i.e. youth justice professionals) should be made primarily responsible for constructing and delivering effective youth justice (although the meaningful participation and engagement of children in design and delivery remains essential) as they hold the power in the youth justice dynamic. The basis of the children-first model is that youth justice must recognise the inherent status and (relative lack of) capacity of the 'child'. Children's ability/capacity to make decisions about their own behaviour and to lead independent lives is restricted by the lack of responsibility, power and voice assigned to them in adult-led societies (Freeman 2007; Such and Walker 2004). Indeed, as argued by critics of 'new youth justice' responsibilisation strategies (see Chapter 5), it would seem that children are not given full social responsibility over any aspect of their life or behaviour apart from their offending behaviour (the irresponsible–responsible dichotomy). Therefore, as children do not have full social responsibilities, so adult youth justice professionals must fully accept their responsibilities towards children (Haines and Case 2015). The principle of responsibilising adults on the basis of the child's relative powerlessness resonates with the progressive youth justice model known as 'moral youth justice' (Arthur 2016) that has been developed by Raymond Arthur, a Professor of Law at Northumbria University. I explored this contemporary model in a 'Conversation' with Raymond in January 2017.

CONVERSATIONS

Moral youth justice

Steve: How did your focus on 'moral youth justice' emerge?

Raymond Arthur: Children and young people are less mature than adults in terms of their judgement and sensation-seeking and they experience difficulties in weighing and comparing consequences when making decisions. These developmental differences suggest that children who offend may not yet be developed enough to understand the wrongfulness of what they have done. As such, they are the least ready to assume the responsibilities associated with autonomous individuality and the most seriously in need of adult help and guidance. However, in England and Wales, young defendants who may not understand the consequence of their offending, including those with impaired mental capacity, are often exposed to the full rigours of the YJS unless their decision-making capacities are impaired by a mental illness. The YJS does not ask whether a child can live up to the moral and psychological components of criminal responsibility; that is, whether a child, by virtue of her or his individual discernment and understanding, can be held responsible for their behaviour. This approach to working with children in conflict with the law effectively constructs such children as non-children who do not deserve to remain children – including having the right to make mistakes. Consequently, the rights of the child when labelled an offender, in particular marginalised and socially excluded children, become invisible and ignored.

Steve: What does your perspective contribute to the field of youth justice?

Raymond: My perspective argues that children have a right to respect for their evolving capacities and that respecting this right would redirect the YJS towards a normative framework better equipped to accommodate the realities of childhood; one which contains a clear foregrounding of the child's experiences and the reality of their daily lives and in which the child's experience of vulnerability and powerlessness is embedded throughout. If such a focus on children's rights were applied to children in conflict with the law it would ensure that criminal liability could only be imposed upon children who had sufficient mental capacity, competence and maturity to understand the nature of their conduct and to exercise volition over their behaviour. Such a rights-based approach to children in conflict with the law could help to achieve recognition of the child's evolving capacities and therefore holds significant potential to address many of the profound theoretical and practical shortcomings of the YJS. Such a rights-based approach would also better serve the twin goals of the YJS to prevent offending by children and young people (Crime and Disorder Act 1998, sec. 37) and to have regard to the welfare of the child (Children and Young Persons Act 1933, sec. 44). This focus on children as rights holders would avoid conflict between the competing rights of young people, parents, victims and the State and instead create a rhetoric which focuses more on adult responsibility and children's needs and has a larger focus on all of the issues affecting the child.

Steve: What do you think is the potential for your perspective to be accepted and integrated across contemporary youth justice systems?

Raymond: What is evident is that the YJS in England and Wales uses an adult template to measure children's criminal responsibility and overlooks children's particular vulnerabilities. This approach ensures that the power imbalance between children and adults is sustained, the special status of childhood is diminished and the child's human rights are violated. As Lord Dholakia stated when introducing the Age of Criminal Responsibility Bill in the House of Lords 'children who are too young to attend secondary school can be prosecuted and receive a criminal record' (*Hansard* HL Deb vol. 749, col. 476, 479, 8 November 2013). In England and Wales, children who are alleged to have broken the law are held accountable for their actions through an adversarial system that prioritises the finding of guilt or innocence and sentencing for a particular offence. This approach deflects blame for the social conditions which underpin youth offending to individual children who are ill-equipped to participate in formal criminal proceedings, even in the specialist youth court. There is a greater need to develop structures to address inequality and disadvantage and to support children to exercise legal capacity, including supported decision-making and a recognition that background social and political contexts are central to facilitating autonomy. In other spheres of law (for example, the right of children to make decisions regarding their own medical treatment), we have seen judicial recognition of autonomy interests and their evolution into autonomy rights.

The UNCRC represents the most comprehensive legally binding statement of children's rights. The UNCRC promotes the view that all children, including those involved in offending behaviour, are invested with important rights, including the right to have their best interests as a primary consideration in all court actions involving them (Article 3) and the right of children accused of engaging in criminal behaviour to be treated in a manner consistent with the promotion of the 'child's sense of dignity and worth . . . and which takes into account the child's age' (Article 40). Compliance with Article 40 of the UNCRC requires that criminal proceedings should consider whether a child can live up to the moral and psychological components of criminal responsibility; that is, whether a child, by virtue of her or his individual discernment and understanding, can be held responsible for their behaviour. The UNCRC recognises that young people under the age of 18 may need special protection because of their age or emotional development. The most recent observations of the UN Committee on the Rights of the Child reiterate that the principle that the child's best interests are taken as a primary consideration is still not reflected in criminal justice law, policy and judicial decision-making in the UK (Concluding observations on the fifth periodic report of the UK of Great Britain and Northern Ireland, CRC 2016: para. 25).

The English judiciary has highlighted the importance of the UN Convention on the Rights of the Child. In *R v G* ([2003] UKHL 50), Lord Steyn believed that the UNCRC created a norm which acknowledged that the YJS should take account of a defendant's age, level of maturity, and intellectual and emotional capacity. Lord Steyn emphasised that ignoring the special position of children in the YJS is not acceptable in a modern civil society. In the same case, Lord Bingham held that it was neither moral nor just to convict a young person on the strength of what someone else would have comprehended if the defendant himself had no such comprehension. More recently, the Court of Appeal stated in *R v L* ([2013] EWCA Crim 991), in the context of young defendants trafficked into the UK who had been convicted of various offences including the production and supply of cannabis and use of a forged passport, that age is always a relevant factor in the case of a child defendant, which may significantly diminish, and in some cases effectively extinguish, their culpability. These judgements offer encouragement and an opportunity for the relevant authorities to consult about the best way forward in respect of a child who is about to be prosecuted for an offence, rather than to embark on a prosecution. For instance, the youth court could be radically reformed and developed into a problem-solving youth court, involving the co-location of relevant children's and youth services in court buildings and provision for review of sentences by the sentencing judge. Such a shift would permit the reinvigoration of the welfare principle (Children and Young Persons Act 1933, sec. 44[1]) and a renewed focus on ensuring children's underlying needs are met. Alternatively, civil proceedings under the Children Act 1989 could be more appropriate than criminal proceedings – a return to welfare-based responses to offending by children under the moral youth justice model.

PYJ contends that it is the responsibility of adult professionals (e.g. youth justice staff, policy-makers, politicians, academics) to design, deliver and evaluate diversionary and promotional youth justice responses, working in partnership with children and families to ensure that decisions and responses at all stages of the YJS are consistently child-friendly/appropriate and evidence based. The principle of responsibilising adults is derived from the children's rights context of the UNCRC, which promotes a series of universally agreed, non-negotiable minimum standards for the civil, cultural, economic, political and social rights of children (UNICEF 1989). Where children-first PYJ moves beyond the UNCRC, however, is in its promotion of *maximum outcomes* for all children, rather than simply *minimum standards* – with these maximum outcomes being the responsibility of adults. This principled aspect of PYJ has clear links to the *Extending Entitlement* youth inclusion strategy in Wales

(National Assembly Policy Unit 2002), which responsibilises adult service providers and policy-makers to ensure that children have unobstructed access to support, services, opportunities and information that enables them to access their universal entitlements (see Section 4 of this chapter). Broadly similar social policies for children ('Every Child Matters'; Department for Education and Skills 2004) and young people ('Youth Matters'; Department for Education and Skills 2005), are promoted in England, setting out 'a series of global objectives for children's well-being in positive terms' (Smith 2011: 173). However, critics have argued that English social policy for children and young people focuses more on risk reduction and making children responsible for taking advantage of the opportunities offered to them, rather than promoting unconditional, universal entitlements to support, guidance and opportunities as in Wales (Case and Haines 2010; Hoyle 2008). The contrasting English social policy (and 'new youth justice') view of access to rights and opportunities as conditional on children's behaviour and the responsibility of children was illustrated by Tony Blair's proclamation while in opposition that there can be 'no rights without responsibilities' (in Giddens 1998: 65). A principled, children-first approach, therefore, challenges the responsibilising excesses of anglicised social and youth justice policy by responsibilising adult stakeholders for the nature of youth justice services and the outcomes that children in the YJS achieve as a result.

To summarise, the principled and progressive children-first model of PYJ was constructed as a direct challenge to the perceived negative, risk-focused, retrospective and adult-centric nature of the 'new youth justice' (Haines and Case 2015). Proponents of PYJ believe that children-first youth justice policy and practice should be child-friendly and child-appropriate, maintaining sensitivity to the status of 'child', to children's universal entitlements and to the inherent responsibilities of adults in all dealings with children, including those who offend. The objective of 'special treatment' of children is pursued through the *normalisation* of everyday childhood behaviour and the normalisation of the treatment that children receive following demonstration of need, deprivation or problems. Accordingly, children should be diverted from the potentially iatrogenic consequences of their contact with the YJS, as opposed to the State and adults seeking to inflict retributive punishment, administer punitive justice or impose adult-centric, needs-led welfare to admonish or cure the child. The PYJ model emphasises *diversion and minimum necessary intervention* with children, challenging the interventionist and net-widening excesses of punishment, justice and welfare models. PYJ prioritises the *promotion of positive behaviours and outcomes* through the *legitimate participation and engagement* of children and their families in youth justice processes, rather than subjecting children to disengaging and inequitable treatment that could result in social exclusion, stigmatisation, marginalisation and further offending. PYJ encourages the *responsibilisation of adults* (practitioners, policy-makers, politicians, parents, researchers) to facilitate specific processes and outcomes: *child-focused decision-making* across the YJS and beyond (systems management), *evidence-based partnership* between children, families, other practitioners, researcher, agencies and the State and the *promotion* of children's universal entitlements, universal rights and capacities in order to realise positive behaviours and outcomes for children who offend.

5 EASY PIECES

5 Children-first positive youth justice: a new frontier

1 *Child-friendly/appropriate*: key stakeholders in the YJS should construct under-standings of youth offending in a principled, 'children-first' way – prioritising the status of the child and their relative physical, cognitive and social immaturity and powerlessness, as opposed to adulterising children.

2 *Diversion and systems management*: PYJ argues for a diversionary and minimum necessary intervention response to children who offend in order to avoid the labelling, stigmatising and iatrogenic consequences of system contact. Children should be worked with and diverted into positive interventions through child-friendly/appropriate decisions made at every stage of the youth justice process (systems management).

3 *Promoting positive behaviours and outcomes*: the focus of a modern, progressive (positive) youth justice should be the promotion of positive behaviours/outcomes for children (not prioritising the prevention of negative behaviour/outcomes) through their legitimate participation in and engagement with the design and delivery of sentences and interventions.

4 *Evidence-based partnership*: the child-friendly/appropriate, diversionary, positive/promotional and participatory principles of PYJ can be animated as strategies by the construction of a meaningful evidence-based partnerships between key stakeholders in the YJS, particularly children, families, youth justice professionals, policy-makers, politicians, civil servants and academic researchers – thus avoiding the reductionist 'programme fetishism' of the 'new youth justice'.

5 *Responsibilising adults*: it should be the responsibility of adult professionals (e.g. youth justice staff, policy-makers, politicians, academics) to design, deliver and evaluate diversionary and promotional youth justice responses, working in partnership with children and families to ensure that decisions and responses at all stages of the YJS are consistently child-friendly/appropriate, diversionary, positive/promotional and evidence based.

Bringing youth justice up to date: the YJB Strategic Plan 2019–2022

The detailed exposition of the 'children first, offenders second' model of Positive Youth Justice (admittedly a slightly biased account from its co-creator!) leads us neatly into a significant legislative and strategic development that brings youth justice in England and Wales right up to date – the *Youth Justice Board for England and Wales Strategic Plan 2019–2022* (YJB 2019a). Following from the Taylor Report (2016) and associated strategic advancements from the police, courts and the YJB in Wales (YJB Cymru), the YJB has committed to a new strategic direction for youth justice, wherein 'all of our [YJB] work will be guided by a child first, offender second principle' (YJB 2019a: 3). Concurrently, the *Youth Justice Blueprint for Wales* has outlined its guiding principle of a 'Child First' approach to youth justice, [to] ensure that it is child-centred rather than service focused' (MoJ and Welsh Government 2019). This strategic change of direction has been consolidated and formalised in a revised National Standards document titled *Standards for Children in the Youth Justice System* (YJB 2019b), which serves as a framework for youth justice (effective) practice, quality assurance, innovation and inspection. The new National Standards state that all youth justice practice must 'align with the YJB's child first, offender second principle' (YJB 2019b: 3).

The official commitment to a 'Child First' strategy of youth justice is a significant development in the progressive trajectory of the YJB – moving youth justice further away from the risk-led ('new youth justice') mechanisms of the post–Crime and Disorder Act decade, building on the diversionary ethos of the subsequent decade and aligning with contemporary priorities for more localised, integrated and child-friendly approaches to delivering youth justice. The Strategic Plan has been published in a context of continued annual decreases in FTEs and custody rates (YJB and MoJ 2020), yet where reoffending rates remain stubbornly fixed within the decreasing cohort of children in the YJS, many of whom experience multiple complex needs (Bateman and Wigzell 2019) and demonstrate challenging behaviour, especially those leaving custody (YJB 2019a). Furthermore, as discussed earlier in this chapter, BAME children remain over-represented across FTE, reoffending and custody cohorts, so disproportionality remains a significant systemic problem, one acknowledged by the Strategic Plan. Finally, the most significant socio-political, economic and global issue looming large over contemporary youth justice is the far-reaching effects of the COVID-19 pandemic since its onset in early 2020. Accordingly, the severe impact of COVID-19 on children in the YJS of England and Wales is examined in a special 'Telling it like it is' feature from Dr Kathy Hampson, which is presented in Appendix 6.

The new, dynamic vision of the YJB is for a fit-for-purpose YJS that addresses contemporary youth justice issues such as multiple complex needs, appropriate diversion, child-friendly justice and BAME disproportionality. The YJB has articulated a strategic plan for:

> A youth justice system that sees children as children, treats them fairly and helps them to build on their strengths so they can make a constructive contribution to society. This will prevent offending and create safer communities with fewer victims.
>
> (YJB 2019a: 6)

Indeed, this 'new' value-base for this progressive approach to youth justice reflects a child-centred, inclusive and collaborative organisation focused on promoting positive outcomes for children (YJB 2019a). Inevitably, the success of the YJB's vision will be judged by the reduction of the numbers of children in the YJS (including in custody) and reduction of reoffending rates. However, more positive-focused, less justice-based outcome measures for children in the YJS have been introduced to complement these traditional prevention/reduction outcomes: improving safety and well-being, improving 'outcomes' (e.g. positive outcomes during and after contact with the YJS) and recognising that solutions can lie outside the YJS (i.e. supporting diversion and integrated service provision). Taken together, therefore, the YJB wishes to pursue a strategic vision to work with 'children as children' using a 'positive approach' to reducing (re)offending, addressing unmet needs and promoting positive outcomes. The vehicle for pursuing this new strategic vision will be 'Child First' youth justice.

What is the YJB's 'Child First' strategic objective?

The YJB's strategy is underpinned and driven by a detailed definition (operationalisation) of 'Child First' as a key strategic objective (YJB 2019a), itself based on an earlier Board Information Paper (YJB 2018). The YJB definition has been explicitly adapted from the 'children first, offender second' principle of Haines and Case (2015) and augmented by elements of the 'constructive resettlement' model (Hazel *et al.* 2017; see later in this chapter). The Strategy outlines the key objectives of the Child First objective as to:

- Prioritise the best interests of children, recognising their particular needs, capacities, rights and potential. All work is child-focused and developmentally informed.
- Promote children's individual strengths and capacities as a means of developing their pro-social identity for sustainable desistance, leading to safer communities and fewer victims. All work is constructive and future-focused, built on supportive relationships that empower children to fulfil their potential and make positive contributions to society.
- Encourage children's active participation, engagement and wider social inclusion. All work promotes desistance through co-creation with children.
- Promote a childhood removed from the justice system, using pre-emptive prevention, diversion and minimal intervention. All work minimises criminogenic stigma from contact with the system.

(YJB 2019a: 7, see also 2019b)

The YJB's Strategic Plan 2019–2022 (YJB 2019a) underpins its vision, values, aims and central principle (Child First) with (at least) two emerging and increasingly evidence-based[13] areas of contemporary youth justice: Trauma Informed Practice and Resettlement and Transitions (typically pursued through Constructive Resettlement).

Trauma-informed practice

At the time of writing (November 2020), Trauma Informed Practice is unequivocally flavour of the month in the youth justice field – an approach benefiting from incremental political, policy and practice support, and consolidated by a growing (although not unproblematic) evidence base. The burgeoning popularity of Trauma Informed Practice is increasingly linked to and informed by the burgeoning Adverse Childhood Experiences (ACEs) movement and the traumas associated/synonymous with ACEs in understandings of children's offending (Lacey and Minnis 2020). The rapidly expanding ACEs evidence base links the cumulative effects of traumatic, adverse experiences in childhood (e.g. psychological, physical and sexual abuse, physical and emotional neglect, household dysfunction, mental illness, substance abuse, divorce) with harmful behaviours and negative outcomes in later life, including offending, aggression, imprisonment, psychiatric disorders, school exclusion, substance use and poverty (cf. Evans *et al.* 2020; McCartan 2018, 2020; MoJ and Welsh Government 2019). The common-sense and readily applicable nature of the ACEs evidence base to children who offend (especially children with multiple complex needs) has led to its acceptance amongst youth justice policy-making and practitioner stakeholders and its integration within much Trauma Informed Practice (McCartan 2020, 2018) as a purportedly holistic, integrated (multisystemic) approach.

The YJB Strategic Plan (YJB 2019a) commits to evaluating Trauma Informed Practice in order to consider it a suitability for further roll-out. The *Youth Justice Blueprint for Wales* goes further still, committing to Trauma Informed Practice as its guiding principle (alongside Child First) for youth justice in Wales. The Blueprint asserts that Trauma Informed Practice is to be embedded at all stages of the YJS and rolled out across the country 'to effect cultural and systemic change' (MoJ and Welsh Government 2019). The YJB Strategic Plan consolidates this commitment asserting that 'success' in relation to 'children first, offender second trauma-informed practice' will be evidenced in terms of reductions in (re)offending and custody, alongside improvements in resilience to trauma, social outcomes (relations with others, engagement with services), resettlement outcomes, transitions from youth to adult services and multi-agency working). However, the current status of Trauma Informed Practice as a runaway train in youth justice is arguably at odds with its relatively underdeveloped evidence base. There is a clear and present danger that the inherently common-sense nature of the seemingly conjoined trauma informed and ACEs agendas (cf. McCartan 2020) could motivate a widespread, uncritical and presumptive acceptance of Trauma Informed Practice across youth justice policy and practice without full and balanced consideration of its applicability, its appropriateness or the validity of the (largely ACEs) research evidence that guides the approach. For example, at least two key areas of evidential presumption can be identified at this early stage of implementation:

1   *Policy pre-emption*: Both the YJB Strategic Plan and the Welsh Blueprint state that Trauma Informed Practice requires further evaluation before its application across England and Wales (see also Evans *et al*. 2020). However, both strategy documents immediately follow their commitment to further evaluation with a commitment to immediate roll-out in policy (e.g. as a central principle of the YJS in Wales) and in practice (e.g. through 'success' measures in England and Wales), regardless of the tentative nature of existing evaluation results (see Cordis Bright 2017) and pre-emptive nature of future evaluation outcomes. This has shades of the 'policy-based evidence' agenda of the 'New Labour' Government (Goldson and Hughes 2010), where evidence was generated through research and consultation with practice to support and validate a pre-empted policy direction (e.g. the Scaled Approach; Haines and Case 2012). The apparent contradiction between under-developed, uncertain evidence base/evaluation outcomes and more developed, definitive policy commitments may be less about pre-emption and more a product of aspirational and overzealous wording at certain points in each strategy document – an expression of policy and practice enthusiasm for a very promising and ostensibly necessary new approach that could clearly align with and facilitate Child First principles (e.g. engagement/relationship-building, legitimacy, responsibilising adults, diversion, evidence-based partnership) if delivered appropriately.

2   *Evidential imputation*: At present, there is a worrying degree of imputation from policy-makers regarding the causal (deterministic) and predictive influence of ACEs on negative behaviours and outcomes in later life. This assumed causality and predictive validity serves as the rationale for retrospective assessments of ACEs/traumas, often leading to a quantified, cumulative and aggregated ACEs score to guide intervention with individuals, which itself could be an invalid and stigmatising approach (Lacey and Minnis 2020). Furthermore, the ACEs evidence base is, as yet, insufficiently developed to have conclusively evidenced causality

or how this causality may work, so we are left with a limited and oversimplistic understanding of how ACEs may influence offending (Lacey and Minnis 2020) or how interventions targeting ACEs (e.g. Trauma Informed Practice) may influence change in behaviour (i.e. What is their 'theory of change'?). Using imputed determinism to underpin an assessment-intervention framework has clear overlaps with the rationale for, and limitations of, the risk factor prevention paradigm (RFPP). Indeed, evaluations of Trauma Informed Practice make these overlaps explicit when discussing the aetiology of offending by children by stating, under the heading of 'Risk Factors', that 'There are factors, warning signs and issues that can alert us to potentially problematic behavior' (McCartan 2018). However, if ACEs and traumas were conceptualised and understood as correlations with later offending (i.e. as more likely to be evidenced in the past lives of children who offend than those who don't) rather than deterministic causes, then they could be understood and addressed in a more valid manner, for example, as historical examples of unmet need that may have influenced past behaviour, attitudes and experiences, but may not be influential now (so may not require intervention). Furthermore, constructing ACEs as unmet needs rather than quantified/factorised indicators of risk (i.e. risk factors) would move Trauma Informed Practice away from the iatrogenic, reductionist and responsibilising excesses of the RFPP, such that it does not become a deficit model by stealth or accident. Crucially, constructing ACEs as needs that correlate with undesirable outcomes could move Trauma Informed Practice towards the YJB's desired Child First strategic objective by enabling more valid and comprehensive (holistic) understandings of the child's current life (e.g. their multiple complex needs) and facilitating the Child First positive identity development and multi-agency working (e.g. diversion into more appropriate services) that can promote positive outcomes (Case and Browning 2021; Hazel *et al.* 2017).

Resettlement and transitions

The YJB Strategic Plan (consolidated by the *Youth Justice Blueprint for Wales*) emphasises that children within the Secure Estate are some of the most vulnerable in our society and that often, their behaviour has the most negative impact on communities (YJB 2019a; MoJ and Welsh Government 2019). The YJB has prioritised the effective and appropriate resettlement of children who transition out of custody, with the objective of promoting positive outcomes and futures for these children, in line with the new Child First strategic objective for youth justice in England and Wales. The effective resettlement priority is underpinned by a new evidence-based approach called Constructive Resettlement, which promotes collaborative working with children to build on their strengths and goals in order to achieve positive outcomes. At its heart, Constructive Resettlement aims to encourage identity development/shift within the child from 'pro-offending' to 'prosocial', crime free and socially included. Constructive Resettlement acknowledges that children in or leaving custody are disproportionately likely to have experienced trauma (e.g. ACEs) and other personal and structural vulnerabilities (e.g. victimisation, discrimination, poverty), which can be exacerbated by their gender and BAME status – all of which can contribute to the development of an identity favourable to offending and unfavourable to effective engagement with the YJS. Accordingly, the YJB has identified five evidence-based principles for effective resettlement support, based on the Beyond Youth Custody research of Hazel *et al.* (2017). These are:

- *Constructive*: strengths based, and future-focused on identity shift and empowering positive choices.
- *Co-created*: inclusive of the child, their family and supporters at every stage.
- *Customised*: individualised wraparound support, incorporating diversity.
- *Consistent*: all agencies focused on resettlement from the start, enabling seamless transitions.
- *Co-ordinated*: managed widespread partnership across agencies and sectors.

The 5Cs of Constructive Resettlement coalesce to promote positive identity shift (also known as transition); a shift about provides the model with its Theory of Change for the behaviour of children. Each element is consistent with the principles of Positive Youth Justice (e.g. child-friendly/appropriate, prospective, promoting positive outcomes, inclusive, legitimate, evidence-based partnership) and the model has been deliberately constructed to facilitate the Child First agenda – as illustrated by the inclusion of the 5Cs in the YJB's operational definition of Child First (YJB 2019a).

A NEWER 'NEW YOUTH JUSTICE'? SO, WHAT DO WE KNOW?

The final chapter of our journey through the socio-historical construction of youth justice has examined the extent and nature of youth justice developments in England and Wales since the 2010 fall of the New Labour Government. The throughgoing focus has been on the extent to which (re)constructions of youth justice over this period constituted a modernised and distinctive approach or were more akin to an updated version of their predecessor's approach – a newer 'new youth justice'. Initially, youth justice developed under the Coalition Government of 2010–2015 through the responsibilising 'Big Society' agenda. In 2010, the associated *Breaking the Cycle* Green Paper (accompanied by an Independent Commission review *Time for a Fresh Start*), offered recommendations for a consolidated emphasis on existing 'new youth justice' strategies of responsibilisation (including restorative justice), prevention and risk-focused intervention. Subsequent revisions to the out-of-court sentencing process under LASPO 2012 and to the assessment and intervention framework through AssetPlus in 2013 indicated some confusion in Coalition youth justice policy (**RTA – conflict and ambivalence**) between building on 'new youth justice' strategies and constructing a contradictory, more PYJ approach underpinned by progressive principles and strategies such as diversion, participation, eliciting young people's voices and enabling practitioner discretion. Evaluation of Coalition youth justice identified several positive statistical outcomes, such as continuing annual decreases in the main KPIs (FTEs, reoffending numbers (not rates) and custody), although the explanations and responsibility for these apparent successes remain contested between the Government, YJB, practitioners and academics. Despite ostensible successes in terms of outcomes, it is difficult to identify significant departures from the 'new youth justice' strategies across Coalition youth justice, with consistent evidence of responsibilisation (e.g. Big Society, *Breaking the Cycle*) and prevention/risk-focused early intervention (e.g. *Breaking the Cycle*, *Prevention Matters*, Early Intervention Grant). Even the 'new era of diversion' ushered in by the LASPO Act 2012 appeared to retain the interventionism and preventative emphasis of the Crime and Disorder Act 1998, while AssetPlus retained significant elements of Asset, such as the desire to predict the likelihood of reoffending by assessing (explanatory) psychosocial factors.

The youth justice of the subsequent Conservative Government that took power in 2015 has been characterised by both ambiguity and inertia, shaped in large part by extreme socio-economic and political changes and insecurities brought on by austerity and Brexit. Despite continued annual decreases in FTEs, both reoffending and custody rates remain problematic, practically and ethically, due to their iatrogenic nature and the UK's continued contravention of the UNCRC in this regard. The most significant youth justice development under the Conservatives thus far has been the wide-ranging review of the YJS by Charlie Taylor (now chair of the YJB), which offered recommendations for improvement that were progressive, including children-first and education-focused youth justice, diversionary children's panels, secure schools (educational custodial institutions), and more local devolution and discretion in the delivery of youth justice. However, these recommendations were largely ignored in the Government response to the report (with the exception of secure schools), in favour of a reiterated commitment to 'new youth justice' strategies of risk-focused intervention and prevention, reintroducing conflict, ambivalence and uncertainty regarding the future of contemporary youth justice.

The penultimate section of the chapter outlined the approach to youth justice that has emerged in Wales and that coheres around principles of children's rights/entitlements, universalism and collective responsibility. The ongoing debate here was whether the Welsh approach can be considered a distinct, 'dragonised' form of youth justice (Haines and Case 2015) or rather a more Welsh-centric model that is to some degree constrained by the requirements of the 'anglicised' Crime and Disorder Act 1998 and its associated strategies of 'new youth justice'. Broadly speaking, it seems that a progressive, positive youth justice (with accompanying, bespoke structures) is discernible in Wales in policy/strategic terms, but that this distinctiveness is less obvious in practice due to adherence to centralised (English) youth justice policy prescriptions, inconsistencies in local YOT practice, and a degree of local mediation of centralised policy and practice guidance (RTA) and charismatic leadership that mitigates the 'new youth justice' (mediation and mitigation that is equally evident in England). This latter point suggests that the 'new youth justice' is not necessarily pervasive in youth justice practice across England (let alone Wales), raising the possibility that a degree of (unofficial) local devolution and discretion/mediation has already distorted the realities of youth justice practice in both countries beyond automated adherence to the 'new youth justice'.

The chapter and indeed our historical journey through the construction of youth justice concluded with a detailed discussion of the children-first PYJ model of progressive and principled youth justice. The children-first model is guided by five principles for PYJ practice with children in the YJS that challenge the negativity of the 'new youth justice': *child-friendly* and *child-appropriate* treatment (not adulterisation), *diversion* (away from system contact and into positive, promotional interventions) and *systems management* (of child-friendly decisions at every stage of the YJS), *promoting positive behaviours* (e.g. educational achievement, engagement, participation) and *outcomes* (e.g. access to universal entitlements), *evidence-based partnership* (between children, families, practitioners, policy-makers, Government and academics) and *responsibilising*

5 EASY PIECES

Recommended further reading

Students keen to further evaluate the recommendations of the Independent Commission report *Time for a Fresh Start* in a broader (thematic) youth justice context are directed to the companion edited text *A New Response to Youth Crime* by David Smith (2010). This book is a source of copious evidence about changing patterns of youth, trends in youth crime figures and youth justice processes, supposed causes of offending, and the impact and effectiveness of interventions, concluding by outlining an ambitious reform programme that could transform the way we approach youth crime.

The progressive, principled and evidence-based model of PYJ is unpacked in critical depth in *Positive Youth Justice: Children First, Offenders Second* by Stephen Case and Kevin Haines (2015). This book provides a highly critical and subjective review of the negative elements of 'new youth justice' and thorough discussions of the scholarly arguments, research and evidence that underpins the principles of PYJ. Of course, I'm biased here, but I'm also incredibly proud of this book and the thought-provoking and progressive perspective that it sets out – one that progresses critique into a practical model for youth justice.

Along the same lines, *Foundations for Youth Justice: Positive Approaches to Practice* by Anne Robinson (2014) is a well-structured, dynamic, radical and ambitious text that sets out a critical, yet realistic model for reconstructing youth justice practice. It is written in a student-friendly and engaging style; offering an ideal complement to the arguments set out in the Case and Haines text.

For a detailed critique of traditional youth justice responses in the Western world (UK, Australasia, North America) and a vision of how agencies could more effectively respond to youth offending, *Responding to Youth Crime: Towards Radical Criminal Justice Partnerships* by Paul Omojo Omaji (2003) is highly recommended. Although certain arguments are now a little dated, the author offers an insightful, accessible, yet challenging evaluation of westernised youth justice.

Finally, if you are interested in a bite-sized summary of the arguments from across this book, you should watch my TEDx presentation, 'Solving the Youth Crime Problem' (www.youtube.com/watch?v=QYWPyiZlpV8). Indeed, this 15-minute presentation may be a good place to start your exploration of youth justice prior to rereading this book. It should certainly consolidate and clarify several of the recurring arguments in language intended for a non-expert audience.

adults (to ensure children-first, promotional practice in partnership with children). The children-first model of PYJ is gaining traction in national and local constructions of youth justice as both a direct challenge to the negative excesses of the 'new youth justice' and as a response to contemporary financial pressures to refine youth justice practice. The model coheres with and consolidates recent progressive youth justice developments such as the diversionary emphasis of the new out-of-court system, the strengths-based, child-focused emphasis of AssetPlus and the recommendations for enhancing local devolution made in the Taylor Review. The children-first ethos has the potential to afford local authorities and practitioners more discretion to innovate and shape their practice around a set of touchstone principles, as opposed to (unprincipled, ad hoc) prescribed practice guidelines that pursue negative-facing, prevention-led strategic goals. The guiding principles of child-first PYJ are slowly becoming embedded at all stages of the YJS; underpinning the *National Strategy for the Policing of Children and Young People* (treating young people as children first in all encounters with the police – NPCC 2015), sentencing guidelines for magistrates/judges (child-focused, avoiding criminalising, acknowledging that children are not fully developed – Sentencing Council 2017) and recommendations for improving YOT practice (children first, children as not fully developed/culpable – Taylor 2016). It is possible to argue that child-first PYJ offers the newest incarnation of an effective, efficient and economical youth justice, but one that is a direct contrast and response to the 'new youth justice' of the Crime and Disorder Act 1998 that originally pursued these goals for the YJS.

NOTES

1   Building on *Breaking the Cycle*, the YJB collaborated with the Children and Young People Now newsletter to produce *Prevention Matters: How Sustained Investment in Prevention Programmes Has Reduced Youth Offending* (Youth Justice Board and CYP Now 2010). *Prevention Matters* detailed the youth justice work conducted over the past ten years aimed at 'preventing children and young people from becoming involved in crime' (Youth Justice Board and CYP Now 2010: 2). Using local case study examples and testimony from children who have desisted from offending, the publication champions 'a robust raft of targeted interventions' (Youth Justice Board and CYP Now 2010: 2), notably YIPs, YISPs, Safer Schools Partnerships and parenting programmes, which have purportedly demonstrated success and cost-effectiveness in reducing offending.

2   This cost-cutting measure was subsequently downsized into recommendations for maintenance of current functions in a reduced capacity (Public Bodies Act; HM Government 2011) and a reduction of YJB independence to make it more accountable to ministers (Triennial Review; Ministry of Justice 2012).

3   Further to this, YOT practitioners have received training in desistance theory (McNeill *et al.* 2012) and the good lives model (Ward 2002) – both of which were developed with adult offenders, but both of which enable greater focus on the individual's strengths and positive behaviours.

4   Protection against and resilience to risk is the absence of a negative element (i.e. harmful exposure to risk), not the presence of a positive element (Case and Haines 2009).

5   Annual youth justice statistics cover the period from April to March in England and Wales.

6   Two notes of caution must be sounded with regards to the practicalities of integrated service provision – cautionary notes for which I am grateful to an anonymous reviewer of this book. Firstly, different departments within local authorities may be reluctant to work together closely unless there is a statutory requirement to do so. This may be truer still of agencies outside the direct governance of local authorities. In order to make Taylor's recommendation work in practice, therefore, there may need to be a change in or amendment to legislation. The relevant agencies and services would still be required to work together, but not necessarily within the old YOT model. Secondly, the inequitable nature of local government finances means that there are large differences in the resources available to local authorities, Smaller and poorer authorities are currently overstretched and might struggle to deliver the same quality of service as richer areas.

7   Articulated by the *Extending Entitlement* youth inclusion strategy outlining unconditional universal entitlement to support, guidance and services in ten key areas of a young person's

life (National Assembly Policy Unit 2002) and the Seven Core Aims for children and young people: (1) flying start in life, (2) access to education, training and learning opportunities, (3) best possible physical, mental social and emotional health, (4) access to play, leisure, sport and cultural activities, (5) be listened to, treated with respect and have racial and cultural identity recognised, (6) safe home and community, (7) not disadvantaged by child poverty (Welsh Government 2004).

8   The WYJAP meets three times a year, with each meeting co-chaired by the Welsh representative on the YJB for England and Wales (a role that predates the creation of YJB Cymru). The panel contains representatives from the Welsh Government (e.g. the Community Safety Division), YJB Cymru, Welsh YOTs, the Secure Estate in Wales, the courts, probation service, police, voluntary sector and academics from the Welsh Centre for Crime and Social Justice (most notably Professor Kevin Haines when he worked in Wales until 2017; occasionally replaced by me). YJB Cymru reports to each meeting on the standing item of 'Wales youth justice performance'. The monitoring and delivery of a Welsh-sensitive youth justice is further supported by the Welsh representative on the YJB for England and Wales (one of 12 representatives), who also works closely with YJB Cymru to ensure that Welsh interests and devolved services for children and young people are accounted for in YJB policy and practice formations (Haines and Case 2015).

9   The Welsh Government adopted the UNCRC as the basis for policy-making for children in Wales in 2004; in 2011, they passed the Rights of Children and Young Persons (Wales) Measure, placing a duty on all Welsh Government ministers to have regard to the UNCRC in all decisions affecting children. The Welsh Government published a Children's Rights Scheme in 2014 specifying how this duty was to be discharged and the accountability arrangements in relation to it. However, unlike other children services, youth justice is not devolved and the extent to which commitment to the children's rights agenda impacts directly on policy is therefore limited (Bateman 2016).

10   Tackling the socio-economic conditions that lead to poverty and inequality, universality and re-engaging the 'social', diversion, child-appropriate justice, abolitionism, de-politicisation and tolerance.

11   Limitations when charging children and young people, minimum/maximum ages for youth court jurisdiction, trained specialists to work with young people, timely decision-making, delegation of decision-making to families, victims and communities, encouraging participation, evidence-based therapeutic approaches, capacity to refer to care and protection services, minimal use of custody, retaining the young person within their family and community.

12   *Youth Justice and Participation in Wales* (Nacro Cymru 2009) outlined the 'minimal essential components' of participation with children to shape their YOT: information, choice, non-discrimination, respect, reciprocity, feedback, practice improvements. The guidance identified a series of challenges and barriers to children's participation and engagement in youth justice processes, notably the enforced, compliance-focused nature of court-ordered disposals, mistrust of adults, communication difficulties and previous unsatisfactory experiences of not being listened to or valued. Several recommendations were offered to address these issues, including empowering children to participate equally in decision-making processes at all stages of their involvement with the YJS – drawing on appropriate consultation methodologies (e.g. online tools, self-assessment), the provision of information, evidence-based practice and research with children and a commitment to promoting children's rights in order to encourage a 'culture of participation'.

13   The broader research evidence base for the 'child first' strategic objective has recently been articulated in a comprehensive report by Case and Browning (2021).

APPENDIX 4

Critiquing *A New Response to Youth Crime*

In general, the text offers a series of informed contributions that ultimately cohere around these key reform themes and which utilise arguments grounded in relevant literature, a large body of (heavily referenced) research and a series of well-rehearsed criticisms of the established order. Where this book fails in my view is that it singularly fails to meet its main objective of offering innovative recommendations for a fresh start to approaching youth crime and antisocial behaviour. Instead, established hegemonic paradigms are privileged, notably those positivist and psycho-developmental in origin (e.g. adherence to official statistics, risk factor research, what works interventions). The book promulgates these paradigms in a selective and uncritical fashion at the expense of arguments drawn from the burgeoning movement of highly relevant critical youth criminology/critical youth justice. Critical youth justice in particular has posited a number of cogent arguments relating to, for example, decarceration (Goldson), responsibilisation (Muncie), closer consideration of the experiences of girls (Phoenix), criticisms of risk factor research (Case, Haines, O'Mahony), promotion of children's rights and children-first approaches (Scraton, Haines), the unblocking of societal access routes (e.g. France, Homel) and critical reflection on practice issues (e.g. Pitts, Bateman, Souhami). Indeed, an implicit positivist and psycho-developmental bias is evident not only from the arguments presented but also from the choice of contributing authors, most of whom have written and researched prolifically around the efficacy of psychosocial risk-based approaches to assessment and intervention (e.g. Smith, Utting, Graham, Hawkins, Welsh, Rutter). The reader is struck by the exclusion of any of the aforementioned critical writers (several of whom were consulted by the report authors) who would have offered the text a much more qualitative, sociological and critically balanced perspective that it is sadly lacking in its current form. An implication here is that authors and research evidence had been cherry-picked in order to confirm the preconceptions of the Independent Commission report. Of particular concern is the lack of cultural sensitivity in areas of the text, notably where conclusions have been informed by two chapters grounded in the North American context: focused on risk factor research and intervention in the US (the Prevention of Youth Crime chapter) and youth justice in Canada. Therefore, certain conclusions are offered with little or no critical consideration of the relative applicability and transferability of these research and practice contexts to England and Wales and with no heed of McAra's sensible caveat that 'particular policy narratives make sense and a very specific conditions' (p. 312). The overarching lack of criticality and lack of cultural sensitivity is typified in the Prevention chapter where the authors make no attempt to address contemporary criticisms of risk factor research (including my own text on the subject) and make insufficient reference to the UK research, policy and practice contexts, which appears at odds with the relative weight to given to the chapter's arguments and the context of their use to inform reform recommendations.

The reader is left with a sense of disappointment and unfulfilled promise upon completing this book. Whilst the central recommendations are worthy, they are neither original nor grounded in a rigorous, comprehensive or critical evaluation of available evidence. There is an internal confusion regarding the central aims of the book, largely centred on the conflation of responses to with the prevention of youth crime and antisocial behaviour, not to mention a general incoherence to the chapter order-ing (e.g. the Causes of Offending and Antisocial Behaviour chapter is situated after the Responding to Youth Crime chapter). Furthermore, the criteria for the inclusion of certain thematic chapters is not made clear. For example, Families and Parenting may be a relevant topic for discussion, but why are the roles of education, neighbourhood or substance use not addressed? Similarly, why is the increasingly salient youth jus-tice context of Welsh devolution overlooked? Perhaps of most concern, why is there no bespoke chapter covering Restorative Justice issues, despite this being a central thematic recommendation of the report? There is also a sense that much of the argu-ment has been made elsewhere in the large body of academic critical youth justice literature in the UK (e.g. arguments by Muncie, Goldson, Haines, Allen, Burney, Roger Smith) and even within the less critical, more textbook style overviews of youth jus-tice (e.g. by Hopkins-Burke, Stephenson et al). Therefore, as an academic text, *A New Response to Youth Crime* is of limited value to students, researchers and lecturers who have already engaged with the academic youth justice literature. These parties would be better served merely reading the report. An exception to this recommendation, however, is the excellent chapter on 'Models of Youth Justice' by Leslie McAra, which offers originality, breadth, insight and criticality to the debate and, as such, is an ideal standalone read for students of criminology. Policy-makers and practitioners may be similarly disappointed in as much as the book constitutes a much weightier and less coherent or digestible version of the report. Consequently, this book (and indeed the report it extrapolates) constitutes something of a damp squib in failing to meet its promise of a new approach to youth justice by proffering recommendations for reform that are partial, uncritical and grounded in well-rehearsed arguments.

(Case 2011: 106–108)

So that's what I thought of the book, but what do YOU think?

APPENDIX 5

CONVERSATIONS

Investigating the YJB and the challenges to policy-making

I spoke with Dr Anna Souhami of Edinburgh University about her ethnographic study of the functioning and policy-making of the YJB for England and Wales. Along with John Drew, Anna offers perhaps the deepest insight into the inner working of the YJB and the challenges it has faced when attempting to influence and implement youth justice policy.

Steve: What was the purpose of your study and what motivated it?

Anna Souhami: My project really began in 1997 when, as a new researcher, I watched the New Labour Government sweep into power. Like many observing the whirlwind of youth justice reform that followed, I was concerned with the punitive tone of their rhetoric about the YJS and the new, interventionist approach they promised. In particular, I was interested in the restructuring that started their reforms off. Removing youth justice from mainstream social services and putting it into these new inter-agency YOTs felt like yet another indication of a hardening of approach towards young people in trouble. What were the implications of having police officers and probation staff delivering youth justice alongside social workers? So, for my PhD I began an ethnographic study of a developing YOT to explore what I thought would be a changing culture of youth justice services (see Souhami 2007). However, as I soon realised, the problems were much more complex than I imagined. Rather than showing a clear difference in approach to work with young people, removing the boundaries between all those professions that worked with young people instead revealed a profound uncertainty about what youth justice work is, what it aimed to do, and what 'success' looked like. But what is more, this uncertainty was thought by practitioners not only to be inevitable but also important: from experience, they knew that what worked for one young person might not work for another. They also knew that practitioner input could and should not be expected to show a direct effect on behaviour, but it could have all kinds of other important outcomes which could not be measured. I was struck by the contrast with the New Labour Government's certainty that they would solve the problem of youth crime. If responses to troubling behaviour are necessarily individual, fluid and uncertain, how do Government officials make broad policies? If there is no clear criteria or mechanism for success, how do governments show themselves to be successful? How do they cope with uncertainty in a political climate in which it is not tolerated? And what becomes of the practice expertise which is so important in how youth justice services work? Does this play a part in how policies are made in central Government, and if so, how?

I wanted to see how policy was made in a climate that was volatile and constantly changing, and in which, to use a phrase loved by policy-makers, there were no 'magic bullets'. At the time, my interest in the YJB was simply that I suspected it was where youth justice policy-making took place. Like most people – including, it turns out, the Home Office, Home Secretary and many in the YJB itself (Souhami

2011) – I didn't know what the YJB was or what it did. Despite the intense debate about Labour's youth justice reforms, the YJB had received almost no attention. If it was mentioned at all it was simply as part of the Home Office: a vehicle for the Home Secretary's reforms. I knew that it was a Non-Departmental Public Body (NDPB, also known as a 'quango'). I knew a bit about what an NDPB was: it wasn't part of the civil service so its staff weren't civil servants, but instead was 'sponsored' by a Government department (then the Home Office, now the Ministry of Justice) to which it had to report. However, I didn't really understand what any of that meant and certainly didn't think it was interesting. Yet, as I soon discovered, its status as an NDPB was the most important feature of the YJB. Every part of the way the staff worked and the decisions they made was underpinned by the self-image of the YJB as a sort-of-independent, expert body. In other words, it was the non-departmental status of the YJB that shaped the form of youth justice policy took, in all kinds of subtle and important ways. To my surprise, my research became a study of the institutions of central Government and the cultures which shape what people in them do.

Steve: Can you describe your experiences of conducting the study – the challenges, obstacles, frustrations, revelations etc?

Anna: The overwhelming feeling for me during the research was astonishment that I was allowed in. The first phase of research involved a year's ethnographic fieldwork during a period (2006–2007) which was particularly turbulent and politically sensitive. Blair was just coming to the end of his reign as Prime Minister amid plummeting popularity and revolt within the Labour Party. During the research period, Home Secretary Charles Clarke was sacked after a bitter dispute, John Reid was appointed to replace him and resigned within the year. The Home Office was rocked by scandals involving foreign national prisoners and knife crime, and was declared unfit for purpose. The YJB was under critical scrutiny over deaths in custody. Staff throughout government feared for their jobs and their careers. Yet the YJB not only invited me in, but ignored all opportunities to throw me out. After a few months, the Chair of the YJB wrote to the then Director of the Research Development and Statistics Directorate of the Home Office to let him know I was conducting my study. The reply came back that Home Secretary Charles Clarke strongly disapproved of this kind of work. I was certain this was the end of my study. Yet the YJB Chief Executive merely shrugged and said 'well, your time-scales are longer than his', and sure enough he was gone by the end of the month. Throughout the research, I tried to work out why I was being kept around. What use did I have for the YJB?

At the outset, it was clear that the YJB felt they were about to be abolished and wanted a record of what they felt was the right way to govern youth justice; as a senior official put it, they wanted 'validation'. Of course, I wasn't there to provide validation and I worried about how critical research would be received. But as the research progressed, I realised my use to the YJB was subtler than this. The tensions that surrounded the YJB were reflected within it. I found myself in an organisation riven with conflict and divided into real and perceived factions. My role became one of neutral confidante, a safe place where staff could express their anxieties and frustrations knowing that they would be understood and would stay confidential. The extent of this only became clear once I'd left the YJB and received an email from a senior official, saying that she'd 'miss our whispered conversations on the stairs'.

However, doing research in such a fraught environment was incredibly challenging too. I had to uncover where the tensions were thought to be and be careful not to be seen to be allied with any particular individual or group. I didn't always get this right: after a very fractious meeting I happened to leave the room at the same time as a senior YJB figure. The following day I was told that 'we all noticed you leaving with him': that was seen as evidence I was on his side. I also had to unpick the status of what I was being told: how was it influenced by the politics of the organisation? And was I being manipulated by any particular interests?

Another challenge is one common to all ethnographers. I really liked the YJB officials. They were funny, smart and passionate. While I often felt frustrated with their working styles or decision-making, these were not the self-interested bureaucratic state officials usually described in criminological research, but people who felt themselves driven by wanting to protect vulnerable young people. I also saw that powerful people can feel very powerless, and I had enormous sympathy for their sense of impotence and fear. How do I keep my critical distance? This was a particular concern as I ended up with a conclusion I was not expecting, namely that I thought the YJB or a body like it was crucial for child-centred policy-making. Had I simply become captivated by these smart, nice people?

In the end, I found three ways of keeping a critical check. The first was simply to be mindful of these concerns. Was any other interpretation possible? Had I developed a skewed view of what I was observing? The second was to seek alternative perspectives. Conducting research with Government Ministers and Ministry of Justice officials outside the YJB was a very useful check on what I had been observing, as was presenting research to colleagues. But the single most useful way of stepping back from the research was time. I returned to conduct more research at two further stages in the YJB's history: when its abolition was debated in 2011 and, in 2014, the aftermath of its eventual reprieve. Through this I saw the organisation in three different political climates, with different staff and regimes. This allowed me to see more clearly the underlying thematic continuities, as well as the ways in which particular personalities and moments affect what organisations do.

Steve: Has your view of the YJB changed due to your experiences?

Anna: My ideas about the YJB and of Government generally changed completely through the research. As a criminologist, I was used to a fiercely critical approach to thinking about State power. I admired greatly the work of critical criminologists who viewed the criminal/youth justice system as a system of oppression to maintain the vested interests of the powerful. Labour's youth justice policy – often attributed to the YJB – was held up to particularly powerful critical scrutiny. Similarly, I was suspicious of quangos like the YJB, the unelected bodies outside the civil service which were allocated important government roles. As academic research and public debate had taught me, these were surely just a way for governments to secretly and undemocratically expand their control of executive government by filling posts with complicit, unelected officials. At the outset of my research, the idea that I would argue for the importance of a government quango at the centre of the YJS (Souhami 2015a) would have been unthinkable. The assumption of youth justice colleagues was that anyone researching youth justice policy-making must surely, as one put it, be writing an 'exposé'.

But through my research I realised what NDPBs were, and how policy-making worked. I saw that as NDPBs aren't part of the civil service, they can appoint specialists in youth justice: youth justice social workers, local government, charity workers, and others. This allows for the absorption into central government of the sorts of practice knowledge I had observed in my PhD. It also made bodies like the YJB exempt from the churn in the rest of the civil service, where people move to different departments every few years, meaning that continuity of expertise could develop within the YJB, something crucial for such a complex policy area. But it was also vital for the effects on the self-image of the YJB. The difference in the institutional culture in which they worked and their professional background encouraged YJB staff to see themselves 'independent' from their ministerial sponsors, allowing them to develop a role as a critical friend. The effect was as a buffer to the populist excesses of ministerial power: persuading, encouraging and at times rebelling against measures deemed counter-productive and damaging to young people in trouble. This caused all kinds of problems of course, and I am sure will lead to the inevitable abolition of the YJB. It also doesn't mean that the people or activities within the YJB are the right ones, nor that the YJB is necessarily the right body: For example, I think a body concerned with young people in trouble should be located within social services and not the Ministry of Justice. But it did show that policy in such a politically volatile and complex area as youth justice should be made at arm's-length from government departments, by dedicated, specialist experts.

I then started to wonder about my initial preconceptions of the YJB and of Government officials more broadly. Given the rich body of nuanced work about youth justice practice, why did I have such a simplistic and negative view of the practice of policy-making and the people that made it? I now realise that this reflects something missing in the way policy is thought about in criminology. Debates about policy have focused solely on 'products' such as legislation, Green Papers or ministerial speeches. It is these that we analyse to understand what the tone and direction of youth justice is. Of course, these are vitally important and powerful instruments in the policy process. However, I saw that policy is something much wider than this (see Souhami 2015b). It isn't made just by senior civil servants and ministers, but by all kinds of people working in government and in partnership elsewhere. It emerges in the spaces between defined parameters of legislation and guidance. And it can diverge in important ways from those 'products' which tend to be the focus of criminological studies. In short, I realised that if we want to understand youth justice policy-making, we need to look at what youth justice policy-makers do – and an understanding of the culture and institutions in which they work is vital to understand the way they do it.

APPENDIX 6

TELLING IT LIKE IT IS

Youth justice in the COVID-19 pandemic

I asked my colleague Dr Kathy Hampson about the impact of the COVID-19 pandemic on policy and practice in the YJS of England and Wales. Kathy is a youth justice expert who has conducted a wealth of research with children and practitioners in the YJS. She works as a lecturer at Aberystwyth University in Wales, having previously been a YOT practitioner, so is ideally placed to explain the impact of COVID-19 on justice-involved children. Kathy told me:

During 2020, the COVID-19 pandemic has arguably posed the greatest global challenge since World War Two and has resulted in policies across the world which are unprecedented. On 23 March 2020, Prime Minister Boris Johnson announced that the UK would effectively lockdown, with new restrictions enforceable by law (YJB 2020a, 2020b). Unfortunately, responses to the pandemic appear to have had a particularly deleterious effect on justice-involved children, already on the fringes of society. As the Chair of the Standing Committee for Youth Justice, Professor Hannah Smithson (2020) put it: 'While the crisis has been referred to in the media as a 'leveller', the reality is that social inequality has been exacerbated and amplified by the pandemic and will have long lasting implications for the most vulnerable in society, including young people in youth justice systems'.

The YJB set out its policy response to COVID-19 as aiming to: minimise numbers of children entering the YJS, maximise early release for children in custody, maximise the use of bail (thereby minimising custodial remand), ensure quick communication throughout sector agencies, and raise concerns regarding such issues as criminalisation and safeguarding under lockdown with government (YJB 2020a). In order to service these aims, initial policies included convening a virtual Heads of Service working group, assisting with the roll-out of a virtual court and expanding the YJB Resource Hub to enable YOTs to share good practice under lockdown (YJB 2020a, 2020b). In addition, national policies related to justice-involved children were amended to address the demands of the pandemic, which included the classification of YOT workers as essential key workers (meaning they could still operate under lockdown), reduction of court activity to essential matters only (including bail/remand hearings, but no trials (not resumed until May 2020) and immediate suspension of all prison, probation and Ofsted/Estyn inspections (YJB 2020b). Additionally, for children in custody, there have been further restrictions, including the suspension of all prison visits (including those from professionals) and children isolated in their cells for extended periods of time (by increasing so-called 'in-room activities'). To mitigate these restrictions, children in custody have been given improved telephone access (including in-room access, 24-hour free access to helplines, additional phone credit), the facility for early release through the introduction of the end of custody temporary release scheme (if within 61 days of release, not convicted of violent offences and resettlement accommodation identified) and plans made for developing video-conferencing to address difficulties caused by the visits ban (YJB 2020a).

Community realities

My informal conversations with several practitioners and managers in England and Wales have revealed that YOTs were quick to adapt to the new restrictions, with many staff being given smart phones so they could keep in contact with children through video call apps. This has allowed appointments to continue, ensuring that children do not miss their contacts and end up in breach, or lose out on important personal support. Referral Order Panels went virtual, and so were able to continue, and many YOTs continued face-to-face contact with those children they considered to be particularly vulnerable (Hampson 2020). Whilst the YJB's Resource Hub evidence base illustrates some really excellent and innovative work, which will no doubt be reflected in the upcoming inspection on YOT processes (not yet available), though this doesn't necessarily mitigate the difficulties caused by mental health and substance misuse appointments generally moving to telephone contacts, which can severely hamper their effectiveness, especially at a time of heightened anxiety more generally.

The practitioners I've spoken to tell me that some children benefit from virtual contact, as they are more likely to 'attend' than they had been doing previously and that children have enjoyed interventions delivered via the internet. Practitioners also noted that, conversely, other children became difficult to locate and some hampered by uncooperative parents, potentially increasing the risk of order breach. Others may have been put at higher risk of harm, with their contacts maintained on a handset belonging to a parent/carer (some children find phone ownership difficult to maintain through loss or the temptation of selling handsets), limiting options for the child to disclose abuse or other concerns. One practitioner revealed his 'massive concerns' about child criminal exploitation at this time, with YOTs relatively powerless to mitigate this issue. Conversely, the greater police capacity resulting from a general reduction in crime during COVID-19 has enabled greater concentration on drug gangs and targeting of child exploitation through County Lines activities (ONS 2020).

Moreover, the added pressures on YOTs at a time when staff could be self-isolating or sick, has meant that in general preventative work has fallen by the wayside in favour of keeping up with statutory cases from court, so vital early interventions have been lost. Further loss has occurred due to the lack of court activity, meaning that cases which YOTs would normally have returned to court for early revocation due to good progress had to continue to the bitter end, this delaying justice, support and potential release. In the case of Referral Orders, early revocation also means earlier consideration of the offence as 'spent', so children have had longer to wait before their convictions could be legally excluded from application forms (more significant since the major job market losers of the pandemic have been children (ONS 2020). These issues, coupled with an increase in criminalisation through COVID-19-specific legislation, could have the effect of *increasing* the criminalisation of children at a time when concerted efforts have significantly reduced the numbers of children drawn into the YJS.

Custody realities

The suspension of most court activity has meant that most active cases were put on hold, with no end date identified. While custody figures during the pandemic have reduced (with children still released at the end of sentence and no new sentencing occurring), the *proportion* of children in custody *on remand* has risen worryingly, with courts still remanding children to custody throughout the lockdown (despite the YJB's stated aim that this should be minimised). In March 2020, 33 per cent of children in custody were there on remand, but by August this had risen to 39 per cent (Youth Custody Service 2020).

The Prisons Inspectorate conducted a first tranche of COVID-themed 'short scrutiny visits' in April within three YOIs to evaluate how restrictions were affecting them (HMIP 2020). It is concerning that whilst video conferencing had been lauded as the 'way forward', no such facilities were available in any of the examined YOIs. It seems that the process of rolling out video conferencing more generally was delayed by the perceived necessity to run a pilot in an adult prison first, showing that no learning appeared to be taken from the already-evaluated Parc YOI Skype project (HMIP 2020). By the time of the second Prisons Inspectorate short scrutiny report in July (encompassing two YOIs not visited in April), 'purple visits' had been established in both YOIs, which was the facility for video-calling on a laptop (HMIP 2020). However, the report also noted that take-up of this facility was limited, indicative of a lack of understanding of these children's backgrounds, as many (especially those 'looked after') had no contacts who could utilise this – some families were deemed ineligible because they had no acceptable ID for this purpose, further disadvantaging the already disadvantaged (HMIP 2020). Disappointingly, the report also commented that take-up by children may have been hampered by the deemed necessity of the 'purple visit' to include a member of staff in the vicinity.

It is also evident that children have been spending far too long locked up alone. The expansion of phone credit in custody allows children more telephone contact with family, a helpful way to maintain vital attachments, but the HMIP scrutiny visit criticised the realities of this, identifying a discrepancy in amounts of credit offered by custodial sites (HMIP 2020). However, the report did *not* question that children were being charged at all for these calls – why not allow free access? Whilst vulnerable children in the community have been enabled to continue in-person schooling, no such facility was initially offered to children in custody, arguably the most vulnerable children in our society. That said, the scrutiny report revealed that privately run and local authority–run custodial institutions had quickly reinstated face-to-face education during COVID-19; contrasting starkly with the YOIs run by the Youth Custody Service, *none* of which yet had any out-of-cell education. By July 2020, despite a significant easing of the community lockdown in all areas of the UK, children were still kept locked up for in excess of 22 hours a day in YOIs (HMIP 2020), with legislation recently passed to extend the ability for Secure Training Centres to legally lock children up for this period of time until 2022 (Grant 2020). The dangers of high levels of isolated lock-in have been well-established elsewhere, with normal adolescent development depending in large part on socialisation with others (cf. Bateman 2020). Further, this detriment to normal development could potentially harden the return routes back into custody after release, further demonstrating the damage visited on justice-involved children by COVID-19 restrictions.

The golden promise of early release, which the YJB proclaimed as a way to reduce the numbers of children in custody at the onset of the pandemic, has in fact facilitated *no* children being released at all; a fact admitted in oral evidence given to the

House of Commons Justice Committee on 2 June 2020 (House of Commons 2020). According to a recent freedom of information request I made to the Ministry of Justice, this was still the case by the time the scheme stopped in August 2020, despite recent figures showing substantial falls in crime over the lockdown period in England and Wales, both in official and self-reported crime statistics (ONS 2020). It is logical to surmise that now may actually constitute the *safest* time to release children from prison, given the drastically reduced opportunities they have for reoffending, thus giving them a better chance of a non-offending future.

A way forward?

The situation is currently balanced on a knife-edge more generally, with rates of COVID-19 infection rising rapidly around the world and the threat of more lockdowns becoming reality in ever-more places. Some lessons have been learned from the first lockdown experience: YOTs are now well practiced at online and mobile phone alternatives where face-to-face meetings are not feasible, many custodial establishments are working out a new normal so that education and visits can continue wherever possible, and video calls are now much more widely available (although issues around their take-up should be addressed). However, none of this addresses the damage caused by the social isolation inherent in all of this for children who are already finding life challenging, nor provides a way for them to seek independent help if they find themselves victims of abuse or exploitation. Notably, children in custody are still being locked up in isolation for excessive periods, reflecting a lack of will to consider alternatives. Consequently, children in the YJS, especially those in custody, still seem destined to remain disproportionately affected by any 'new normal' emerging from the pandemic.

Bibliography

Abramson, B. (2000) '*Juvenile Justice: The Unwanted Child of State Responsibilities*. International Network on Juvenile Justice/Defence for Children International'. Available at: www.defence-for-children.org.

Agnew, R. (2005) *Why Do Criminals Offend? A General Theory of Crime and Delinquency*. Oxford: Oxford University Press.

Aichhorn, A. (1925) *Wayward Youth*. New York: Meridian Books.

Akers, R.L. (1985) *Deviant Behavior: A Social Learning Approach*. Belmont, CA: Wadsworth.

Akers, R.L. (1991) Self-control as a general theory of crime. *Journal of Quantitative Criminology*, 7: 201–211.

Akers, R.L. and Sellers, C.S. (2013) *Criminological Theories: Introduction, Evaluation, and Application*. Los Angeles, CA: Roxbury.

Alder, C. and Wundersitz, J. (1994) 'New directions in juvenile justice reform in Australia'. In: C. Alder and J. Wundersitz (eds) *Family Conferencing and Juvenile Justice: The Way Forward or Misplaced Optimism?* Canberra: Australian Institute of Criminology.

Allen, R. (1991) Out of jail: The reduction in the use of penal custody for male juveniles 1981–1988. *Howard Journal*, 30(1): 30–52.

Allen, R. (2011) '*Written Evidence to the Justice Committee on the Proposed Abolition of the Youth Justice Board*'. Available at: https://publications.parliament.uk/pa/cm201012/cmselect/cmjust/1547/1547vw07.htm.

Andrews, D.A. and Bonta, J. (2010) *The Psychology of Criminal Conduct*. London: Routledge.

Ariès, P. (1962) *Centuries of Childhood: A Social History of Family Life*. New York: Random House.

Armstrong, D. (2004) A risky business? Research, policy, governmentality and youth offending. *Youth Justice*, 4(2): 100–116.

Arnull, E. and Fox, D. (2016) *Cultural Perspectives on Youth Justice. Connecting Theory, Policy and International Practice*. London: Palgrave Macmillan.

Arseneault, L., Tremblay, R.E., Boulerice, B. and Saucier, J. (2002) Obstetrical complications and violent delinquency: Testing two developmental pathways. *Child Development*, 73(2): 496–508.

Arthur, R. (2016) *The Moral Foundations of Youth Justice*. Abingdon, UK: Routledge.

Ashford, M., Chard, A. and Redhouse, N. (1997) *Defending Young People in the Criminal Justice System*. London: Legal Action Group.

Audit Commission. (1996) *Misspent Youth*. London: Audit Commission.

Audit Commission. (2004) *Youth Justice 2004*. London: Audit Commission.

Bailleau, F. and Cartuyvels, Y. (eds). (2002) La justice pénale des mineurs en Europe. *Déviance et Société*, 26(3), special issue.

Baker, K. (2005) Assessment in youth justice: Professional discretion and the use of Asset. *Youth Justice*, 5: 106–122.

Baker, K., Jones, S., Roberts, C. and Merrington, S. (2002) *Validity and Reliability of Asset*. London: YJB.

Baker, K., Jones, S., Roberts, C. and Merrington, S. (2005) *Further Development of Asset*. London: Youth Justice Board.

Bandalli, S. (2000) 'Children, responsibility and the new youth justice'. In: B. Goldson (ed.) *The New Youth Justice* (pp. 81–95). Lyme Regis, UK: Russell House.

Bandura, A. (1973) *Aggression: A Social Learning Analysis*. Englewood Cliffs, NJ: Prentice Hall.

Barry, M. (2006) *Youth Offending in Transition*. London: Routledge.

Barry, M. and McNeill, F. (2009) *Youth Offending and Youth Justice*. London: Jessica Kingsley.

Baskerville, D. and Goldblatt, H. (2009) Learning to be a critical friend: From professional indifference through challenge to unguarded conversations. *Cambridge Journal of Education*, 39(2): 205–221.

Bateman, T. (2011) Punishing poverty: The 'scaled approach' and youth justice practice. *Howard Journal of Penal Reform*, 50(2): 171–183.

Bateman, T. (2012) *Children in Conflict with the Law: An Overview of Trends and Developments – 2010/2011*. London: NAYJ.

Bateman, T. (2014) Where has all the youth crime gone? Youth justice in an age of austerity. *Children and Society*, 28(5): 416–424.

Bateman, T. (2015) *The State of Youth Justice 2015: An Overview of Trends and Developments*. London: NAYJ.

Bateman, T. (2016) *The State of Youth Custody*. London: NAYJ.

Bateman, T. (2017) *The State of Youth Justice 2017: An Overview of Trends and Developments*. London: NAYJ.

Bateman, T. (2020) Unjust pains: The impact of COVID-19 on children in prison. *Journal of Children's Services*. Available at: www.emerald.com/insight/content/doi/10.1108/JCS-07-2020-0045/full/html

Bateman, T. and Wigzell, A. (2019) Exploring recent trends in youth justice reconvictions: A challenge to the complexity thesis. *Youth Justice*. Online first.

Bateman, T., Hazel, N. and Wright, S. (2013) *Resettlement of Young People Leaving Custody: Lessons from the Literature*. London: Beyond Youth Custody.

Bateman, T. and Pitts, J. (2005) *The RHP Companion to Youth Justice*. Lyme Regis, UK: Russell House.

Bates, K. A., Bader, C. D. and Mencken, F. C. (2003) Family structure, power-control theory and deviance: Extending power-control theory to include alternate family forms. *Western Criminology Review*, 4(3): 170–190.

Baumgartner, E. (2012) And then there were the men – masculinity and the youth justice system in England and Wales. *Graduate Journal of Social Sciences, Special Edition: 'Gendered Subjects'*, 9(3): 79–86.

Baumgartner, E. (2014) *Boys Will Be Boys, or Will They? A Study of Youth Offending Team Practitioners' Constrictions of Masculinity of the Young Men with Whom They Work*. Unpublished Thesis, Durham University. Available at: http://etheses.dur.ac.uk/10607/.

Beccaria, C. (1963, first English edition 1767) *On Crimes and Punishment*, translated by H. Paolucci. Indianapolis, IN: Bobbs-Merrill Educational.

Beck, U. (1992) *Risk Society: Towards a New Modernity*. London: Sage.

Becker, H. (1963) *Outsiders: Studies in the Sociology of Deviance*. New York: Free Press.

Beckman, M. (2004) Neuroscience. Crime, culpability, and the adolescent brain. *Science*, 30: 596–599.

Behlmer, G. (1998) *Friends of the Family: The English Home and its Guardians, 1850–1940*. Stanford, CA: Stanford University Press.

Bell, C. and Haines, K. (1991) 'Managing the transition: Implications of the introduction of a youth court in England and Wales – a moving frontier'. In: T. Booth (ed.) *Juvenile Justice in the New Europe*, Social Services Monographs: Research in Practice. Sheffield: University of Sheffield.

Bell, E. (2011) *Criminal Justice and Neoliberalism*. Basingstoke, UK: Palgrave Macmillan.

Benstead, J. (1994) Men working with men in groups: Masculinity and crime. *Groupwork*, 7(1): 37–49.

Bentham, J. (1970) *An Introduction to the Principles of Morals and Legislation*, edited by J. H. Burns and H. L. A. Hart. London: Athlone Press.

Bernard, T. J., Snipes, J. B., Gerould, A. L. and Vold, G. B. (2015) *Vold's Theoretical Criminology*. Oxford: Oxford University Press.

Bessant, J., Hill, R. and Watts, R. (2003) *Discovering Risk: Social Research and Policy Making* (vol. 18). New York: Peter Lang.

Bishop, D. M. and Farber, H. B. (2007) Joining the legal significance of adolescent developmental capacities with the legal rights provided by in re gault. *Rutgers Law Review*, 60(1).

Bishop, D. M. and Feld, B. C. (2012) *The Oxford Handbook of Juvenile Crime and Juvenile Justice*. Oxford: Oxford University Press.

Blair, T. (1994) 'Crime and society', Fabian society, what price a safe society? In: *Fabian Pamphlet 562, Proceedings of the 1994 Fabian New Year School*. London: Fabian Society.

Blunkett, D. (2003) *'Foreword' to Home Office: A Guide to Antisocial Behaviour Orders*. London: Home Office.

Boeck, T., Fleming, J. and Kemshall, H. (2006) The context of risk decisions: Does social capital make a difference? *Forum: Qualitative Social Research*, 7(1), Article 17. Available at: www.qualitative-research.net/fqs-texte/1–06/06–1-17-e.htm.

Bone, J. D. (2012) The neo-liberal phoenix: the big society or business as usual. *Sociological Research Online*, 17(2): 16.

Bottoms, A. E. (2002) 'The divergent development of juvenile justice policy and practice in England and Scotland'. In: M. Rosenheim *et al.* (eds) *A Century of Juvenile Justice*. Chicago, IL: University of Chicago Press.

Bottoms, A. E. and McClintock, F. H. (1973) *Criminals Coming of Age. A Study of Institutional Adaptation in the Treatment of Adolescent Offenders*. London: Heinemann.

Box, S. (1981) *Deviance, Reality, Society*. Canada: Holt, Rinehart and Winston.

Braithwaite, J. (2002) *Restorative Justice and Responsive Regulation*. New York: Oxford University Press.

Bredo, E. (2005) 'Reconstructing educational psychology'. In: P. Murphy (ed.) *Learners, Learning and Assessment*. London: Paul Chapman.

Briggs, D. (2013) Conceptualising risk and need: the rise of actuarialism and the death of welfare? Practitioner assessment and intervention in the youth offending service. *Youth Justice*, 13(1): 17–30. Bristol, UK: Policy Press.

Brown, S. (1998) *Understanding and Listening to Youth*. Buckingham, UK: Open University Press.

Brown, S. (2005) *Understanding Youth and Crime. Listening to Youth?* Maidenhead, UK: Open University Press.

Browning, K., Huizinga, D., Loeber, R. and Thornberry, T. P. (1999) *Causes and Correlates of Delinquency Program. Fact Sheet*. Washington, DC: U.S. Department of Justice, Office of Justice Programs, Office of Juvenile Justice and Delinquency Prevention.

Bruce, N. (1985) *Juvenile Justice in Scotland: A Historical Perspective?* Paper presented at a Franco-British Workshop, The Best Interests of the Child, Edinburgh.

Burfeind, J. W. and Bartusch, D. J. (2006) *Juvenile Delinquency: An Integrated Approach*. Burlington, MA: Bartlett and Jones.

Burfeind, J. and Bartusch, D. J. (2016) *Juvenile Delinquency: An Integrated Approach*. London: Routledge.

Burr, V. (2003) *Social Constructionism*. London: Routledge.

Burt, C. (1925) *The Young Delinquent*. London: University of London Press.

Cabinet Office. (2010) *Building the Big Society*. London: Cabinet Office.

Cabot, R. (1940) A long-term study of children: the Cambridge-Somerville youth study. *Child Development*, 11(2): 143–151.

Cameron, D. (2008) *'Fixing Our Broken Society'*. Speech in Gallowgate, Glasgow, 7 July. Available at: www.conservatives.com/News/Speeches/2008/07/David_Cameron_Fixing_our_Broken_Society.

Cameron, D. (2009) *The Big Society. Hugo Young Memorial Lecture*. Available at: www.conservatives.com/News/Speeches/2009/11/David_Cameron_The_Big_Society.

Cameron, D. (2011) *'Building a Bigger, Stronger Society'*. Speech 23 May. Available at: www.conservatives.com/News/Speeches/2011/05/David_Cameron_Building_a_bigger_stronger_society.

Case, S. P. (2006) Young people 'at risk' of what? Challenging risk-focused early intervention as crime prevention. *Youth Justice*, 6(3): 171–179.

Case, S. P. (2007) Questioning the 'evidence' of risk that underpins evidence-led youth justice interventions. *Youth Justice*, 7(2): 91–106.

Case, S. P. (2008) 'Systems management'. In: B. Goldson (ed.) *The Dictionary of Youth Justice*. Cullompton, UK: Willan.

Case, S. P. (2010) 'Preventing and reducing risk'. In: W. Taylor, R. Earle and R. Hester (eds) *Youth Justice Handbook*. Cullompton, UK: Willan.

Case, S. P. (2011) A new response to youth crime (D. J. Smith). *Youth Justice*, 11(1): 106–108.

Case, S. P. (2014) Strategic complexities and opportunities in Welsh youth justice: Exploring YJB Cymru. *Safer Communities*, 13(3): 109–119.

Case, S. P. and Browning, A. (2021) *Child First Justice: The Research Evidence-Base*. Loughborough: UKRI.

Case, S. P., Clutton, S. and Haines, K. R. (2005) Extending entitlement: A Welsh policy for children. *Wales Journal of Law and Policy*, 4(2): 187–202.

Case, S. P., Ellis, T., Haines, K. R. and Hayden, C. (2011) A tale of two cities: Exploring localised public opinion about young people and anti-social behaviour. *Crime Prevention and Community Safety*, 13(3): 153–170.

Case, S. P. and Haines, K. R. (2009) *Understanding Youth Offending: Risk Factor Research, Policy and Practice*. Cullompton, UK: Willan.

Case, S. P. and Haines, K. R. (2010) 'Juvenile delinquency: Manifestations and causes'. In: M. Herzog-Evans (ed.) *Transnational Criminology Manual*. Nijmegen: Wolf Legal.

Case, S. P. and Haines, K. R. (2012) Supporting an evolving and devolving youth justice board. *Criminal Justice Matters*, 88(1): 38–40.

Case, S. P. and Haines, K. R. (2014) 'Reflective friend research: the relational aspects of social scientific research'. In: K. Lumsden (ed.) *Reflexivity in Criminological Research*. Basingstoke, UK: Palgrave Macmillan.

Case, S. P. and Haines, K. R. (2015a) Children first, offenders second positive promotion: Reframing the prevention debate. *Youth Justice Journal*, 15(3): 226–239.

Case, S. P. and Haines, K. R. (2015b) 'Risk management and early intervention'. In: B. Goldson and J. Muncie (eds) *Youth, Crime and Justice*. London: Sage.

Case, S. P., Johnson, P., Manlow, D., Smith, R. S. and Williams, K. H. (2017) *Criminology*. Oxford: Oxford University Press.

Catalano, R. F. and Hawkins, J. D. (1996) 'The social development model: A theory of anti-social behaviour'. In: J. Hawkins (ed.) *Delinquency and Crime: Current Theories*. Cambridge: Cambridge University Press.

Catalano, R. F., Park, J., Harachi, T. W., Haggerty, K. P., Abbott, R. D. and Hawkins, J. D. (2005) 'Mediating the effects of poverty, gender, individual characteristics and external constraints on antisocial behaviour: A test of the social development model and implications for developmental life-course theory'. In: D. P. Farrington (ed.) *Integrated Developmental and Life-Course Theories of Offending*. New Brunswick, NJ: Transaction.

Cavadino, M. and Dignan, J. (2006) *Penal Systems: A Comparative Approach*. Thousand Oaks, CA and New Delhi: Sage.

Chambliss, W. J. (1975) Toward a political economy of crime. *Theory and Society*, 2(1): 149–170.

Chapman, T. and O'Mahony, D. (2007) 'Youth and criminal justice in Northern Ireland developments in social work with offenders'. In: G. McIvor and P. Raynor (eds) *Developments in Social Work with Offenders*. London: Jessica Kingsley.

Chesney-Lind, M. and Shelden, R. G. (2004) *Girls, Delinquency and Juvenile Justice* (3rd edition). Belmont, CA: Wadsworth.

Children's Commissioner for England. (2015) *Unlocking Potential: A Study of the Isolation of Children in Custody in England*. London: Children's Commissioner.

Christiansen, K. O. (1974) 'Seriousness of criminality and concordance among Danish twins'. In: R. Hood (ed.) *Crime, Criminology and Public Policy*. New York: Free Press.

Clarke, R. V. G. (1987) 'Rational choice theory and prison psychology'. In: B. J. McGurk, D. Thornton and M. Williams (eds) *Applying Psychology to Imprisonment: Theory and Practice*. London: HMSO.

Cloward, R. and Ohlin, L. (1960) *Delinquency and Opportunity*. New York: Free Press.

Cohen, A.K. (1955) *Delinquent Boys: The Culture of the Gang*. New York: Free Press.

Cohen, L.E., Kluegel, J. and Land, K. (1981) Social inequality and predatory criminal victimization: An exposition and test of a formal theory. *American Sociological Review*, 46: 505–524.

Cohen, S. (1973) *Folk Devils and Moral Panics*. London: MacGibbon and Kee.

Cohen, S. (1985) *Visions of Social Control: Crime, Punishment and Classification*. London: Polity Press.

Cohen, S. (2011) Whose side were we on? The undeclared politics of moral panic theory. *Crime Media Culture*, 7(3): 237–243.

Collier, R. (1998) *Masculinities, Crime and Criminology: Men, Heterosexuality and the Criminal(ised) Other*. London: Sage.

Colvin, M. (2000) *Crime and Coercion: An Integrated Theory of Chronic Criminality*. New York: St Martin's Press.

Committee on Children and Young Persons. (1964) *Children and Young Persons, Scotland: Report by the Committee Appointed by the Secretary of State for Scotland [Chairman: Lord Kilbrandon]* Cmnd 2306. Edinburgh: Her Majesty's Stationery Office.

Committee on the Rights of the Child (CRC). (2002) *UNCRC Concluding Observations*. Geneva: UNICEF.

Committee on the Rights of the Child (CRC). (2008) *UNCRC Concluding Observations*. Geneva: UNICEF.

Committee on the Rights of the Child (CRC). (2016) *UNCRC Concluding Observations*. Geneva: UNICEF.

Connell, R.W. (1995) *Masculinities*. Cambridge: Polity Press.

Connell, R.W. (2005) *Masculinities*. London: Polity Press.

Coote, A. (1993) Boys who can't grow up: Men use crime to prove their masculinity because they have lost their role as breadwinner. *The Independent*, 14 November.

Cordis Bright. (2017) *Evaluation of the Enhanced Case Management Approach*. Cardiff: Cordis Bright.

Council of Europe. (2008) *European Rules for Juvenile Offenders Subject to Sanctions or Measures: Basic Principles 2008*. Strasbourg: Council of Europe.

Council of Europe. (2010) *The Guidelines of the Committee of Ministers of the Council of Europe on Child-friendly Justice*. Strasbourg: Council of Europe.

Cousin, G. and Deepwell, F. (2005) Designs for network learning: A communities of practice perspective. *Studies in Higher Education*, 30(1): 57–66.

Cowburn, M. (2010) Invisible men: Social reactions to male sexual coercion-bringing men and masculinities into community safety and public policy. *Critical Social Policy*, 30: 225–244.

Cox, P. (2003) *Gender, Justice and Welfare Bad Girls in Britain, 1900–1950*. London: Palgrave Macmillan.

Crawford, A. and Newburn, T. (2003) *Youth Offending and Restorative Justice: Implementing Reform in Youth Justice*. Cullompton, UK: Willan.

Creaney, S. and Smith, R. (2014) Youth justice back at the crossroads. *Safer Communities*, 13(2).

Crofts, T. (2009) Catching up with Europe: Taking the age of criminal responsibility seriously in England. *Criminal Law and Criminal Justice*, 17(4): 267–291.

Cuneen, C., White, R. and Richards, K. (2015) *Juvenile Justice: Youth and Crime in Australia*. Oxford: Oxford University Press.

CYP Now. (2011) Interview with Crispin Blunt. 8 February.

Davies, B. (1982) Juvenile justice in confusion. *Youth and Policy*, 1(2).

Davies, J.S. and Pill, M. (2012) Empowerment or abandonment? Prospects for neighbourhood revitalization in the big society. *Public Money and Management*, 32(3): 193–200.

Davis, H. and Bourhill, M. (1997) 'Crisis: the demonization of children and young people'. In: P. Scraton (ed.) *Childhood in Crisis?* London: UCL Press.

Davis, J.S. (1990) *Youth and the Condition of Britain*. London: Athlone Press.

Day-Sclater, S. and Piper, C. (2000) Remoralising the family – family policy, family law and youth justice. *Child and Family Law Quarterly*, 12(2): 135–151.

Department for Education and Skills. (2004) *Every Child Matters*. London: DfES.

Department for Education and Skills. (2005) *Youth Matters*. London: DfES.

Department of Health. (1994) *Responding to Youth Crime: Findings from Inspections of Youth Justice Sections in Five Local Authority Social Services Departments*. London: HMSO.

Dominelli, L. (2002) *Feminist Social Work: Theory and Practice*. Hampshire, UK: Palgrave Macmillan.

Douglas, G. (1998) The child's right to make mistakes: Criminal responsibility and the immature minor. In: G. Douglas and L. Sebba (eds) *Children's Rights and Traditional Values*. Aldershot, UK: Ashgate.

Downes, D. and Rock, P. (1998) *Understanding Deviance* (3rd edition). Oxford: Oxford University Press.

Drake, D.H., Fergusson, R. and Briggs, D.B. (2014) Hearing new voices: Re-viewing youth justice policy through practitioners? Relationships with young people. *Youth Justice*, 14: 22–39.

Drakeford, M. (2010) Devolution and youth justice in Wales. *Criminology and Criminal Justice*, 10: 137–154.

Dugdale, R.L. (1877) *The Jukes*. New York: Putnam.

Dunkel, F. (2006) *Crime Policy in Europe: Good Practices and Promising Examples*. Strasbourg: Council of Europe.

Dunkel, F. (2014) Juvenile justice systems in Europe – reform developments between justice, welfare and 'new punitiveness'. *Criminological Studies*, 1.

Dunkel, F., Gryzywa, J., Horsfield, P. and Pruin, I. (2010) *Juvenile Justice Systems in Europe, Vols. 1–4*. Monchengladbach: Forum Verlag Godesberg.

Durkheim, E. (1895/1964) *The Division of Labor in Society*. New York: Free Press.

Durkheim, E. (1933 originally 1893) *The Division of Labour in Society*. Glencoe, IL: Free Press.

Edwards, A. and Hughes, G. (2009) 'The preventive turn and the promotion of safer communities in England and Wales'. In: A. Crawford (ed.) *Crime Prevention Policies in Comparative Perspective*. Cullompton, UK: Willan.

Elliott, D.S., Ageton, S.S. and Canter, J. (1979) An integrated theoretical perspective on delinquent behaviour. *Journal of Research in Crime and Delinquency*, 16: 3–27.

Elliott, D.S., Huizinga, D. and Ageton, S.S. (1985) *Explaining Delinquency and Drug Use*. Beverly Hills, CA: Sage.

Ericson, R.V. (1991) Mass media, crime, law and justice. *British Journal of Criminology*, 31(3): 219–249.

Etzioni, A. (1995) *The Spirit of Community*. London: Fontana.

Evans, K. (2011) Big society in the UK: A policy review. *Children and Society*, 25(2): 164–171.

Evans, J., Kennedy, D., Skuse, T. and Matthew, J. (2020) Trauma informed practice and desistance theories: Competing or complementary approaches to working with children in conflict with the law. *Salus Journal*, 8(20): 55–76.

Eysenck, H.J. (1970) *Crime and Personality*. London: Granada.

Fagan, J. and Zimring, F. (2000) *The Changing Borders of Juvenile Justice*. Chicago, IL: University of Chicago Press.

Farrington, D.P. (1996) *Understanding and Preventing Youth Crime*. New York, UK: JRF.

Farrington, D.P. (2000) Explaining and preventing crime: the globalization of knowledge. *Criminology*, 38(1): 1–24.

Farrington, D.P. (2005) 'The integrated cognitive antisocial development (ICAP) theory'. In: D.P. Farrington (ed.) *Integrated Developmental and Life-Course Theories of Offending*. New Brunswick, NJ: Transaction.

Farrington, D.P. (2007) 'Childhood risk factors and risk-focused prevention'. In: M. Maguire, R. Morgan and R. Reiner (eds) *The Oxford Handbook of Criminology*. Oxford: Oxford University Press.

Feeley, M.M. and Simon, J. (1992) The new penology: Notes on the emerging strategy of corrections and its implications. *Criminology*, 30: 449–474.

Feld, B.C. (1999) *Bad Kids: Race and the Transformation of the Juvenile Court*. Oxford: Oxford University Press.

Feld, B.C. and Bishop, D.M. (2011) *The Oxford Handbook of Juvenile Crime and Juvenile Justice*. Oxford: Oxford University Press.

Fergusson, R. (2007) Making sense of the melting pot: Multiple discourses in youth justice policy. *Youth Justice*, 7(3): 179–194.

Ferri, E. (1895) *Criminal Sociology*. London: Unwin.

Flanagan, R. (2008) *The Review of Policing: Final Report*. London: HMCIC.

France, A. (2008) Risk factor analysis and the youth question. *Journal of Youth Studies*, 11(1): 1–15.

France, A. and Homel, R. (2006) Societal access routes and developmental pathways: Putting social structure and young people's voices into the analysis of pathways into and out of crime. *Australian New Zealand Journal of Criminology*, 39(3): 295–309.

France, A. and Homel, R. (2007) *Pathways and Crime Prevention. Theory, Policy and Practice*. Cullompton, UK: Willan.

Freeman, M. (2007) Why it remains important to take children's rights seriously. *International Journal of Children's Rights*, 15: 5–23.

Freud, A. (1952) 'Adolescence'. *Psychoanalytical Study of the Child*, 13: 255–278.

Friday, P.C. and Ren, X. (2006) *Delinquency and Juvenile Justice Systems in the Non-Western World*. New York: Criminal Justice Press.

Garland, D. (1985) *Punishment and Welfare: A History of Penal Strategies*. London: Gower.

Garland, D. (1996) The limits of the sovereign state: Strategies of crime control in contemporary society. *British Journal of Criminology*, 36(4): 445–471.

Garland, D. (2001) *The Culture of Control*. Oxford: Oxford University Press.

Gatrell, V. (1990) 'Crime, authority and the policeman-state'. In: F. M. L. Thompson (ed.) *Cambridge Social History of Britain 1750–1950*. Cambridge: Cambridge University Press.

Gelsthorpe, L. and Morris, A. (1994) 'Juvenile justice 1945–1992'. In: M. Maguire, R. Morgan and R. Reiner (eds) *The Oxford Handbook of Criminology*. Oxford: Clarendon Press.

Gelsthorpe, L. and Sharpe, G. (2006) 'Gender, youth crime and justice'. In: B. Goldson and J. Muncie (eds) *Youth Crime and Justice*. London: Sage.

Giddens, A. (1998) *The Third Way. The Renewal of Social Democracy*. Cambridge: Polity Press.

Giedd, J.N., Blumenthal, J., Jeffries, N.O., Castellanos, F.X., Liu, H., Zijdenbos, A., Paus, T., Evans, A.C. and Rapoport, J.L. (1999) Brain development during childhood and adolescence: A longitudinal MRI study. *Nature Neuroscience*, 2(10): 861–863.

Gillis, J.R. (1975) The evolution of juvenile delinquency in England 1890–1914. *Past and Present*, 67: 96–126.

Gittell, J.H. (2003) 'A theory of relational coordination'. In: K.S. Cameron, J.E. Dutton and R.E. Quinn (eds) *Positive Organizational Scholarship: Foundations of a New Discipline*. San Francisco, CA: Berrett-Koehler.

Glueck, S. and Glueck, E. (1930) *500 Criminal Careers*. New York: Alfred Knopf.

Glueck, S. and Glueck, E. (1937) *Later Criminal Careers*. New York: Commonwealth Fund.

Glueck, S. and Glueck, E. (1950) *Unraveling Juvenile Delinquency*. New York: Commonwealth Fund.

Goddard, H.H. (1914) *Feeblemindedness: Its Causes and Consequences*. New York: Palgrave Macmillan.

Goddard, T. and Myers, R. (2017) Against evidence-based oppression: Marginalized youth and the politics of risk-based assessment and intervention. *Theoretical Criminology*, 21(2): 151–167.

Goldson, B. (2000) *The New Youth Justice*. Lyme Regis, UK: Russell House.

Goldson, B. (2005) 'Taking liberties: Policy and the punitive turn'. In: H. Hendrick (ed.) *Child Welfare and Social Policy*. Bristol, UK: Policy Press.

Goldson, B. (2007) 'New Labour's youth justice: A critical assessment of the first two terms'. In: G. McIvor, P. Raynor and J. Lishman (eds) *Developments in Social Work with Offenders* (pp. 23–39). London and Philadelphia, PA: Jessica Kingsley.

Goldson, B. (2008) *The Dictionary of Youth Justice*. Cullompton, UK: Willan.

Goldson, B. (2011) The independent commission on youth crime and antisocial behaviour: Fresh start or false dawn? *Journal of Children's Services*, 6(2): 77–85.

Goldson, B. (2013) 'Unsafe, unjust and harmful to wider society': Grounds for raising the minimum age of criminal responsibility in England and Wales. *Youth Justice*, 13(2): 111–130.

Goldson, B. (2014) Youth justice in a changing Europe: Crisis conditions and alternative visions. *Perspectives on Youth*, 1: 39–52.

Goldson, B. and Hughes, G. (2010) Sociological criminology and youth justice: Comparative policy analysis and academic intervention. *Criminology and Criminal Justice*, 10(2): 211–230.

Goldson, B. and Jamieson, J. (2002) Youth crime, the 'parenting deficit' and state intervention: A contextual critique. *Youth Justice*, 2: 82–99.

Goldson, B. and Muncie, J. (2006) Rethinking youth justice: Comparative analysis, international human rights and research evidence. *Youth Justice*, 6(2): 91–106.

Goldson, B. and Muncie, J. (2009) 'Editors introduction'. In: B. Goldson and J. Muncie (eds) *Youth Crime and Juvenile Justice* (vol. 2, Juvenile Corrections). London: Sage.

Goldson, B. and Muncie, J. (2012) Towards a global 'child friendly' juvenile justice? *International Journal of Law, Crime and Justice*, 40(1): 47–64.

Goldson, B. and Muncie, J. (2015) *Youth Crime and Justice*. London: Sage.

Gottfredson, M.R. and Hirschi, T. (1990) *A General Theory of Crime*. Stanford, CA: Stanford University Press.

Grant, H. (2020) 'It's just too long': Children in detention may face Covid-19 restrictions until 2022. *The Guardian*. Available at: www.theguardian.com/global-development/2020/jul/21/its-just-too-long-children-in-detention-may-face-covid-19-restrictions-until-2022 (accessed 21 July, 2020).

Gray, P. (2005) The politics of risk and young offenders' experiences of social exclusion and restorative justice. *British Journal of Criminology*, 45: 938–957.

Greenough, W.T., Black, J.E. and Wallace, C.S. (1987) Experience and brain development. *Child Development*, 58(3): 539–559.

Griffiths, P. (2002) 'Juvenile delinquency in time'. In: P. Cox and H. Shore (eds) *Becoming Delinquent: British and European Youth, 1650–1950*. Aldershot, UK: Ashgate.

Grove, W.M. and Meehl, P.E. (1996) Comparative efficiency of informal (subjective, impressionistic) and formal (mechanical, algorithmic) prediction. *Psychology, Public Policy and Law*, 2: 293–323.

Hagan, J. (1989) *Structural Criminology*. New Brunswick, NJ: Rutgers University Press.

Hagell, A. and Hazel, N. (2001) Macro and micro patterns in the development of secure custodial institutions for serious and persistent young offenders in England and Wales. *Youth Justice*, 1(1): 3–16.

Haines, A., Goldson, B., Haycox, A., Houten, R., Lane, S., McGuire, J., Nathan, T., Perkins, E., Richards, S. and Whittington, R. (2012) *Evaluation of the Youth Justice Liaison and Diversion (YJLD) Pilot Scheme. Final Report*. Liverpool, UK: University of Liverpool.

Haines, K.R. (1996) *Understanding Modern Juvenile Justice: The Organisational Context of Service Provision*. Avebury, UK: Palgrave Macmillan.

Haines, K.R. (1999) Crime is a social problem. *European Journal on Criminal Policy and Research*, 7: 263–275.

Haines, K.R. and Case, S.P. (2008) The rhetoric and reality of the risk factor prevention paradigm approach to preventing and reducing youth offending. *Youth Justice*, 8(1): 5–20.

Haines, K.R. and Case, S.P. (2011) Risks, rights or both? Evaluating the common aetiology of negative and positive outcomes for young people to inform youth justice practice. *Social Work Review*, 2: 109–122.

Haines, K.R. and Case, S.P. (2012) Is the scaled approach a failed approach? *Youth Justice*, 12(3): 212–228.

Haines, K.R. and Case, S.P. (2015) *Positive Youth Justice: Children First, Offenders Second*. Bristol, UK: Policy Press.

Haines, K.R., Case, S.P., Charles, A.D. and Davies, K. (2013) The Swansea bureau: A model of diversion from the youth justice system. *International Journal of Law, Crime and Justice*, 41(2): 167–187.

Haines, K.R. and Drakeford, M. (1998) *Young People and Youth Justice*. London: Palgrave Macmillan.

Haines, K. R. and O'Mahony, D. (2006) 'Restorative approaches, young people and youth justice'. In: B. Goldson and J. Muncie (eds) *Youth Crime and Justice*. London: Sage.

Hall, S., Clarke, J., Critcher, C., Jefferson, T. and Roberts, B. (1975) *Newsmaking and Crime. Occasional Paper*. Birmingham Centre for Contemporary Cultural Studies, Birmingham University, Birmingham.

Hammersley, R., Marsland, L. and Reid, M. (2003) *Substance Use by Young Offenders: The Impact of the Normalisation of Drug Use in the Early Years of the 21st Century. Home Office Research Study No. 261*. London: Home Office.

Hampson, K. (2020) Youth justice in a pandemic: The situation in England and Wales. *London School of Economics Social Policy Blogspot*. Available at: https://blogs.lse.ac.uk/socialpolicy/2020/07/24/youth-justice-in-a-pandemic-the-situation-in-england-and-wales/

Harding, C. J. and Beecroft, A. J. (2013) *10 Characteristics of a Good Youth Justice System*. A Paper for The Pacific Judicial Development Programme Family Violence and Youth Justice Workshop, Port Vila, Vanuatu.

Harris, R. (1985) Towards just welfare. *British Journal of Criminology*, 25(1): 31–45.

Hart, D. (2014) *What's in a Name? The Identification of Children in Trouble with the Law*. London: SCYJ.

Hart, D. and Thompson, C. (2009) *Young People's Participation in the Youth Justice System*. London: NCB.

Hatty, S. E. (2000) *Engendering Violence. Masculinities, Violence and Culture*. London: Sage.

Hawes, M. (2013) *Legitimacy and Social Order: A Young People's Perspective*. Unpublished PhD Thesis, Swansea University, Swansea, UK.

Hawkins, J. D. and Weis, J. G. (1985) The social development model: An integrated approach to delinquency prevention. *Journal of Primary Prevention*, 6: 73–97.

Hay, C. and Forrest, W. (2009) 'The implications of family poverty for a pattern of persistent offending'. In: J. Savage (ed) *The Development of Persistent Criminality*. Oxford: Oxford University Press.

Hazel, N. (2008) *Cross-National Comparison of Youth Justice*. London: Youth Justice Board.

Hazel, N., Goodfellow, P., Liddle, M., Bateman, T. and Pitts, J. (2017) *Now All I Care About is My Future: Supporting the Shift: Framework for the Effective Resettlement of Young People Leaving Custody (Full Report)*. London: Beyond Youth Custody.

Heidensohn, F. (2000) *Sexual Politics and Social Control*. Milton Keynes, UK: Open University Press.

Heimer, K. and De Coster, S. (1999) The gendering of violent delinquency. *Criminology*, 37(2): 277–318.

Hendrick, H. (1990) 'Constructions and reconstructions of British childhood: An interpretive study 1800 – present'. In: A. James and A. Prout (eds) *Constructing and Reconstructing Childhood*. London: Falmer Press.

Hendrick, H. (1994) *Child Welfare: England, 1872–1989*. London: Routledge.

Hendrick, H. (2015) 'Histories of youth crime and youth justice'. In: B. Goldson and J. Muncie (eds) *Youth Crime and Justice*. London: Sage.

Henriques, U. R. Q. (1972) The rise and decline of the separate system of prison discipline. *Past and Present*, 54(1): 61–93.

Herrnstein, R. J. and Murray, C. (1994) *The Bell Curve*. New York: Basic Books.

Hill, M., Lockyer, A. and Stone, F. (2007) *Young People and Child Protection*. London: Jessica Kingsley.

Hine, J. (2005) Early intervention: the view from on track. *Children and Society*, 19(2): 117–130.

Hine, J. (2006) *Young People, Pathways and Crime: Context and Complexity*. Pathways Into and Out of Crime: Taking Stock and Moving Forward: International Symposium, Leicester, UK, April.

Hine, J., France, A., Dunkerton, L. and Armstrong, D. (2007) 'Risk and Resilience in Children Who Are Offending, Excluded from School or Who Have Behaviour Problems'. Available at: www.pcrrd.group.shef.ac.uk/reports/project_1.pdf (accessed July 2007).

Hirschi, T. (1969) *Causes of Delinquency*. Berkeley: University of California.

HM Government. (2003) *Respect and Responsibility: Taking a Stand Against Antisocial Behaviour*. London: HM Government.

HM Government. (2008) *Youth Crime Action Plan 2008*. London: HM Government.

HM Government. (2011) *Public Bodies Act*. London: HM Government.

HM Government. (2012) *Legal Aid, Sentencing and Punishment of Offenders Act*. London: HMSO.

HMI Probation. (2009) *Joint Inspection Findings of Youth Offending Teams in Wales 2003–2008*. London: HMI Probation.

HMI Probation (HMIP). (2020) *Report on Short Scrutiny Visits to Young Offender Institutions Holding Children*. Available online at www.justiceinspectorates.gov.uk/hmiprisons/wp-content/uploads/sites/4/2020/07/YOI-SSV-2.pdf (accessed 7 July, 2020).

Home Office. (1994) *The Cautioning of Offenders. Circular 18/1994*. London: Home Office.

Home Office. (1997) *No More Excuses: A New Approach to Tackling Youth Crime in England and Wales*. London: HMSO.

Home Office. (1998) *Crime and Disorder Act 1998*. London: Home Office.

Home Office. (2001) *Criminal Justice: The Way Ahead*. London: Home Office.

Home Office. (2002) *Offences Brought to Justice*. London: Home Office.

Home Office. (2003) *Respect and Responsibility – Taking a Stand Against Anti-social Behaviour*. London: Home Office.

Home Office. (2011) *More Effective Responses to Antisocial Behaviour*. London: Home Office.

Home Office. (2012) *Assessing Young People in Police Custody: An Examination of Triage Schemes*. London: Home Office.

Hope, T. (2005) Pretend it doesn't work: the 'anti-social' bias in the Maryland scientific methods scale. *European Journal on Criminal Policy and Research*, 11(3): 275–296.

Hope, T. and Walters, R. (2008) *Critical Thinking About the Uses of Research*. London: Centre for Crime and Justice Studies.

Hopkins-Burke, R. (2013) *An Introduction to Criminological Theory*. Cullompton, UK: Willan.

Hopkins-Burke, R. (2016) *Young People, Crime and Justice*. Abingdon, UK: Routledge.

Hough, M. and Roberts, J. (1998) *Attitudes to Punishment. HORS 179*. London: HMSO.

House of Commons. (2012) *The Big Society: Further Report with the Government's Response to the Committee's Seventh Report of Session 2010–2012*. London: HMSO.

House of Commons. (2020) *Justice Committee Oral evidence: Children and Young People in Custody*. Available at: https://committees.parliament.uk/oralevidence/509/pdf/ (2 June, 2020).

Hoyle, D. (2008) 'Problematizing Every Child Matters'. Available at: www.infed.org/socialwork/every_child_matters_a_critique.htm (accessed March 2014).

Huizinga, D. and Espiritu, R. (1999) *Delinquent Behavior of Youth in the Juvenile Justice System*. Pittsburgh, PA: National Center for Juvenile Justice.

Huizinga, D., Weiher, A.W., Espiritu, R.C. and Esbensen, F. (2003) 'Delinquency and crime: Some highlights from the Denver youth survey'. In: T.P. Thornberry and M. Krohn (eds) *Taking Stock: An Overview of Findings from Contemporary Longitudinal Studies* (pp. 47–92). New York: Kluwer Academic and Plenum.

Independent Commission on Youth Crime and Antisocial Behaviour. (2010) *Time for a Fresh Start*. Available at: www.youthcrimecommission.org.uk/.

Jacobson, J., Bhardwa, B., Gyateng, T., Hunter, G. and Hough, M. (2010) *Punishing Disadvantage: A Profile of Children in Custody*. London: Prison Reform Trust.

Jamieson, J. (2006) New Labour, youth justice and the question of respect. *Youth Justice*, 5(3): 180–193.

Jeffery, C.R. (1977) *Crime Prevention Through Environmental Design*. Beverly Hills, CA: Sage.

Jeffs, T. and Smith, M. (1996) Getting the dirtbags off the streets – curfews and other solutions to juvenile crime. *Youth and Policy*, 52: 1–14.

Jenks, C. (1996) *Childhood*. London: Routledge.

Jepsen, J. (2006) 'Juvenile justice in Denmark: From social welfare to repression'. In: E. Jensen and J. Jepsen (eds) *Juvenile Law Violators, Human Rights and the Development of New Juvenile Justice*. Oxford: Hart.

Jewkes, Y. (2004) *Media and Crime*. London: Sage.

Johnston, J., MacDonald, R., Mason, P., Ridley, L. and Webster, C. (2000) *Snakes and Ladders: Young People, Transitions and Social Exclusion*. Bristol, UK: Policy Press.

Jones, A.P., Laurens, K.R., Herba, C.M., Barker, G.J. and Viding, E. (2009) Amygdala hypoactivity to fearful faces in boys with conduct problems and callous-unemotional traits. *American Journal of Psychiatry*, 166: 95–102.

Jones, C. (1993) Auditing criminal justice. *British Journal of Criminology*, 33(3): 187–202.

Jones, D. (2001) 'Misjudged youth'. A critique of the audit commission's reports on youth justice. *British Journal of Criminology*, 41(2): 362–380.

Jones, R. (1984) Questioning the new orthodoxy. *Community Care*, 11 October, 26–29.

Jordan, L. and Farrell, J. (2013) Juvenile justice diversion in Victoria: A blank canvas? *Current Issues in Criminal Justice*, 24(3): 419–437. Sydney: University of Sydney, Law School Institute of Criminology.

Joyce, P. (2017) *Criminal Justice: An Introduction*. London: Routledge.

Katz, J. (1988) *Seductions of Crime*. New York: Basic Book.

Kelly, L. (2012) Representing and preventing youth crime and disorder: Intended and unintended consequences of targeted youth programmes in England. *Youth Justice*, 8(1): 21–37.

Kelly, L. and Armitage, V. (2015) Diverse diversions: Youth justice reform, localized practices, and a 'new interventionist diversion'? *Youth Justice*, 15(2): 117–133.

Kemshall, H. (2003) *Understanding Risk in Criminal Justice*. Maidenhead, UK: Open University Press.

Kemshall, H. (2008) Risk, rights and justice: Understanding and responding to youth risk. *Youth Justice*, 8(1): 21–38.

Kemshall, H., Marsland, L., Boeck, T. and Dunkerton, L. (2006) Young people, pathways and crime: Beyond risk factors. *Australian and New Zealand Journal of Criminology*, 39(3): 354–370.

King, P. (2006) *Crime and Law in England, 1750–1840*. Cambridge: Cambridge University Press.

King, P. and Wincup, E. (2008) *Doing Research on Crime and Justice*. Oxford: Oxford University Press.

Kisby, B. (2010) The big society: Power to the people. *Political Quarterly*, 81(4): 484–491.

Kohlberg, L. (1958) *The Development of Modes of Thinking and Choices in Years 10 to 16*. PhD Dissertation, University of Chicago, Chicago, IL.

Kohlberg, L. (1984) *The Psychology of Moral Development: The Nature and Validity of Moral Stages (Essays on Moral Development, Volume 2)*. New York: Harper & Row.

Krisberg, B. (2006) 'Rediscovering the juvenile justice ideal in the United States'. In: J. Muncie and B. Goldson (eds) *Comparative Youth Justice*. London: Sage.

Krohn, M.D. (1986) The web of conformity: A network approach to the explanation of delinquent behavior. *Social Problems*, 33: 581–593.

Ksenych, E. (2011) *Exploring Deviance in Canada*. Oxford: Oxford University Press.

Lacey, R. and Minnis, H. (2020) Practitioner review: Twenty years of research with adverse childhood experience scores – Advantages, disadvantages and applications to practice. *Journal of Child Psychology and Psychiatry*, 61(2): 116–130.

Lammy, D. (2017) *An Independent Review Into the Treatment of, and Outcomes for Black, Asian and Minority Ethnic Individuals in the Criminal Justice System*. London: HM Government.

Laub, J. and Sampson, R. (2003) *Shared Beginnings, Divergent Lives. Delinquent Boys to Age 70*. London: Harvard University Press.

Lave, J. and Wenger, E. (2002) 'Legitimate peripheral participation in community of practice'. In: R. Harrison, F. Reeve, A. Hanson and J. Clarke (eds) *Supporting Lifelong Learning: Perspectives on Learning*. London and New York: Routledge Falmer.

Lawrence, J. (2007) 'Taking the developmental pathways approach to understanding and preventing antisocial behaviour'. In: A. France and R. Homel (eds) *Pathways and Crime Prevention*. Cullompton, UK: Willan.

Lawy, R. (2002) Risk stories: Youth identities, learning and everyday risk. *Journal of Youth Studies*, 5(4): 407–423.

Lea, J. and Young, J. (1984) *What Is to Be Done About Law and Order?* Harmondsworth, UK: Penguin.

Lemert, E. (1951) *Social Pathology*. New York: McGraw-Hill.

Lemert, E. (1972) *Human Deviance, Social Problems, and Social Control*. New York: Prentice-Hall.

Lipscombe, S. (2012) *The Age of Criminal Responsibility in England and Wales*, Standard Note SN/ HA/3001, 18 April. London: House of Commons Library.

Loader, I. and Sparks, R. (2010) *Public Criminology*. Abingdon, UK: Routledge.

Lockyer, A. and Stone, F. (eds). (1998) *Juvenile Justice in Scotland*. Edinburgh, UK: T. & T. Clark.

Loeber, R., Farrington, D. P., Stouthamer-Loeber, M., Moffitt, T. E., Caspi, A., White, H., Wei, E. and Beyers, J. M. (2003) 'The development of male offending. Key findings from fourteen years of the Pittsburgh youth study'. In: T. P. Thornberry and M. D. Krohn (eds) *Taking Stock of Delinquency: An Overview of Findings from Contemporary Longitudinal Studies*. New York: Kluwer.

Loeber, R. and Hay, D. F. (1997) Key issues in the development of aggression and violence from childhood to early adulthood. *Annual Review of Psychology*, 48: 371–410.

Lombroso, C. (1875) *L'uomo delinquente (The Criminal Man)*. Milan: Hoepli.

Losada, M. and Heaphy, E. (2004) The role of positivity and connectivity in the performance of business teams: A nonlinear dynamics model. *American Behavioral Scientist*, 47(6): 740–765.

Lupton, D. (1999) *Risk*. New York: Routledge.

Macdonald, R. (2007) Social exclusion, youth transitions and criminal careers: Five critical reflections on "risk"'. In: A. France and R. Homel (eds) *Pathways and Crime Prevention. Theory, Policy and Practice*. Cullompton, UK: Willan.

Macdonald, R. and Marsh, J. (2005) *Disconnected Youth? Growing Up in Britain's Poor Neighbourhoods*. Basingstoke, UK: Palgrave Macmillan.

Magarey, S. (1978) The invention of juvenile delinquency in early nineteenth century England. *Labour History*, 34: 1–27.

Maguire, M., Morgan, R. and Reiner, R. (2007) *Oxford Handbook of Criminology* (4th edition). Oxford: Oxford University Press.

Marshall, T. F. (1999) *Restorative Justice: An Overview*. London: Home Office.

Martinson, R. (1974) What works? – Questions and answers about prison reform. *Public Interest*, 35: 22–54.

Mason, P. and Prior, D. (2008) *Engaging Young People Who Offend*. London: YJB.

Matza, D. (1964) *Delinquency and Drift*. New York: Wiley.

Matza, D. (1969) *Becoming Deviant*. New York: Prentice-Hall.

May, M. (1973) Innocence and experience: the evolution of the concept of juvenile delinquency in the mid-nineteenth century. *Victorian Studies*, xvii: 7–29.

May, T. (2010) *Moving Beyond the ASBO*. Speech to the Coin Street Community Centre, 28 July.

McAra, L. (2006) 'Welfare in crisis? Key developments in Scottish youth justice'. In: J. Muncie and B. Goldson (eds) *Comparative Youth Justice*. London: Sage.

McAra, L. (2010) 'Models of youth justice'. In: D. J. Smith (ed.) *A New Response to Youth Crime*. Cullompton, UK: Willan.

McAra, L. and McVie, S. (2005) The usual suspects? Street-life, young offenders and the police. *Criminal Justice*, 5(1): 5–36.

McAra, L. and McVie, S. (2007) Youth Justice? The impact of system contact on patterns of desistance from offending. *European Journal of Criminology*, 4(3): 315–345.

McAra, L. and McVie, S. (2010) Youth crime and justice: Key messages from the Edinburgh study of youth transitions and crime. *Criminology and Criminal Justice*, 10: 211–230.

McAra, L. and McVie, S. (2015) 'The case for diversion and minimum necessary intervention'. In: B. Goldson and J. Muncie (eds) *Youth Crime and Justice*. London: Sage.

McCartan, K. (2018) *Understanding and Use of Trauma Informed Practice*. Presentation to the Academy for Social Justice Commissioning. Available at: https://assets.publishing.service.gov.uk/ government/uploads/system/uploads/attachment_data/file/746766/Trauma_informed_practice_seminar_SW_8_Oct_2018_slides.pdf (accessed October 2020).

McCartan, K. (2020) *Trauma-Informed Practice*. Manchester: HMIP.

McCord, J. (1978) A thirty-year follow-up of treatment effects. *American Psychologist*, 33(3): 284–289.

McCord, J. and McCord, W. (1959) A follow-up report on the Cambridge-Somerville youth study. *The Annals of the American Academy of Political and Social Science*, 322(1): 89–96.

McNeill, F., Farrall, S., Lightowler, C. and Maruna, S. (2012) *How and Why People Stop Offending: Discovering Desistance*. University of Glasgow, UK: IRISS.

McQuail, D. (1993) *Media Performance*. London: Sage.

McSweeney, B. (1988) Accounting for the audit commission. *Political Quarterly*, 59(1): 28–43.

Mednick, S.A. (1977) 'A biosocial theory of the learning of law-abiding behavior'. In: S.A. Mednick and K.O. Christiansen (eds) *Biosocial Bases of Criminal Behavior*. New York: Gardner.

Mednick, S.A., Moffitt, T.E. and Stack, S. (eds). (1987) *The Causes of Crime: New Biological Approaches*. Cambridge: Cambridge University Press.

Mednick, S.A. and Volavka, J. (1980) 'Biology and crime'. In: N. Morris and M. Tonry (eds) *Crime and Justice: An Annual Review of Research* (vol. 2). Chicago, IL: University of Chicago Press.

Merton, R.K. (1938) Social structure and anomie. *American Sociological Review*, 3: 672–682.

Messerschmidt, J.W. (1993) *Masculinities and Crime: Critique and Reconceptualization of Theory*. Lanham, MD: Rowman & Littlefield.

Messerschmidt, J.W. (2012) *Gender, Heterosexuality, and Youth Violence: The Struggle for Recognition*. Plymouth, UK: Rowman & Littlefield.

Messerschmidt, J.W. and Tomsen, S. (2017) 'Masculinities, crime, and criminal justice'. In: M. Tonry (ed.) *Oxford Handbooks Online*. New York: Oxford University Press.

Miller, J.M. (ed.) (2009) *21st Century Criminology: A Reference Handbook (Volumes I-II)*. Thousand Oaks, CA: Sage.

Ministry of Justice (MoJ). (2010) *Breaking the Cycle: Effective Punishment, Rehabilitation and Sentencing of Offenders*. London: Ministry of Justice.

Ministry of Justice (MoJ). (2012) *Youth Justice Board for England and Wales (Triennial Review)*. London: Ministry of Justice.

Ministry of Justice (MoJ). (2016) *The Government Response to Charlie Taylor's Review of the Youth Justice System*. London: Ministry of Justice.

Ministry of Justice (MoJ) and Youth Justice Board (YJB). (2016) *Youth Justice Statistics: 2014 to 2015*. London: Ministry of Justice.

Ministry of Justice (MoJ) and Youth Justice Board (YJB). (2017) *Youth Justice Statistics: 2015 to 2016*. London: Ministry of Justice.

Ministry of Justice (MoJ) and Welsh Government. (2019) *Youth Justice Blueprint for Wales*. London: Ministry of Justice.

Moffitt, T.E. (1993) Adolescent-limited and life-course-persistent antisocial behavior: A developmental taxonomy. *Psychological Review*, 100: 674–701.

Moffitt, T.E., Caspi, A., Rutter, M. and Silva, P.A. (2001) *Sex Differences in Antisocial Behaviour*. Cambridge: Cambridge University Press.

Morgan, R. (2002) *Annual Lecture of the National Centre for Public Policy*. Swansea, UK: Swansea University.

Morgan, R. (2007) A temporary respite. Jailing young people in ever larger numbers is not the answer to tackling youth crime. *The Guardian*, 19 February.

Morgan, R. (2009) *Report to the Welsh Assembly Government on the Question of Devolution of Youth Justice Responsibilities*. Cardiff, UK: Welsh Government.

Morgan Harris Burrows. (2003) *Evaluation of the Youth Inclusion Programme*. London: MHB.

Morris, A., Giller, H., Geach, H. and Szwed, E. (1980) *Justice for Children*. London: Palgrave Macmillan.

Muller, P. (1973) Childhood's changing status over the centuries. In: L.M. Brockman, J.H. Whiteley and J.P. Zubak (eds) *Child Development: Selected Readings*. Toronto: McClelland and Stewart.

Mullins, C.W. (2006) *Holding Your Square: Masculinities, Streetlife and Violence*. Cullompton, UK: Willan.

Muncie, J. (1984) *'The Trouble with Kids Today': Youth and Crime in Post-war Britain*. Dover, NH: HarperCollins.

Muncie, J. (2004) *Youth and Crime*. London: Sage.

Muncie, J. (2008) The 'punitive' turn in juvenile justice: Cultures of control and rights compliance in Western Europe and the USA. *Youth Justice*, 8(2): 107–121.

Muncie, J. (2009) *Youth and Crime*. London: Sage.

Muncie, J. (2010) The United Nations, children's rights and juvenile justice. In: W. Taylor, R. Hester and R. Earle (eds) *Youth Justice Handbook* (pp. 200–210). London: Routledge.

Muncie, J. (2014) *Youth and Crime*. London: Sage.

Muncie, J. and Goldson, B. (eds). (2006) *Comparative Youth Justice: Critical Issues*. London: Sage.

Muncie, J. and Goldson, B. (2015) Towards a global 'child friendly' juvenile justice? *International Journal of Law, Crime and Justice*, 40(1): 47–64.

Muncie, J., Hughes, G. and McLaughlin, E. (2002) *Youth Justice: Critical Issues*. London: Sage.

Murray, C. (ed.) (1990) *The Emerging British Underclass*. London: Institute of Economic Affairs Health and Welfare Unit.

Murray, C. (1994) *Underclass: The Crisis Deepens*. London: Institute of Economic Affairs.

Nacro. (2003) *A Failure of Justice*. London: Nacro.

Nacro. (2011) *Reducing the Number of Children and Young People in Custody*. London: Nacro.

Nacro Cymru. (2009) *Youth Justice and Participation in Wales*. Cardiff, UK: Nacro Cymru.

National Assembly Policy Unit. (2002) *Extending Entitlement: Support for 11 to 25 Year Olds in Wales. Direction and Guidance*. Cardiff, UK: National Assembly for Wales.

National Association of Youth Justice. (2012) *For a Child Friendly Youth Justice System*. London: NAYJ.

National Police Chiefs' Council. (2015) *Child-Centred Policing. National Strategy for the Policing of Children and Young People*. London: NPCC.

Nye, F.I. (1958) *Family Relationships and Delinquent Behaviour*. New York: Wiley.

OHCHR. (2013) *Access to Justice for Children: Report of the United Nations High Commissioner for Human Rights*. Geneva: United Nations.

O'Mahony, D. and Doak, J. (2017) *Reimagining Restorative Justice: Agency and Accountability in the Criminal Process*. West Sussex, UK: Hart.

O'Mahony, P. (2009) The risk factors paradigm and the causes of youth crime: A deceptively useful analysis? *Youth Justice*, 9(2): 99–115.

ONS. (2020) *Coronavirus and Crime in England and Wales: August 2020*. Available at: www .Ons.Gov.Uk/Peoplepopulationandcommunity/Crimeandjustice/Bulletins/Coronavirusand crimeinenglandandwales/August2020

Park, R. and Burgess, E. (1925) *The City*. Chicago, IL: University of Chicago Press.

Pavlov, I. (1927/1960) *Conditioned Reflexes: An Investigation of the Physiological Activity of the Cerebral Cortex*. New York: Dover.

Paylor, I. (2010) Youth justice in England and Wales: A risky business. *Journal of Offender Rehabilitation*, 50(4): 221–233.

Pearson, G. (1983) *Hooligan: A History of Respectable Fears*. Basingstoke, UK: Palgrave Macmillan.

Perry, B.D. (2001) *'Violence and Childhood: How Persisting Fear Can Alter the Developing Child's Brain'*. Available at: www.childtrauma.org/CTAMATERIALS/Vio_child.asp.

Phillips, C. (2011) Institutional racism and ethnic inequalities: An expanded multilevel framework. *Journal of Social Policy*, 40(01): 173–192.

Phoenix, J. (2009) 'Whose account counts? Politics and research in youth justice'. In: W. Taylor, R. Hester and R. Earle (eds) *Youth Justice Handbook* (pp. 73–82). Cullompton, UK: Willan.

Phoenix, J. (2016) Against youth justice and governance, for youth penalty. *British Journal of Criminology*, 56: 123–140.

Phoenix, J. and Kelly, L. (2013) 'You have to do it for yourself': Responsibilization in youth justice and young people's situated knowledge of youth justice practice. *British Journal of Criminology*, 53(3): 419–437.

Piaget, J. (1932) *The Moral Judgment of the Child*. London: Kegan Paul, Trench, Trübner.

Pilkington, E. (1993) Boys guilty of Bulger murder – Detention without limit for 'unparalleled evil'. *The Guardian*, 25 November.

Pinchbeck, I. and Hewitt, M. (1973) *Children in English Society*. London: Routledge.

Pinchbeck, I. and Hewitt, M. (1981) 'Vagrancy and delinquency in an urban setting'. In: M. Fitzgerald, G. McLennan and J. Pawson (eds) *Crime and Society*. London: Routledge.

Pitts, J. (1988) *The Politics of Juvenile Crime*. London: Sage.

Pitts, J. (2001) Korrectional karaoke: New Labour and the zombification of youth justice. *Youth Justice*, 1(2): 3–16.

Pitts, J. (2003) *The New Politics of Youth Crime: Discipline or Solidarity?* Lyme Regis, UK: Russell House.

Platt, A. (1969) *The Child Savers: The Invention of Delinquency*. Chicago, IL: University of Chicago.

Platt, A. (2009) 'The triumph of benevolence: the origins of the juvenile justice system in the United States'. In: B. Goldson and J. Muncie (eds) *Youth Crime and Juvenile Justice*. London: Sage.

Platt, T. and Takagi, P. (1977) Intellectuals for law and order: A critique of the new realists. *Crime and Social Justice*, 40(1): 30–58.

Pollock, L.A. (1983) *Forgotten Children: Parent-Child Relations from 1500 to 1900*. Cambridge: Cambridge University Press.

Powers, E., Witmer, H. and Allport, G.W. (1951) *An Experiment in the Prevention of Delinquency. The Cambridge-Somerville Youth Study*. New York: Columbia University Press.

Pratt, J. (1989) Corporatism: the third model of juvenile justice. *British Journal of Criminology*, 29(3): 236–254.

Pratt, J. (2005) *Penal Populism*. London: Routledge.

Pratt, J. and Eriksson, A. (2012) 'In defence of Scandinavian exceptionalism'. In: T. Ugelvik and J. Dullum (eds) *Penal Exceptionalism? Nordic Prison Policy and Practice*. London: Routledge.

Prior, D. and Paris, A. (2005) *Preventing Children's Involvement in Crime and Antisocial Behaviour*. Birmingham: Children's Fund.

Put, J. and Walgrave, L. (2006) 'Belgium: From protection to accountability'. In: J. Muncie and B. Goldson (eds) *Comparative Youth Justice*. London: Sage.

Quételet, M.A. (1842) *A Treatise on Man*. Edinburgh, UK: William and Robert Chalmers.

Quinney, R. (1974) *Critique of Legal Order*. Boston, MA: Little Brown.

Radzinowicz, L. and Hood, R. (1986) A History of the English Criminal Law and its Administration from 1750. Volume 5. *The Emergence of Penal Policy*. London: Stevens & Son.

Raine, A., Brennan, P. and Mednick, S. (1997) Interaction between birth complications and early maternal rejection in predisposing individuals to adult violence: Specificity to serious, early-onset violence. *American Journal of Psychiatry*, 154(9): 1265–1271.

Redmond, A. (2015) *Children in Custody 2014–15: An Analysis of 12–18-Year-Olds' Perceptions of Their Experience in Secure Training Centres and Young Offender Institutions*. London: HMIP.

Reich, A. (2010) *Hidden Truth – Young Men Navigating Lives in and Out of Juvenile Prison*. Berkeley, CA: University of California Press.

Reiss, A.J. (1951) Delinquency as the failure of personal and social controls. *American Sociological Review*, 16: 213–239.

Renshaw, J. and Perfect, M. (1997) Out of order. *Community Care*, 8 January, 20–21.

Richards, K. (2014) Blurred lines: Reconsidering the concept of 'diversion' in youth justice systems in Australia. *Youth Justice*, 14(2): 122–139.

Robinson, A. (2014) *Foundations for Youth Justice: Positive Approaches to Practice*. Bristol, UK: Policy Press.

Rose, N. (2000) Government and control. *British Journal of Criminology*, 40: 321–339.

Royal Society. (2011) *Brain Waves Module 4: Neuroscience and the Law*. London: Royal Society Science Policy Centre.

Rush, P. (1992) The government of a generation: the subject of juvenile delinquency. *Liverpool Law Review*, 14(1): 3–43.

Rutherford, A. (2002) *Growing Out of Crime – The End of an Era*. Winchester, UK: Waterside Press.

Rutter, M. and Giller, H. (1983) *Juvenile Delinquency: Trends and Perspective*. Harmondsworth, UK: Penguin.

Sampson, R.J. and Laub, J.H. (1993) *Crime in the Making: Pathways and Turning Points Through Life*. Cambridge, MA: Harvard University Press.

Sampson, R.J. and Laub, J.H. (1997) 'A life-course theory of cumulative disadvantage and the stability of delinquency'. In: T.P. Thornberry (ed.) *Developmental Theories of Crime and Delinquency*. New Brunswick, NJ: Transaction.

Sampson, R.J. and Laub, J.H. (2004) 'A general age-graded theory of crime: Lessons learned and the future of life-course criminology'. In: D.P. Farrington (ed.) *Advances in Criminological Theory*. Cambridge: Cambridge University Press.

Sampson, R.J. and Laub, J.H. (2005) A life-course view of the development of crime. *Annals of the American Academy of Political and Social Science*, 602: 12–45.

Sampson, R.J., Raudenbush, S.W. and Earls, F. (1997) Neighborhoods and violent crime: A multilevel study of collective efficacy. *Science*, 15: 918–924.

Schlesinger, P. and Tumber, H. (1994) *Reporting Crime: The Media Politics of Criminal Justice*. Oxford: Clarendon Press.

Scraton, P. and Haydon, D. (2002) 'Challenging the criminalisation of children and young people: Securing a rights-based agenda'. In: J. Muncie, G. Hughes and E. McLaughlin (eds) *Youth Justice: Critical Issues* (pp. 311–328). London: Sage.

Sentencing Council. (2017) *Sentencing Children and Young People*. Overarching Principles and Offence Specific Guidelines for Sexual Offences and Robbery. Definitive Guidelines. London: Sentencing Council.

Sharp, C. and Budd, C. (2003) *Offending, Crime and Justice Survey*. London: Home Office.

Sharpe, G.H. (2011) *Offending Girls: Young Women and Youth Justice*. Abingdon, UK: Routledge.

Sharpe, G.H. (2015) Precarious identities: 'Young' motherhood, desistance and stigma. *Criminology and Criminal Justice*, 15(4): 407–422.

Sharpe, G.H. and Gelsthorpe, L. (2015) 'Girls, crime and justice'. In: B. Goldson and J. Muncie (eds) *Youth Crime and Justice*. London: Sage.

Shaw, C.R. (1930) *The Jack-Roller: A Delinquent Boy's Own Story*. Chicago, IL: University of Chicago Press.

Shaw, D.S., Ingoldsby, E., Gilliom, M. and Nagin, D. (2003) Trajectories leading to school-age conduct problems. *Developmental Psychology*, 38: 480–491.

Shelden, R.G. (1999) *An Evaluation of the Detention Diversion Advocacy Program*. Washington, DC: Juvenile Justice and Delinquency Prevention.

Sheldon, W.H. (1949) *Varieties of Delinquent Youth*. London: Harper.

Sherman, L.W., Gottfredson, D., MacKenzie, D., Eck, J., Reuter, P. and Bushway, S. (1998) *Preventing Crime: What Works, What Doesn't, What's Promising*. Department of Criminology and Criminal Justice. Baltimore: University of Maryland.

Sherman, L.W. and Strang, H. (2007) *Restorative Justice: The Evidence*. London: Smith Institute.

Shore, H. (1999) *Artful Dodgers. Youth and Crime in Early 19th-Century London*. Woodbridge, UK: Boydell Press.

Shore, H. (2011) Reforming the juvenile in nineteenth- and early-twentieth-century England. *Prison Service Journal*, 197: 4–9.

Silk Commission. (2014) *Empowerment and Responsibility: Legislative Powers to Strengthen Wales*. Cardiff, UK: Commission on Devolution in Wales.

Skinner, B.F. (1938) *The Behaviour of Organisms*. New York: Appleton Century Crofts.

Smart, C. (1977) *Women, Crime and Criminology*. London: Routledge and Kegan Paul.

Smart, C. (1990) Feminist approaches to criminology: Or postmodern woman meets atavistic man'. In: L. Gelsthorpe and A. Morris (eds) *Feminist Perspectives in Criminology*. Buckingham, UK: Open University Press.

Smith, C. and Thornberry, T.P. (1995) The relationship between childhood maltreatment and adolescent involvement in delinquency. *Criminology*, 33(4): 451–481.

Smith, D.J. (2006) *Social Inclusion and Early Desistance from Crime* (p. 12). Edinburgh: Study of Youth Transitions and Crime Research Digest.

Smith, D.J. (2010) *A New Response to Youth Crime*. Cullompton, UK: Willan.

Smith, D.J. and Ecob, R. (2007) An investigation into causal links between victimization and offending in adolescents. *British Journal of Sociology*, 58(4): 633–659.

Smith, D.J. and McAra, L. (2004) *Gender and Youth Offending, Edinburgh Study of Youth Transitions and Crime Research Digest No. 2*. Edinburgh, UK: Edinburgh University.

Smith, D.J. and McVie, S. (2003) Theory and method in the Edinburgh study of youth transitions and crime. *British Journal of Criminology*, 43(1): 169–195.

Smith, R. (2005) Welfare versus justice – Again! *Youth Justice*, 5(1): 3–16.

Smith, R. (2011) *Doing Justice to Young People: Youth Crime and Social Justice*. Cullompton, UK: Willan.

Smith, R. (2014) Reinventing diversion. *Youth Justice*, 14(2): 109–121.

Smithson, H. (2020) *Marginalised yet Vulnerable: The Impact of COVID-19 on Young People in the Youth Justice System*. Avilable at: *https://www.mmu.ac.uk/news-and-events/news/story/12283/*

Snacken, S. and Dumortier, E. (2012) 'Resisting punitiveness in Europe? An introduction'. In: S. Snacken and E. Dumortier (eds) *Resisting Punitiveness in Europe? Welfare, Human Rights and Democracy*. London: Routledge.

Social Exclusion Unit. (2001) *National Strategy for Neighbourhood Renewal*. London: SEU.

Solanki, A., Bateman, T., Boswell, G. and Hill, E. (2006) *Anti-Social Behaviour Orders*. London: Youth Justice Board.

Solomon, E. and Garside, R. (2008) *Ten Years of Labour's Youth Justice Reforms: An Independent Audit*. London: Centre for Crime and Justice Studies, Kings College London.

Souhami, A. (2007) *Transforming Youth Justice. Occupational Identity and Cultural Change*. Cullompton, UK: Willan.

Souhami, A. (2011) Inside the youth justice board: Ambiguity and influence in New Labour's youth justice. *Critical Social Policy*, 10(3): 7–16.

Souhami, A. (2015a) The central institutions of youth justice: Government bureaucracy and the importance of the youth justice board for England and Wales. *Youth Justice*, 14: 209–225.

Souhami, A. (2015b) Creating the youth justice board: Policy and policy-making in English and Welsh youth justice. *Criminology and Criminal Justice*, 15: 152–168.

Soung, P. (2011) Social and biological constructions of youth: Implications for juvenile justice and racial equity. *Northwestern Journal of Law and Social Policy*, 6(2): 428–444.

Sousa, W. and Kelling, G. (2006) 'Of "broken windows", criminology and criminal justice'. In: D. Weisburd and A. Braga (eds) *Police Innovation: Contrasting Perspectives*. Cambridge: Cambridge University Press.

Sowell, E.R., Thompson, P.M., Holmes, C.J., Jernigan, T.L. and Toga, A.W. (1999) *In vivo* evidence for post-adolescent brain maturation in frontal and striatal regions. *Nature Neuroscience*, 2: 859–861.

Springhall, J. (1986) *Coming of Age: Adolescence in Britain 1860–1960*. Dublin: Gill and Palgrave Macmillan.

Squires, P. and Stephen, D. (2005) *Rougher Justice: Antisocial Behaviour and Young People*. Cullompton, UK: Willan.

Standing Committee for Youth Justice. (2017) *SCYJ Response to Charlie Taylor's Review of the Youth Justice System and the Government's Response*. London: SCYJ.

Stanley-Hall, G. (1904) *Adolescence*. New York: D. Appleton.

Stephenson, M., Giller, H. and Brown, S. (2007/2011) *Effective Practice in Youth Justice*. Cullompton, UK: Willan.

Straw, J. (1995) *Safer Communities, Safer Britain: Labour's Proposals for Tough Action on Crime*. London: Labour Party.

Straw, J. and Michael, A. (1996) *Tackling the Causes of Crime: Labour's Proposals to Prevent Crime and Criminality*. London: Labour Party.

Such, E. and Walker, R. (2004) Being responsible and responsible beings: Children's understanding of responsibility. *Children and Society*, 18: 231–242.

Sutherland, A. (2009) The 'scaled approach' to youth justice. Fools rush in. . . *Youth Justice Journal*, 9(1): 44–60.

Sutherland, E.H. (1940) White-collar criminality. *American Sociological Review*, 5: 1–12.

Sutherland, E.H. (1947) *Principles of Criminology* (4th edition). Philadelphia, PA: Lippincott.

Sutherland, E.H. and Cressey, D.R. (1960) *Criminology* (5th edition). Philadelphia, PA: Lippincott.

Tankebe, J. (2008) Colonialism, legitimacy and policing in Ghana. *International Journal of Law, Crime and Justice*, 6: 68–70.

Tannenbaum, F. (1938) *Crime and the Community*. New York: Columbia University Press.

Taylor, C. (2016) *Review of the Youth Justice System in England and Wales*. London: Ministry of Justice.

Taylor, I. (1981) Crime waves in post-war Britain. *Contemporary Crises*, 5: 43–62.

Taylor, I., Walton, P. and Young, J. (1973) *The New Criminology: For a Social Theory of Deviance*. London: Routledge and Kegan Paul.

Taylor, J. (2003) *An Evaluation of Probation Practice in Relation to Masculinity and Offending Behaviour: Are We Addressing the Issue?* Unpublished MA Dissertation, Northumbria University, Newcastle upon Tyne, UK.

Taylor, W., Earle, R. and Hester, R. (2010) *Youth Justice Handbook Theory, Policy and Practice*. Cullompton, UK: Willan.

Thomas, W. I. (1907) *Sex and Society*. Chicago, IL: University of Chicago Press.

Thomas, W. I. (1923) *The Unadjusted Girl*. New York: Harper and Row.

Thornberry, T. P. (1994) *Violent Families and Youth Violence. OJJDP Fact Sheet 21*. Washington, DC: OJJDP.

Thornberry, T. P., Huizinga, D. and Loeber, R. (2004) The causes and correlates studies: Findings and policy implications. *Juvenile Justice*, 10(1): 3–19.

Thornberry, T. P. and Krohn, M. D. (2003) *Taking Stock of Delinquency. An Overview of Findings from Contemporary Longitudinal Studies*. New York: Kluwer.

Thorpe, D., Smith, D., Green, C. and Paley, J. (1980) *Out of Care – The Community Support of Juvenile Offenders*. London: George Allen and Unwin.

Tittle, C. R. (2000) 'Control balance'. In: R. Paternoster and R. Bachman (eds) *Explaining Criminals and Crime: Essays in Contemporary Theory*. Los Angeles, CA: Roxbury.

Turnbull, G. and Spence, J. (2011) What's at risk? The proliferation of risk across child and youth policy in England. *Journal of Youth Studies*, 14(8): 939–959.

Tutt, N. and Giller, H. (1987) Manifesto for management – the elimination of custody. *Justice of the Peace*, 151: 200–202.

Tyler, T. (2006/1990) *Why People Obey the Law*. Princeton, NJ: Princeton University Press.

Tyler, T. (2007) *Legitimacy and Criminal Justice: International Perspectives*. New York: Russell Sage Foundation.

Ugwudike, P. (2015) *Critical Criminology*. Bristol, UK: Policy Press.

Uhrig, N. (2016) *Black, Asian and Minority Ethnic Disproportionality in the Criminal Justice System in England and Wales*. London: Ministry of Justice. Available at: https://www.gov.uk/government/uploads/system/uploads/attachment_data/file/568680/bame-disproportionality-in-the-cjs.pdf

Ungar, M. (2004) A constructionist discourse on resilience. Multiple contexts, multiple realities among at-risk children and youth. *Youth and Society*, 35: 341–365.

UNICEF. (1989) *United Nations Convention on the Rights of the Child 1989*. Geneva: United Nations.

United Nations General Assembly. (1985) *UN Standard Minimum Rules for the Administration of Juvenile Justice*. Geneva: United Nations.

United Nations General Assembly. (1990a) *UN Guidelines on the Prevention of Delinquency*. Geneva: United Nations.

United Nations General Assembly. (1990b) *UN Rules for the Protection of Juveniles Deprived of Their Liberty*. Geneva: United Nations.

Urwin, J. (2015) *A Return to Rawls: Applying Social Justice to Mental Health Provision in the Youth Offending Service*. Unpublished PhD Thesis, De Montfort University, Leicester, UK.

Vold, G. B., Bernard, T. J. and Snipes, J. B. (1998) *Theoretical Criminology* (4th edition). Oxford: Oxford University Press.

Wacquant, L. (2008) *Urban Outcasts: A Comparative Sociology of Advanced Marginality*. Cambridge: Polity Press.

Wacquant, L. (2009) *Punishing the Poor: The Neoliberal Government of Social Insecurity*. Durham, NC: Duke University Press.

Walker, J. and McCarthy, P. (2005) 'Parents in prison: the impact on children'. In: G. Preston (ed.) *At Greatest Risk: The Children Most Likely to be Poor*. London: Child Poverty Action Group.

Walker, J., Thompson, C., Laing, K., Raybould, S., Coombes, S., Proctor, S. and Wren, C. (2007) *Youth Inclusion and Support Panels: Preventing Crime and Antisocial Behaviour?* London: DfES.

Wallace, N. and Jacobsen, G. (2012) Children reoffend as system goes soft. *Sydney Morning Herald*, 28 April, 1.

Walton, P. and Young, J. (1998) *The New Criminology Revisited*. London: Palgrave Macmillan.

Weatherburn, D., McGrath, A. and Bartels, L. (2012) Three dogmas of juvenile justice. *University of New South Wales Law Journal*, 35(3): 781–809.

Webster, C. (2018) "Race', ethnicity, social class and juvenile justice in Europe'. In: B. Goldson (ed) *Juvenile Justice in Europe*. London: Routledge.

Webster, C., MacDonald, R. and Simpson, M. (2006) 'Predicting criminality: Risk/protective factors, neighbourhood influence and desistance'. *Youth Justice*, 6(1): 7–22.

Webster, C., Simpson, D., MacDonald, R., Abbas, A., Cieslik, M., Shildrick, T. and Simpson, M. (2004) *Poor Transitions: Social Exclusion and Young Adults*. Bristol, UK: Policy Press.

Welsh Assembly Government and Youth Justice Board. (2004) *All Wales Youth Offending Strategy*. Cardiff, UK: WAG.

Welsh Assembly Government and Youth Justice Board. (2009) *All Wales Youth Offending Strategy: Delivery Plan 2009–2011*. Cardiff, UK: WAG.

Welsh Government. (2011) *Devolution of Youth Justice: Cabinet Briefing*. Cardiff, UK: Welsh Government.

Welsh Government. (2012) *Proposals to Improve Services in Wales to Better Meet the Needs of Children and Young People Who Are Risk of Entering, or Are Already in, The Youth Justice System*. Cardiff, UK: Welsh Government.

Welsh Government and Youth Justice Board. (2014) *Children and Young People First*. Cardiff, UK: Welsh Government and YJB.

Wenger, E. (1998) *Communities of Practice: Learning, Meaning and Identity*. Cambridge: Cambridge University Press.

West, D.J. (1982) *Delinquency: Its Roots, Careers and Prospects*. London: Heinemann.

West, D.J. and Farrington, D.P. (1973) *Who Becomes Delinquent?* London: Heinemann.

West, D.J. and Farrington, D.P. (1977) *The Delinquent Way of Life*. London: Heinemann.

Whitehead, P. and Arthur, R. (2011) 'Let no one despise your youth': A sociological approach to youth justice under New Labour 1997–2010. *International Journal of Sociology and Social Policy*, 31(7/8): 469–485.

Whyte, B. (2009) *Youth Justice in Practice*. London: Policy Press.

Whyte, B. (2014) Young people in conflict with the law in Scotland – 50 years after the Kilbrandon report. What does contemporary policy and practice tell us about our progress since and about the legacy of Kilbrandon? *Scottish Journal of Residential Child Care*, 13(3).

Wigzell, A. and SCYJ. (2017) Truss strips YJB of youth custody role. *Children and Young People Now*, 24 February.

Wikstrom, P.-O. (2008) 'In search of causes and explanations of crime'. In: R. King and E. Wincup (eds) *Doing Research on Crime and Justice*. Oxford: Oxford University Press.

Wikstrom, P.-O. and Butterworth, D. (2006) *Adolescent Crime: Individual Differences and Lifestyles*. Cullompton, UK: Willan.

Wikstrom, P.-O. and Loeber, R. (2000) Do disadvantaged neighborhoods cause well-adjusted children to become adolescent delinquents? A study of male juvenile serious offending, risk and protective factors and neighborhood context. *Criminology*, 38(4): 1109–1142.

Wikstrom, T. and Loeber, R. (1998) 'Individual risk factors, neighbourhood SES and juvenile offending'. In: M. Tonry (ed.) *The Handbook of Crime and Punishment*. New York: Oxford University Press.

Wilcox, A. (2004) *National Evaluation of the Youth Justice Board's Restorative Justice Projects*. London: YJB.

Wilkins, L. (1964) *Social Deviance*. London: Tavistock.

Williamson, B. and Cairns, L. (2005) *Working in Partnership with Young People: From Practice to Theory*. Durham, UK: Investing in Children and Research in Practice.

Wilson, J.Q. (1975) *Thinking About Crime*. New York: Basic Books.

Wilson, J. Q. and Herrnstein, R. J. (1985) *Crime and Human Nature*. New York: Simon and Schuster.

Winlow, S. (2002) *Badfellas: Crime, Tradition and New Masculinities*. Oxford: Berg.

Wundersitz, J. (1996) *The South Australian Juvenile Justice System: A Review of Its Operation*. Adelaide: South Australia Office of Crime Statistics.

Yates, J. (2012) What prospects youth justice? Children in trouble in the age of austerity. *Journal of Social Policy and Administration*, 46(4): 432–447.

YOT Managers Cymru. (2013) Available at: www.yotmanagerscymru.org.uk/.

Young, J. (1974) 'Mass media, drugs and deviance'. In: I. Taylor, P. Walton and J. Young (eds) *Deviance and Social Control*. London: Tavistock.

Young, J. (1986) 'The failure of criminology: the need for a radical realism'. In: R. Matthews and J. Young (eds) *Confronting Crime*. London: Sage.

Young, J. (2007) *The Vertigo of Late Modernity*. London: Sage.

Young, J. (2011) *The Criminological Imagination*. London: Polity Press.

Younge, S. L., Oetting, E. R. and Deffenbacher, J. L. (1996) Correlations among maternal rejection, dropping out of school, and drug use in adolescents. *Journal of Clinical Psychology*, 52(1): 96–102.

Youth Justice Board. (2000) *ASSET: Explanatory Notes*. London: YJB.

Youth Justice Board. (2003) *Assessment, Planning Interventions and Supervision*. London: YJB.

Youth Justice Board. (2004) *National Standards for Youth Justice Services*. London: YJB.

Youth Justice Board. (2006) *Onset Referral and Screening – Guidance*. London: YJB.

Youth Justice Board. (2008) *Assessment, Planning Interventions and Supervision*. Source Document. London: YJB.

Youth Justice Board. (2009a) *Youth Justice: The Scaled Approach. A Framework for Assessment and Interventions*. Post-consultation version two. London: YJB.

Youth Justice Board. (2009b) *Girls Offending – Patterns, Perceptions and Interventions*. Ministry of Justice. London: YJB.

Youth Justice Board. (2010) *Process Evaluation of the Pilot of a Risk-Based Approach to Interventions*. London: YJB.

Youth Justice Board. (2012) *Key Performance Indicators*. London: YJB.

Youth Justice Board. (2013) *Assessment and Planning Interventions Framework – AssetPlus*. Model Document. London: YJB.

Youth Justice Board. (2014) *AssetPlus Rationale*. London: YJB.

Youth Justice Board. (2016) *Participation Strategy: Giving Young People a Voice in Youth Justice*. London: YJB.

Youth Justice Board. (2017) *Academic/YOT Partnership Working Guide*. London: YJB.

Youth Justice Board. (2018) *Board Information Paper*. London: YJB.

Youth Justice Board. (2019a) *Youth Justice Board for England and Wales Strategic Plan 2019–2022*. London: YJB.

Youth Justice Board. (2019b) *Standards for Children in the Youth Justice System*. London: YJB.

Youth Justice Board. (2020a) *Youth Justice Partner COVID-19 Update*. Available at: https://yjresourcehub.uk/covid-19-resources-for-youth-justice/item/download/852_458b6afb3bcb42adcbfbf1ef0592940e.html

Youth Justice Board. (2020b) *Covid-19. Youth Justice Update*. Available at: https://youthjusticeboard.newsweaver.co.uk/yots2/lop5s0cnmrztdt3xlq5agw?lang=en&a=1&p=56949841&t=21098985

Youth Justice Board and Cymru. (2012) *A Blueprint for Promoting Effective Practice and Improving Youth Justice Performance in Wales*. London: YJB.

Youth Justice Board and CYP Now. (2010) *Prevention Matters*. London: YJB.

Youth Justice Board and Ministry of Justice. (2012) *Youth Justice Annual Statistics 2011–2012*. London: YJB and MoJ.

Youth Justice Board and Ministry of Justice. (2020) *Youth Justice Statistics 2018/19 England and Wales*. London: YJB and MoJ.

Youth Justice Board and Welsh Government. (2015) *Children and Young People First: Children and Young People at Risk of Entering, or Who Are in, the Youth Justice System Must Be Treated as Children First and Offenders Second in All Transactions with Services.* Cardiff, UK: Welsh Government.

Youth Custody Service. (2020) *Monthly Youth Custody Report – August 2020.* Available at: https://assets.publishing.service.gov.uk/government/uploads/system/uploads/attachment_data/file/924426/youth-custody-report-august-2020.xlsx

Zehr, H. and Mika, H. (1998) Fundamental concepts of restorative justice. *Contemporary Justice Review*, 1: 47–55.

Zimring, F. E. (2000) The common thread: Diversion in juvenile justice. *California Law Review*, 88(6): 2477–2496.

Zimring, F. E. (2011) *The City That Became Safe: New York's Lessons for Urban Crime and Its Control.* Oxford: Oxford University Press.

Znaniecki, F. and Thomas, W. I. (1918) *The Polish Peasant in Europe and America.* Boston, MA: Gorham Press.

Index

Page numbers in *italic* indicate a figure and page numbers in **bold** indicate a table on the corresponding page.

Printed in Great Britain
by Amazon

23914820R00213